Deliberation, Participation and Democracy

Deliberation, Participation and Democracy

Can the People Govern?

Edited by

Shawn W. Rosenberg
Professor of Political Science and Psychology
University of California, Irvine, USA

palgrave
macmillan

First published in 2007 by
PALGRAVE MACMILLAN
Houndmills, Basingstoke, Hampshire RG21 6XS and
175 Fifth Avenue, New York, N.Y. 10010
Companies and representatives throughout the world.

PALGRAVE MACMILLAN is the global academic imprint of the Palgrave
Macmillan division of St. Martin's Press, LLC and of Palgrave Macmillan Ltd.
Macmillan® is a registered trademark in the United States, United Kingdom
and other countries. Palgrave is a registered trademark in the European
Union and other countries.

ISBN-13: 978–0–230–51735–6 hardback
ISBN-10: 0–230–51735–8 hardback

This book is printed on paper suitable for recycling and made from fully
managed and sustained forest sources. Logging, pulping and manufacturing
processes are expected to conform to the environmental regulations of
the country of origin.

A catalogue record for this book is available from the British Library.

Library of Congress Cataloging-in-Publication Data

    Deliberation, participation and democracy : can the
people govern? / Shawn W. Rosenberg, editor.
        p. cm.
    ISBN 0–230–51735–8 (alk. paper)
        1. Political participation. 2. Democracy. I. Rosenberg,
Shawn W., 1951–

JF799.D44 2007
321.8—dc22   2007018316

10 9 8 7 6 5 4 3 2 1
16 15 14 13 12 11 10 09 08 07

Printed and bound in Great Britain by
Antony Rowe Ltd, Chippenham and Eastbourne

Contents

List of Tables

List of Figures

Notes on Contributors

André Bächtiger is Senior Assistant at the Institute of Political Science at the University of Bern (Switzerland). His research interests lie in the fields of deliberative democracy, institutional theory and democratization processes in Africa and Asia. He is co-author of *Deliberative Politics in Action. Analysing Parliamentary Discourse* (Cambridge University Press, 2004). He was Research Fellow at the University of North Carolina (Chapel Hill) and Swiss Chair/ Jean Monnet Fellow at the European University Institute (Florence).

Joshua Cohen is Professor of Political Science, Philosophy and Law at Stanford University. Cohen is also co-editor of *Boston Review* and of more than twenty-five Boston Review Books (published with Beacon, Princeton, Oxford and MIT). He has written extensively on democratic theory, and is author of several essays on the subject of deliberative democracy, including "Deliberation and Democratic Legitimacy," "Procedure and Substance in Deliberative Democracy," "Democracy and Liberty" (with Charles Sabel) "Directly-Deliberative Polyarchy," "Privacy, Pluralism, and Democracy," and (with Joel Rogers) "Power and Reason."

Fay Lomax Cook is Director of the Institute for Policy Research at Northwestern University and Professor of Human Development and Social Policy in the School of Education and Social Policy with a joint appointment in the Department of Political Science. She has been President of the Gerontological Society of America (2000); a fellow at the Center for Advanced Study in the Behavioral Sciences (1997–1998) and a Visiting Scholar at the Russell Sage Foundation (1987–1988). Her research focuses on the interrelationships between public opinion and social policy, the politics of public policy and the dynamics of public support for Social Security and other social programs for older Americans. She is the author or co-author of many scholarly articles and book chapters as well as four books, including *Support for the American Welfare State: The Views of Congress and the Public* (with Edith J. Barrett) (New York: Columbia University Press, 1992); *The Journalism of Outrage: Investigative Reporting and Agenda Building in America* (with David Protess et al.) (New York: Guilford Publications, Inc., 1991); and *Navigating Public Opinion: Polls, Policy and the Future of American Democracy* (with J. Manza and B. Page, Eds.) (New York: Oxford University Press, 2002).

Michael X. Delli Carpini is Dean of the Annenberg School for Communication. Prior to joining the University of Pennsylvania faculty in July of 2003, Professor Delli Carpini was Director of the Public Policy program of the Pew Charitable Trusts (1999–2003), and member of the Political

Science Department at Barnard College and graduate faculty of Columbia University (1987–2002), serving as chair of the Barnard department from 1995 to 1999. His research explores the role of the citizen in American politics, with particular emphasis on the impact of the mass media on public opinion, political knowledge and political participation. He is author of *Stability and Change in American Politics: The Coming of Age of the Generation of the 1960s* (New York University Press, 1986), and *What Americans Know About Politics and Why It Matters* (Yale University Press, 1996), and *A New Engagement: Political Participation, Civic Life, and the Changing American Citizen* (Oxford University Press, 2006), as well as numerous articles, essays and edited volumes on political communications, public opinion, and political socialization.

John Dryzek is Head of the Social and Political Theory Program at the Australian National University. Before joining the Program he taught at Ohio State University, the University of Oregon and the University of Melbourne. He is a former editor of the Australian Journal of Political Science and Fellow of the Academy of the Social Sciences in Australia. Aside from being a political theorist, Dryzek does work in environmental politics, comparative politics, international relations and public policy. His recent books include *Green States and Social Movements: Environmentalism in the United States, United Kingdom, Germany and Norway* (with David Downes, Christian Hunold and David Schlosberg) (Oxford University Press, 2003), *Post-Communist Democratization: Political Discourses across Thirteen Countries* (with Leslie Holmes) (Cambridge University Press, 2002), *Deliberative Democracy and Beyond: Liberals, Critics, Contestations* (Oxford University Press, 2002), *The Politics of the Earth: Environmental Discourses* (Oxford University Press, 1997).

Archon Fung is an Assistant Professor of Public Policy at Harvard's John F. Kennedy School of Government. His research examines the impacts of civic participation, public deliberation, and transparency upon public and private governance. His *Empowered Participation: Reinventing Urban Democracy* (Princeton University Press, forthcoming 2003) examines two participatory-democratic reform efforts in low-income Chicago neighborhoods. His recent books and edited collections include *Deepening Democracy: Institutional Innovations in Empowered Participatory Governance* (Verso Press, 2003), *Can We Eliminate Sweatshops?* (Beacon Press 2001), *Working Capital: The Power of Labor's Pensions* (Cornell University Press 2001) and *Beyond Backyard Environmentalism* (Beacon Press 2000).

Lawrence R. Jacobs is Land Grant-McKnight Professor at the University of Minnesota and Adjunct Professor in the Hubert H. Humphrey Institute and Director of its 2004 Elections Project. His most recent books are *Healthy, Wealth, and Fair* (Oxford University Press, 2004) and *Politicians Don't Pander: Political Manipulation and the Loss of Democratic Responsiveness* (University of Chicago Press, 2000), which received three awards. He also authored, *The Health of Nations: Public Opinion and the Making of Health Policy in the U.S. and*

Britain (Cornell University Press, 1993) as well as several edited volumes and articles in scholarly journals.

Christopher F. Karpowitz is Assistant Professor of Political Science at Brigham Young University and a Research Fellow at the Center for the Study of Elections and Democracy. Prior to his arrival at BYU, he served as the Postdoctoral Fellow in Democracy and Human Values and Associate Director of the Program in Ethics and Public Affairs at Princeton's University Center for Human Values. His research explores how citizens experience democratic institutions and processes, with special attention to democratic and deliberative theory and practice. He is a co-author of *Democracy at Risk: How Political Choices Undermine Citizen Participation, and What We Can Do About It* (Brookings, 2005), and his work has appeared in a number of scholarly journals.

Christian List is a Professor of Political Science and Philosophy at the London School of Economics. He graduated in mathematics, philosophy and politics from the University of Oxford. He held postdoctoral and visiting positions at Nuffield College, Oxford, the Australian National University, Harvard University, Princeton University, University of Konstanz and MIT. His main research areas are formal and normative political theory and the philosophy of social science.

Jane Mansbridge is the Adams Professor at the Kennedy School of Government at Harvard University. She is the author of *Beyond Adversary Democracy* and *Why We Lost the ERA*, both in their own ways about deliberative democratic processes. She is also editor of *Beyond Self-Interest*, co-editor with Susan Okin of *Feminism* and co-editor with Aldon Morris of *Oppositional Consciousness*. She has written a number of journal articles and book chapters on deliberative democracy.

Lorraine M. McDonnell is Professor and Chair of the Department of Political Science at the University of California, Santa Barbara. McDonnell has authored major studies of teacher unions, immigrant education, and the politics of student testing. With Stephen Weatherford, she is currently working on a project surveying the use of deliberative democratic processes in local education decision-making. McDonnell has been the author of numerous articles and reports on educational policy. Recently she edited *Rediscovering the Democratic Purposes of Education* (with P. Michael Timpane and Roger Benjamin) (University Press of Kansas, 2000).

Tali Mendelberg is Associate Professor of Politics at Princeton University. She is the author of *The Race Card: Campaign Strategy, Implicit Messages, and the Norm of Equality* (Princeton University Press, 2001) and winner of the American Political Science Association's 2002 Woodrow Wilson Foundation Award for "the best book published in the United States during the prior year on government, politics or international affairs". In 2002 she received the

Erik H. Erikson Early Career Award for Excellence and Creativity in the Field of Political Psychology.

Shawn Rosenberg is Professor of Political Science and Psychology and Director of the Graduate Program in Political Psychology at the University of California, Irvine. He is currently a Visiting Fellow at the University Center for Human Values, Princeton University. He has also been a Visiting Professor at Leiden University, the University of Amsterdam and the University of California, Berkeley. A political psychologist, Rosenberg has done research on the nature of political ideology, political cognition and democratic deliberation. He has also written on issues of philosophy of social science with specific reference to the conduct of interdisciplinary research. He is the author of three prize wining books, *Political Cognition and Reasoning* (with D. Ward and S. Chilton) (Duke University Press, 1988), *Reason Ideology and Politics* (Princeton University Press, 1988) and *The Not So Common Sense: How People Judge Social and Political Life* (Yale University Press, 2002).

Markus Spörndli has been a researcher at the University of Bern and visiting scholar at the Social Science Research Center Berlin (WZB). There, he explored the effects of deliberation on political outcomes (published in German, VS-Verlag, 2004) and co-authored the book *Deliberative Politics in Action* (with Steiner, Bächtiger and Steenbergen) (Cambridge University Press, 2005). After having been a journalist for Swiss newspapers, he tried to put deliberation into action as a delegate of the International Committee of the Red Cross in Kashmir. He is currently the communication officer of the Swiss Agency of Economic Development and Cooperation.

Marco R. Steenbergen is Associate Professor of Political Science at the University of North Carolina, Chapel Hill. His research and teaching interests lie in the fields of quantitative methods and political psychology with a specific focus on voting behavior, public opinion, measurement and multi-level inference. He has co-authored *Deliberative Politics in Action* (with Steiner, Bächtiger and Sporndli) (Cambridge University Press, 2005) and an edited volume about the contestation of European Integration (co-edited with Gary Marks).

Jürg Steiner has taught for many years both at the University of North Carolina at Chapel Hill and the University of Bern. Now he is Emeritus at both universities, but still moves back and forth between the two places. In 2003/2004 he held the Swiss Chair at the European University Institute in Florence. More recently he was visiting professor at the Central European University in Budapest and the Externado University in Bogota. His most recent books are *Deliberative Politics in Action* (with Bächtiger, Spörndli, and Steenbergen) (Cambridge University Press, 2004) and *European Democracies*, fifth edition (with Crepaz) (Longman 2007).

Katherine Cramer Walsh (B.A. University of Wisconsin-Madison 1994, Ph.D. University of Michigan 2000) is an assistant professor in the Department of Political Science. Her primary research and teaching interests include public opinion, political communication and civic engagement. She is the author of *Talking about Race: Community Dialogues and the Politics of Difference* (University of Chicago Press, forthcoming) and *Talking about Politics: Informal Groups and Social Identity in American Life* (University of Chicago Press, 2004). She is currently a member of the American Political Science Association's Task Force on Civic Education and Civic Engagement.

Mark E. Warren is Professor of Government at Georgetown University. Warren teaches late modern and contemporary political theory, with an emphasis on continental political thought and democratic theory. He came to Georgetown in 1988 after having served as a Mellon Fellow in Philosophy at Rice University, and teaching at Northwestern. Publications include *Nietzsche and Political Thought* (MIT Press, 1988), *Democracy and Trust* (ed., Cambridge University Press, 1999) and *Democracy and Association* (Princeton University Press, 2001) as well as articles on continental political thought, political psychology and philosophy of social science.

M. Stephen Weatherford is Professor of Political Science at the University of California, Santa Barbara. His research has ranged over questions of representation, political behavior and political economy, mainly in the context of US politics. Two active research projects include a survey of US economic policymaking in the post-Second World War years and a study of community- and state-level innovations in deliberative democracy. His contribution to this volume is part of a larger project, undertaken with Lorraine McDonnell, which examines community- and state-level innovations in deliberative democracy.

1
An Introduction: Theoretical Perspectives and Empirical Research on Deliberative Democracy

Shawn W. Rosenberg

Since the fall of the Berlin Wall in 1989, political scientists have once again turned their attention to a critical examination of the state of democratic governance in their home countries. The trends of the last half century are troubling. In most Western democracies, citizen's trust and interest in politicians and political institutions have declined. People increasingly see politics as a remote arena populated by powers beyond their control pursuing interests that do not reflect the needs of the public at large. Political cynicism is widespread and it is often accompanied by a withdrawal from politics. Where voting is not a legal requirement, rates of participation in elections have also declined. For both citizens and political scientists, this has raised concerns about the well-being and legitimacy of democratic governance in those countries where it is most firmly established (e.g. Pharr et al., 2000; Pharr and Putnam, 2000).

This erosion of the polity in the Western democracies has been accompanied by indications that society itself is at risk. Apart from occasional minor reversals, the post–World War II period has been marked by increasing crime rates and growing prison populations, an indication of a weakening of social norms. Perhaps more significant, the commonality of those norms appears to be disintegrating. The mass migrations of the twentieth century have transformed Western societies into a collage of groups, each of which constitutes a local source of normative direction and social identification for its members. Partly this has been a matter of the dominant cultures giving more place and voice to immigrant groups. Although some governments (like the French) have actively resisted these changes, the trend is evident in most of the Western democracies, particularly in the former colonial states of Canada, Australia and the United States. However, the result is not the hoped for creation of some abstract community wherein cultural and individual differences are celebrated while a commitment to shared principles is sustained.[1] Instead, there has been a balkanization of society in which social affiliations, values and trust are increasingly limited to one's particular ethnic, racial and religious groups. In the view of some commentators, the social fabric of the advanced industrial societies of the Western democracies is unraveling.

From the perspective of democratic governance, a most troubling consideration is that electoral democracy may itself be contributing to this emerging state of affairs. As strategic competitions for support, electoral campaigns typically highlight differences in belief, value and social identity in a way that divides segments of the population against one another. To mobilize voters, electoral campaigns regularly identify subpopulations of voters and emphasize how their beliefs, values and policy interests are in conflict with and are threatened by the concerns of other subpopulations. The elections that follow do not yield a shared judgment, but simply produce the victors and vanquished of the moment. As a result, no common views are forged, little legitimacy is conferred and no trust develops. In largely homogeneous societies, an existing sense of a shared community (and with it a common past, present and future) naturally operates to minimize the divides that elections accentuate and to reassert the social bonds that have been called into question. Similarly, an existing shared culture operates to reassert overarching, common beliefs and values. However, in multicultural societies a sense of shared community is weak and cultural commonalities are thin. Here there is little to counter the social fragmentation and distrust of the opposition that electoral campaigns actively foster.

To address these problems, a number of political theorists have advocated a more deliberative form of democratic practice as a supplement to more conventional electoral democracy (e.g. Habermas, 1987, 1996; Gutmann and Thompson, 1996, 2004; Cohen, 1996, 1997; Bohman, 1997; Dryzek, 2000; Benhabib, 1996, 2002; and Chambers, 2003). They claim that citizens brought together to discuss public policy in a setting that emphasizes equal participation, mutual respect and reasoned argument will be more likely to bridge differences. They will also be more likely to produce policy decisions that are both perceived as more legitimate and are in fact more consensual, rational and just. These theorists also argue that deliberative institutions are better suited to realize the core democratic values of autonomy and equality and to foster citizen concern for the public good. Deliberative democracy is thus presented as at least a partial remedy for the social and political deterioration of the established democracies and as preventive medicine for the emerging ones.

This turn to deliberation is also evident in political practice. Reliance on deliberative fora of different types has become an increasing reality of political life. Books such as *The Deliberative Practitioner* (Forester, 1999; Fung and Wright, 2003) detail exemplary cases of deliberation in the United States, South America and Europe to illustrate the nature, difficulties and potential of citizen deliberation. My own investigation of deliberative efforts in the

United States suggests that citizen deliberations have been central in major city, school board, county and regional decision-making in over 1000 localities over the last 15 years. Deliberative political practice is also evident in the turn to 'citizen juries' in England, Germany, Denmark and Australia. The European Union has increasingly emphasized deliberative (sometimes referred to as collaborative) practices as central to the process of integration and public policy formulation. Even more authoritarian regimes have turned to some form of citizen deliberation to deal with particularly intractable problems. A good example here is the recent reliance of the Chinese government on deliberations in villages to deal with economic dislocations and consequent unrest in a number of rural areas.

Despite this surge of interest in deliberation, relatively little systematic research has been done. Initially a number of cases studies were conducted that involved more or less informal observation of single instances where citizens participated in some form of political or public policy deliberation (e.g. Mansbridge, 1980; Button and Mattson, 1999). However, little systematic research has been done. As a result, relatively little is known about the general quality and dynamics of deliberative processes or about the effect these processes have either on the collective decisions made or on the individuals who participate. Only recently has research of this kind begun. The present volume is an attempt to provide the reader with a coherent and somewhat comprehensive introduction to the panorama of work now being conducted. Thus the topics studied range from the extent and sites of ordinary citizen talk about politics to citizen deliberation about local policy-making to the deliberation of elected representatives in formal governmental institutions. A broad array of approaches is also represented, including survey research, informal and formal observational study, public choice analysis and experimental research.

In addition to providing an introduction to the empirical work now being conducted by the leading researchers in the field, this volume also represents an attempt to bring this research to the attention of some political theorists who have been central to the development of the theory of deliberative democracy. This is done with two goals in mind. One aim is to ask the theorists to provide empirical researchers with some feedback regarding their research. The central concern here is the relevance of the questions addressed in that research and the adequacy with which key theoretical concepts are operationalized. A second aim is to ask theorists to consider the theoretical implications of the results of the research presented. The goal here is to use the evidence presented on actual deliberation to further develop the theory of democratic deliberation. Overall the hope is to use the encounter between empirical research and theory to realize the potential that John Dryzek speaks of in his chapter, "Today, research on deliberative democracy is at the cutting edge of the integration of political theory and empirical social science. The empirical findings are quite capable of discomforting theorists, just as theorists are quite capable of discomforting empirical researchers." This volume is, in part, an effort to create productive discomfort.

In the remainder of this chapter, I provide the reader with a brief introduction to the family of ideas that comprise the theory of deliberative democracy. In so doing I first sketch the overarching view shared by most theorists who advocate for more deliberative democratic practice. I then focus on some basic differences in how deliberative democracy is conceived. Here I address the often underestimated difference between Anglo-American and continental approaches to the understanding of deliberation. I then offer a brief introduction to both the empirical and theoretical chapters that follow.

1.1   The idea of deliberative democracy: Commonalities and differences in theory

In presenting the idea of deliberative democracy, I begin with how it is conceptualized from an Anglo-American perspective. As Jane Mansbridge points out in her chapter, this conception of deliberative democracy underlies most English language theorizing and most empirical studies of democratic deliberation. I then present the more continental alternative understanding of deliberation offered by Jurgen Habermas. Although many deliberative democrats are quite content to cite both Anglo-American and Habermasian theorists as progenitors of the perspective they adopt, their positions differ significantly. Building on different epistemological assumptions, these two theoretical perspectives suggest different understandings of individuality, political relationships and political communication. As such they offer different direction for the analysis and implementation of democratic deliberation.

1.1.1   Deliberative democracy: The Anglo-American view

Although democracy is a contested concept, much of this contest begins with substantial agreement. In the Anglo-American approach, theorizing is anchored by a focus on the nature and value of the individual citizen. There follows a normative consideration of personal rights, namely individual autonomy and its social corollary, equality. The problem of democratic governance is conceived accordingly. It is one of crafting institutions that facilitate collective decision-making in a manner consistent with these fundamental values and thus with a good that is common to all. Beyond this quite general orientation, significant divergence emerges over how individuals are conceptualized and consequently over how autonomy and equality should be defined. Division over how best to institutionalize democratic governance follows.

Deliberative democratic theory emerged in the 1990s partly as a response to the "aggregative" view of democracy advanced by rational choice theorists. In this latter view, the individual is conceived as rational in a very limited sense. She is postulated to have a set of preferences that are ordered according to his/her desirability. Taking into consideration the constraints and opportunities present, he/she is then assumed to make choices that will lead to the satisfaction of these preferences.[2] The individual as citizen is conceived accordingly, that is as a self-directing actor who orients his/her initiatives in the political arena so as to realize his/her interests. Building on this conception of the citizen, autonomy is defined as the ability to freely affect collective decisions in a manner consistent with the pursuit of one's own preferences. In complementary fashion, equality is defined as a social relationship in which individuals have equivalent opportunity to freely pursue their interests in this collective, political domain. In this light the institutions of governance are designed so as to allow this free and equal pursuit of interest. The key mechanism developed is the political election complemented by a notion of government by law. In the attempt to better realize these political goals, the specific contours of governance are developed differently in theories of direct or representative democracy, but the foundational assumptions remain largely the same.

Endemic to this aggregative view of democracy is the potential conflict between personal preferences and the collective choice. With it emerge questions of legitimacy and compliance. Why would individuals oriented by their own interests accept outcomes that are inconsistent with those interests? Why would the losers in an election accept the outcome and abide by its consequences when this contravenes the rational pursuit of their interests? Rational choice theorists answer by suggesting that the conditions render apparently undesirable outcomes acceptable. Losers abide by electoral outcomes precisely because it is in their interest to do so. They may have lost in the recent election but they may win in the next. Accepting the present outcome supports the legal arrangement that insures that today's winners will accept their future loss. Moreover, government has the means to enforce the results of elections and the ensuing public policy, thereby increasing the cost of defection. Some have also argued that these expressly political forces must be supplemented by a reservoir of social trust or "social capital" that binds people to one another and to the political arrangements they create (e.g. Putnam 1993). In sum, the conditions of action bring the pursuit of personal interest into line with the requisites of the political system, thereby reducing problems of legitimacy and compliance. Critics suggest that while this solution may obtain when conditions are ideal, it is less workable in fragmented, complex societies where minority groups may have little hope of ever winning an election, where the use of executive power to force compliance from those who do not accept the law can be costly and is often ineffective, and where social trust is systematically undermined both by a multiculturalism that reinforces social cleavages and by an ethos of individualism that erodes all social ties and commitments.

Deliberative democrats offer a very different view of individuals and a commensurately different understanding of basic political values and how to best realize them in the design of political institutions. Their perspective is guided both by a modern liberalism, one well articulated by John Rawls' recent elaboration of a concept of political justice, and by the nineteenth-century contributions made by John Stuart Mill with his focus on public debate. Although deliberative theory explicitly rejects Rawls' reliance on the veil of ignorance, it does draw on the liberal conception of the individual so clearly articulated by Rawls in his theory of political justice (Rawl, 1993). Here the individual citizen is defined to have significantly greater cognitive capacities and moral potential than in rational choice theories. According to Rawls, all individuals are (or more exactly, must be) logical, rational and reasonable. In their logic, individuals are explicitly assumed to have the basic cognitive capacity to argue with reasons, to recognize criteria of justification, to understand rules of evidence, to be logical (to follow rules of inference and deduction) and to reflect on their own presuppositions. Implicitly it is assumed that individuals have the cognitive capacity to construct systems of interrelated propositions and abstract principles of relationships and to effectively use these constructions for the purpose of interpretation, explanation and evaluation. In their rationality, individuals are assumed to be able to consider and order their specific preferences and values relative to their overall life plan and their sense of a higher-order good. In their reasonableness, they are assumed to be able to take the perspective of the other and thus can fairly consider the claims of another person in that other person's terms. They are also able to consider not only the personal value of specific actions or outcomes, but also the common value of general principles of interaction (constitutional essentials). Individuals therefore have the capacity to make judgments that are guided by a sense of justice as fairness.

Rawls vacillates in his faith that individuals, even theoretically defined ones, can be relied upon to realize these capacities. Responding to concerns that individuals' motivations are naturally egocentric, he suggests the use of the "veil of ignorance" and the "original position" as a cognitive device to negate the influence of particular, selfish desires and to encourage the consideration of more general, social concerns. Rawls concludes that armed with this orienting cognitive device and their own natural capacities, individuals can critically reflect on their own views, fairly consider other's needs as well as their own and participate in defining the common good. Consequently, the interests that these individuals define for themselves are more broadly conceived. Any conflict between personally and collectively defined interests is thereby reduced and the problem of political conflict and the perceived illegitimacy of outcomes is diminished commensurately.

Although they adopt a theory of the citizen quite similar to the one articulated by Rawls, more deliberatively oriented theorists suggest that the personal reflection, even when guided by the use of a cognitive device, is not sufficient to insure that citizens approach political questions with the requisite reasonableness, rationality and logic. Instead these theorists argue that the desired critical self-reflection and fair orientation to the other can only be realized in an actual encounter with the beliefs, values and arguments of other citizens. The institutional demand to come to agreement on a course of action that others find workable and worthwhile emphasizes the need for perspective-taking, justification and the elaboration of a common good while rendering ineffective any claims that either are not justified or are justified on solely selfish grounds. Thus participation in deliberation leads individuals to reflect and interact in a way that is more logical (Gutmann and Thompson, 1996), rational (Benhabib, 2002), just, considerate of others (Gutmann and Thompson, 1996; Cohen, 1997), self-critical (Dryzek, 2000) and oriented to the common good (Cohen, 1997; Benhabib, 2002). The implicit assumption here is that, even if individuals have not fully developed the aforementioned capacities, they still have the requisite ability to participate in deliberation and can readily develop their skills as required in this context.

In the deliberative view, an individual is not only a rational actor who makes choices and acts to satisfy personal interests, he/she is also an ethical and moral agent who reflects and collaborates. Guided by reflections on his/her own overarching sense of the good life, a consideration of the interests of others and an understanding of the common good, he/she is able to reorder existing interests and create new ones. Following Mill (1861), deliberative theorists argue that this process is facilitated by constructive conversation in which others' views are expressed and one's own are given feedback. The democratic values of autonomy and equality are reconceived accordingly. The concept of political autonomy is redefined in recognition of the individual's increased capacities and broader bases of evaluation. The focus extends beyond the pursuit of one's own particular interests through freedom of expression and choice and centers on the process whereby personal interests and the common interest are revealed and perhaps modified through reflection and open, cooperative discussion. This recognition of the social dimension of the process of interest formation suggests an expansion of the concept of autonomy to include the freedom to participate with others in a joint attempt to elaborate each other's specific and general interests, to formulate just rules of interaction and to develop a shared sense of the common good. This also leads to a re-conceptualization of the notion of political equality. It can no longer be regarded just as a matter of an equivalent opportunity to affect specific collective decisions, for example through voting. Political equality requires equal opportunity to participate actively in a cooperative process of discussing public policy problems and the overarching values that should orient this policy-making effort.

In this deliberative conception, equality and autonomy require each other. On the one hand, equality is a necessary precondition of autonomy. It is only in a cooperative exchange between equals that the self-expression and critical self-reflection required for the self-reflective construction of one's understandings and interests is possible (e.g. Warren, 1992). Where the self dominates, self-criticism truncates and narrows. Where the other dominates, self-expression is suppressed. In either case, the self that is constructed is a distortion, and any true autonomy is compromised. On the other hand, equality requires autonomy. Deliberative equality is equality of effective participation (e.g. Bohman, 1996, 1997; Knight and Johnson, 1997). The latter can only be achieved by citizens who have full deliberative autonomy and thus have the capacity to express their own interests in a way that others can comprehend, and to reflect on those interests in light of ideas and aims voiced by other people. Where autonomy is compromised, meaningful equality cannot be achieved.

Typically this understanding of autonomy and equality suggests that they must not only be realized in informal political conversation, but that they must also be realized through participation in governance. Again this participation not only serves as an expression of autonomy, but also serves to sustain and develop it. This view is reflected in Mill's argument:

> "There is no difficulty in showing that the ideally best form of government is that in which the sovereignty, or supreme controlling power in the last resort, is vested in the entire aggregate of the community; every citizen not only having a voice in the exercise of that ultimate sovereignty, but being, at least occasionally, called on to take an actual part in the government, by the personal discharge of some public function, local or general. ... more salutary is the moral part of the instruction afforded by the participation of the private citizen, if even rarely, in public functions. He is called upon, while so engaged, to weigh interests not his own; to be guided, in the case of conflicting claims, by another's rules rather than his private partialities; to apply, at every turn, principles and maxims which have for their reason of existence the common good: and he finds associated with him in the same work, minds more familiarized than his own with these ideas and operations, whose study it will be to supply reasons to his understanding, and stimulation to his feeling for the general interest. He is made to feel himself one of the public and whatever is for their benefit to be for his benefit." (Mill, (1861) 1991)

The problem of democratic governance is reconsidered in this light. Given the broader conception of autonomy and equality, the emphasis on the design of institutions such as elections or referenda that allow individuals to freely pursue their personal interests by equally contributing to collective decision-making are regarded as inadequate. Instead the focus is on constructing institutional arrangements that create the opportunity for full and equal participation by citizens in a joint, cooperative process of clarifying, elaborating and revising common conceptions and values in the course of defining specific problems and determining how they should be addressed.

The solution is governance by citizen deliberation. Most of the theoretical efforts of deliberative democrats have focused on elaborating the conditions, procedures and salutary effects of the political institution of deliberation. This has been supplemented by recent work on deliberative policy analysis which has focused on the role of citizen deliberation in governmental decision-making (e.g. Fischer and Forester, 1987; Forester, 1999; Hajer and Wagenaar, 2003).

Deliberative democrats suggest a number of conditions that must be met if an interaction is to be a fully deliberative democratic exercise. Several prior conditions must be met before the deliberation actually begins.

1. There must be a suspension of action to create the political space for the deliberation to take place. There must be some assurance that decisions will not be taken and practical action will not be initiated until after the deliberation has been completed.
2. Once the political space for deliberation is created, it must be inclusive. This requirement is variously elaborated as the inclusion of all those parties potentially affected or of all the relevant points of view.
3. The deliberation must be public so that all those affected but not directly involved can be apprised of and can potentially respond to the substance of the deliberations (e.g. Gutmann and Thompson, 1996).
4. The results of the deliberation must be binding on all those involved (Cohen, 1997). Participants must not be able to circumvent the outcome of the deliberation by recourse to alternative means of affecting policy.
5. The deliberation must have some bearing on the formulation of public policy. This may involve playing an advisory role relative to elected officials or public administrators. Alternatively, the deliberation body may be more directly involved in the formulation of law or policy. (Forester, 1999; Hajer and Wagenaar, 2003)

Apart from meeting these prior conditions, the practice of deliberation must itself meet certain standards of conduct.

1. The practice of deliberation must be governed by a concern for autonomy. On the one hand, this requires that participation in the deliberation be free. The participants must be able to formulate and express their own views of the various issues that are raised. On the other hand, it necessitates that the integrity and value of each participant be acknowledged. This demands that each not only is free to speak, but that each also is heard with respect and consideration. Deliberation must foster communication that facilitates the expression of one's own views in a way that can be understood and accepted by the other and the expression of others' views in a way that one can understand their meaning and value in others' terms. One important means to accomplish this is

through argument with reasons. The value of the latter is its potential to link the differing beliefs or judgments of opposed parties to underlying claims of truth and value that both might accept. In Rawls' terms, it is a means to reveal an underlying or overlapping consensus on fundamentals that opposed parties may share. Argument is of course not the only means for communicating beliefs and feelings in ways that others can appreciate. This can also be done through joking, storytelling or personal narratives. The latter may be particularly important when there are significant differences in the relevant lived experiences of the different participants.

2. The deliberation must be guided by the concerns of equality. Each participant must have an equal opportunity to speak and to persuade his audience (e.g. Bohman, 1997; Knight and Johnson, 1997).

3. The outcomes of deliberation must be consistent with the associated values of justice as fairness and democracy as governance oriented to the common good and guided by the principles of autonomy and equality. For some theorists such as Gutmann and Thompson (1996), such an orientation to justice and democracy can only be insured by the stipulation of constitutional constraints. For others such as Benhabib (1996), Cohen (1996, 1997) and Knight (1999), the conditions of deliberative practice themselves not only embody these goals but also orient participants toward achieving them.

The claim here is that when these prior conditions are met and the standards of conduct are followed the ensuing discussion will be fully deliberative. As such it will consist of a respectful and reciprocal expression, correction, revision and restatement of views. In the process, thinking will become more logical and self-reflection will become deeper and more critical. As a result, personal beliefs, values and preferences will change. At the same time, this will encourage the discovery of a common ground for agreement, one that will yield more just and legitimate recommendations for public policy.[3] This in turn will provide a basis for both a renewal of interest and faith in democratic governance (thus addressing current problems of declining interest and participation in politics) and a means for social reintegration (thus addressing the problems of a socially destructive individualism and a socially disintegrative multiculturalism).

1.1.2   Continental European alternatives – from individuality to sociality[4]

While there is a common analytical focus on deliberation and democracy and a shared advocacy of the values of autonomy and equality, the continental European conception of deliberative democracy is quite different from that of the Anglo-American perspective presented in the preceding section. At its core, the difference is an epistemological one. This underlies significant differences in how individuals and social life are conceptualized and consequently how autonomy and equality are understood. This in turn suggests somewhat different direction for how deliberations should be instituted. This continental perspective is best exemplified in the work of Jurgen Habermas (1984/7, 1996). It is worth noting that with the very significant exception of an assumed rational foundation to discourse, many of the key assumptions of this perspective are also shared by poststructuralists. The latter have been among the most strident critics of both Habermasian and Anglo-American views of democratic deliberation (e.g. Mouffe, 2000 or Keenan, 2003).

A key point of departure for continental theorizing is the assumption that rationality or thinking is sociohistorically relative. The claim here is that how people think, that is how they perceive, define and integrate information, and consequently the quality of the product of their thinking, the understandings and values they construct, may vary across societies and historical epochs. An example of this is the historical differences in the understanding of what it means to be a person. In the late middle ages and the early enlightenment period, the definition of the character or nature of a person included a consideration of the property they owned. That property was considered an attribute of the person in much the same sense as her intelligence or good humor. Such a concept of a person is quite alien to more contemporary Western conceptions of a person as being defined by set of internal dispositions (character) and capacities. Another example is offered by a comparison of the structure of early European folk tales of the same period and the more contemporary narratives of the nineteenth-century novel (or, for that matter, current television dramas). The latter are characterized by a clear linear causal structure to the narrative. Early events have causal impact on latter ones. The terms of coherence of the whole story is dictated by this causal structure so that the meaning and relevance of early events are ultimately revealed by their relationship to final outcomes. The structure of early folk tales is quite different. By comparison they seem to include a series of rather discreet episodes that seem to follow one another in a rather haphazard sequence. A later event is not caused by an earlier one; it simply follows it in time. In this sense the only coherence to the story seems to be that its sequence of events is typically, if not always, populated by the same central character. In both the case of the propertied individual and the meandering folk tale, the quality of the understanding constructed was readily comprehensible to people of the time; however, it appears alien to more contemporary Western understandings. The inference drawn from such examples is that as we move from one society or historical period to another, not only do the substance of people's beliefs and preferences change, but so may the formal quality of how they think and thus of the understandings and values they construct. Translated into the terms of Anglo-American theorizing, the suggestion is that the quality of the logic, rationality and reasonableness of individuals' thinking is not universal, but may vary across societies and history.

In this vein, Habermas rejects a subjectivist concept of thinking that highlights the universal qualities of mind in favor of a more sociohistorical view of thinking as something that occurs in the interaction between people in a way that is conditioned by the social and cultural conditions of their interpersonal exchange. The activity of thinking – the making of connections and the defining of the objects thereby connected – is no longer explicated with reference to the activity of the subject, to the connections he/she makes in his/her head, but instead with regard to the interaction between several subjects and to the connections made in the course of their acting upon one another. The latter connections are viewed as the means whereby significant relationships and ultimately systems of meaning are constructed. When attention does turn to an individual's cognitive activity, it is largely understood to be a product of the discourses or social interactions in which she participates (e.g. Habermas, 1979). Consistent with the historical considerations mentioned earlier, the form of intersubjective engagement and consequentially the qualities of individual's subjectivity are understood to be socially and historically conditioned (e.g. Habermas, 1987).

Such a view of thought and meaning leads to a distinctive conceptualization of democratic deliberation. This is evident in the different understanding of the autonomy of individuals and the desired relationship between individuals that is generated. In the Anglo-American view, autonomy is a natural attribute of all individuals, the political manifestation of the inherent capacity for self-direction that follows from their ability to be logical, rational and self-reflective. In the continental view, the abilities assumed by Anglo-American theorists are regarded as specific achievements that are not universally shared. Similarly autonomy is not viewed as something that naturally exists and has a singular form, but rather as something that is socially constructed and may take a variety of forms. In this regard, it is possible to refer to greater and lesser forms of autonomy and to understand each kind of autonomy as an achievement that reflects a particular form of social engagement and the cognitive capacities which that form of social engagement fosters in the individuals involved. (For an example of such analysis, see my Chapter 7 on the kinds of citizenship different forms of deliberative discourse fosters.)

Related to this conception of autonomy is a distinctive understanding of the form of political relationships. No longer do political relationships just provide a venue for the expression of an inherent individuality, either by translating personal choices into collective decisions (as in the aggregative view) or by stimulating reflection on preferences through the provision of more information or counterargument (as in the more deliberative view). Instead, political relationships are understood to enable social interaction in a way that affects the development of individuals' cognitive capacities and the quality of the understanding and values they construct. Thus the normative focus shifts away from considerations of a simple equality of opportunity (either of choice or of voice) among interdependent, but largely self-directing actors. It turns instead to the quality of social interaction, as it pertains to how individuals are constituted as subject/actors. Considerations of equality are thus coupled with considerations of complementarity. While a question of the kind, "Do all participants have equal voice?" remains a concern, the question, "Are people engaging one another in a manner that contributes to their capacity have their own voice?" is raised as more fundamental.[5] It should be noted here that this emphasis on connection naturally leads to a consideration not only of the intersubjective, cognitive elements of political relationships, but also of their emotional and empathic aspects.

While sharing many of the prescriptions of the Anglo-American view, the continental understanding of cognition, sociality and society leads to a distinctive approach to the institutionalizing of democratic deliberation. This approach is oriented by several key assumptions: (a) communication in a deliberation is not an amorphous or neutral medium, but instead has a form or structure which orchestrates how individuals can engage one another, (b) this communicative structure shapes the cognitive capacities, socioemotional orientation and communicative competence of individuals in fundamental ways, (c) this structure may take different forms, depending on the nature of the larger social and cultural context, (d) variation in the formal structure of deliberative communications will effect how people can talk to one another, the kind of understandings and values they can collectively construct, and thus the kind of persons that the individual participants can be.

The foregoing assumptions suggest a very different approach to democratic deliberation than the one implied by the Anglo-American view. In the latter view, people have the requisite cognitive capacities and communicative competence such that the potential for effective, cooperative and fair deliberation inheres in any deliberative context. The key problem that may emerge is one of externally induced inequalities (such as those of class, education, income and race) that then interfere with the full and fair expression of the autonomy of the participants. The design of deliberations is thus evaluated with the goal of protecting otherwise capable, autonomous actors from these external interferences and constraints.

In the continental view, the problem goes deeper than this. The capacities and autonomy of the participants are not regarded as given, but rather as something that must be created. Thus the focus of institutional design questions shifts to the construction of the capacities and autonomy that most democratic theories simply assume or stipulate. This leads to two related considerations. The first is more descriptive and analytical. The focus here is on the existing social conditions of the proposed deliberation. Several questions are raised in this regard: What are the dominant forms of discourse present in the larger society? What kinds of social cooperation and what kinds of collaborative meaning-making and judgment do these dominant discourses enable or prevent? What implications do these discourses have for how the potential participants in a deliberation are likely to be constituted? That is, what are the probable cognitive capacities (and thus the kind of logic, rationality and reasonableness) of the participants and how are they likely to engage one another in the deliberation? The second type of consideration is more normative and remedial. The concern here is an emancipatory one. The critical question is as follows: Given the limitations imposed by the larger social/discursive context and the consequent limitations of the participants, how can the deliberation be structured so as to foster a more adequate (that is more fully deliberative and democratic) form of intersubjective engagement and, in so doing, enable better forms of cooperative decision-making and foster the development of the greater autonomy of the participants?

As indicated by the foregoing concerns, the continental view suggests that deliberation must not simply be thought of and institutionalized as a "free" space that is created by warding off external sources of inequality. This is not enough. This will only allow for the re-enactment of the prevalent, if subtle, ways in which individuals' autonomy is limited and their relationships are defined in undemocratic, subdemocratic or antidemocratic ways. Rather, deliberation must be institutionalized so as to address limitations that inhere in the construction of how citizens engage one another and in who they are as individuals. This leads to an institutional design considerations that focus on the dynamics of deliberative exchange and how they may be influenced by some form of pedagogically and democratically oriented facilitation.

In sum, there are significantly different approaches to deliberative democracy. I have tried to highlight some of these differences by comparing the Anglo-American and continental approaches. I have argued that these two differ because they are oriented by different epistemologies that in turn suggest different understandings of human capacities and the role played by social communication in individual psychology, the formation of communities and the quality of deliberative decision-making. As a result the two approaches generate different understandings of the limits and potential of citizen deliberation and address different concerns when considering the design of deliberative institutions. Despite these differences, these two streams of deliberative democratic theory are united by a common focus on citizen participation in governance through public discourse on the problems they as a community confront. This leads to many shared concerns regarding the free, open and cooperative quality of deliberative decision-making. It also leads to a shared faith that democratic deliberation offers a form of democratic governance that can contribute to (a) the making of more effective and just policy decisions, (b) the building of more united communities that embrace group and individual differences, (c) the facilitating of more equal, caring and cooperative social relations, and (d) the fostering of greater levels of cognitive and social development of individual citizens. Most of these concerns, both divergent and shared, are addressed by the empirical research presented in this volume.

1.2 The empirical study of deliberation: An overview of the chapters

Whereas deliberative democratic theory may vary in its assumptions and in its consequent analytical and normative trajectory, its various streams share the problem of a dearth of systematic empirical research on a core concern, deliberative discourse. The result is a great deal of stipulation and conjecture and very little relevant evidence. The first chapters in this volume exemplify the recent efforts of empirical political scientists to fill this gap. The last chapters were solicited in the attempt to encourage theorists to seriously consider this empirical research. I had two goals in mind here. The first was to provide theorists with the opportunity to critically assess the nature and direction of the empirical research and, in this way, help make it more relevant to democratic theory. The second was to have theorists draw on the evidence of deliberation offered in the work to critically assess deliberative democratic theory and thus make it more relevant to the realities and practices of everyday political life.

1.2.1 Empirical studies of democratic deliberations: An overview of Chapters 2–9

Like its theoretical counterpart, this empirical effort is characterized by a variety of focal concerns and methodologies. Some research focuses on political talk more generally. In research of this kind, there is less attention to the substance or quality of the talk or to the conditions under which it occurs. Other research considers more particular kinds of political talk such as the dialogue which occurs in settings designed to foster cross-cultural understanding or the specifically political deliberation that occurs in institutional contexts designed to produce collective decisions. In the latter instance researchers have studied a variety of groups and settings ranging from students in university experiment to citizens in a deliberation on local policy to legislators participating in parliamentary debate. Each of these topical concerns is represented in the empirical studies reported in this volume. These studies also vary in the research designs they employ. Various methods for data are used including close-ended questionnaires, open-ended self-report, rational or social choice analysis, informal observation and systematic content analysis. A number of different research designs are represented, including a focus on specific interesting populations, random sampling, case studies and both laboratory and field experiments.

In Chapter 2, entitled "Who Deliberates? Discursive Participation in America," Fay Lomax Cook, Michael Delli Carpini and Lawrence Jacobs explore how and to what degree Americans talk about politics. To this end, they distinguish four kinds of political talk: traditional talk (the personal, face-to-face discussion about politics people have with friends, family and fellow workers), face-to-face deliberation in formal settings (including formal organized citizen deliberations related to policy-making and more open-ended discussions on issues organized by schools, churches or other associations) and Internet communication, either Internet discussion (of the kind that occurs in chat groups or on message boards) or email exchange. To discover who is engaging in what kind of talk, the authors conducted a national telephone survey in which subjects reported on their political talk over the preceding year. Among an array of interesting results, two findings stand out. One is on the amount of talk. Two-thirds of Americans report engaging in some of kind of regular political talk and one-fourth report having participated in at least one organized forum in the preceding year. A second particularly interesting finding bears on the determinants of talk. Contrary to common expectation, socioeconomic status had no consistent effect on engaging in political talk. A factor that did emerge as critical was group membership.

In Chapter 3, entitled "The Democratic Potential of Civic Dialogue," Kathy Cramer Walsh focuses on a particular style of talk, civic dialogue. Civic dialogue is a kind of conversation that is encouraged in organized settings that aim to foster greater understanding and empathy among participants who come from different, often mutually antagonistic, racial or ethnic groups. In the course of describing examples of efforts to promote civic dialogue, Walsh juxtaposes this kind of discourse to democratic deliberation as normally conceived. In so doing, she distinguishes civic dialogue as more oriented to exploring and revealing differences, privileging personal experience and emotional expression and as aiming to creating interpersonal connections. In a complementary way, she suggests that conventionally conceived deliberation is defined as more concerned with reaching agreement. It consequently tends to marginalize minority perspectives and to privilege argument in a way that renders emotional expression and personal narratives irrelevant or inappropriate. In this context, Walsh points to the democratic value of civic dialogue as a form of discourse that respects differences by encouraging the expression of minority and conflicting understandings and values.

In Chapter 4, entitled "Deliberation and Agreement," Christian List utilizes a social choice theory approach to explore the value of deliberation as a mechanism for correcting the limitations of voting as a means for making collective choices. His focus is the limitations highlighted by Kenneth Arrow's impossibility theorem. Exploring the indeterminacy that voting sometimes produces, List suggests that the underlying problem is the lack of structure to the preferences being aggregated. He argues that where there is considerable disagreement on specific alternatives, the problem can be resolved if agreement can be reached on the underlying characterization of the problem and the alternative policies being discussed. Specifically, a kind of "meta-agreement" must be reached on the underlying dimension of the problem along which individuals' various preferences may be arrayed. With this in place, voting does yield a determinate result. List argues that it is in this context that purpose and value of democratic deliberation becomes clear. Through deliberation, participants may come to the requisite meta-agreement on the issue dimension underlying the problem they are addressing and then use this dimension to locate their preferences relative to one another. The subsequent aggregation of their preferences avoids the indeterminacy dilemma suggested by Arrow and Condorcet.

In Chapter 5, entitled "Deliberation in Legislatures," Andre Bachtiger, Markus Sporndli, Marco Steenbergen and Jurg Steiner explore the nature of deliberation in the formal political institution of a parliament. In so doing, they examine deliberations in the national legislatures of Switzerland, Germany, the United Kingdom and the United States. Apart from its focus on the special case of parliamentary discourse, their chapter contributes to the study of deliberation in two ways. On the one hand it offers a tool for the analysis of deliberative exchange, the Discourse Quality Index. Inspired by the definition of communicative action defined by Jurgen Habermas, the DQI offers a way of examining deliberative discourse that measures the respect accorded to others and their arguments, the content and level of justifications of arguments that are made, and the willingness to change position. On the other hand it offers evidence on the impact that institutional arrangements and issue conflict have on the quality of discourse and on the impact that the quality of discourse has on deliberative outcomes. Among a number of intriguing results, they find that the qualities of the different chambers of a legislature affect their willingness to change positions and the publicity of the deliberation affects both the level and the content of the justifications offered. With regard to the effects of discourse, they find that discourse quality influences the ability to come to agreement, but has no effect on the justice or fairness of the decision reached.

In Chapter 6, entitled, "How People Deliberate about Justice," Tali Mendelberg and Christopher Karpowitz examine deliberation through a secondary analysis of student discussion and decisions in a deliberative justice experiment. In their analysis, they focus on the impact of group norms and decision rules on the equity of the decision reached by the various student groups. Examining how the gender makeup of the group affects the norm invoked, Mendelberg and Karpowitz discover that norms do have a significant impact on the generosity the group was willing to show to disadvantaged groups. Where most members were female, groups were more generous. Where most members were male, groups were stingier. This effect was enhanced when the group decision required consensus rather than a majority vote. Evidence of this interactive effect of norms and decision rule was also evident in how participants talked to one another during the discussion. Turning to deliberative democratic theory, the authors argue that their research suggests that rather than being a vehicle for the open and rational exploration of a problem and its alternative solutions, deliberation may instead operate so as to reinforce the norms of the dominant group in the deliberation and to marginalize minority perspectives.

In Chapter 7, entitled "Types of Discourse and the Democracy of Deliberation," I explore the nature of deliberative discourse through the observation of two citizen groups convened to make recommendations regarding K-12 education in their town. Eschewing the strategy of postulating a single ideal form of discourse and then measuring the degree to which existing discourses match that ideal, the chapter offers a typology of the different forms the discourse may take. These include (1) protodiscourse in which talk is a secondary means that individuals utilize by drawing on their personal understandings to realize immediate private goals, (2) conventional discourse that draws on shared representations and politeness rules in order to choose the correct course of action and to maintain existing social relationships among the interlocutors, (3) collaborative discourse that entails the exchange of information and reasoned arguments to reach agreement on the nature of the problem, the value of alternative solutions and the appropriateness of the way in which the deliberation is being conducted, and (4) transformative discourse that involves an awareness of basic differences in participants' understandings and critical reflection on the discourse situation with the goal of solving a policy problem in a way that fosters a self-aware, caring and cooperative construction of the individuality of the participants and of the culture of the deliberative group they are forming. The prevalence of these different types of discourse in actual citizen deliberations was examined through an observation of two deliberative groups. In a way that was presumed to favor higher-level discourse, the groups included well-educated, high-income and empowered participants. The results suggest that the deliberations were mostly conventional and to a lesser degree protodiscursive. Rational discourse was rare and transformative discourse did not occur at all. Drawing out the relevance of these results to democratic theory, the chapter concludes with a consideration of how different types of discourses might shape interaction and thus delimit who individuals can be and how they can relate to one another in a deliberative setting. In this light, the kind of autonomy and political relationship each type of discourse fosters is explored.

In Chapter 8, entitled "Minipublics: Deliberative Designs and Their Consequences," Archon Fung develops a typology of forms of deliberative institutions and then illustrates its utility by briefly discussing five case studies of deliberation. Adopting a structural functional approach, Fung builds his typology of deliberative institutions by distinguishing the different aims they are intended to achieve (e.g. educational, advisorial, collaborative or governing) and the means by which these aims are pursued. In the latter case, he poses Harold Lasswell's questions of the "who" (who participates and who doesn't), "what" (the personal significance of the issues addressed), "when" (the length and frequency of meetings) and "how" (modes of expression fostered) of the design of deliberations. With these distinctions in hand, Fung then theorizes about the consequences of the design choices that have been made. Here he considers the kind of participation that is fostered (e.g. mobilizing potential, inclusion biases), the effect on the participants (e.g. the information to which they are exposed and the democratic skills they learn), the effect on policy-making (e.g. effectiveness of policy produced and the accountability of government officials that is fostered) and the potential for mobilizing citizens who are not direct participants in the deliberation. With this framework of aims, means and outcomes, Fung ends the chapter by turning to the examination of the five illustrative cases, ranging from deliberative polls of the opinions of randomly sampled people to the deliberative governance of budgetary issues in Porto Alegre, Brazil.

In Chapter 9, entitled, "Deliberation with a Purpose: Reconnecting Communities and Schools," Stephen Weatherford and Lorraine McDonnell explore the impact of citizen deliberations on public policy by examining five communities in South Carolina who engaged in the Reconnecting Community and Schools project. They examine the causal impact of such factors as the quality of the recommendations that are made, the relationship of the citizen body to agencies with decision-making power, and the political history and culture of the local area. Through their examination of the communities involved, Weatherford and McDonnell draw a number of interesting conclusions. One is the important observation that it is possible to have a civil discourse about schools, even in communities with a history of divisiveness. A second significant observation is that these deliberations draw a more diverse group than one might expect and than are normally in attendance at other venues for participating in schools. A third conclusion was that citizen forums work best when information is provided by relevant experts, in this case educators, but only if that information is provided in an nonauthoritarian fashion. A fourth is that citizen groups have a greater policy impact when there is a positive working relationship with relevant governmental agencies and, in a related way, when there is a political culture and history of citizen–government trust and cooperation. A final conclusion is that, although citizen forums may significantly affect governmental agencies, they appear less able to mobilize the public in desired ways. They also have difficulty in motivating citizens to take up considerations that go beyond their own schools and neighborhoods.

1.2.2 Theoretical reflections on the empirical research: An overview of Chapters 10–13

In Chapter 10, entitled "Deliberative Democracy," Joshua Cohen offers an analysis of democratic and deliberative qualities of deliberative democracy and then considers the empirical research on two of its most significant, theoretically stipulated features – the use of reasoning and reasons as central to the process of collective decision-making and the quality of the decisions that are thereby produced. Addressing the nature of deliberative democracy, Cohen argues that democratic deliberation combines a deliberative concern with weighing reasons when making a decision and a democratic concern with equality and making regulatory decisions that connect to the interests of those regulated. As such, deliberative democracy subjects power to the discipline of talk and to the reasoning of equal persons. Turning to the empirical research chapters, Cohen considers how that work illuminates two key concerns of deliberative democratic theory: (1) the role played by reasoning in the deliberative process and (2) the quality of the outcomes of deliberation, that is their justice, their impact on the preferences and knowledge of individual participants and their effect on the way in which people regard one another and their community. Focusing on the quality of deliberative discourse, he raises questions about the substantive focus of some research (e.g. the focus on political talk more generally or on civic dialogue in particular). Responding to evidence of the inadequacies of deliberative discourse, Cohen notes the apparent fragility of deliberation and the consequent significance of the manner in which it is instituted. Addressing the research on deliberative outcomes, Cohen argues that insufficient attention has been paid to possible effects on the perceived legitimacy of outcomes, the mutual respect among participants and the development of community.

In Chapter 11, entitled "Theory, Evidence and the Tasks of Deliberation," John Dryzek considers the interface of theory and empirical research on deliberation. He begins with a critical discussion of how evidence has been used and misused in the discussion of democratic deliberation. While clearly noting the importance of evidence, Dryzek adopts a cautionary tone by emphasizing how advocates have often avoided any consideration of the "facts" of deliberation by simply stipulating what they must be. Similarly, he chastises critics for stylizing or distorting the facts or for drawing on facts gathered through inappropriate methods. Having offered these caveats, Dryzek turns to an analysis of the tasks of deliberation. These include fostering a certain kind of discourse, changing preferences, legitimating policy, affecting the substance of policy, enhancing the rationality of problem-solving, rendering collective choice more tractable, fostering political equality and enhancing citizenship. Using this framework, Dryzek reviews both the strengths and weaknesses of the empirical chapters in the book and some additional research published elsewhere.

In Chapter 12, entitled "Deliberative Democracy or Democratic Deliberation," Jane Mansbridge offers her understanding of the difference between a more philosophical, European view of 'deliberative democracy' and a more political science, American view of what she terms 'democratic deliberation.' Using the example of Habermas' early writings on the public sphere, she argues that the European philosophical focus on reasoning as a critical aspect of the process and on justice as its critical outcome is inappropriately narrow. By contrast, she suggests that the American political science view is more open in its consideration of democratic processes recognizing the value of fair aggregation (i.e., voting). Adopting the American view, Mansbridge advocates a more plural approach to deliberative democracy. This involves recognizing that there is considerable, normatively appropriate variation in what can constitute the giving of reasons, how the common good can be understood, how legitimacy can be conferred and how deliberation may conducted. In her review of the empirical chapters, Mansbridge focuses on the topics studied and concludes that the work is overwhelmingly oriented by the concerns of the more pluralistic American conception of democratic deliberation that she adopts and commensurately little attention is paid to the concerns of the more narrow European alternative.

In Chapter 13, entitled "Institutionalizing Deliberative Democracy," Mark Warren takes a somewhat different approach than the preceding chapters. In those chapters, the authors draw on their existing theoretical understandings of deliberative democracy and examine the empirical research in that light. Warren is more interested in drawing on the research to interrogate the limits of the theory and suggest direction for both future theory and research. In this vein, Warren begins by discussing deliberative democratic theory, suggesting that it is distinguished by a commitment to a particular medium of conflict resolution rather than to particular institutions or civic virtues. However, his aim here is not to highlight what the theory offers, but rather to focus on what it fails to offer. He argues that the empirical research indicates that democratic deliberation is very demanding and is not readily realized in actual practice. Deliberative democratic theory must recognize this fact, and in so doing it must offer an account of deliberation that connects to questions of institutional design. This requires analysis of the dynamics of democratic deliberation and the kinds of institutional arrangements and incentives that might lead that dynamic toward better outcomes. This entails getting clear on the types and social psychology of the discourses that occurs in deliberative settings and then determining which institutional conditions that are likely to produce more deliberative democratic effects. With this, Warren sets the agenda both for theory and empirical research on deliberative democracy. Considering the larger political context, he also suggests that deliberation must be understood as only one locus of decision-making and organization among others in the broader systems of a democracy.

Notes

1. For a discussion of this kind of community, see Habermas's (1996, Appendix 2) discussion of "constitutional patriotism" and the critical considerations of Markell (2000).

2. There is very little attention to psychological processes. Thus the question of how a preference ordering is constructed is regarded as a secondary consideration and left unclear. Similarly, the nature of cognitive processes is not specified, but rather is loosely conceived in terms of some vague notions of logic and common sense.

3. This common ground is sometimes assumed to already exist either explicitly or implicitly in the larger, shared political culture of the participants. This is suggested by the relativism of the later Rawls (1993) with his invocation of the critical role of a pre-existing "overlapping consensus." For most deliberative theorists, this common ground is conceived in more universalist terms and inheres in the essential quality of the human condition. For liberals this resides in the nature of the individual. For theorists who follow Habermas (1984/87), this common ground is found in the structure of the intersubjective engagement inherent in discourse itself.

4. The term "European perspective" is employed as a matter of convenience. While the English Channel and North Atlantic are important intellectual as well as geographic markers, they are an imperfect way of drawing boundaries. For example, there is an American tradition, one that builds on the pragmatism of John Dewey which adopts a more traditionally European concern for forms of intersubjective engagement and associated differences in the quality of individual cognition or subjectivity.

5. A somewhat misleading, but familiar and suggestive, parallel is offered in Lukes' well-known analysis of different kinds of power (Lukes, 1974). He discusses three kinds: the power to tell people what to do, the power to control the agenda of discussion regarding what things might be done, and the power to shape what people want and believe. The distinctions I draw here suggest that the Anglo-American view leads to a focus on the first two kinds of power and the continental view, although it focuses more on the qualities of thinking than that on particular wants and beliefs, is much more concerned with the third kind.

Part I

Empirical Studies of Democratic Deliberation

2
Who Deliberates? Discursive Participation in America[1]

Fay Lomax Cook, Michael X. Delli Carpini, and Lawrence R. Jacobs

Much contemporary analysis of American democracy sounds the alarm that citizens are retreating from the political process. Voter turnout appears to have declined over the past thirty years, with this trend most notable among the young. Many public attitudes and opinions about candidates, parties, elected officials, and the campaign and policy processes, more generally, all show disturbing signs of decay (Texiera, 1992; Rosenstone and Hansen, 1993; Patterson, 2002). Similar trends can be seen in several measures of citizens' cognitive and affective engagement in politics and government, as well as their sense of government officials' responsiveness to their wants and wishes (Texiera, 1992; Rosenstone and Hansen, 1993; Erikson and Tedin, 2001; Patterson, 2002). More ominously, many observers of American public life conclude that low or declining participation in the electoral process reflects a broader civic disengagement that is rooted in the erosion of community networks and the decline in "social capital" (Rahn and Transue, 1998; Putnam, 2000), or new elite strategies geared toward the affluent and professionals (Skocpol, 2003).

Perhaps unsurprisingly, some scholars dispute these trends. McDonald and Popkin (2001) argue that reported declines in voter turnout are inflated by treating immigrants, felons, and other individuals who cannot vote as if they were eligible, though even the adjusted turnout rates are below those found in the 1960s. Many measures of civic and political engagement (e.g., political interest, political knowledge, internal political efficacy, and several measures of campaign-related behavior) show little consistent evidence of decline over time (Abramson, 1983; Smith, 1989; Delli Carpini and Keeter, 1996). And evidence of a wholesale decline in social capital has been challenged on a number of fronts (Ladd, 2000; Skocpol and Fiorina, 2000; Skocpol, 2003). Without question, portions of the public remain concerned – at times intensely – about a range of issues. Many Americans are engaged in debates over competing social issues related to gay marriage and abortion, conflicts over economic redistribution through taxation and government revenues, and the clash of values and interests witnessed, for instance, in the battles between environmentalists and economic developers. Marches by thousands of Americans who favored and opposed the war in Iraq also appeared to reflect deep interest in government policy even as participation in the "headline" politics of electoral and legislative processes is atrophying. The debate is further complicated by the possibility that while some forms of participation (e.g., voting or membership in traditional neighborhood associations) may be declining, other, less well-understood or measured forms of engagement (e.g., online "communities" and "associations") may be growing.

Nonetheless, one need not accept the most Cassandra-like warnings of the collapse of civic and political life to be concerned about the health of American democracy. Participation in the electoral process has traditionally been disappointingly low in the United States when compared to other advanced democracies, a point which should not be ignored simply because its roots are deep. Although engagement in civic life may not be decaying to the extent that some have argued, Putnam and others have amassed enough evidence of a decline in associational life to give one pause. While more Americans have shown a willingness to engage in acts of compassion and charity than is sometimes acknowledged (as witnessed, for example, in the aftermath of the September 11 terrorist attacks) such involvement appears to be sporadic and usually lacks any direct connection to broader issues of policy or politics. Finally, and perhaps most importantly, most forms of civic and especially political engagement in the United States – whether declining or not – are skewed in favor of socially and economically advantaged citizens (Verba, Schlozman, and Brady, 1995), leading to Schattschneider's classic and still apt conclusion that "the flaw in the pluralist heaven is that the heavenly chorus sings with a strong upper class accent" (1960: 35).

A central question that underlies this multilayered debate about the civic and political health of the nation is "How do Americans voice their preferences on public issues?" In this chapter we address the question using some results from a larger project. We explore an important and to our minds understudied outlet for civic and political engagement by citizens – what we call "discursive participation." By discursive participation we mean the various ways in which citizens can talk in public settings about issues that affect the community, state, or nation in which they live – from one-on-one conversations to e-mail exchanges to more formal meetings. Such participation does not always provide the kind of institutional guarantees found in electoral and legislative politics. But it may nevertheless bolster the capacities and resources of citizens to understand opposing views and articulate their own views, motivate them to participate, and recruit them into organizations and activities to further their views and interests. Ultimately, we believe that discursive participation by individual citizens can enhance participatory resources, motivations, and recruitment, though the extent and representativeness of these enhancements remain to be established.

More specifically, this chapter addresses three simple but important questions regarding discursive participation in the United States. First, what forms does discursive participation take and how common are they? Second, what are the demographic, political, and social characteristics of citizens who engage in these various forms of discursive participation? And third, which of these characteristics are most important in predicting who deliberates. We begin by reviewing existing theory and research on public deliberation and our concept of discursive participation. After describing our data and measures, we present evidence regarding the extent and types of discursive participation currently occurring in the United States and examine the demographic, social, and political characteristics of Americans who engage in these different forms of public talk.

2.1   Theory and research on public deliberation

A large group of scholars, foundations, and public intellectuals agree with Benjamin Page that "public deliberation is essential to democracy" (1996: 1). The celebration of public deliberation by citizens has a long history that flows from the city-states of ancient Greece to the town hall meetings of colonial New England to the salons and cafes of Paris. Democratic theory has long designated public deliberation as a cornerstone of participatory democracy and representative government (Dewey, 1927; Habermas; 1962; Mansbridge, 1980; Connolly, 1983; Barber, 1984; Dahl, 1989; Fishkin, 1992; 1995). The practice of public deliberation has also been a subject of scholarly research. This tradition of research ranges from case studies of group deliberations (Mansbridge, 1980; Gamson, 1992; Gastil, 2000; Lindeman, 2002) to quasi-experimental designs built around face-to-face (Luskin and Fishkin, 1998; 1999) or online (Price and Cappella, 2001) discussions, to extrapolations from the psychological literature on small group dynamics (Mendlberg, 2002) to explorations of "mass mediated" (Page, 1996) or "survey based" (Lindeman, 2002) deliberation.

Public deliberation is also enjoying a renaissance outside of the academy. President Clinton's initiative on race in the early 1990s was premised on the power and value of public discussion regarding a divisive but often unspoken issue. Televised initiatives such as James Fishkin's "deliberative polls," town-hall meeting style presidential debates, *Nightline's* or *Hardball's* occasional public forums, even talk shows such as *Oprah* all try to capture the spirit of public deliberation, albeit in ways that are more spectator sport than active involvement for the vast majority of American citizens. For others, the Internet holds the potential key for blending the advantages of face-to-face discussion with the scale and convenience of modern communications technology. Public deliberation has been supported by non-profits such as the Kettering Foundation's "national issues forums," the Study Circles Resource Center, and the Pew Charitable Trusts.

This eclectic group of promoters has been attracted to public deliberation for varied reasons, but three tend to stand out. First, public deliberation is a means for citizen education and training. Page credits it with "ensuring that the public's policy preferences – upon which democratic decisions are based – are informed, enlightened, and authentic" (1996: 1). In addition to educating citizens, deliberation can also be a tool for building a sense of efficacy and trust in political institutions and in fellow citizens. Second, participation in public deliberation has been cited as a tool for the moral (and not simply instrumental) development of citizens. Publicly talking about issues of community concern forces citizens to consider competing interests and values and to accept responsibility not only for themselves but also for the well-being of others (Pateman, 1970; MacPherson, 1977; Barber, 1984). Third, public deliberation has been singled out as a unique mechanism for producing collective decisions. Policy entrepreneurs as diverse as urban planners and ecologists have embraced public deliberation as a tool for reconciling competing perspectives. For instance, public deliberation has been used as a method for discussing and negotiating such diverse issues as how to safely produce genetically modified organisms, encourage economic development, and develop efficient and environmentally sustainable uses of energy (e.g., Forester, 1999; Kapuscinski et al., 2003. In an era of great divisiveness over policy issues and partisan positions, the traditional tools of electoral and legislative avenues to collective decision making remain essential. But they have also become deadlocked or have alienated large parts of America. Public deliberation has emerged as a potentially valuable way of breaking (or at least sidestepping) this deadlock.

Although scholars and practitioners appreciate the promise of public deliberation, there remain deep doubts about its practicality, political significance, and even appropriateness as a core feature of a vibrant democracy. The holding of civic forums is often considered too infrequent and uncommon to deserve much attention, despite the visibility of occasional efforts. Still others are concerned that public deliberation is little more than another enclave of "gated democracy" – a practice reserved for the same group of affluent Americans who disproportionately deploy their checkbooks to lure candidates to their favorite positions or who are well endowed with social capital. Yet another complaint is that civic forums are "just talk" – idle chat that is cut off from government decision making about important issues of the day. Perhaps most damning, some argue that many citizens are unable to participate effectively in such deliberative settings, that public deliberation can produce unintended consequences such as "opinion polarization ... shifts in opinion in new and risky directions ... [and] social-normative pressures that can subvert sound judgment" (as summarized by Price et al., 2003: 5. See also Mansbridge, 1980; Sanders, 1997; Schudson, 1997; Brown, 2000; Sunstein, 2001; Hibbing and Theiss-Morse, 2002b). Put simply, the strong and persistent presumption is that public deliberation is so infrequent, unrepresentative, and disconnected from actual decisionmaking as to make it an impractical mechanism for determining the public will at best and misleading or dangerous at worst.

There is, however, a noticeable disjuncture between on the one hand the growing debate regarding the potential and pitfalls of public deliberation, and on the other hand the relative scarcity of research on it. As noted above, much of the existing research is based on case studies of specific deliberative forums, experiments, or extrapolations from research on non-political small group interactions. In addition, there have been some efforts to use survey-based research to examine discrete aspects of public deliberation – how often citizens attend meetings (Verba, Schlozman and Brady, 1995), talk about politics and public affairs (Bennett, 1995) or try to convince others on how to vote (Huckfeldt et al., 1998; Keeter et al., 2002). But, to our knowledge, there has been no systematic analysis of the extent to which Americans engage in discursive participation, the specific forms this participation takes, and the traits of those who do and do not participate. Our research starts to fill this significant gap.

2.2 Discursive participation and its relationship to public deliberation

In the most formal sense, public deliberation is "discussion that involves judicious argument, critical listening, and earnest decision making" (Gastil, 2000: 22). Fishkin (1995) adopts a similarly strict definition, but allows for a more realistic assessment by introducing the notion of "incompleteness" by arguing that "In practical contexts a great deal of incompleteness must be tolerated. Hence, when we talk of improving deliberation, it is a matter of *improving* the completeness of the debate and the public's engagement in it, not a matter of perfecting it" (p. 41).

How far one is willing to take the notion of "incompleteness" before a particular activity can no longer be considered deliberation is, however, far from clear or agreed upon. For example, Page (1996) acknowledges the "face-to-face ideal" underlying most traditional notions of deliberation and goes on to argue that in modern, mass democracies deliberation is largely "mediated" through professional communicators "who not only help policy experts communicate with each other, but also assemble, explain, debate, and disseminate the best available information and ideas about public policy, in ways that are accessible to large audiences of ordinary citizens" (p. 5). Lindeman (2002) argues that deliberation need not even involve direct exchanges between two or more citizens, but can also occur through the survey process or within the thought processes of an individual citizen. And while not always explicitly using the term deliberation, research on other forms of public talk (e.g., talk radio; interpersonal persuasion between a friend, neighbor or co-worker; contacting the media or a public official about an issue; having informal conversations about a community concern) all intersect conceptually with more formal definitions of public deliberation.

Our concept of discursive participation builds on the more formal definition of public deliberation to define it as a distinctive form of political and civic engagement. We define discursive participation as citizens coming together with others in formal or informal settings – face-to-face or via the telephone or the internet – to discuss local, national, or international issues. Specifically, our conceptualization of discursive participation has five principal characteristics. First, and most obviously, the primary form of activity we are concerned about is discourse with others – talking, conversing, discussing, or deliberating. Second, we consider public discourse as a form of *participation*. While analyses of civic and political participation have become more sensitive to the variety of ways in which citizens can act, they seldom include public "talk" as a measure of engagement, focusing instead on activities such as voting, attending rallies, working for a political party, lobbying, joining and actively participating in voluntary organizations, protest, and the like (Brady, 1999; Ladd, 2000; Putnam, 2000; Skocpol and Fiorina, 2000). But talking in public with other citizens is a form of participation, one that reflects and contributes to participatory resources, motivations, and recruitment – that is, it enhances the opportunity for individuals to develop and express their views, learn the positions of others, identify shared concerns and preferences, come to understand and reach judgments about matters of public concern, and become integrated into networks of citizens. Such exchanges are a central way for expressing and negotiating deep divisions over material interests and moral values; they are also critical for publicly airing disagreements that have not been articulated or at least incompletely stated because so many citizens have withdrawn from electoral and legislative politics (Michelman 1988; Habermas, 1989; Dryzek, 1990; Benhabib 1992;1996; Etzioni, 1996; Gutmann and Thompson, 1996; Elster, 1998).

Third, discursive participation can include but is not limited to the formal institutions and processes of civic and political life. As such it can involve private individuals in informal, unplanned exchanges; those who convene in public, but who do so outside the realm of the normal process of government operations (e.g., in such places as libraries, schools, homes, churches, and community centers); and those who are brought together in settings such as town hall meetings of political representatives and their constituents. Fourth, discursive participation can occur through a variety of mediums, ranging from face-to-face exchanges to phone conversations to e-mail exchanges to Internet forums. And fifth, discursive participation is focused on formal and informal discourse about local, national, or international issues of public concern, and does not include meetings or conversations about personal lives that are *unrelated* to issues of broader public concern.

2.3 National survey of discursive participation in America

In order to understand the prevalence, types, distribution, sources, and impact of discursive participation in the United States, we designed a national telephone survey of American adults age 18 and over. Conducted by the Center for Research and Analysis at the University of Connecticut, the survey consisted of a random sample of 1,001 respondents and an over sample (N = 500) of what we call "Face-to-Face Deliberators" – those who had attended a formal or informal meeting to discuss a local, national, or international issue of public importance. For the analyses in this chapter, we combined and weighted both samples into a single, nationally representative sample (N = 1501).

The survey was in the field from February 10 to March 23, 2003. We asked respondents about their discursive participation in the time since January of the preceding year. This period included not only the 2002 election cycle and debates about state and national budgets, but also a number of post-September 11 related issues such as the ongoing war against terrorism, follow-up from the invasion of Afghanistan, and (less anticipated) the build-up and early stages of the war against Iraq. Given this active period with unusually spirited debates about local, national, and international issues, our analyses of the levels of discursive participation in general and face-to-face deliberation, in particular, should be viewed as what evaluators call a "best case study."

The survey instrument itself included several questions designed to gauge the extent to which citizens engaged in four distinct types of deliberation: what we call face-to-face deliberation, traditional talk, Internet deliberation, and Internet talk.[2] As just discussed, for many observers face-to-face deliberation is at the heart of discursive participation. As Page (1996) notes, the "exemplars of deliberation, and many of the ideals and normative standards that we associate with it, are based on situations involving face-to-face talk among small numbers of people" (23). Respondents in our survey fell into this group – which we call *Face-to-Face Deliberators* – if they indicated that they had "attended a formal or informal [organized] meeting" since January 2002 to discuss a local, national, or international issue.[3]

Participation in face-to-face group discussions may be the epitome of public deliberation, but it also imposes high costs on individuals in terms of their time (i.e., travel, preparation, and participation), psychological commitment and discursive skills – especially, public speaking and the tension associated with disagreeing with another person in public. With this in mind we measured three arguably less demanding forms of discursive participation. One form – what we call *Traditional Talkers* – involves participation in informal conversations about public issues. Respondents in our survey fell into this category if they indicated that they had "informal face-to-face or phone conversations or exchanges with people you know about public issues that are local, national, or international concerns" at least "a few times a month."[4]

The Internet has been heralded as a promising means for re-engaging a disconnected and atomized citizenry in political life. Our third measure of discursive participation – which we call *Internet Deliberators* – are respondents who indicated they participated since January 2002 in "internet chat rooms, message boards, or other on-line discussion groups organized to specifically discuss a local, national, or international issue." Finally, *Internet Talkers* are those who report having used e-mail or instant messaging to talk informally about issues of public concern at least several times a month.[5]

We examine all four types of discursive participation in the subsequent analyses.[6] In addition, we also examine what we call *discursive intensity*, defined as the extent to which respondents engaged in multiple forms of discursive participation. *Discursive intensity* was measured as a simple additive index coded 0 to 4, with "0" indicating that the respondent did not engage in any of the four types of discursive participation we measured, and "4" indicating that the respondent participated in all four types.

In addition to assessing the overall extent of discursive participation in the United States, a second goal of this chapter is to analyze which members of the public are most active in public deliberation. We examine sub-group differences in discursive participation across key demographic variables (race, education, gender, age, and income) and standard measures of political identity (ideology and party identification). Finally, we explore the additional influence of four measures of social capital (organizational membership, religious attendance, length of residence, and social trust) and four measures of political engagement (political trust, political knowledge, political interest, and political efficacy) on the likelihood and type of discursive participation.

2.4   Mapping discursive participation

Our analysis is divided into three sections: the frequency of different types of discursive participation, who engages in these various forms of discursive participation, and which configurations of citizen characteristics are most related to different modes of deliberation.

2.4.1   The frequency of discursive participation

Despite the general caricature of the average citizen as being uninterested in "politics," our national survey suggests that a sizable portion of Americans are engaging in various forms of discursive participation (Table 2.1). Not surprisingly, informal conversations about public issues seem to be the most common form of such politically relevant talk. Two-thirds of Americans report they have conversations about public issues at least several times a month – what we call "traditional talking" – and of these, the vast majority say they frequently have discussions of five minutes or longer.

Table 2.1 The frequency of engaging in different types of discursive activity

Types of discursive activity	Number	Percent of total
Traditional talking	1018	68%
Formal face-to-face deliberation	379	25%
Internet talking	360	24%
Internet deliberation	61	4%
No discursive activity	387	26%
Total N = 1501		

Notes: Respondents could engage in more than one form of discursive activity. Therefore, the numbers add to more than the total number of respondents, and the percentages add to more than 100.

A far more difficult and time consuming type of discursive participation is attending a formal or informal meeting to discuss a local, national, or international issue – what we label "formal face-to-face deliberation." Nonetheless, one-in-four Americans reported having attended at least one such meeting in the past year. Given the time, interest, and effort required to attend such meetings, coupled with the fact that 85 percent of those who said they had *not* attended a meeting to discuss public issues reported they had never been invited to do so, this degree of deliberative engagement strikes us as surprisingly high. A similar percentage (24 percent) of Americans report e-mailing or instant messaging with others about policy issues several times a month or more ("internet talking"). However, only four percent engaged in what we call "internet deliberation" – participation in internet chat rooms, message boards, or other online discussion groups – to discuss a local, national, or international issue.

As another way of examining the extent of political talk in the United States, we created a summary variable ("discursive intensity") based on a simple additive index of our four specific measures. Based on this measure, fully 74 percent of Americans reported having engaged in at least one *type* of discursive act in the last year. More specifically, 40 percent engaged in one type of discursive act in the last year, 24 percent reported having engaged in two types of such activities, nine percent reported having engaged in three, and two percent said they engaged in all four. It is important to note that this index measures the percentage of people reporting that they engaged at least once in each type of discursive participation in the last year. The actual number of total acts is significantly greater since many individuals would have engaged in each type of participation (talking about policy issues, attending forums to discuss policy issues, emailing, etc.) several times a year. Although these percentages suggest that the extent of public talk in America is substantial, it is important to also note that 26 percent of our survey respondents reported having engaged in *no* form of discursive participation in the last year. Nonetheless, taken as a whole, we find it impressive that such a relatively large proportion of Americans engage in some form of discussion about public issues, and conclude that discursive participation in contemporary America is surprisingly robust.

2.4.2   Who deliberates?

Analysis of political participation typically focuses on the impact of standard social and economic status (SES). The findings from this research are that political participation is stratified, with greater participation associated with those who have higher levels of income, education, and other markers of affluence and advantage (Milbrath and Goel, 1977; Verba, Schlozman, and Brady, 1995). The critical question posed by research on political participation is whether discursive participation is similarly stratified. Answering this question requires an analysis of who is engaged in political talk of different kinds, including attending deliberative forums.

Research on civic life in America suggests we should study not only the standard measures of SES – education and income – but also age, gender, race, and the political characteristics of party identification and ideology. Individuals with strong ideological and partisan identities are especially motivated to participate in politics (Smith, 1989; Delli Carpini and Keeter, 1996; Patterson, 2002). In addition, government policy legacies and political identity (based on ideology or party) can increase political participation and activism (Soss, 1999; Mettler, 2002; Campbell, 2003; Skocpol, 2003). Research on well-developed government programs such as Medicare and the Social Security program, which largely – but not exclusively – benefit seniors, finds that these generate higher participation by their recipients (Campbell, 2003).

Table 2.2 shows that Americans at all education levels are participating in discursive politics. There are, though, small but consistent patterns indicating that those with a high school degree or less are underrepresented in discursive politics, while those with at least some college (and especially those with at least a college degree) are overrepresented. For example, whereas 25 percent of our sample has a college or postgraduate degree, 39 percent of face-to-face deliberators, 42 percent of internet deliberators, 38 percent of internet talkers, and 31 percent of traditional talkers are college educated. The one exception to this pattern is the overrepresentation of those with less than a high school degree among internet deliberators, which we attribute to the greater number of young people who go online. The differences are less striking by income, though those with reported family incomes below $30,000 are noticeably less likely to be engaged in discursive activities than their proportion in the population would expect, all other things being equal.

Age differences in discursive participation are particularly intriguing, especially in internet talking and internet deliberation. Many political commentators bemoan the lack of political participation among the young, and it is

Table 2.2 The percentage of Americans by demographic and political characteristics who engage in different types of discursive participation

	Whole sample	Face-to-face deliberators	Internet deliberators	Internet Talkers	Traditional talkers	Non discursive participants
			Percentages			
Demographic characteristics						
Race						
African American	8	9	5	7	6	11
Hispanic	7	4	5	2	4	14
White	78	77	84	81	82	68
Other	8	10	6	10	8	7
	(N = 1458)	(N = 366)	(N = 60)	(N = 350)	(N = 988)	(N = 373)
Education						
< HS Degree	10	5	15	5	5	22
HS degree only	37	26	5	23	32	48
Some college	28	30	38	35	32	18
College degree	16	22	19	22	19	9
Post Grad. Degree	9	17	23	16	12	3
	(N = 1466)	(N = 368)	(N = 61)	(N = 355)	(N = 996)	(N = 375)
Gender						
Male	48	46	58	49	48	48
Female	52	54	42	51	52	52
	(N = 1501)	(N = 379)	(N = 61)	(N = 360)	(N = 1018)	(N = 387)
Age						
18–29	23	24	31	32	24	24
30–39	17	18	12	16	17	16
40–49	22	24	33	19	23	20
50–64	21	22	20	22	21	18
65+	16	12	4	14	11	22
	(N = 1460)	(N = 365)	(N = 61)	(N = 351)	(N = 994)	(N = 372)
Family Income						
< $30,000	32	21	21	23	27	51
$30K–$50K	21	23	20	21	21	20
$50K–$75K	23	24	29	27	25	16
$75K–$100K	12	17	16	16	12	10
>$100K	12	14	13	13	14	4
	(N = 1128)	(N = 307)	(N = 53)	(N = 299)	(N = 791)	(N = 256)
Political characteristics						
ideology						
Strong liberal	8	14	15	16	9	2
Liberal	13	11	12	11	14	12
Moderate	42	42	49	43	42	44
Conservative	20	16	8	16	19	23
Strong conservative	17	17	16	15	16	19
	(N = 1302)	(N = 350)	(N = 60)	(N = 341)	(N = 919)	(N = 294)
Party ID						
Democrat	35	32	43	33	41	39
Independent	26	28	25	25	28	25
Republican	25	27	25	29	21	18
Other ID	13	12	8	12	10	16
	(N = 1480)	(N = 745)	(N = 105)	(N = 1159)	(N = 480)	(N = 200)

true that young adults aged 18 to 29 are less likely than older adults to vote and to engage in a number of other political activities (Keeter et al., 2002). However, our data show that they are a good deal *more* likely than adults over age 30 to deliberate about policy issues on the internet. Of course, it is not surprising that they are more likely than older adults to use the still relatively new internet technology, but given the concerns over their overall low rates of political participation, it is important to note that commentators may have missed this heretofore unnoticed way for the young to make their voices heard. The other age-related pattern worth noting is that despite elderly (age 65 and over) Americans' high rates of voter turnout, their discursive participation rates are generally slightly lower than their proportion in the population would predict.

In terms of race and ethnicity, African Americans appear to be slightly underrepresented among internet deliberators and traditional talkers, Hispanics are slightly underrepresented among all forms of discursive participation, and whites are slightly overrepresented among internet deliberators, internet talkers and traditional talkers. Overall, however, these distortions are relatively modest. The one gender difference of note is that men are overrepresented among internet deliberators.

Turning to our two political variables, there is some evidence that those who identify themselves as "strong liberals" are slightly overrepresented among discursive participants, though this distortion is slight. And Democrats are somewhat overrepresented among internet deliberators and traditional talkers.

Another way of exploring group differences in discursive participation is to examine those who *do not* engage is this type of activity. The last column in Table 2.2 does just this, showing the breakdown among groups for the 26 percent of our sample who told us they had not engaged in any of our four types of political talk in the last year. Among this group, those with a high school degree or less, those with reported family incomes under $30,000 a year, African Americans and Hispanics, and those over 65 years of age were over represented, while those with at least some college education, those earning $50,000 a year or more, whites, strong liberals, and self-identified Republicans were underrepresented.

What do we make of this first cut at our data? The traditional biases that have been found in other forms of political and civic participation appear to also exist for discursive participation. Although these disparities in political participation are important, the biases appear to be modest in size, and it appears that citizens from all backgrounds and walks of life are talking about politics and public issues.

2.4.3   A closer look at who engages in discursive participation

While the initial descriptive data suggests some disparities in representation, we do not yet know what is driving discursive participation. In this section, we examine the determinants. First, we include the seven demographic and political characteristics presented in Table 2.2 as independent variables in a set of logit analyses. Results of the first set of these analyses are provided in Table 2.3.

Consistent with prior findings regarding other forms of political and civic participation (Verba, Schlozman, and Brady, 1995), we find that even when controlling for other factors education has a consistent and positive impact on three of the four types of discursive participation we measured. The one exception to this pattern is internet deliberation, which while showing a positive impact, does not reach statistical significance (undoubtedly due to the small sample size of internet deliberators).

Beyond education, however, the group characteristics we measure show little consistent impact on discursive participation. Contrary to the expectations of the SES model, income does not have a significant effect on the likelihood of engaging in any of our individual discursive acts. While income may be an important resource in many participatory acts such as campaign contributions and contacting public officials, it may be less important in terms of its direct effect on whether an individual decides to engage in discussions about policy issues.

Age has a significant impact on three of our four measures of discursive participation, but unlike most other forms of civic or political engagement,

Table 2.3 Demographic and political determinants of deliberation

	Face-to-Face deliberators	Internet deliberators	Traditional talkers	Internet talkers	Nondiscursive participants
Demographic characteristics					
Race					
African American	.23(.31)	−.73(.65)	−1.1(.40)**	−.30(.35)	.70(.45)
Hispanic	−.70(.41)	−.61(.77)	−1.1(.49)*	−1.3(.59)*	1.4(.51)**
Other	.30(.31)	−.44(.53)	−.67(.35)	−.26(.33)	.94(.39)*
Education	.36(.07)***	.30(.25)	.47(.10)***	.37(.09)***	−.42(.12)***
Gender	.14(.16)	−.38(.36)	.08(.21)	−.08(.19)	−.20(.25)
(m = 0; f = 1)					
Age	−.01(.01)	−.03(.01)**	−.01(.01)*	−.02(.01)**	.01(.01)
Income	.09(.06)	.04(.10)	.05(.08)	.02(.07)	−.24(.11)*
Political characteristics					
Ideology	−.09(.08)	−.19(.14)	−.32(.11)**	.02(.07)	.30(.12)*
Party ID					
Democrat	−.04(.22)	.29(.49)	−.64(.29)*	−.28(.27)	.70(.35)*
Nonidentifier	−.02(.20)	−.08(.43)	−.76(.29)**	−.74(.26)**	.72(.25)*
Constant	−1.4(.50)**	−1.2(1.0)	2.2(.74)**	.62(.63)	−2.1(.87)*
Total N	1099	1099	1099	1099	1099
Pseudo R square	0.05	0.06	0.11	0.08	0.14

*: $p < .05$; **: $p < .01$; ***: $p < .001$

Notes: The first numbers are logit coefficients. The numbers in parentheses are robust standard errors. Ideology is coded such that 1 = strong liberal and 5 = strong conservative.

this effect is negative, meaning young people are *more* likely than older ones to engage in internet deliberations, internet talk and, surprisingly, traditional public talk. Being African American suppresses traditional talk, but is unrelated to the other three types of discursive participation, while being Hispanic suppresses both traditional talk and internet talk. Gender shows no significant relationship with any of our four measures of discursive participation. Being more conservative has a negative impact on engaging in traditional talk, but then so too does being a self-identified Democrat. And those with no party affiliation are less likely to talk about public issues via the internet or through more traditional means.

A pattern that is somewhat more consistent with the traditional SES model emerges when we look at the impact of our seven group characteristics on the likelihood of not participating in *any* discursive act (last column of Table 2.3). Interpreting these results, we find that having low levels of education and income and being Hispanic and a Democrat increases the likelihood that one engages in no form of discursive activity. Surprisingly, however, ideology also has an effect: the more likely citizens are to be conservative, the more likely they are to be among those who don't engage in acts of public talk. Age and gender show no significant relationship.

Taken as a whole, the results of these analyses, much like those presented earlier, suggest that discursive participation suffers from some of the biases found in other forms of civic and political participation – most noticeably and consistently through education. But they also suggest that these biases are relatively modest and inconsistent, holding out some hope that public talk – including fairly demanding activities such as deliberative forums – may be more equitably distributed within the U.S. population than other forms of engagement.

As an additional attempt to better understand the predictors of discursive participation, we move beyond the simple SES model, adding a number of additional measures of social capital (organizational membership, religious attendance, length of residence in the community, and social trust) and political engagement (political trust, political knowledge, political interest, and political efficacy) to the model presented in Table 2.3. Results of these analyses are presented in Table 2.4.

Eight findings resulting from the addition of measures of social capital and political engagement to the model are worth noting. First, and not surprisingly, the expanded model explains a larger percentage of the overall variance (as indicated by the R2s). Second, it dampens many, though not all, of the few effects found in our initial logit analyses, indicating that these earlier effects (most notably education) operate indirectly through other attitudes and behaviors. Third, the most consistent relationship with most forms of discursive participation is organizational membership, which is positively associated with attending face-to-face deliberative forums, participating in internet deliberative chat rooms, and engaging in traditional talk. Fourth,

Table 2.4 Determinants of deliberation: The full model of determinants

	Face-to-Face deliberators	Internet deliberators	Traditional talkers	Internet talkers	Nondiscursive participants
Demographic characteristics					
Race					
African American	.35(.37)	−.83(.76)	−1.3(.43)**	−.06(.38)	1.0(.50)*
Hispanic	−.41(.49)	−.38(.84)	−.54(.59)	−1.2(.60)	1.1(.62)
Other	.70(.42)	−.36(.61)	−.55(.44)	−.16(.39)	.87(.50)
Education	.01(.10)	−.04(.19)	.28(.13)*	.11(.11)	−.11(.15)
Gender	.09(.19)	−.43(.41)	.15(.26)	−.08(.22)	−.13(.31)
(m = 0; f = 1)					
Age	−.02(.01)	−.03(.01)*	−.02(.01)*	−.01(.01)	.01(.01)
Income	−.03(.07)	.05(.12)	−.16(.11)	−.11(.09)	−.07(.12)
Political characteristics					
Ideology	−.12(.10)	−.22(.17)	−.40(.13)**	−.19(.11)	.31(.14)*
Party ID					
Democrat	.21(.28)	.23(.49)	−.80(.34)*	.25(.32)	.58(.39)
Nonidentifier	.43(.24)	−.23(.58)	−.74(.34)*	−.32(.31)	.42(.40)
Social capital					
Organizational membership	1.3(.19)***	1.2(.40)**	.76(.26)**	.14(.22)	−.94(.35)**
Religious attendance	.09(.05)*	.01(.08)	.03(.06)	.04(.05)	−.13(.07)
Length of residence	.00(.01)	−.01(.01)	.00(.01)	−.02(.01)*	.01(.01)
Social Trust	.00(.10)	−.25(.14)	.15(.13)	.09(.11)	−.03(.16)
Political engagement					
Political trust	.14(.11)	−.17(.21)	−.02(.14)	.09(.13)	−.13(.16)
PolitikKnowledge	.04(.08)	−.06(.17)	.11(.10)	.20(.09)*	.00(.12)
Political interest	.15(.04)***	.07(.11)	.18(.05)***	.04(.05)	−.17(.05)
Political efficacy	.12(.05)*	.07(.10)	−.08(.07)	.14(.05)**	.05(.08)
Constant	−3.0(.69)***	−.66(1.8)	2.0(.95)*	−1.3(.78)	−1.5(1.1)
Total N	865	865	865	865	865
Pseudo R square	0.15	0.1	0.17	0.12	0.16

*: p< .05; **: p< .01; ***: p< .001

Notes: The first numbers are logit coefficients. The numbers in parentheses are robust standard errors. Ideology is coded such that 1 = strong liberal and 5 = strong conservative.

those who have lived in an area for a short time are more likely than others to engage in internet talk. Fifth, religious attendance increases the likelihood of attending face-to-face deliberative forums. Sixth, political interest is positively associated with participation in face-to-face deliberative forums and in traditional talking. Seventh, political knowledge is positively associated with internet talking. And eighth, political efficacy is positively associated with both face-to-face deliberation and internet talking.

The findings in Table 2.4 modify the SES model, suggesting an organizational and political explanation for discursive participation. This model shows the strong effects of organizational membership, indicating that the impact of education is indirect. In addition, political factors like political interest and political knowledge are also important influences on discursive participation.

As a final step to understanding the predictors of discursive participation, we return to our measure of discursive intensity. Recall that this index ranges from 0 to 4, with 0 indicating that a respondent participated in none of our four types of discursive activities in the last year and 4 indicating he/she participated in all four types. Table 2.5 gives the results of two regression analyses – the first using only demographic and political characteristics and the second adding the variables that measure social capital and political engagement.

Our analysis of discursive intensity replicates our previous findings of an organizational and political model of public deliberation. Looking first

Table 2.5 Determinants of deliberative intensity

	Deliberative intensity			
	Model 1		Model 2	
	Unstandardized	Standardized	Unstandardized	Standardized
Demographic characteristics				
Race				
African American	−.26(.15)	−.06	−.25(.16)	−.06
Hispanic	−.55(.16)**	−.14	−.34(.20)	−.09
Other	−.12(.16)	−.03	.00(.19)	.00
Education	.24(.03)***	.27	.06(.04)	.07
Gender (m = 0; f = 1)	.01(.06)	.00	.02(.08)	.01
Age	−.01(.00)***	−.14	−.01(.00)**	−.14
Income	.03(.03)	.04	−.05(.03)	−.07
Political characteristics				
Ideology	−.14(.04)***	−.15	−.13(.04)***	−.14
Party ID				
Democrat	−.15(.10)	−.07	−.03(.11)	−.02
Nonidentifier	−.28(.09)**	−.13	−.12(.10)	−.06
Social capital				
Organizational membership			.45(.08)***	.23
Religious attendance			.03(.02)	.06
Length of residence			.00(.00)	−.05
Social trust			.03(.04)	.03
Political engagement				
Political trust			.03(.04)	.03
Political knowledge			.05(.03)	.08
Political interest			.07(.01)***	.19
Political efficacy			.03(.02)	.08
Constant	1.8(.24)***		1.2(.28)***	
Total N	1099		865	
R square	0.18		0.26	

*: p< .05; **: p< .01; ***: p< .001

Notes: The first column in each model are unstandardized regression coefficients. The numbers in parentheses are robust standard errors. The second column in each model are standardized coefficients. Ideology is coded such that 1 = strong liberal and 5 = strong conservative.

at Model 1, education increases the likelihood of discursive participation, while lower levels of participation are associated with being Hispanic, older, conservative, or having no party identification. When we add measures of social capital and political engagement (Model 2) the effects of education and Hispanic status become statistically insignificant, indicating that they operate primarily through other factors, though age and ideology continue to have a direct effect on discursive intensity. As in our analyses of individual types of discursive participation, discursive intensity is positively affected by organizational membership and interest in politics.

2.5 Conclusions

Scholars and practitioners express two common concerns about the health of American democracy. The first is that participation in the electoral process and in other forms of civic and political engagement such as working for campaigns, making campaign and charitable contributions, contacting officials, and informal community involvement is low in comparison to the past, as well as in comparison to normative standards of what critics think it should be. The second is that the citizen participation that does exist is not equally distributed across the population, often showing biases in favor of those with higher levels of income and education. Since civic and political participation provides avenues for citizens to communicate their opinions, interests, and needs, these worries are important. But there are other outlets for citizens to express their political preferences on public issues. In this chapter we have explored one such alternative outlet – discursive participation, or the ways that people talk about, discuss, and deliberate with each other on public issues that affect the community, state, or nation in which they live.

Clearly our analyses in this chapter provide only a glimpse into the world of discursive politics, and they represent only the first step in a larger project on this topic. Nonetheless the findings are tantalizing. It appears that two-thirds of Americans engage in at least some kind of regular political talk, and that a quarter participate in forums and meetings that begin to approximate accepted definitions of "public deliberation." While we find evidence of the unrepresentativeness and bias found in other forms of political engagement, these distortions appear to be less consistent or extreme in the case of discursive participation. These findings suggest that discursive participation may be a promising, undertheorized and underexamined pathway into public life.

Two of our most tantalizing findings have to do with the roles of SES and age. It is well established in the civic participation literature that people with high levels of income and education are most likely to participate. Our findings about *discursive* participation are somewhat different. In multivariate analyses, income appears to have no significant effect on discursive participation. This runs counter to findings of direct income stratification found in other forms of political participation and may suggest an encouraging opportunity to expand equitable involvement of citizens in public life. For example, fully 85 percent of those who had not attended a deliberative forum or meeting in the last year reported that *they had never been asked to do so*. Perhaps one way to increase citizen involvement is simply to make clear to citizens the routes open to their participation and to be sure they are invited to participate.

The story about education is more complicated. When taking into account only demographic characteristics and political identity, education has a large statistically significant effect on participating in discursive activities. People with higher levels of education appear to be more likely to engage in face-to-face deliberative forums, traditional talking, and internet talking. They are also more likely to engage in multiple types of discursive activities (i.e., discursive intensity). But when we add measures of social capital (especially organizational membership) and political engagement (especially political interest) the effect of education is largely eliminated. Thus, it is not education *per se* that shapes discursive participation; it is instead belonging to organizations and being interested in political issues. This suggests an organizational and political model of discursive participation.

The important role of organizational membership has been noted by a range of scholars, especially Putnam (2000) and Skocpol (2000). If one is a member of an organization, one has some type of social network, which enhances the resources, motivations, and recruitment of individuals into politics. The central premise of social capital theory is that community networks generate trust, reciprocity, information, and cooperation that have significant individual and group effects. Our work on discursive participation shows the value of organizational membership in enhancing the likelihood of citizens engaging in discussions about policy issues.

The role of political interest is not surprising. Measures of psychological engagement with politics have long played a central role in theories of political participation. It is also a central component of the civic voluntarism theory of Verba, Schlozman, and Brady, 1995.

The second intriguing finding relates to age. Many commentators bemoan the low electoral participation of young adults (Keeter et al., 2002), and research on senior political activism (Campbell, 2003) points to the high participation of the elderly in contrast to that of adults under age 65. But our survey uncovered areas where the young are more likely participants, and the old are less active. Young adults aged 18 to 29 engage in conversations about policy issues on the internet, as well as in person, at a level greater than would be predicted based on their proportion in the population; a finding that survived a number of our more elaborate tests. Political talk may be a largely unnoticed way for the young to make their voices heard in social networks (though not necessarily in the halls of government). Clearly more work is needed to fully support these conclusions. And discursive participation, in and of itself, is not a substitute for other important forms of civic and political engagement. Nonetheless we find these results encouraging. Discursive participation is one pathway into public life, a pathway that appears to be more common than oftentimes assumed. At a minimum, the research presented in this chapter suggests it is an area of inquiry deserving of more attention and study than it has received to date. And, perhaps, it may prove to be a way to help counter the steady erosion of political and civic life in America.

Notes

1. The research was supported by a grant from the Pew Charitable Trusts. We would like to thank Sam Best of the Center for Survey Research and Analysis for his advice and assistance in designing and conducting the survey. We are also grateful to Dan Stevens, Dukhong Kim, Melanie Burns, and Dan Bergan for their assistance in analyzing the survey results.
2. While not part of the analysis we present in this chapter, the vast majority of the survey was devoted to items designed to tap respondents' experiences with and reactions to face-to-face deliberative forums of various kinds. While some of these questions focused on respondents' overall participation in such forums (e.g., how many such meetings they attended since January 1st 2002), most asked more specifically about "the last meeting" they had attended during the past year. We chose this approach to allow for a more detailed, nuanced description of the deliberative experience (e.g., what issues were discussed, where it was held, how many people attended) and respondents' reaction to it (e.g., did they feel the discussions were balanced, did they take any action as a result of the meeting).
3. We treated respondents as "formal face-to-face deliberators" if they answered "yes" to the following question: "Since the beginning of last year – that is since January of 2002 – have you attended a formal or informal meeting organized by yourself, by someone else you know personally, or by a religious, social, civic, governmental or political group to specifically discuss a local, national, or international issue – for example, neighborhood crime, housing, schools, social security, election reform, terrorism, global warming, or any other public issue that affects people?"
4. The question was the following: "How often do you have informal face-to-face or phone conversations or exchanges with people you know about public issues that are local, national, or international concerns? I'm talking about exchanges or conversations of any length. Would you say you do this everyday, a few times a week, once a week, a few times a month, or less often than this." Respondents were considered "face-to-face talkers" if they indicated that they engaged in this form of deliberation "everyday," "a few times a week," "once a week," or "a few times a month."
5. This group of discursive participants is based on the following question: "How often do you use e-mail or instant messaging to talk INFORMALLY with people you know about public issues that are local, national, or international concerns. Would

you say you do this everyday, a few times a week, once a week, a few times a month, or less often than this." Respondents were treated as "internet talkers" if they indicated "everyday", "a few times a week", "once a week," or "a few times a month."

6. As can be seen, all of these screener questions refer explicitly to conversations (whether informal or formal) that were to discuss a "local, national, or international issue." Our reasoning here was to tap into citizens' discussions about issues related to public life, rather than more general discussions that are of a more personal, less publicly-relevant nature. In addition we attempted to distinguish one-to-one public talk from participation in more collective conversations by defining "public deliberation" as participation in a "formal or informal meeting organized by yourself, by someone else you know personally, or by a religious, social, civic, governmental or political group" (in the case of face-to-face deliberation) and in "any INTERNET chat rooms, message boards, or other on-line discussion groups" (in the case of on-line deliberation).

3
The Democratic Potential
of Civic Dialogue[1]
Katherine Cramer Walsh

How can deliberative democracy work in contexts of cultural heterogeneity? Some say that one of the great values of deliberation is not just its ability to enhance the decision task at hand, but also its ability to bridge divides rather than perpetuate them. By legitimating governing procedures, the argument goes, deliberation brings together the governed and the governing and reduces conflict among cultural groups (Benhabib, 2002). Participation in deliberation is expected to confer greater tolerance for opposing views (Gutmann and Thompson, 1996; Dryzek, 2000), and more civil interactions among people in a society (Barber, 1998).

The problem, however, is that the communities that are most in need of improved bonds between people are also those in which deliberation is the most problematic: heterogeneous, multicultural communities. Theorists who are critical of, yet sympathetic to, deliberation have clearly outlined the problematic nature with deliberation in such contexts. In order to succeed in deliberation, people must put their arguments in the language that is understandable and persuasive to the largest array of people, by definition disadvantaging minority concerns and exacerbating inequality (Young, 1996; 2001; Sanders, 1997; Williams, 2000).

These critics do not claim, however, that intercultural communication is in general ineffective. Instead they recommend forms of communication other than deliberation such as testimony (Sanders, 1997), storytelling, greeting, rhetoric (Young, 1996), and discursive communication (Dryzek, 2000). Each of these forms relaxes some of the rules of deliberation.[2] One of the tasks for empiricists interested in the possibilities of deliberative democracy, then, is to consider how opening the deliberative system to these alternative forms of public talk might improve the capacity of citizens to connect with one another across cultural divides.

In this chapter, I investigate the potential of one such type of communication: civic intergroup dialogue programs. Since the early 1990s, over 400 cities across the United States, and many cities throughout the world (Varshney, 2002, 293–295; Nelson et al., 2004) have turned to civic dialogue

45

as a means of confronting public issues that involve intercultural conflict (Du Bois and Hutson, 1997; Schoem and Hurtado, 2001).[3] I illuminate how these programs might contribute to the task of forging connections between people by comparing them to everyday conversation among naturally occurring groups of people, and then to ideals of good deliberation. Through the comparisons, I argue that intentionally including dialogue in deliberative systems has the potential to improve intercultural connections by enabling participants to construct a balance between unity and diversity.

3.1 What form might connections through public talk take?

To analyze the potential of civic dialogue, I will refer to the varieties of communication that are intentionally generated among members of a community to address public issues such as public talk. I do this to encompass both deliberation and dialogue. Although political theorists often use the terms "deliberation" and "dialogue" interchangeably, or together (Deveaux, 2003: 781), communications scholars distinguish dialogue from deliberation quite explicitly. Drawing on theorists including Habermas, Bakhtin, Gadamer, and Buber, they describe dialogue as the act of sharing information about perspectives, rather than debate (Pearce and Littlejohn, 1997; Burkhalter et al., 2002; Cissna and Anderson, 2002; Anderson et al., 2004). Often dialogue is described as an essential precursor to deliberation when participants view the policy issue at hand from disparate cultural perspectives (Pearce and Littlejohn, 1997; Burkhalter et al., 2002). The expectation is that if participants keep an open mind and allow themselves enough time, shared understandings can develop. Dialogue is regarded as an act of communication in which participants actively create connections with one another. If given enough time, this can take the form of shared understandings, or a new "language" jointly understood by all parties. At a less advanced stage, it can take the form of active listening or empathy (Burkhalter et al., 2002).

These are just some of the positive psychological bonds among people that public talk can foster that enable future cooperation.[4] In general, such connections can take the form of consensus, tolerance, or common ground. Consensus could appear as agreement on which topics are issues of joint concern (Ackerman, 1989), agreement on ends, or agreement on the means to meet mutually desired ends. Public talk can enable different degrees of tolerance, from a willingness to extend civil liberties to disliked groups (Prothro and Grigg, 1960; Sullivan, Pierson, and Marcus, 1979), to a respect for differences or empathy for members of other social groups.

The third type of connection that public talk could enable is "common ground," which could consist of identification with a common, overarching, category, such as mutual residence in a geographic area, or membership in the overarching category of human beings (Gaertner et al., 1999). Common ground could also mean solidarity with one another in the sense of emotional ties, or concern for others' well-being.

Is dialogue uniquely capable of forging some or more of these types of connections? To consider, a useful point of comparison is informal political talk. This is not public talk, in the sense of intentional, organized talk about public issues, but talk about public issues that arises spontaneously in the course of casual, social interaction. It is conducted primarily for the purposes of *maintaining* social connections, not for addressing public issues.

In a previous project, I studied processes of political understanding among naturally occurring groups of people who met regularly in voluntary associations (Walsh, 2004). I spent three years observing several groups of people, primarily a group of retired, white, self-proclaimed middle-class men who met every morning over coffee in a neighborhood corner store in Ann Arbor, Michigan. By visiting with them and watching their physical behavior in the small store, I learned how they clarified their connections with one another. Many of these people, who called themselves the Old Timers, had known each other a long time. Most of them had grown up in Ann Arbor, had gone to school together, played sports together, married into one another's families, and attended church together. These overlaps in acquaintances and experiences typically formed their reasons for joining the group. And yet every morning they further clarified their connections to one another.

They did this most clearly with reference to outgroups. When their plastic cups ran dry of coffee, one of them would get the "decaf" and "regular" coffee pots from behind the counter, and pour the others a round. Notably, the person doing coffee duty would not walk the ten steps across the room to fill the cups of the other regulars in the store. These others were not a part of the Old Timers' circle. They were women, African Americans, and white blue-collar workers. Several of the Old Timers called this part of the room the Dunbar Center, after a former community center in the African American part of the city.

There were other ways that the Old Timers reinforced the boundaries of their group. In the mid-1980s they made themselves membership cards just for fun. They often collectively signed and sent birthday or get-well cards to other members. And if a person was brought up in conversation that one of the group did not recognize, a common question was, "Is he one of us?"

In other words, through their talk and their behavior, they clarified their social identities, or their psychological attachments to social groups ranging from the Old Timers, to Ann Arborites, to middle-class whites. These conceptions of "who we are" and "us and them" did not exist in full before spending time at the corner store. Through their interaction, they clarified questions such as, can Republicans like us vote for Colin Powell? Can native Ann Arborites like us move to another town to avoid tax increases? Those kinds of processes are valuable for democracy. They help people notice the relevance of public issues to their private lives, and they may even help mobilize political participation. But the bonds such informal political talk enables have downsides as well. They do little to create connections across cultures or social groups. In making sense of political issues with people who view the world in similar ways, the Old Timers received little practice in understanding the concerns and interests of others in the community. Because of the tendency of people to congregate with others they perceive to be like themselves, everyday informal political talk is not likely to involve communication across social divides and therefore holds little potential for improving connections among people.

One antidote to the lack of talk about public issues across cultural divides is to intentionally generate this type of communication, rather than wait for it to arise in the course of everyday interaction. Communities around the country have done just this in the form of intergroup dialogue programs. To examine the potential that this type of talk has for enhancing democracy in contexts of cultural differences, I turn now to a comparison of it with deliberation.

3.2   The widespread practice of civic dialogue

In a civic intergroup dialogue program, a nonprofit organization or local government recruits diverse groups of volunteers (typically about 12–15 people per group) from the community to engage in facilitator-led discussion about race relations, immigration, crime, housing, or other issues that involve intercultural relations. Groups meet repeatedly over a series of several weeks to several months. Curricula vary, but typically the facilitators are volunteers from the community who are trained to lead people through discussions about their experiences with intercultural difference and discrimination, their perceptions of intercultural relations in the community, and in many cases, their ideas for individual and collective actions people can take to improve relations in the community.

The programs function under such names as Study Circles on Race, Dialogue on Race Relations, and Honest Conversations. Their proliferation in the past 15 years has been spurred in part by national umbrella organizations such as the Study Circles Resource Center (SCRC), the Hope in the Cities program, the YWCA, the National Conference for Communities and Justice, the National League of Cities, and President William Jefferson Clinton's Initiative on Race (*One America*, 1998; also see Reichler and Dredge, 1997: ch. 2; Leighninger and McCoy, 1998; Sirianni and Friedland, 2001: ch. 6). They were used to reconcile racial tension in Los Angeles following the Rodney King verdict (Jones-Correa, 2000), and in many cities to address tensions including immigrants and people of Islamic faith after the September 11, 2001 terrorist attacks.[5]

3.3 Comparing deliberation and dialogue

These dialogue programs are typically started to improve relations among people in a community, not to complete a decision making task; they are distinct from deliberation. But does their nature suggest that this form of talk can compensate for some of deliberation's shortcomings when it comes to intercultural conflict? Is this form of public talk uniquely suited to forge connections in contexts of difference? To compare the two, it is useful to begin with an outline of the characteristics of good deliberation. I say "good deliberation" intentionally to note that I seek an ideal-type of deliberation that may not match the actual practice of any one example of deliberation, but serves as a standard of comparison. Mansbridge (1999: 221–227) offers up seven characteristics of good deliberation based on her reading of a broad range of deliberative theory: equality, publicity, reciprocity, reasonableness, freedom from power, accountability, and a focus on consensus or common ground.[6]

To characterize the communication within intergroup dialogue programs, I used several sources of data. First, I conducted participant observation of a 10-session round of a Study Circles on Race program in Madison, Wisconsin, in the Fall of 2000 to gain an understanding of the nature of the communication within intergroup dialogue programs. Second, I conducted in-depth interviews with eight representatives of national organizations either conducting or promoting civic dialogue with respect to race relations,[7] and analyzed the content of facilitator guides issued by three national organizations sponsoring and promoting intergroup dialogue programs. Several of the interviews and a study of the most effective strategies of Study Circle programs around the country (Houlé and Roberts, 2000) suggested that individual programs commonly modify the guides and formats of the curricula provided by the national organizations to fit local needs. Therefore, I interviewed 31 state and local government officials and nonprofit organization employees administrating intergroup dialogue programs in 11 medium-sized census-designated central cities in the central United States.[8]

These individuals were chosen to provide variation in program type (i.e., Study Circles, Honest Conversations, etc.), government sponsorship (ranging from government sponsored and administrated, partial government financial support, government verbal support, to no ties with a local government), and racial heterogeneity of the population. In addition, the interviews were limited to programs located in cities that have a population between 100,000 and 225,000 people, according to the 2000 census, and are located in the central United States. These parameters were chosen in order to limit the scope of the study and to enable additional related investigations.[9] To check this information against programs conducted in larger cities, I conducted additional in-person interviews with practitioners in two larger metropolitan areas.[10]

All of the interviews were examined for remarks relevant to each of the above seven criteria, analyzed for similarities and differences across cities, and then compared and contrasted to ideal deliberation.

One of the most apparent differences between dialogue and deliberation is their purpose. Even though dialogue practitioners at times use the term "deliberation" to describe the activity involved in intergroup dialogue programs (SCRC, 1997: 28),[11] they regularly emphasize that dialogue is not *debate*. Guidelines for discussions organized through the NCCJ read "Dialogue is not a debate, in which one can expect to id a 'winner' or a 'loser'. In dialogue, the goal is not for one party to impose ideas on the other; rather, to see afresh issues or positions that seemed non-negotiable" (Los Angeles NCCJ: 1005). A guide for a program in St. Louis called Bridges Across Polarization similarly says, "Keep in mind that a Bridges group discussion is designed for dialogue and not debate" (FOCUS St. Louis, 2002: 15). Unlike deliberation, dialogue programs are not about reaching a decision or a policy choice. "Exploration, not agreement, is the objective" reads a pamphlet describing the Kenosha/Racine Diversity Circles. The SCRC guide includes an entire page outlining the distinction between debate and dialogue (SCRC, 1997: 47). Statements in civic dialogue programs are expected to take the form of testimony or personal stories, not statements on behalf of a particular stance on an issue, especially in the earlier meetings of the group (SCRC, 1997: 7).

This distinction suggests that the connections dialogue enables are somewhat unique from those made possible through deliberation. Interaction with people of different racial backgrounds does not in itself promote tolerance (Allport, 1954). The extensive research in the wake of Allport's contact hypothesis has supported his claims that in order to reduce prejudice between groups, the contact should involve cooperation, not competition; involve working toward a common goal; take place among people of equal status; and be supported by authorities (see Pettigrew and Tropp, 2000, for a meta-analysis). Whether this ideal contact reduces conflict because it encourages people to think of others as individuals, not as members of a disliked group (Brewer and Miller, 1984), or because it encourages members of in-groups and out-groups to think of themselves as members of the same "superordinate" category, it seems that public talk that is explicitly not about competition or debate but about sharing perspectives and gaining understanding might play a unique role in creating positive bonds among people.

3.3.1   Equality

Let us now consider how the practice of dialogue matches up to the seven characteristics of ideal deliberation. Civic dialogue practitioners, consistent with theories of good deliberation, strive for the first criterion, equality, or the inclusion of all views. The SCRC discussion guide instructs organizers to "Recruit participants from a broad cross section of the community. This is easier, of course, if your working group [steering committee] is representative of the community and can recruit from its ranks" (SCRC, 1997: 38). Achieving this inclusivity is difficult. Dialogue programs are often criticized for "preaching to the choir" or only attracting people who already perceive that racism in their community is a problem and are willing to do something about it. At least one practitioner involved in each of the 11 programs studied in detail here reported that his or her program has a difficult time recruiting people of color. Dean Lovelace, a Dayton, Ohio, city commissioner who started the Dayton Dialogues, stated that as an African American city official, in a city in which a majority of the elected city officials are African American and 43 percent of the population is identified as Black in 2000, his recruitment concerns are dominated by the dilemma of attracting Blacks who are particularly upset with the state of race relations. He said, "My concern is, 'How do you get angry brothers and sisters involved?'"

Practitioners often recommend combining dialogue with deliberation as a way to overcome this problem. While theorists critical of deliberation suggest dialogue-type communication as a way to make the deliberative system more just, in order for dialogue to attract marginalized voices, practitioners assert that it needs to be connected to formal channels of decision making. Without the incentive of a potential impact on policy, why, indeed, would angry brothers and sisters choose to be involved? As these programs have developed, practitioners have concluded that recruiting a diverse array of participants is much easier if those traditionally left out of decision making perceive that their participation will result in visible change in their communities.[12]

3.3.2 Publicity and reciprocity

Considering other criteria further reveals that using both dialogue and deliberation may enhance the bridging ability of the deliberative system. To see this, consider publicity, or the criterion that deliberation be open to public scrutiny. The hope, expressed by Bohman (1996) for example, is that the legitimacy of outcome decisions is enhanced if the reasons given in debate are publicly acceptable reasons, or reasons that all citizens can at least understand, if not agree with.[13] However, what constitutes an acceptable reason is a subjective question. In the glare of public light, participants may be less likely to offer up reasons that are unpopular or unfamiliar with the majority, thereby perpetuating intercultural misunderstanding. Dialogue programs relax the constraint of publicity by requiring that the communication is private and *removed* from public scrutiny. Participants commonly create their ground rules collectively, and these often include an agreement to keep the conversations confidential. Facilitator and participant guides instruct people to "speak with confidentiality" (Corcoran and Greisdorf, 2001: 112), and respect confidentiality (FOCUS St. Louis, 2002: 12).

Analyzing publicity requires an analysis of reciprocity as well. Reciprocity requires a willingness to listen to and potentially agree with others' reasons.

It is the criterion of open-mindedness, mutual respect, and civility.[14] Relaxing
the criterion of publicity may have a positive loosening of the constraints of
reciprocity as well. Civic dialogue programs *do* strive for civility – but they
simultaneously allow for a bit of incivility as well. Program guides and
administrators ask participants to be civil in the sense of listening to all
reasons, stories, and viewpoints – especially if they do not find them acceptable at first. Participants are asked to keep their minds open, and to try to
understand others' views, especially when they conflict with one's own. The
following series of "Tips for study circle participants," published in the SCRC
guide given to participants and facilitators (SCRC, 1997: 46) illustrates:

1. Make a good effort to attend all meetings. The comfort level and depth
   of conversation depend upon familiarity with other participants.
2. Think together about what you want to get out of your conversation.
3. Help keep the discussion on track. Make sure your remarks are relevant.
4. Speak your mind freely, but don't monopolize the conversation.
5. Really try to understand what others are saying and respond to their
   ideas, especially when their thinking is different from yours. (In other
   words, seek first to understand, then to be understood.)
6. Be open to changing your mind. This will help you really listen to
   others' views.
7. When disagreement occurs, don't personalize it. Try to identify the
   ideas that are in conflict. Search for the common concerns beneath
   the surface.
8. Don't waste time arguing about points of fact. For the time being, you
   may need to agree to disagree and then move on. You might decide to
   check out the facts together before your next meeting.
9. Value one another's experiences. Think about how your own experiences have contributed to your thinking.
10. Help to develop one another's ideas. Listen carefully, and ask clarifying
    questions.

Instructions to "Really try to understand what others are saying" (tip
number 5), and "Be open to changing your mind" (tip number 6) illustrate
the ways in which dialogue programs encourage participants to keep an
open mind.

The guide for the Hope in the Cities program likewise urges facilitators to
"make it clear [to participants] that there are no right or wrong responses for
the purposes of these dialogues" and to show respect to each member of the
group (Corcoran and Greisdorf, 2001: 112). It also suggests that the groups
adopt the following as one of their ground rules: "We will listen carefully
and respectfully to each other" (113). Likewise, a handout on dialogue produced by the NCCJ states that the "Primary requirements are a willingness to
act civilly, both in listening to the other and in expressing one's convictions.

It also involves a willingness to learn from others, to clarify, even change perceptions without forfeiting individual values and identity" (Los Angeles Region NCCJ, 1995). The St. Louis Bridges program similarly uses the terms "open mind" and "respect" to describe the form that comments should take during discussion (FOCUS St. Louis, 2002: 7–8).

Although dialogue programs do strive for civility, the dangers of such a goal are well known. An atmosphere of open-mindedness may make people more comfortable and thus perhaps more likely to contribute, but it does not necessarily make the talk more beneficial when the goal is social justice. As Young suggests, to give due consideration to marginalized voices, democracy needs a space in which these voices can "rupture a stream of thought" (2001: 687). Civil contexts are not synonymous with listening. "[S]ubordinates sometimes need the battering ram of rage" (Mansbridge, 1999: 223). And, "Democracy may sometimes require that your interlocutor does not wait politely for you to finish but shakes you by the collar and cries, 'Listen! For God's sake!'" (Schudson, 1997 : 308). Rather than enhance the quality of decisions, calls for civility have at times been used to alienate some members of the public from participation at times (Herzog, 1998; Sapiro, 1999).

How does a democracy create a space in which people are both willing to participate and yet willing to say publicly unpalatable things? The dialogue practitioners' answer is "safety," or relaxing the criterion of publicity.[15] According to Mary Jane Hollis, the Executive Director of the Aurora Community Study Circles program, the "key to the discussions is safety, openness, and that people feel valued." Program guidebooks and organizers espouse these goals, and participants themselves reiterate them. In response to pre-participation questionnaires administered to participants in the City of Madison [Wisconsin] Study Circles on Race and the Aurora [Illinois] Circles of Understanding, a typical response to, "What do you hope the Study Circles will achieve?" is, "I hope the circles will help members interact in a 'safe' (psychologically) but multiracial setting. I hope I'll be more comfortable talking about race relations." The participant guidelines cited above suggest that the goal is to provide a forum in which people can say whatever is on their mind (tip number 4), but not be hurt by the comments of others (tip number 7). This is civility, but it is simultaneously an attempt to not restrict what gets said.

3.3.3 Considered debate

The role that emotions ought to play in good deliberation is, ironically, hotly contested. Some expect that deliberation ought to be the careful consideration of opinions (e.g., Cohen, 1989), or the cool voice of reason (according to the founders of the United States, as Bessette (1994) describes). Yet outlawing emotion ignores evidence that citizens use affect as a source of information when trying to make sense of public issues (Sniderman, Brody, and Tetlock, 1991: ch. 6; Marcus, Neuman, and MacKuen, 2000; Marcus, 2002).

Moreover, emotions such as compassion and solidarity are important contributions to public debate, suggesting that we ought to strive for "considered" rather than "reasoned" deliberation (Mansbridge, 1999: 225–226). Dialogue practitioners tend to privilege the expression of emotion. For example, the SCRC guide starts with a "note to readers" that acknowledges, "It is hard to talk about race. Conversations are likely to touch on power and privilege, fear and anger, hope and disappointment" (SCRC, 1997: 5). The guide to Hope in the Cities Honest Conversations describes the expression of emotions as a sign of attaining a goal of the program:

How to Know … When You are Having an Honest Conversation
When you say the things you *need* to say
When you say things to *reveal* your feelings
When you say things to *disclose* your own reality
When you say things that you *really* believe
When you say things in such a way that indicates an openness to *growth* and the *future*

INSTEAD OF
When you say things you *want* to say
When you say things to *accuse* others
When you say things to *control* another person's reality
When you say what's *expected* or *stereotypical*
When you speak only to the *past*
(Corcoran and Greisdorf, 2001: 74, emphasis in original)

The Hope in the Cities program focuses on "racial reconciliation," a large part of which practitioners argue is acknowledging history. One way in which they do this is by taking "walks through history," guided tours of the city during which the participants consider significant events in the history of race relations in that community. The program guide specifies a significant role for emotions in this part of the dialogue program. "Facts are important, but historical memory may be more powerful. Facts have emotional components which are attached to our hearts and spirits. We need to look within the 'package of pain' where historical facts are packed. It is not the facts that challenge us racially; it is the pain that we choose to not get beyond" (Corcoran and Greisdorf, 2001: 11).

Guidelines to NCCJ dialogues make a similar claim that emotions are in fact valued and perhaps essential parts of the discussion. "Dialogue is not an argument, which is a logical process using reflective reasoning. While reasoned argument may be used in the service of dialogue, it is not always an effective tool, since positions are usually formed by historical circumstances, emotions and experiences as much as reason" (Los Angeles NCCJ, 1995). A related handout reads "Every participant has the right to express emotions and ideas to be heard" (NCCJ, 2002). These statements are indicative of the way practitioners expect that the conversations will involve a good deal of emotional expression. Under a scenario "What If Group members ... get angry and threaten to leave?" in the St. Louis Bridges guide, the advice is "Remind them that disagreement is part of the dialogue process. Ask them to help the group understand their feelings and use the opportunity to learn from each other" (FOCUS St. Louis, 2002: 21).

Some programs actually treat the discussions as a kind of *haven* for emotions. For example, Roseann Mason who runs the Kenosha/ Racine Diversity Circles has held discussions among prison inmates. While talking about the importance of confidentiality, she noted that the discussions are perhaps the one opportunity in prison life where the expression of emotions is acceptable.

The welcoming of passion into public talk might seem a danger to the attempts to forge connections between people. Fueling tempers rather than dampening them might exacerbate hostility. But this aspect of dialogue underscores that a deliberative system that includes dialogue might enable a unique kind of connection – one based not on de-emphasizing conflict, but built on an airing of difference.

3.3.4 Free from power

This next criterion further suggests that dialogue is as much about revealing difference as striving for a kind of unity. The prescription that good deliberation be "free from power" is the idea that inequalities in society should be prohibited from influencing deliberation. There is, of course, reason to wonder whether any form of communication can be free from power (Mansbridge, 1999: 224). How can civic talk – whether deliberation or dialogue – ever be free from power since it is highly unlikely that those with and those without power are equally familiar and comfortable using the same set of symbols (Young, 2001)?

Rather than chase the elusive condition of being free from power, a deliberative system could continually try to redress imbalances in power by focusing on them directly. In many respects, this is what dialogue programs attempt to do. That is, they take as their topic imbalances in power and differences in understanding, things that interfere with communication. For example, the curriculum guide for the second session of Study Circles on race relations suggests that groups discuss "What is the nature of the problem?" Participants are given five different viewpoints, and then are asked to discuss which comes closest to their own view. These viewpoints include: (1) "History is at the root of the problem," (2) "The real problem is institutional racism," (3) "The problem is that many people of color lack economic opportunity," (4) "The problem is that too many people of color are not taking advantage of the opportunities available to them," and (5) "Separation and prejudice are still our major problems."

The goal of focusing on imbalances in power puts a premium on encouraging testimony and storytelling about experience with these disparities. In practice, this results in attempts to include as many people of color as possible and attempts to ensure equality in participation during the conversations. Tips for Study Circles' facilitators include instructions such as "It is important to hear from everyone ... [and] ... Don't let anyone dominate; try to involve everyone" (SCRC, 1997: 44). Other programs set similar goals such as "We will insure the participation of all" (Corcoran and Greisdorf, 2001: 112) and instructions to not sit at tables, but place all chairs in one circle so that there is no back row (111). The SCRC and the St. Louis Bridges program both advise discussion groups to have a racially diverse team of co-facilitators to make speaking up as comfortable as possible for people of a variety of racial backgrounds. While some of these instructions are obviously attempts to minimize the tendency for some people to monopolize discussion, other suggestions such as the placement of chairs are intended to minimize the power differentials that exist in the society beyond the discussion groups.

3.3.5   Accountability

Ideal deliberation requires that the participants are accountable to their constituents.[16] This might seem to be irrelevant to civic dialogue programs, since the participants are neither elected nor formal representatives of any constituency. In fact program guides urge facilitators to not treat individual participants as representatives of any given social group.[17] However, part of what nonformal modes of deliberation accomplish is the clarification of notions of "to whom am I responsible?" (Walsh, 2004). Neither interviews with practitioners nor the dialogue program literature analyzed for this study revealed the use of the term accountability or phrases related to it such as "responsibility to others" or "obligation to others." However, there was an occasional emphasis on common good and "unity," suggesting that some expect dialogue programs will lead participants to be sensitive to a broader cross-section of the community. It is this aspect of public talk to which I now turn.

3.3.6   Focus on consensus or common good

The point of this comparison between dialogue programs and ideal deliberation is to conceptualize what kinds of connection are made possible by dialogue. The final criterion – of focus on consensus or common ground – is directly related to the types of connection that result from public talk. The belief that good deliberation consists of a focus on consensus or common good suggests that deliberation tends to address intercultural difference by focusing on unity. However, the place of unity is ambiguous among deliberative theorists. Various deliberative theorists have argued that the focus on consensus evident in Habermas and in Cohen (1989) is unwarranted (see Benhabib, 1996; Mansbridge, 1999). Recent summaries of the field question whether deliberative theorists in general advocate such a focus (Dryzek, 2000: 72; Chambers, 2003: 318). Similar disagreements also show up in the practice of dialogue. The SCRC materials promoting civic dialogue programs encourage participants to not strive for consensus, but nevertheless seek unity in the sense of common concerns. For example, instructions to Study Circles facilitators read: "Help participants identify 'common ground,' but don't force consensus" (SCRC, 1997: 45) and "While our differences may separate us on some matters, we have enough in common as human beings to allow us to talk together in a constructive way" (45). And yet some dispute resolution organizations that incorporate dialogue do advocate consensus to the point of including the word in the organization's title (e.g., Consensus Council, Inc.)[18] Postings on the listserve for the National Coalition for Dialogue and Deliberation also show disagreement over the utility of consensus versus common ground in addressing tensions in a community.

3.4 What kind of connections can dialogue forge?

Whether or not dialogue strives for consensus or common ground, it sets the stage for acknowledging difference. Although participants are urged to not carve up the world into us and them, civic dialogue often proceeds with the implicit assumption that experiences and perspectives differ by racial and ethnic background.[19] While people may be using these dialogue programs to create unity, the nature of the problems they seek to address and the distinctiveness of this form of public talk suggest the processes involved are about seeking unity while paying attention to cultural difference, rather than focusing on unity in spite of difference.

A brief review of the nature of civic dialogue and its comparison to deliberation will illuminate. These programs arise to address problems related to relations between people of different cultural backgrounds. They do so by trying to bring diverse groups of people together. The privacy of dialogue enables the airing of difference (publicity). Also, the explicit focus on conceptions of power (free from power) and constituency (accountability) could draw attention to existing inequalities and patterns of discrimination. Finally, the encouraging of expressions of emotion suggests that the communication is infused with the passion attached to these perceptions – perceptions held by people who were sufficiently motivated to volunteer for the program in the first place.

In the abstract we might expect that togetherness is best achieved through privileging unity. But this analysis of dialogue shows that the set-up of civic dialogue does little to obscure difference. Instead, it creates a forum that combines an emphasis on unity with a focus on diversity.

Thus dialogue may be making a unique and valuable contribution to deliberative democracy. However, dialogues have their downsides as well.

For example, if it is nearly impossible to have public talk that is free from power, perhaps the deliberative system needs forms of communication in which inequalities regarding who controls decision making (deliberative) processes are directly discussed. However, is it actually the case that we end domination by recognizing it? Or do we perpetuate it by bringing it into the limelight? One African American woman, during the last session of her Study Circles round in Madison, Wisconsin suggested the latter. "I would like to say something as someone who has dreaded coming to just about every one of these sessions." She said that she thought the sessions were a good idea, but that they had not taught her anything new. "I wanted to be surprised." She said that she had wanted to learn that the gap in understanding between whites and blacks was smaller than she thought, or that it was shrinking, but she was not able to conclude either. A white participant interjected that she was glad this woman had been a part of the circles. A facilitator said, "How do you feel about that?" The African American woman replied, "Not very good. This is selfish, but that doesn't address what these circles have done for me. What didn't get said here is that it is the Blacks that do the teaching in these circles." She said that she was not necessarily speaking on behalf of all people of color, but "I am probably like the other Blacks in the circle. I think about race every day. These things aren't new to me." When she said this, at least one other African American participant nodded in affirmation.

If it is the case that ending discrimination requires that members of dominant groups recognize their own complicity in discriminatory practices, hearing the stories of people who have been discriminated against could help. But when the burden of this work falls predominantly on members of marginalized groups, who has the power? Members of marginalized groups who get to place their stories at least temporarily front and center? Or the powerful who get to move one step closer to "getting it?" Because the answer is not clear, it is possible that civic dialogue, like other forms of public talk, perpetuate power imbalances that exist outside the discussion (Kim, 2000; McPhail, 2004).[20]

Whether we are considering deliberation, dialogue, or another form of public talk, understanding the connections it can forge requires considering it from majority and minority points of view. Even when a dialogue program is convened under the guise of promoting shared understanding or common ground, it is hard to imagine that members of dominant groups and members of subordinate groups strive for unity in an identical fashion, or that the airing of difference has identical implications for people of different levels of status. Let's assume that the perspectives of dominant groups in a community are considered the norm, and the standard against which other views are judged. Then, for people who are members of a dominant group, participating in dialogue may allow them to become aware of the viewpoints of nondominant groups. This in turn accomplishes two things. One, it enables dominant group members to more fully consider the concerns of members of marginalized groups when making political choices that will impact members of these groups. Second, it may lead dominant group members to realize that they are not fully equipped to speak on behalf of others – that they need additional information, or perhaps need to hear directly from the others they purport to represent.

I mean to distinguish this from the argument that the more views included in deliberation the more informed the outcome decisions. The potential of civic dialogue is that it is not just one policy decision that gets illuminated. Instead, the focus on differences in perspective, power inequalities, and conceptions of community means that it is the civic fabric itself that is created through the interaction.

Let's now consider the processes and implications of constructing community through awareness of difference for members of a nondominant group. If it is people of color in civic intergroup dialogues who "do the teaching," then the process they experience is not necessarily the act of recognizing difference, but the act of watching dominant group members become aware of difference and the extent of discrimination in a community. Several things might occur because of this witnessing. Nondominant group members might become more willing to engage in collective action with dominant group members, due to the possibility that the dominant group members will actively listen to and respect their concerns. They might also forge connections across various marginalized groups, laying the basis for action in opposition to the status quo.

This raises yet another possible downside of dialogue: instead of enabling connections, it may exacerbate divides. If what goes on in these dialogues is partly about airing differences, how can that be construed as a positive bond that lays the groundwork for future cooperation? If a connection contains opposition, isn't it more of a distancing than a bond between people? Such rhetorical questions overlook conceptions of public life that allow for opposition and difference and ignore another way that dialogue may be contributing to the deliberative system.

In *The Human Condition*, for example, Hannah Arendt describes the public realm as the space in which the many opposing perspectives comprising a society collectively give meaning to a common topic of concern ([1958] 1998). In her conception, all individuals have a unique perspective, and it is the diversity of perspectives in the public realm that allows for a more complete understanding of a topic. An analogy is that each person's perspective is like a flashlight, shining on a common issue. It is when many beams of light are at work, each catching a different part of the surface, that the topic is fully illuminated.

Arendt reminds us that people can create understandings of their communities that are based on – not disrespectful of – differences. None of the types of connection that I identified in the introduction – consensus, tolerance, or common ground – fully capture the kind of balance between unity and diversity suggested by Arendt or made possible by the unique character of dialogue. Providing a space in which people of a given geographic community – both members of dominant and marginalized groups – can voice their perspectives and listen to those of others, treats conflict not as something to be gotten past (cf. Gould, 1996: 172), but as a force that can be harnessed.

One final aspect of civic dialogue further illuminates why this form of public talk deserves the attention of scholars of democracy. In many cities, local governments sponsor the dialogue programs. This poses a challenge to our conception of civil society. In these forums of public talk, people are apparently constructing the fabric of civic life. And yet a strict interpretation of civil society treats it as a sphere of interaction that is distinct from the state. But if informal talk does little to foster intercultural communication, then state intervention might be necessary. But won't state intervention mean the perpetuation of domination that critics of deliberation caution against?

The practice of civic dialogue calls into question conventional interpretations of the role of the government in civil society. When cities sponsor and fund civic dialogue, they are providing a means by which marginalized groups can communicate their experiences with discrimination and in which members of dominant groups volunteer to listen. This act of majoritarian governments opening themselves to criticism from marginalized voices is unexpected behavior and worthy of further scrutiny.

Incorporating dialogue in the deliberative system may demonstrate to minorities that their views are actively being considered in the decision making process. However, these signals reach members of majorities, too, some of whom may interpret them as indications that the local government is intent on fueling intercultural conflict. Using civic dialogue represents a stance that connections among people in a community are healthiest in the long run when conflict is addressed, rather than obscured with the demand of politeness or assumptions of underlying harmony. Such a position should be reason to rethink our assumptions about the kinds of civic connection governments are encouraging as well as the types of bonds citizens are attempting to create in contexts of difference.

Notes

1. Special thanks to the people who agreed to be interviewed or observed for this study. Thank you to Kristine Berg, Tim Bagshaw, Patrick Guarasci, Patty LeBaron, Zach Mesenbourg, Hillary Schulman, and Adam Busch for their research assistance. My gratitude to members of the Political Behavior Research Group at the University of Wisconsin-Madison, participants in the National Election Studies Fellows Workshop at the University of Michigan, seminar participants in the Departments of Political Science and Psychology at the University of Minnesota, Joe Soss, Richard Merelman, and William Scheuerman for very helpful feedback on this project.

2. This prescription is also evident in Mansbridge's explanation of the deliberative system, the *range* of acts of communication that collectively comprise deliberative democracy (1999). This system includes acts ranging from "the representative assembly (Bessette, 1994), to the public assembly producing a binding decision (Cohen, 1989; Gutmann and Thompson, 1996), to the 'public sphere' (Habermas, [1962] 1989), to the most informal venues of everyday talk" (227).

3. For more information on the count of programs, see Walsh, 2007, ch. 1. President Clinton's Initiative on Race represents an effort by federal governments to do this as well (*One America* 1998; Kim, 2000; Oskamp and Jones, 2000; Goering, 2001). I use the term intercultural to refer to interracial and interethnic conflict.

4. Thanks to Joe Soss for his insight on these conceptions.

5. For more background on these programs, please see Walsh, 2007: ch. 1.

6. She derives publicity, accountability, and reciprocity from Gutmann and Thompson's *Deliberative Democracy*. The remaining are adapted primarily from Cohen (1989). These labels closely map on to the criteria that Mendelberg and Oleske "distill" from these and other theories (2000).

7. Telephone interviews were conducted in the spring and summer of 2002 with Martha McCoy, Executive Director of the Study Circles Resource Center; Molly Holme Barrett, Project Coordinator and Assistant Editor of the SCRC; Robert Corcoran, National Director of Hope in the Cities; and William Barnes, Director, Center for Research and Program Development of the National League of Cities. In addition, program evaluators for the Study Circles programs, Rona Roberts and Steve Kay, were interviewed in person on 26 June 2002. Interviews ranged in length from 40 to 75 minutes. Also, several in-person and telephone conversations were conducted with Gwen Wright, Project Coordinator, Racial Justice and Race Relations, National League of Cities, and Deborah George, Manager of Local Government Services at the National League of Cities, as well as numerous additional consultations with McCoy.

8. Interviewees include Mary Jane Hollis, Executive Director of the Aurora Community Study Circles; Audrey Norman Turner, Program Coordinator of the Dayton Dialogues on Race; Dean Lovelace, City Commissioner, Dayton, Ohio; Rudy Simms, Executive Director of the National Conference for Community and Justice (NCCJ), Iowa Region; Jesse Villalobos, Des Moines Regional Program Director for the NCCJ; Cliff Kessler, Director of the Neighborhood Circles program in Des Moines; Floyd Jones, Executive Director of the Des Moines Human Rights Commission; Jessica Dumas of the Community Conversations in Kansas City, Missouri; Roseann Mason of the Diversity Circles in Kenosha and Racine, Wisconsin; Ellen Rice Parks, of the YWCA in Lexington, Kentucky; Rona Roberts, Speak Out Lexington (Ky.) and Lexington Study Circles; Steve Kay, Speak Out Lexington (Ky.) and Lexington Study Circles; Roy Fuller, Executive Director of the Louisville NCCJ; Lt. Col. Stan Mullen, Louisville Police Department; Mona Winston, Study Circles Program Coordinator, Greater Madison Urban League; Stephen Braunguinn, President/CEO, Greater Madison Urban League; Susan Bauman, Mayor of the City of Madison, Wisconsin; Hedi Rudd, Madison Study Circles on Race Program Coordinator; Sandi O'Brien, Siouxland Study Circles Program Coordinator, Sioux City Iowa; Richard Hayes, Executive Director of the Human Rights Commission, Sioux City; Chief Joseph Frisbee, Sioux City Police Department; Sandy Robinson, Director of the Springfield Department of Community Relations in Springfield, Illinois; Kathryn Harris, Director of the Illinois State Historical Library and a former Springfield Study Circles facilitator;

Walter Reed, Executive Director of the Human Rights Commission, Waterloo, Iowa; John Crews, Mayor of Cedar Falls, Iowa and Waterloo Study Circles facilitator; Lanette Watson program administrator of Waterloo, Iowa, Study Circles; Jim Day, Waterloo Study Circles; Virgill Powell, Waterloo Study Circles facilitator and Chief, Waterloo Fire Department; Lt. John Daws, Waterloo Police Department; Walter Rooff, Mayor, Waterloo, Iowa; Don Grove, former Director, Iowa Human Rights Commission. All interviews were conducted in person (except for the interviews with Grove, Kessler, Fuller, and Rooff, and one of several conversations with Hayes). Interviews were conducted during the summers of 2002 and 2003 and ranged in length from one to three hours. All were tape-recorded and transcribed.

9. This study is part of a larger project that analyzes the conditions under which cities choose to use civic dialogue to address public problems and the nature of the discussions that occur in these programs (Walsh, 2006; 2007). Walsh, 2007 reports the results of more extensive participant observation of these groups than is reported here.

10. In July 2002, I interviewed Chip Harrod, the Executive Director of the National Conference for Community and Justice in Cincinnati, Ohio, and Barbara Levin, the coordinator of the Bridges Across Racial Polarization program administered through FOCUS St. Louis in St. Louis, Missouri.

11. This is especially the case when practitioners describe discussions that are intended to create plans for future collective action (SCRC, 1997: 28).

12. Leighninger (2002); Bill Barnes (personal interview). Responses to questionnaires administered to participants in the Madison Study Circles on Race similarly show a racial divide in what participants want the program to achieve.

Despite the difficulties with racial and ethnic inclusivity, dialogue programs do, however, appear to improve the equality of the deliberative system with respect to gender. Although women in the United States tend to speak less during jury and legislative deliberation (Marder, 1987; Sanders, 1997; Kathlene, 1994), small group discussions (Guzzetti and Williams, 1996), the public forum of talk radio (Bolce, De Maio, and Muzzio, 1996; Davis and Owen, 1998: 146), and in everyday political discourse (Huckfeldt and Sprague, 1995: ch. 10; Hansen, 1997), the volunteers for dialogue programs tend to be female.

13. See also Fung and Wright (2001: 19).

14. Mansbridge points out that Gutmann and Thompson include many more criteria under this dimension. "Gutmann and Thompson group under the heading of 'reciprocity' the values of mutual respect, the goals of consistency in speech and consistency between speech and action, the need to acknowledge the strongly held feelings and beliefs of others, and the values of open-mindedness and 'economy of moral disagreement' (seeking rationalities that minimize the rejection of an opposing position)" (1999: 222). She continues on to note that their definition includes Sanders's (1997) call for testimony.

15. As Mansbridge notes, the early stages of deliberation require a mixture of protection and publicity.

16. Mansbridge (1999) interprets this criterion as responsibility to others, but Chambers states that the treatment of accountability in recent deliberative theory is "primarily understood in terms of 'giving an account' of something, that is publicly articulating, explaining, and most importantly justifying public policy" (2003: 308). I use Mansbridge's treatment as my point of departure since Chambers's definition overlaps with the criterion of reciprocity.

17. "We will speak in the first person. We will not speculate on what 'they' think or feel" (Corcoran and Greisdorf, 2001: 112). "We will focus on those person [*sic*] or persons present. We will not focus on an historic person or group" (Corcoran and Greisdorf, 2001: 113).
18. Available at http://www.usconsensuscouncil.org/.
19. This focus has been criticized for privileging differences to the extent of essentializing (Kim, 2000).
20. This dynamic reflects the antipathy toward participatory democracy many Black Americans exhibited during the civil rights movement (Polletta, 2002: chs. 3–4). Polletta argues that Blacks perceived participatory democracy as "unappealingly moralistic, self-indulgent, and white" (206). I address these issues at greater length in Walsh, 2007.

4
Deliberation and Agreement
Christian List[1]

4.1 Introduction

A central problem of democracy is decision making among individuals with conflicting preferences or judgments. Democracy is sometimes thought to be about finding 'the will of the people', but if different individuals have radically different 'wills', it may be hard to extract from these 'individual wills' a consistent 'popular will'. To illustrate, imagine a group of people in which a third prefers option x to option y to option z, a second third prefers option y to option z to option x, and the last third prefers option z to option x to option y. Then a majority prefers x to y, a majority prefers y to z, and a majority prefers z to x – a 'cyclical' majority preference. So the plausible democratic procedure of pairwise majority voting fails to generate a consistent 'popular will' here. This is Condorcet's paradox.

More generally, Kenneth Arrow's impossibility theorem (1951/1963) shows that this problem is not just an artefact of majority voting. Consider a group of individuals, a committee, legislature, or perhaps entire society. Suppose we want to find a procedure for aggregating the preferences of these individuals into corresponding preferences for the group as a whole. And suppose we want our democratic procedure to satisfy some minimal conditions. First, the procedure should accept as its admissible input all possible combinations of individual preferences ('universal domain'). Second, whenever all individuals agree that option x is preferable to option y, the procedure should respect this unanimous preference ('the weak Pareto principle'). Third, the social preference over any two options x and y should depend only on individual preferences over x and y, and not on individual preferences over third alternatives, thus ruling out various forms of manipulation ('independence of irrelevant alternatives'). Fourth, there should be no dictator ('non-dictatorship'). And, fifth, social preferences should be consistent, in particular there should be no 'cycles' as in Condorcet's paradox above ('collective rationality'). In short, these five conditions require that the democratic procedure should work for all possible inputs that might arise in a pluralistic society, that its outputs should be democratically responsive to

64

its inputs, and that these outputs should themselves be consistent. Can we find such a procedure? Arrow's theorem gives a negative answer to this question. When there are three or more decision options, no procedure will simultaneously satisfy Arrow's five conditions.

Of course, the difficulties posed by democratic decision making depend on how much disagreement there is between different individuals' preferences or judgments. In the rare case of unanimity the difficulties disappear. If everybody had exactly the same preferences or judgments, there would be no conflict to resolve. But although unanimity is sufficient for resolving the problems identified by Condorcet and Arrow, it is not necessary. Since Duncan Black's seminal work (1948), it is known that Condorcet's paradox can be traced back to a 'lack of structure' in the combination of preferences across individuals. Black proved that 'single-peakedness', a structure condition on preferences discussed formally below, is sufficient (but not necessary) for avoiding Condorcet paradoxes.[2] A well-known corollary of Black's result is that Arrow's impossibility theorem ceases to apply if the domain of admissible input to the decision procedure is restricted to combinations of individual preferences satisfying single-peakedness.

At first sight, Black's result may only seem to confirm what we already know, namely that, if disagreement in a group stays within certain limits – limits that are somehow transcended in the example of Condorcet's paradox – then familiar majoritarian procedures can be used for making consistent democratic decisions. But Black's result teaches us more than that. It highlights an important distinction between two different types of agreement. The two types are 'substantive agreement' on the one hand and 'meta-agreement' on the other. My aim in this chapter is to explore this distinction.

I discuss two different contexts of democratic decision making. The first is the familiar context of preference aggregation, the second the less familiar one of judgment aggregation. In Sections 4.2 and 4.3, I explore the two types of agreement in the context of preference aggregation, and in section 4.4, I discuss the significance of meta-agreement for a deliberative democratic response to Condorcet's and Arrow's problems. In Section 4.5, I introduce the context of judgment aggregation, and in Sections 4.6 and 4.7, I explore the two types of agreement in that context. My main suggestion is that, when agreement is conceptualized in democratic theory and when it is sought in democratic practice, more emphasis should be placed on meta-agreement than is commonly done. In Section 4.8, I take a step back and ask to what extent it is acceptable for the stability of democratic procedures to depend on special empirical contingencies. In Section 4.9, I make some brief concluding remarks.

4.2 Substantive agreement

How can we define 'substantive agreement'? Two or more individuals are in substantive agreement to the extent that their preferences or judgments are the same. Perfect substantive agreement requires identical preferences or judgments across different individuals. In this section, I focus on preferences; I turn to judgments in Section 4.6 later.

In response to Condorcet's and Arrow's problems, it is natural to suggest that collective decisions should be preceded by a period of democratic deliberation, so as to reduce the level of conflict between different people's preferences and to bring about consensus on what decision option should be chosen. Jon Elster summarizes this view succinctly:

> The core of the theory [of deliberative democracy] ... is that rather than aggregating or filtering preferences, the political system should be set up with a view to changing them by public debate and confrontation. The input to the social choice mechanism would then not be the raw, quite possibly selfish or irrational, preferences ..., but informed and other-regarding preferences. Or rather, there would not be any need for an aggregation mechanism, since a rational discussion would tend to produce unanimous preferences. (Elster, 1986: 112)

If successful, the view outlined by Elster seems attractive. But there are at least two problems. The first, and practical, problem is that it is often un-realistic to expect democratic deliberation to produce unanimity. People may agree on all relevant facts and arguments concerning different political options, and yet disagree on their most preferred option. They may agree on what the environmental effects of a new industrial development would be, and yet disagree on whether these effects should be given more weight than the expected economic benefits of the new development. Indeed, as discussed in more detail later, experiments on group deliberation have pro-duced little evidence of post-deliberation unanimity (List et al., 2000/2005). Moreover, Cass Sunstein has presented striking empirical evidence that deliberation, especially in homogeneous groups whose members reinforce each other's views, can sometimes lead to polarization of opinion rather than convergence to a centrist position (Sunstein, 2002). This is not to deny the benefits of substantive agreement, if it can be reached. But clearly, democracy needs to have alternative resources for dealing with conflicts of preferences in those plausible and numerous cases in which deliberation fails to produce unanimity.

The second, and more theoretical, problem with the view outlined by Elster is that it is unclear whether convergence towards substantive agreement – falling short of perfect unanimity – is the most promising strategy for avoiding Condorcet's and Arrow's aggregation problems. William Gehrlein has devised measures of preference homogeneity capturing how closely a given combination of preferences across individuals approximates substan-tive agreement. Using these measures, he has shown that, although there is a positive correlation between preference homogeneity and the avoidance of Condorcet paradoxes, the correlation is weaker than one might have expected (Gehrlein, 2000).

4.3 Meta-agreement

Black's insight is to ask not whether two or more individuals have the same preferences over a set of decision options, but rather whether their preferences can be rationalized in terms of the same underlying 'left-right' dimension. Suppose the decision options are somehow aligned on a single axis, such as from left-most to right-most. We say that an individual has 'single-peaked' preferences on this axis if he or she has a most preferred position somewhere on the axis with decreasing preference as options get more distant in both directions from the most preferred position. If *all* individuals' preferences are single-peaked on the *same* axis, then we say that the entire combination of preferences across individuals is 'single-peaked'. A shared axis on which all individuals' preferences are single-peaked, if it exists, is called a 'structuring dimension'. Figure 4.1 shows an example of two preference orderings over five options that are single-peaked on the left-right axis x, y, z, v, w. By contrast, Figure 4.2 shows a preference ordering that is not single-peaked on that axis. (In both figures, the options are plotted on the horizontal axis, and ordinal preference intensity is plotted on the vertical axis.)

The terms 'left' and 'right' are used here in a purely geometrical sense. Any one-dimensional alignment of the options could serve as a structuring dimension, whether it orders the options from most socialist to most capitalist, from most urban to most rural, from most secular to most religious, from most architecturally avant-garde to most architecturally conservative, or in any other, however esoteric, way. While the term 'structuring dimension' refers only to a geometrical alignment of the decision options, we may use the term 'issue dimension' to refer to a broader interpretation underlying such an alignment, such as one of the interpretations just given.

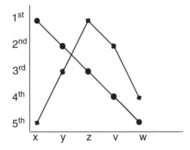

Figure 4.1 Single-peaked preferences

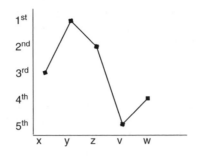

Figure 4.2   Non-single-peaked preferences

Black's concept of single-peakedness inspires the following definition of 'meta-agreement'. Two or more individuals are in meta-agreement to the extent that they agree on a common issue dimension in terms of which a given decision problem is to be conceptualized – and in terms of which preferences are to be rationalized. They may reach perfect meta-agreement while at the same time disagreeing substantively on what the most preferred option is.

Single-peakedness may be an *implication* of meta-agreement. If the individuals agree on a common issue dimension and rationalize their preferences in terms of that dimension, then the resulting combination of individual preferences will satisfy single-peakedness, provided the common (semantic) issue dimension translates into a common (geometrical) structuring dimension. However, as single-peakedness is only a formal structure condition on individual preferences, single-peakedness is logically weaker than meta-agreement. A group of individuals may accidentally have single-peaked preferences on a certain (geometrical) structuring dimension without explicitly rationalizing their preferences in terms of a common (semantic) issue dimension.

Further, single-peakedness is not merely a consistency condition on individual preferences. Take the preferences of a single individual (over a finite set of options). Unless we refer to a specific structuring dimension, it is vacuously true that the individual has single-peaked preferences *on some dimension* (supposing the individual is able to rank the options in a clear order of preference). We can simply define the individual's most preferred option as the left-most option, his or her least preferred option as the right-most option, aligning all other options from left to right in the individual's order of preference. On this artificially constructed structuring dimension, the individual's preference ordering is clearly single-peaked, though uninformatively so, as the constructed structuring dimension has little independent meaning. The condition of single-peakedness becomes non-vacuous only when we *either* refer to a specific structuring dimension *or* apply the condition to several individuals' preferences. In the latter case, we can ask whether there exists at least one *common* structuring dimension on which *all* individuals' preferences are single-peaked. If individual preferences are as in Condorcet's paradox, then there exists no such dimension. Regardless of how we align the options from left to right on some axis in that example, some individuals' preferences will fail to be single-peaked on that axis. On the other hand, if only two of the three different preference orderings in Condorcet's example were held among the individuals (eg., just the first two but not the third), then the resulting combination of individual preferences would be single-peaked on a common structuring dimension. This is the sense in which single-peakedness captures an implication of *agreement*, albeit at a meta-level.

Now Black proved the following simple, yet remarkable result. Given a combination of preferences across individuals satisfying single-peakedness, align the individuals from left-most to right-most in terms of their most preferred position – their 'peak' – on the corresponding structuring dimension. With respect to this left-right alignment of the individuals, the 'median individual' is the one who has an equal number of individuals to the left and to the right (assuming, for simplicity, that the number of individuals is odd). Then the most preferred option of the median individual will beat, or at least tie with, all other options in pairwise majority voting. A simple corollary of this result is that, if the domain of admissible input to the democratic procedure consists only of individual preference combinations satisfying single-peakedness, then pairwise majority voting is guaranteed to generate collective preferences in accordance with Arrow's minimal conditions (except of course 'universal domain').

Moreover, several studies have shown that consistent majority preferences are still likely to exist even if not all individuals, but only a sufficiently large proportion of them (sometimes as few as 75 per cent) have preferences that are single-peaked on a common structuring dimension (Niemi, 1969; Tullock and Campbell, 1970; Gehrlein, 2004). So perfect meta-agreement, with single-peaked preferences among all individuals, is sufficient but not necessary for avoiding Condorcet's and Arrow's problems; partial meta-agreement, with single-peaked preferences among a sufficiently large proportion of the individuals, will often suffice.

4.4   Deliberation and meta-agreement

Black's result suggests an alternative response to the challenge posed by Condorcet and Arrow. Rather than seeking convergence towards substantive agreement through deliberation, which may be hard to achieve, we might seek convergence towards meta-agreement. A recent strand of thinking on deliberative democracy advocates precisely this idea (Miller, 1992; Knight and Johnson, 1994; Dryzek and List, 2003; 2004; List et al., 2000/5). On this view, the key to a deliberative democratic response to Condorcet and

Arrow lies not in deliberation-induced substantive agreement, but rather in deliberation-induced meta-agreement. As the proponents of this view emphasize, it is more realistic, though still demanding, to expect deliberation to produce agreement on what the relevant dimension is than to produce agreement on what option should be chosen. Or, more figuratively, it is often easier to reach agreement on what the questions are than on how to answer them. The view can be stated as a three-part hypothesis:

1. Group deliberation leads people to identify a common (semantic) issue dimension in terms of which to conceptualize the decision problem at stake.
2. For a given such issue dimension, group deliberation leads people to agree on how the decision options are aligned from left to right with respect to that issue dimension; so people determine which (geometric) structuring dimension best represents the given (semantic) issue dimension.
3. Once a (semantic) issue dimension and a corresponding (geometric) structuring dimension have been identified as relevant, group deliberation leads each individual to determine a most preferred position (his or her 'peak') on that dimension, with decreasing preference as options get increasingly distant from the most preferred position.

The combination of parts 1, 2 and 3 is, in essence, the hypothesis that group deliberation brings about meta-agreement, which then surfaces in the form of single-peakedness. Neither part of the hypothesis is trivial. And each part raises difficult social-psychological issues, which I am not able to address here. But let me make some suggestions about the status of each part of the hypothesis, albeit in rather simplistic terms.

First, the question of what semantic issue dimension is relevant to a given democratic decision problem is a *normative* question. For example, if society has to choose between different industrial policy options, it is a normative matter whether the choice should be conceptualized in terms of a classical socio-economic left-right dimension, in terms of a trade-off between short-term economic growth and the environment, in terms of a different trade-off between urban and rural development, or in terms of some other issue dimension. This normative question may not have an independently 'true' answer. Rather, different societies might give different answers, depending on their shared values, histories, demographic and ideological circumstances and other factors.

Second, the question of how decision options are aligned from left to right with respect to a given issue dimension is a *factual* question, albeit one on which there may be considerable disagreement (and where the debate may not always be entirely value-free). For example, if society has agreed that its choice between different industrial policy options should be conceptualized in terms of a trade-off between short-term growth and the environment, it is then a complex factual matter how exactly the proposed policy options are positioned in terms of that trade-off, that is, which policy option is most environmentally friendly, which one leads to the greatest short-term growth, and what the relative positions of the intermediate options are in terms of their impact on growth and the environment.

Third, the question of whether an individual's preferences are single-peaked on a given structuring dimension is a question of *rationality*, provided (crucially) that the individual has recognized this structuring dimension (and its underlying semantic issue dimension) as the relevant one. Suppose an individual has come to accept that a given industrial policy decision should be conceptualized in terms of the trade-off between growth and the environment, and suppose further he or she has come to accept that, among different policy options, option x is the most growth-friendly one, option y the most environmentally friendly one, and other options lie in a particular order in between x and y. Would the individual then have single-peaked preferences on this structuring dimension? It would seem that, *if* the individual genuinely believes the given dimension to be the relevant one, *then* he or she should indeed rationalize his or her preferences in terms of that dimension, that is, the individual should determine his or her most preferred position on that dimension and then prefer options less as they get more distant from the most preferred position.

If my remarks are correct, what does the success of the three-part hypothesis depend on? Let me first address parts 2 and 3 of the hypothesis and then turn to part 1.[3] The success of part 2 depends on whether group deliberation can bring about agreement on factual matters, for instance by clarifying and supplying information on the properties of the various decision options. The success of part 3 depends on whether group deliberation can induce rationality in individuals. Both of these requirements are not undemanding, but they are clearly not completely implausible.

The success of part 1, by contrast, depends on whether group deliberation can make one particular issue dimension sufficiently salient, so as to produce agreement on the relevance of that issue dimension. This in turn depends on whether deliberation can bring about agreement on what normative considerations are relevant for a given decision problem, a demanding requirement in many cases.

In some cases, an appeal to public reasons and generalizable interests – something that deliberative democrats advocate – may lead to the identification of a single publicly relevant issue dimension and thereby to meta-agreement, as required by part 1 of the hypothesis. But in other cases an appeal to such reasons or interests alone may not suffice, because individuals might still disagree about what is in the public interest or whether economic growth or the environment should be given priority when such interests are in conflict.

Even mainstream rational choice theorists are likely to agree that parts 2 and 3 of the hypothesis are relatively undemanding, and that the demanding part is part 1. Mueller (1989: 89–90), for example, argues, '[g]iven that we have a single-dimensional issue, single-peakedness does not seem to be that strong an assumption. What is implausible is the assumption that the issue space is one dimensional.'

Obviously, the question of whether deliberation induces single-peakedness is ultimately an empirical matter that cannot be settled by pure theorizing. In a recent study, List et al. (2000/2005) have used data from James Fishkin and Robert Luskin's deliberative polls to test the hypothesis empirically (on the method of deliberative polling, see Fishkin, 1997). They have studied a set of deliberative polls on topics ranging from energy provision in Texas to the future of the monarchy in Australia. In these polls, participants were first interviewed on their preferences and opinions, then invited to participate in a weekend of group deliberation, and finally interviewed again, being asked exactly the same questions as in the pre-deliberation interviews. This research design allows the comparison of pre-deliberation and post-deliberation levels of single-peakedness, measured in terms of the proportion of individuals whose preferences are single-peaked on a common structuring dimension. The study has shown that the post-deliberation levels of single-peakedness were either strictly greater than the corresponding pre-deliberation levels or at least on a par with them. Moreover, the questionnaires also included factual questions revealing how well-informed participants were before and after deliberation about the issues at stake. Among those participants who emerged best informed from the deliberative process, there was a consistent increase in the level of single-peakedness in all deliberative polls under investigation. Finally, the deliberative process did not appear to lead to a consistent increase in the level of substantive agreement, which suggests that deliberation's effect on meta-agreement is more marked than its effect on substantive agreement.

Of course, these findings are not the final word on the introduced hypothesis. Some situations may be favourable to its success, such as when a certain issue dimension – for example, a trade-off between growth and the environment – is easily identified as the salient one. But other situations may be less favourable to its success, such as when a decision problem is perceived to be inherently multidimensional or when different people's values clash. In such cases, people neither agree on what the correct answer is, nor even on how to think about the problem. (On favourable and unfavourable conditions, see also List et al., 2000/2005.)

4.5   From preferences to judgments

So far my focus has been on preference aggregation. But sometimes democratic decision making bodies are faced with the task of judgment aggregation, that is, they have to make collective judgments on multiple propositions on the basis of conflicting individual judgments on these propositions. Further, the propositions may be logically interconnected, so the judgments on some propositions may constrain the judgments that can consistently be held on others. Judgment aggregation problems arise, for example, when complex systems of policy or legislation are to be designed, where multiple issues are involved, with interconnections between these issues, and where consistency across different issues matters. (For recent discussions of judgment aggregation, see Chapman, 2002; List and Pettit, 2002; 2004; List, 2004a, b; Pauly and van Hees, 2005; Dietrich, 2005.)

A simple example illustrates the problem. Suppose a multi-member government has to make judgments on three policy propositions:

P: A budget deficit is affordable.
If P then Q: If a budget deficit is affordable, then spending on education should be increased.
Q: Spending on education should be increased.

For simplicity, let there be three individual government members, with judgments on the propositions as shown in Table 4.1. Each member's judgments are individually consistent.

If majority votes are taken on each of the three propositions, then a majority accepts P, a majority accepts 'If P then Q', and yet a majority rejects Q, an inconsistency. So proposition-by-proposition majority voting over a set of interconnected propositions can lead to an inconsistent set of collective judgments. Moreover, this can happen even when all individuals hold perfectly consistent individual judgments, as in the present example. This problem is sometimes called the 'discursive dilemma' (Chapman, 1998; Brennan, 2001; Pettit, 2001; the present example is given in Dietrich, 2005).

Just as Arrow's impossibility theorem shows that Condorcet's paradox is not just an artefact of majority voting, we may ask whether the present 'paradox' of judgment aggregation hints at a more general problem. A recent theorem by List and Pettit (2002; 2004) addresses this question. Again consider a group of individuals, and suppose we want to find a procedure for aggregating the judgments of these individuals into corresponding judgments for the group as a whole. Also, suppose we want the judgment

Table 4.1   A combination of individual judgments

	Individual 1	Individual 2	Individual 3
P	Yes	Yes	No
If P then Q	Yes	No	Yes
Q	Yes	No	No

aggregation procedure to satisfy some minimal conditions, similar in spirit to Arrow's conditions on preference aggregation. First, the procedure should accept as its admissible input all possible combinations of individual judgments, so long as these judgments are individually consistent ('universal domain'). Second, the procedure should give equal weight to all individuals' judgments ('anonymity'). Third, the collective judgments on each proposition should depend only on individual judgments on that proposition and different propositions should be treated equally ('systematicity'). And, fourth, collective judgments should be consistent, in particular there should be no collective inconsistencies as in the 'discursive dilemma' example ('collective rationality'). As in the case of Arrow's conditions, the essence of the conditions is that the judgment aggregation procedure should work for all possible inputs, that its outputs should be responsive to its inputs, and that these outputs should themselves be consistent. Can we find such a procedure? Again, the answer is negative. Except in special cases when the propositions under consideration are largely unconnected, no judgment aggregation procedure will simultaneously satisfy the four conditions just introduced.

Once again, the difficulties posed by this result depend on how much disagreement there is between different individuals' judgments. I now suggest that the two different types of agreement I have identified in a preference aggregation context can also be identified in a judgment aggregation context, and that they here, too, point towards two different responses to the problems of aggregation. I also argue that Sunstein's idea of an 'incompletely theorized agreement' can be seen as a special case of a substantive agreement (Sunstein, 1994).

4.6   Substantive agreement revisited

In the context of judgment aggregation, two or more individuals are in substantive agreement to the extent that their judgments are the same on the given propositions. As before, one might try to solve judgment aggregation problems by encouraging a period of deliberation prior to forming collective judgments, so as to bring about greater substantive agreement among the individuals involved in the decision. I have already noted in the context of preference aggregation that substantive agreement may be hard to attain in practice. Now, if we are dealing not just with preferences over separate policy options, but with judgments over an entire set of interconnected propositions, then substantive agreement may become even harder to attain.

There is, however, a special case of substantive agreement that may seem more practically attainable, although it is still demanding (for a more detailed discussion, see List, 2004b). This special case is a version of an 'incompletely theorized agreement', which Sunstein originally proposed for the legal realm. Often different individuals' judgments on fundamental moral and political issues are mutually incompatible, as they reflect genuinely different views of politics and morality, including different supporting reasons even for those judgments on which there is agreement (such as 'killing is wrong'). But, on less fundamental and more pragmatic issues, there may be more agreement. Given someone's overall set of moral and political judgments, this set will contain some judgments that the individual considers fundamental, perhaps even 'axiomatic', and others that he or she considers less fundamental, or more pragmatic. Now it is possible that different mutually incompatible fundamental judgments may nonetheless have certain implications in common at a less fundamental level. This is possible because, if there is a relation of logical entailment between someone's fundamental judgments and his or her less fundamental ones, this relation is usually a one-way entailment. The more fundamental judgments entail the less fundamental ones, but not vice-versa. The less fundamental and more pragmatic judgments are usually logically insufficient to tell us what the underlying fundamental judgments are. The same pragmatic judgments may be consistent with more than one fundamental system of supporting reasons.

For example, consider how many different fundamental reasons one might give to support a particular social welfare policy. One might believe in social justice and equality for liberal reasons or for religious reasons. Or one might believe that the main objective of the state is to keep the streets safe and to prevent crime and social disorder, and that welfare policies are the best way to achieve this. Or consider how many different fundamental reasons one might give for an environmental protection policy. One might believe in the rights of future generations; or one might believe that the rights of non-human animals ought to be respected, or that ecosystems should be treated as 'ends in themselves'. Or one might believe that environmental disasters would ruin the economy and that the best way to secure long-term economic stability would be to protect the environment.

An incompletely theorized agreement requires the identification of a certain set of non-fundamental or pragmatic propositions such that substantive agreement *on these propositions* is feasible, even when there is no substantive agreement on any underlying reasons. In the example of Table 4.1, individuals 2 and 3 both hold that spending on education should not be increased, that is, they both reject proposition Q, even though they fundamentally disagree on *why* it is that spending on education should not be increased. Individual 2 holds that, although a budget deficit is affordable, education would not be a good way to spend additional funds. By contrast, individual 3 holds that education would be a good way to spend additional funds if a budget deficit were affordable, but a deficit simply cannot be afforded. So individuals 2 and 3 are in substantive agreement on proposition Q (to be precise, on its rejection), but not on any of the other propositions; so their substantive agreement on proposition Q is an incompletely theorized one.

It is an open question whether, and under what conditions, political deliberation can bring about substantive agreement – albeit perhaps an incompletely theorized one – on a sufficiently broad range of issues. In this brief discussion, however, two points should have become clear. First, a substantive agreement on a restricted range of issues is easier to achieve than a substantive agreement on all issues. Second, the idea of an incompletely theorized agreement is clearly different from that of a meta-agreement. In an incompletely theorized agreement, the individuals agree on certain judgments, without necessarily agreeing on the supporting reasons for these judgments. They agree on certain answers, without necessarily agreeing on what the more fundamental questions are. Meta-agreement, by contrast, requires agreement on questions, but not necessarily on answers.

4.7   Meta-agreement revisited

Meta-agreement is defined as agreement on a common issue dimension in terms of which a given decision problem is to be conceptualized – and in terms of which preferences or judgments are to be rationalized. In a preference aggregation context, I have argued that single-peakedness may be an implication of meta-agreement. Specifically, if the individuals rationalize their preferences in terms of a common issue dimension, then the resulting combination of individual preferences will satisfy single-peakedness, provided the common issue dimension also corresponds to a common structuring dimension.

While Black's structure condition of single-peakedness itself is not applicable to a judgment aggregation context, I will now show that an alternative structure condition can be devised for the latter context too (List, 2003). Moreover, the new structure condition, like single-peakedness, can be interpreted as an implication of meta-agreement.

Again, the question is not whether two or more individuals hold the same judgments, but now it is whether there exists a single alignment of the individuals (as opposed to options in the preference aggregation context) from left-most to right-most such that, for every proposition under consideration, the individuals accepting the proposition are either all to the left, or all to the right, of those rejecting it. If there exists a left-right alignment of the individuals with this property, then the given combination of judgments across individuals satisfies 'unidimensional alignment'. Once again, a left-right alignment of the individuals with this property is called a 'structuring dimension'.

It is easy to see that the judgments in Table 4.1 violate unidimensional alignment. No matter how the individuals are aligned from left to right, it is impossible to get the pattern of acceptance and rejection required for unidimensional alignment. By contrast, the judgments of the five individuals in Table 4.2 below satisfy unidimensional alignment: there exists a single left-right alignment of the five individuals – namely, 1, 2, 3, 4, 5 – with respect to which, for every proposition, the individuals accepting the proposition are either all to the left, or all to the right, of those rejecting it.

Table 4.2   Unidimensionally aligned judgments

	Individual 1	Individual 2	Individual 3	Individual 4	Individual 5
P	No	No	No	No	Yes
If P then Q	Yes	Yes	Yes	Yes	No
Q	Yes	Yes	No	No	No

Now a result similar to Black's result on single-peakedness can be proved (List, 2003). Given a combination of judgments across individuals satisfying unidimensional alignment, align the individuals from left-most to right-most on the corresponding structuring dimension. As before, the 'median individual' with respect to this alignment is the one who has an equal number of individuals to the left and to the right (again assuming an odd number of individuals, for simplicity). Then the judgments held by that median individual – the judgments of individual 3 in Table 4.2 – will be accepted in proposition-by-proposition majority voting. And provided the median individual's judgments are internally consistent, so are the resulting collective judgments. Again, a simple corollary is that, if the domain of individual input to a judgment aggregation procedure consists only of judgment combinations satisfying unidimensional alignment, then proposition-by-proposition majority voting is guaranteed to generate collective judgments in accordance with the minimal conditions on judgment aggregation introduced above (except of course 'universal domain').

The claim that unidimensional alignment is an implication of meta-agreement may seem less straightforward than the analogous claim for single-peakedness, but here is a way of making it plausible. Suppose, first, that there is a common issue dimension in terms of which all the propositions are conceptualized by the individuals, and suppose that each individual takes a certain position on that dimension. For simplicity, let me call it a left-right dimension, but again a range of interpretations is possible. And suppose, second, that, for each proposition, the extreme positions on that left-right dimension correspond to either clear acceptance or clear rejection of the proposition; and, further, there exists an 'acceptance threshold' on the dimension (possibly different for different propositions) such that all the individuals to the left of the threshold accept the proposition and all the individuals to its right reject it or vice-versa. If these two conditions are met, then we have a situation of unidimensional alignment.

As in the case of single-peakedness, unidimensional alignment requires no substantive agreement at all. In the case of Table 4.2, the left-most and right-most individuals disagree about *every* proposition; yet their judgments are unidimensionally aligned. Unidimensional alignment requires only a common left-right alignment of the individuals, which systematically structures their pattern of acceptance and rejection over the various propositions.

Once again, my claim is only that unidimensional alignment may be an *implication* of meta-agreement. Like single-peakedness, unidimensional alignment is logically weaker than meta-agreement. A combination of judgments across individuals may accidentally have the right formal structure for unidimensional alignment without the individuals conceptualizing all propositions in terms of a common issue dimension.

Moreover, like single-peakedness, unidimensional alignment is not merely a consistency condition on individual judgments. The judgments of a single individual always vacuously satisfy unidimensional alignment, though uninformatively so. Like single-peakedness, unidimensional alignment becomes non-vacuous only when we apply the condition to several individuals' judgments. In this sense unidimensional alignment also captures an implication of *agreement*, albeit again at a meta-level.

Unlike in the case of single-peakedness, however, no empirical research has been done on whether group deliberation can induce unidimensional alignment or on whether there are any non-trivial real-world situations in which the judgments across different individuals satisfy unidimensional alignment. But the mere observation that substantive agreement is often hard to attain, while unidimensional alignment is a less demanding condition, should lead us to give more attention to that condition.

4.8   Empirical contingencies and the design of democratic procedures

A critic might be unconvinced that deliberation-induced meta-agreement and corresponding structure conditions such as single-peakedness or unidimensional alignment open up attractive escape-routes from the paradoxes and impossibility results of social choice theory. The critic might argue as follows. Let us grant that, *if* empirical circumstances are such that individual preferences or judgments satisfy (or approximate) the relevant conditions, *then* familiar democratic procedures will indeed generate consistent collective outcomes. But, as soon as empirical circumstances are different, the very same procedures will fail to do so. Social choice theorists can even predict when such collective inconsistencies will occur. The procedures work well in some empirical circumstances (such as for certain combinations of preferences or judgments) but not in others. Further, the impossibility theorems tell us that this problem is not just an artefact of specific majoritarian procedures, but that it is a much more general problem. No democratic procedure will avoid that problem, unless we are willing to sacrifice some seemingly attractive minimal conditions.

Consider an analogy from engineering. One would not like to design a house merely on the basis that there are some empirical circumstances in which the house would be stable, while there are others in which it would collapse. Rather, one would seek to design a house on the basis of careful physical calculations confirming its stability. Analogously, the critic might argue, it is a risky strategy to use familiar majoritarian decision procedures and to rely on the observation that for some empirical circumstances (such as situations of meta-agreement) these procedures will work well, while ignoring the fact that for others they will not. Like a house, a democratic procedure should be designed so as to work well in *all* relevant circumstances (i.e., for all possible combinations of preferences or judgments). A procedural designer should not rely on the hope that problematic empirical circumstances will not arise. Rather, the designer should make sure that the procedure guarantees consistent outcomes whatever the circumstances are. So far the critic's objection.

The objection raises an important question. Should democratic procedures be designed in such a way as to work robustly under *all* possible empirical circumstances or is it acceptable for such procedures to rely on specific empirical contingencies that are exogenous to, and not guaranteed by, them? At first sight, the critic's objection has some force. After all, democratic procedures that rely on specific contingencies may seem prone to erratic behaviour, just as a house that is stable only under specific conditions may seem unsafe. But, on closer inspection, the objection loses some of its force. Even the best-designed house will collapse under *some* circumstances; for example, if there is a sufficiently strong earthquake. It is simply not true that a well-designed house will be stable in *all* circumstances. The critic might respond that official building standards take that problem into account. In earthquake zones like California, houses are required to meet more demanding building standards than in earthquake-free zones like Britain. But, if an exceptionally strong earthquake were to occur, even a house built according to the most demanding standards might collapse.

We can make the following observation from these points. Whenever something is to be designed, be it a house or a democratic procedure, there is a domain of possible empirical circumstances that might arise. In some of these circumstances (call them type 1) the house will be stable and the procedure will work well, while in others (call them type 2) the house will collapse and the procedure will generate inconsistent outcomes. Rather than trying to design a house or procedure for which there are no type 2 circumstances, which may be difficult if not impossible, a more reasonable strategy would be the following. First, consider the probability distribution over the relevant domain of circumstances, and then ask whether the probability of type 2 circumstances is sufficiently low to make the risk of their occurrence bearable. For example, even in Britain the probability of a massive earthquake is presumably non-zero. But as this probability is low, it is considered acceptable for houses in Britain not to be built to withstand massive earthquakes. In California, the probability distribution is different, and building standards are adjusted accordingly. Generally, if the stability of a house or procedure across *all* possible circumstances cannot be achieved, the building standards for houses or procedures would have to be adjusted to how probable the various possible circumstances are. The idea would be to design a house or procedure so as to ensure a high probability of type 1 circumstances and a low probability of type 2 circumstances.

Suppose the democratic culture in a group or society is such that the achievement of (sufficient) meta-agreement is highly probable (with single-peakedness or unidimensional alignment as an implication), while the occurrence of preference or judgment combinations leading to majority inconsistencies is highly improbable. Then the use of familiar majoritarian procedures for democratic decision making is as defensible as building houses in Britain that do not meet Californian building standards.[4] But suppose the democratic culture is different and combinations of preferences or judgments leading to majority inconsistencies are quite probable. Then the use of such procedures is much less defensible. The defensibility of a democratic procedure is therefore sensitive to the relevant probability distribution over the set of all possible inputs that might come up. This probability distribution, in turn, depends on a range of empirical features of the relevant group or society, their values, beliefs, ideological attitudes, psychological dispositions, and so on. Of course, deliberative democrats would not simply take this probability distribution as given. Rather, they would encourage deliberative arrangements specifically with the aim of transforming it in such a way as to increase the probability of type 1 circumstances and decrease that of type 2 circumstances. Whether, and how, this can be achieved is of course a difficult empirical question, on which much further research is required.

If we take these considerations seriously, then the defensibility of a particular democratic procedure is no longer an *a priori* matter, as sometimes thought in social choice theory, but dependent on empirical contingencies, which may differ from context to context.

4.9   Concluding remarks

The distinction between substantive agreement and meta-agreement was motivated by Duncan Black's insight into how Condorcet's paradox can be avoided. And, indeed, in the context of preference aggregation – the focus of Black's own work – there are both theoretical and empirical results in support of the view that deliberation-induced meta-agreement can facilitate democratic decision making in the face of conflicting individual preferences.

In the context of judgment aggregation, on the other hand, my conclusions must remain much more tentative. Again, the two types of agreement can be identified, and their logical status, even in terms of avoiding majority inconsistencies, is very similar to that of their more well-known counterparts in the context of preference aggregation. But whether deliberation-induced meta-agreement is practically attainable in this new context remains an open question for democratic theory and a challenge for democratic practice. In conclusion, many important questions remain open. Most importantly, we will need to tackle the question of whether a certain minimal level of cohesion among individual preferences or judgments is necessary for collective decisions to be both sufficiently democratic and sufficiently consistent, or whether democratic decision procedures can be made so robust as to cope with even the most extreme cases of disagreement. The impossibility results of social choice theory would certainly seem to apply in the latter cases.

Notes

1. This chapter presents earlier arguments and material from List (2002) in a substantially rewritten, redeveloped and extended form. I thank many colleagues for helpful feedback and discussions, including Geoffrey Brennan, Franz Dietrich, John Dryzek, Stephen Elkin, James Fishkin, Robert Goodin, Robert Luskin, David Miller, and Philip Pettit.
2. Jointly with the (harmless) technical condition that the number of individuals is odd.
3. The three parts of the hypothesis concern independent mechanisms. It is *logically possible* for different individuals to agree on a semantic issue dimension without agreeing on how exactly options are geometrically aligned with respect to that dimension. For example, a certain industrial policy option (like a nuclear technology option) may be considered extremely environmentally friendly by some, and extremely environmentally unfriendly by others. Likewise, it is *logically possible* for someone to consider a certain geometrical structuring dimension (and its underlying semantic issue dimension) to be relevant without having single-peaked preferences on that dimension. For example, one might strongly disprefer centrist options on that dimension and strongly prefer extremist ones. However, it is not clear that one would hold such a non-single-peaked preference if one genuinely recognized the given dimension as relevant. Rather, holding such a preference might reflect a tacit appeal to a different dimension.
4. Under arguably undemanding conditions on the probability distribution over combinations of preferences, it can be shown that the probability of cyclical majority preferences as in Condorcet's paradox converges to 0 with an increasing number of individuals (see the appendix on the probability of cycles in List and Goodin, 2001). Unfortunately, the conditions required for avoiding majority inconsistencies in judgment aggregation are more demanding (List, 2005).

5
Deliberation in Legislatures: Antecedents and Outcomes

André Bächtiger, Markus Spörndli,
Marco R. Steenbergen, Jürg Steiner

5.1 Introduction

In the study of deliberation, classical representative institutions such as legislatures have been largely neglected.[1] While students of deliberation have mainly focused on the deliberation in the civic sphere, students of legislatures have mainly concentrated on formal outcomes (e.g., votes) and how these are affected by institutional rules and legislators preferences. One reason for neglecting the topic of deliberation in the context of legislatures is that many political scientists do not conceive of them as genuine deliberative bodies. A fairly typical example is Uhr (1998) who argues that while the major purpose of legislatures is indeed debate and diversity, it does not imply unanimity and rational consensus. While we certainly do not deny that adversarial and rhetorical forms of debate play an important role in legislative interactions, we think that genuine and consequential deliberation is possible in legislatures, but – in line with new institutionally oriented research programs on legislatures (see Döring, 1995) – that this is largely dependent on favorable institutional contexts.

In our research project (Bächtiger/Steenbergen, 2004; Spörndli, 2004, Steiner et al., 2004; Bächtiger, 2005;), we addressed two questions. First, we tried to identify specific contexts – in particular political institutions – which are favorable to a more deliberative mode of policy-making, a topic which has been largely neglected both by deliberative theorists and institutionalists. Focusing on four national legislatures – Switzerland, United States, Germany, and Great Britain, – we hypothesized that consensus institutions, presidentialism, second chambers, non-public arenas, and low issue polarization are conducive to a more deliberative mode of policy-making. Second, we also tried to address the "so what" question, namely whether deliberation affects policy outcomes. Again, the literature on this topic is speculative and vague, with concrete empirical research almost completely lacking. For the outcome dimension, we distinguished between procedural and substantive outcomes. Concerning procedural outcomes, we examined whether a high discourse quality increases the probability of decisions made by unanimity. Concerning substantive outcomes, we investigated whether a high discourse quality increases egalitarian decisions in the sense that the most disadvantaged in society are particularly helped. The outcome dimension was analyzed in a single institutional context, the German Conference Committee (*Vermittlungsausschuss*), a body which tries to reconcile conflicts between the Federal Diet (*Bundestag*) and the Federal Council (*Bundesrat*). And third, we also tried to overcome the dearth of measurement instruments that allow researchers to operationalize and quantify the quality of discourse. We developed a "Discourse Quality Index" (DQI) which represents an attempt to put the diverse concepts of deliberation in operational terms.

We proceed as follows. We start with the presentation of our hypotheses on preconditions and outcomes of deliberation in legislative interactions; this is followed by the operationalization of the variables (including our measurement instrument for deliberation, the DQI); then we present the results of our analyses; in the concluding section, we discuss some implications of our findings for the theoretical and philosophical debate on deliberation.

5.2 Favorable conditions for parliamentary deliberation: institutions and issues

Our first research aim was to identify contextual factors – institutions and issues – that are favorable to a more deliberative mode of policy-making in legislatures. We identified five such favorable contextual factors.

Consensus versus competitive systems. At the cradle of the consensus model of democracy lies communication. The pre-modern German philosopher Johannes Althusius (1563–1638) developed a political theory revolving around the covenant or "consociatio." The covenant was an arrangement in which people would live together in mutual benevolence, striving for consensus by way of open communication. This "deliberative" conception of the Althusian convenant can be transposed to Lijphart's (1999) seminal distinction between consensus and competitive systems. One institutional mechanism of consensus systems is particularly important in furthering deliberation: the existence of grand coalitions. Grand coalitions generate, first of all, a logic of joint decision-making where argumentative rationality might be necessary for coping with differences in situational definitions, cognitive problem representations, factual understanding, and standards of appropriateness, fairness, and justice (see Risse, 2000; Holzinger, 2001). Moreover, to maintain the stability of the coalition and to ensure a successful government record, actors will need to adopt a cooperative attitude vis-à-vis their coalition partners comprising a willingness to discuss differences in a constructive and respectful way. Two other mechanisms enhance further the deliberative potential in grand coalitions. First, grand coalitions also obfuscate policy-making clarity, which reduces the possibility that actors can use political successes for partisan electoral advantages (Powell and Whitten, 1993). Second, when grand coalition arrangements are made permanent and parties obtain relatively secure power positions (e.g., obtain a fixed seat), the importance of electoral competition among them is reduced. These factors open up an additional "deliberative" space that allows parties to deliberate in a less politicized way and to engage in true argumentative exchanges. The situation in competitive systems is quite different. Here the party in government can safely ignore the opposition and usually stands to gain little by arguing its policies and treating the opposition with respect. Moreover, opposition parties who are "cooperative" must always fear that voters tend to assign political successes to the parties in government (see Lewis-Beck, 1988). Such an environment is not conducive to an open discourse, not even in a problem solving situation (Scharpf, 1997: 192).

Presidentialism versus parliamentarism.   The quality of deliberation in parliaments might also be affected by another classic institutional variable: presidentialism versus parliamentarism. Using Strom's (2000: 265) minimal definition, parliamentarism refers to a system where the government and the legislature are in a confidence relationship. This creates a situation of "bound mandates" which Elster (1998: 3) considered to be deleterious for deliberation: legislators have both incentives and pressures to defend the proposals of their government, whereby argumentative lines often have been fixed before the debate. In a presidential system, to the contrary, where the executive is not dependent on legislative confidence, party discipline is lower and consequently, legislators have more leeway to transcend party boundaries and to be open to argument and argumentative change.

However, combining the parliamentary-presidential distinction with competitive and consensus systems leads to complex interactive effects. We expected the combination of a competitive system and a parliamentary regime to strengthen the competitive logic and to largely undermine constructive policy discourses. Here, legislators are not only pressured to defend the proposals of their government, party competition also requires them to steadily attack the political opponent. If a competitive system is combined with a presidential regime, then there should be more space for deliberation, as legislators can be more receptive to arguments across partisan lines. In the combination of a consensus system with parliamentarism, the management of disagreements – the essence of Habermasian discourse ethics – is mostly "stalled" among coalition Members of Parliament (MPs). Since deliberation and policy redrafting on the part of government MPs always threatens government stability, disagreements are settled in the executive, in coalition committees or in intra-coalition summits. Therefore, to observe the management of disagreements among coalition MPs, the focus was on "presidential" or "non-parliamentary" consensus systems only where MPs are more independent in drawing up legislation[2] – and hence the comparison between presidentialism and parliamentarism was limited to competitive systems. In the context of competitive systems, we expected the quality of deliberation to be higher in presidential than in parliamentary regimes.

Second chambers versus first chambers. From the times of the ancient Greeks onward, there have been staunch advocates, such as Aristotle, Cicero, Mill, and Madison, of a council of elders who could bring their experience and wisdom to the government. The literature frequently conceives of second chambers as a place where policy proposals can be given more thorough thought before they are enacted into law. Several factors lubricate this deliberative process: members of the second chamber usually have greater political experience, are usually elected for longer terms, and work in a smaller chamber than their first chamber peers. In addition, second chambers are also said to have "civility" norms which favor deliberation (Loomis, 1990).

Nonpublic versus public arenas. Observing parliamentary debates in the French National Assembly of the eighteenth century, the conservative philosopher and advocate of more tranquil politics, Edmund Burke found it anything but deliberative. He considered it a sham: the French parliamentarians were playing "the farce of deliberation with as little decency as liberty. They act like the comedians of a fair before a riotous audience; they act amidst the tumultuous cries of a mixed mob of ferocious men, and of women lost to shame, who, according to their insolent fancies, direct, control, applaud, explode them, and sometimes mix and take their seats amongst them, domineering over them with a strange mixture of servile petulance and proud, presumptuous authority" (Burke, 1987: 60). In a study of the constituent assemblies in Philadelphia in 1787, Paris in 1789–1791, and Frankfurt in 1848–1849, Elster (1998) found that speaking in public was indeed not conducive to calm and impartial deliberation. Behind closed doors, however, actors talked much more seriously (although there also was more bargaining). However, Elster (1998) has also pointed out that public discourses tend to have a "civilizing effect" on the participants in the sense that explicitly selfish interests can rarely be justified in the public sphere. Following Elster, we hypothesized that non-public arenas such as parliamentary committees allow legislators to deliberate without external interference, lower the pressures of following constituent demands, and thus make it easier for politicians to reflect, to show respect for the claims of others, or even to change their opinions. Conversely, we expected the public parliamentary arena to increase common good orientations as well as justification rationality, since publicity forces participants to adhere to rough standards of reasoned argument.

Low versus high issue polarization. So far, we have only considered institutional determinants of deliberation. But institutional scholars increasingly recognize the importance of the interaction between political institutions and issues. Of particular importance in this regard is the distance in the policy preferences of actors, what one could call the ideational (or more narrowly, ideological) dimension of policy issues. Hereby, we distinguished between polarized and less polarized issues. Less polarized issues are characterized by a consensus of the elites on key values and goals, while polarized issues are marked by sharp disagreements on these matters. When an issue is not very polarized, then we expected more cooperative attitudes among the political actors. And even those actors whose self-interest is in conflict with the values of the discursive consensus might be rhetorically constrained as it is difficult and costly to undermine a prior discursive consensus or a highly valued goal. This should promote more consensual decision-making and, as such, should lead to higher levels of discourse.

5.3   Procedural and substantive outcomes of parliamentary deliberation

What outcomes are associated with parliamentary deliberation? Does it matter if a policy was derived through extensive parliamentary deliberation, or is talk cheap and inconsequential as some rational choice theorists have argued (see Austen-Smith, 1992)? This question was the focus of the second part of the project. In parliamentary politics, two dimensions of a decision can be identified, a *procedural* dimension which concerns the degree of unification in a decision, and a *substantive* dimension on the effects of a decision on social justice.

Procedural outcomes.   Advocates of deliberative politics typically argue that a deliberative process leads to a genuine, rational consensus consensus, due to the "non-coercive coercion of the better argument" (Habermas, 1983: 132). In contrast to compromise, a genuine consensus is not simply a negotiated agreement of the participants, but includes a transformation of preferences. Yet, it is widely considered to be unrealistic to assume that deliberation would massively transform the preferences of participants in normatively attractive ways. Thus, deliberation may only touch aspects of an actor's worldview, without affecting the fundamentals of this view (Chambers, 1996: 249). Hence, one should allow that unification also refers to compromises, that is, agreements between actors that do not involve a fundamental change in preferences. As Dryzek (2000) notes, consensus and compromise can be both considered discursive, as long as they are reasoned.

In even sharper contrast to such moderate conceptions, some theorists argue that deliberation may actually lead to a radicalization of an initially moderate dissent (Shapiro, 1999: 31). Nonetheless, we thought that if actors take the trouble in deliberation, justify their positions, respectfully weigh arguments, and submit constructive proposals, then the chances for unification is greater.

Substantive outcomes. Regarding the substantive dimension of deliberatively reached decisions, the literature is surprisingly vague. There is a strong current of deliberative theory which simply assumes that a decision after deliberation is legitimate, since the process of deliberation is thought to be more legitimate than other processes of decision-making. However, John Rawls (1996: 428) convincingly argues that the deliberative model of democracy cannot generate the legitimacy of its policies through the legitimacy of its deliberative procedure alone: "legitimacy allows an undetermined range of injustice that justice might not permit" (Rawls, 1996: 428). This seems to be especially true in the real world of politics where an ideal deliberation is virtually impossible and a genuine consensus can hardly be reached. Some deliberative theorists, too, demand that the discourse principle needs to be controlled by higher substantial principles (Cohen, 1996).

However, many deliberative theorists still imply that genuine deliberative processes do produce "good" decisions of a certain kind. Gutmann and Thompson (1996: 208–218), for instance, make an argument for a "deliberative perspective on opportunity," which is strongly related to Rawls's difference principle and thus concerned with distributive justice. Gambetta (1998), in turn, attempts to justify why deliberation can have a positive effect on decisions.

Generally, evidence from several areas of the social sciences suggests that conceptions of justice situated in the ambit of egalitarianism are most likely to be relevant for decisions growing out of deliberative processes (e.g., Deutsch, 1975). To judge whether outcomes are "just", we build on Rawls's difference principle implying that "social and economic inequalities are to be arranged so that they are [...] to the greatest benefit of the least advantaged" (Rawls, 1971: 83). In practice, this implies an egalitarian doctrine of social justice (Rawls, 1996). Specifically, the difference principle is associated with a weak form of egalitarianism, which treats equality as a means toward the end of improving the situation of the least advantaged. In contrast with the principle of strong equality, which stresses the leveling of social differences as the main goal (Niño, 1996), weak inequality tolerates differences.[3]

We hypothesized that the higher the general discourse quality of a debate, the more probable a substantively egalitarian decision becomes a decision also in the real world. Even when assuming that many arguments within a debate are based upon principles of the common good are hypocritical, the presence of such arguments can lead to an increased readiness to make concessions to the other side. This could in turn enable decisions which increase the common good. In particular, the more justifications are framed in egalitarian conceptions of justice, the more probable a substantively egalitarian decision becomes.

5.4   Methodology

5.4.1   Measuring political deliberation

One of the major goals of our research project was to find measures that allow to put the mainly philosophical conception of deliberation into operational terms. The DQI represents an attempt to measure political deliberation in a general, valid, and reliable way (Steenbergen et al., 2003). It mainly draws on Habermasian discourse ethics, but also incorporates elements of other deliberative models. The unit of analysis of the DQI is a *speech act*, that is, the discourse by a particular individual delivered at a particular point in a debate. For each speech, we distinguish between relevant and irrelevant parts, and only the relevant parts are coded. A relevant part is one that contains a *demand*, that is, a proposal on what decision should or should not be made. Our emphasis on demands stems from the fact that they constitute the heart of the deliberation. That is, demands stipulate what ought to be and what ought not to be done, and this normative character puts them at the center of discourse ethics. The DQI is composed of seven indicators. Despite the considerable complexity of parliamentary debates, we attempt to keep the coding categories relatively easy, so as to ensure a high level of reliability. We discuss the seven indicators under four headings (a more detailed coding scheme of the seven indicators can be found in Appendix).

1. *Participation.* Participation constitutes a fundamental precondition for deliberation. In parliamentary settings of Western democracies, this type of basic participation can usually be seen as given for the elected representatives. Normal participation is only assumed to be impaired if a speaker is cut off by a formal decision, or if she feels explicitly disturbed in the case of a verbal interruption by other actors.[4]

2. *Justification.* Fruitful discourse requires the justification of assertions and validity claims. That is, assertions should be introduced and critically assessed through "the orderly exchange of information and grounds between parties" (Habermas, 1992: 370). The major problem here is that since the ideal speech situation itself has no content, one cannot apply external standards to what constitutes a good reason; otherwise one would also predetermine the result of a discourse. Hence, we only judge to what extent a speech gives complete justifications for demands and thus makes it accessible to rational critique. The first indicator of the concept of justification is the *level of the justification*, whereby we distinguish between five levels. No justification forms the lowest level of the indicator. Next comes inferior justification, that is, a reason Y is given why X should or should not be done, but no linkage is made between X and Y (this code also applies if a conclusion is merely supported with illustrations). This is followed by qualified justification where one such linkage is made. Then come two categories of sophisticated justification: the first category of sophisticated justification is given when at least two complete

justifications are given. The second category of sophisticated justification is given when at least two complete justifications are given for a demand and one justification is also embedded in at least two complete inferences. The second indicator of the concept of justification is the *content of the justification*. The importance of referring to the common good is mainly stressed by deliberative theorists drawing on Rawls (e.g., Gutmann/Thompson, 1996). This indicator measures whether the argumentation within a statement is cast in terms of a conception of the common good or in terms of narrow group or constituency interests. With regard to the common good, we distinguish between the common good stated in utilitarian terms, that is, as the best solution for the greatest number of people (Mill, 1998) and the common good expressed through the difference principle, that is, the common good is served when the least advantaged in a society are helped (Rawls, 1971). However, one has always to be aware that a given reference to the common good may be not much more than "cheap talk," being purely rhetorical and intended to attract potential voters.

3. *Respect.* Respect is a prerequisite for serious listening, which in turn is essential for deliberation. Even more importantly, respect also captures the idea of preference change. Several dimensions of respect play a role in discourse. First, it is important to see whether speakers show *respect toward the groups which would be helped* with the demand under discussion. This indicator is a translation of Habermas's (1991: 73) postulate of empathy into the parliamentary context. The lowest category is reserved for speeches in which there are only negative statements about the groups. The next category is implicit respect, that os. there are neither explicitly negative nor positive statements about the groups. The highest category is assigned if there is at least one explicitly positive statement about the groups. Second, in a similar vein, deliberation requires that both sides show *respect toward demands* under discussion. Macedo (1999: 10) regards the recognition of the "merit in [the] opponents' claims" as being one of the principal purposes of deliberation. This indicator uses the same categories as the group respect indicator, with one exception: the highest category here is accepting a demand. However, to get this code, a demand needs to be both accepted *and* positively valued. Third, discursive participants need to show *respect toward counterarguments* to their own position. Respect toward counterarguments is a necessary condition for the weighing of alternatives, which some view as an essential element of deliberation (Chambers, 1999; Luskin/Fishkin, 2002). The lowest coding categories apply when counterarguments are degraded or ignored. This is followed by a neutral category where speakers include counterarguments but neithermake positive nor negative statements about them. The next category applies for speakers who explicitly value counterarguments. The highest coding category is accepting a counterargument (even if this does not cause a transformation of his or her preferences vis-à-vis a demand). Under the rubric of counterarguments we also include personal or partisan attacks and praises.

4. *Constructive politics*. The last indicator, *constructive politics*, is based upon the principal goal of Habermasian discourse ethics to reach a genuine consensus. Here we distinguish between four levels. Positional politics form the lowest level of the indicator. This is followed by alternative proposals, that is, proposals that attempt to mediate but that do not fit the current agenda. The next category is "consensus appeals." Consensus appeals are calls for compromise and consensus that are pertinent to the current agenda but that are unspecific. For example, a call to "bridge our differences" would be a consensus appeal if it did not contain a specific mediating proposal. The highest level of constructive politics is mediating proposals that fit the current agenda.

Habermasian discourse ethics would also require authenticity or truthfulness (*Wahrhaftigkeit*), which is the absence of deception in expressing intentions. The stated preferences should be sincere rather than strategic so that the discourse can develop in an open and honest manner. While we do acknowledge the importance of truthfulness for deliberative theory, it causes the greatest difficulties from a measurement perspective. To judge whether a speech act is truthful is to make a judgment about a person's true versus stated preferences. This is exceedingly difficult, since the true preferences are not directly observable. The speculative nature of such a judgment is bound to introduce large amounts of (possibly systematic) measurement error and for this reason we have decided to drop this category for our current research.

In a series of tests, we could demonstrate that the "inter-coder reliability" of the DQI ranges between good and excellent: for the debates analyzed here, the rate of coder agreement, which is bounded between 0 and 1, ranged from a low of .919 (respect toward counterarguments) to a high of 1 (content of justification and participation – see Steiner et al., 2004: ch. 3).

A final remark: discourse quality is not a unidimensional phenomenon but a complex cluster of elements. Considering all coded speech acts, we find that the different dimensions of the DQI are only weakly (though positively) correlated. This meant for our empirical analyses that quite often we had to break down the DQI into its individual elements.

5.4.2   Research design

Both the precondition and the outcome part used a combination of qualitative and quantitative methodology. In the precondition part, the case selection builds on typological or theoretical sampling. In contrast to random sampling, cases were purposively selected to fill out the theoretically specified categories. The reason for not using a random sampling was twofold. First, there are no lists of parliamentary debates that permit us to draw a random sample. Of course, one could lay one's hands on listings of bills, but that sampling frame is insufficiently detailed because a bill can trigger multiple debates. Second, we wanted to select debates that matter. A random sample might have yielded a selection of debates on relatively minute issues. That might have been correct from a statistical viewpoint, but it would have been of little theoretical interest.

As to the legislatures, we selected Switzerland – a "non-parliamentary" or quasi-presidential consensus system, the United States – a competitive presidential system, Germany and the United Kingdom – competitive-parliamentary systems, albeit of different kinds with the German system offering more veto points than the British system.[5] In addition, we needed to be able to study debates in two legislative chambers and in two different arenas, public and non-public. To shed light on the effect of second versus first chambers, we considered the German, Swiss, and U.S. legislatures. Each of these legislatures is bicameral and in each case the second chamber can be considered a powerful actor. Our analysis of non-public versus public arenas focused on the German and Swiss cases, as both in the United States' Congress and the British House of Commons committee meetings are usually public and there are few other forums in which legislators deliberate behind closed doors.

We selected a total of 52 debates, mostly from the late 1980s and the 1990s, from the four countries. They involved polarized issues such as social and economic policies and abortion, and less polarized issues such as disability rights, animal welfare, and crime prevention. The distinction between polarized and less polarized issues was based on Kriesi's (2001) work, as well as close readings of the history of different issues in the respective countries. We consider as polarized those issues on which key parties have been divided on policy fundamentals over a long period of time. These are typically economic and social issues that are tied to the left-right ideological divide in a country. By contrast, less polarized issues are those on which there is broad consensus about (1) the need to address a problem and (2) the policy fundamentals of a solution. Less polarized issues tend to be issues about which partisan divisions are related to the specifics of a solution, not the need for and general character of a solution.

Concerning the outcome part, we expected that political outcomes vary with institutional designs. To overcome this risk we have opted to keep institutional features constant so that we can establish an effect of discourse quality that is not confounded with institutional designs. Moreover, we wanted a "discourse-friendly environment" entailing chances for high discourse quality as well as sufficient degree of variation in discourse quality between the debates. A setting that fulfilled these criteria was the German Conference Committee or *Vermittlungsausschuss* (VA). The VA is a constitutionally mandated institution that is concerned with mediating conflicts between the Federal Diet (*Bundestag*) and the Federal Council (*Bundesrat*). Not only is the VA by definition a deliberative body, at least one study already concluded that it has a high capacity for deliberation (Lhotta, 2000).

The selected VA debates stem from the time period of 1969–1982, where the Federal Diet and the Federal Council were controlled by different partisan majorities. During such periods of "divided government," the VA plays its most significant role because partisan conflicts are most likely to produce deadlock between the two legislative chambers under those circumstances. The case selection included 20 debates on economic issues, as well as social issues, since these questions define key partisan conflicts that might benefit the most from deliberation.

Measures of procedural and substantive outcomes.   While our measure of the procedural dimension of outcomes is relatively simple – running from a narrow majoritarian decision to a unanimous decision – the measure of the substantive dimension of outcomes is considerably more complicated. The substantive dimension focuses on the question of whether a decision reveals a (weak) egalitarian principle or whether it instead corresponds to a non-egalitarian principle such as equity. Our measure of substantive outcomes focused on the decisions reached by the VA and codes their fairness relative to the goals in the original legislative proposals. When coding those decisions we focused on the fundamental direction that they take, rather than trying to obtain an absolute measure of their fairness implications.

5.5   Results

What did we find? We offer here an overview of our main findings. More detailed discussions of the results can be found in Bächtiger and Steenbergen (2004), Bächtiger (2005), Spörndli (2004), and Steiner et al. (2004). First, we shall focus on the effects of political institutions and issues on the quality of deliberation. In Table 5.1, we conducted a series of "bivariate" tests of our contextual predictors on discourse quality. These tests allowed us control in selecting debates that were truly comparable. As mentioned before, discourse quality does not constitute a unidimensional phenomenon. Therefore, we created four indices of discourse quality.[6] The first one – "overall respect" – is an additive scale of respect toward demands, counterarguments, and groups; this scale ranges from 0 to 9. The other three indices are dichotomized, with one indicating speech acts that approach the ideal discourse on a particular dimension. Thus, level of justification was recoded so that a score of one is given to sophisticated justifications (of both the broad and in depth variety – see Appendix). Appeals to the common good were recoded so that a score of one indicates the presence of such an appeal (categories 2 and 3 of the DQI – see Appendix). Finally, we created a dichotomous constructive politics measure where one indicates the presence of consensus appeals, alternative proposals, or mediating proposals and zero indicates positional politics. While dichotomization reduces the information that is contained in the DQI, it has the advantage of singling out those speech acts that signify ideal Habermasian discourse.[7]

Table 5.1 Predictions of different dimensions of deliberation

	Sophisticated justifications (Logit)	Common good appeals (Logit)	Respect overall (OLS)	Constructive politics (Logit)
Consensus vs. competitive systems				
Switzerland vs. United Kingdom	1.547** (.335) (N=231)	.420 (.313) (N=231)	.828** (.219) (N=231)	.223 (.372) (N=231)
Switzerland vs. Germany	.796** (.151) (N=1384)	.130 (.203) (N=1314)	411** (.071) (N=1384)	.824** (.170) (N=1384)
Switzerland vs. United States/Germany[8]	−.147 (.106) (N=2409)	N/A	.250** (.057) (N=2409	−.003 (.126) (N=2409)
Presidential vs. parliamentary system	−1.130** (.211) (N=498)	.149 (.241) (N=498)	.377** (.143) (N=498)	−.709* (.316) (N=498)
Second vs. first chambers	.059 (.080) (N=3695)	−.473** (.132) (N=2579)	.296** (.044) (N=3695)	.181[+] (.097) (N=3695)
Non-public vs. public arena	−2.258** (.105) (N=3087)	−1.848** (.148) (N=2167)	.186** (.064) (N=3087)	.184 (.123) (N=3087)
Low vs. high issue polarization				
Less\p Polarized issues vs. polarized economic and social issues	.608** (.088) (N=2996)	.155 (.125) (N=2704)	.402** (.045) (N=2996)	.175[+] (.100) (N=2996)
Less polarized issues vs.polarized abortion debates	.428** (.097) (N=2196)	N/A	.505** (.054) (N=2196)	.322** (.120) (N=2196)

Notes: Entries are logit coefficients and unstandardized OLS coefficients (robust standard errors in parentheses). The estimations are based on a factorial design which takes into account that the observations are nested in constellations. Due to space limitations, we do not report any statistical results for the constellation dummies. However, these results are available on request from the authors.** $p < .01$; * $p < .05$; + $p < .1$ (two-sided).

As Table 5.1 shows, contextual variables matter for the quality of political deliberation. Our data suggest that *respect* is most sensitive to institutional and issue attributes. The results go in the expected directions: we found that consensus institutions, presidential regimes, second chambers, non-publicity, and low issue polarization further respectful exchanges among participants.

Our overall respect indicator yields highly significant score differences ranging between .19 and .82.

For the level of justification, we found that justification rationality is much higher in public debates ($b = -2.258$, $p < .01$, whereby the impact of publicity on the odds ratio is almost 10). That public arenas greatly improved sophisticated justification clearly supports the argument that publicity strengthens "civility" in that actors want to appear reasonable in public and therefore forward more extended arguments. Moreover, sophisticated justifications were more frequent in the context of low issue polarization as well as in two (out of three) comparisons between consensus and competitive settings. Finally, we also note one counterintuitive effect on the level of justification, whereby parliamentary systems produced more sophisticated justifications ($b = -1.130$, $p < .01$). Clearly, more theoretical development is required to account for this result.

For the content of justification, we found that common good appeals were more frequently uttered in the public sphere ($b = -1.848$, $p < .01$, with a strong impact of publicity on the odds ratio of about 6). Apparently, in public, actors seem to have a stronger pressure to make appeals to the common good in order to respond to the moral claims of their constituents. A similar effect seems to occur in first chambers: again, legislators in the more publicized first chambers seem to have a stronger incentive to make appeals to the common good than their second chamber peers ($b = -.473$, $p < .01$).

The constructive politics dimension showed remarkable resilience to institutional variation. Only in some comparisons did we find an institutional effect in the expected direction, namely in the comparison between the Swiss consensus system and the German competitive system as well as in the comparison between less polarized issues and polarized abortion debates. Otherwise, levels of constructive politics looked very similar across institutional settings, with positional politics being the norm.

Finally, we can demonstrate that when favorable contextual conditions combine, that is, when a less polarized issue is debated in a second chamber of a consensus setting, we find debates that have in parts features of "ideal discourses" with actors being highly respectful, reflective, open, reasoned, and constructive. In terms of respect, both the public and the non-public debate on the Swiss language bill in the second chamber achieve remarkable scores. In the public debate, the score of disrespectful speech acts is almost zero (one single disparaging speech in the public debate (out of 55) and 3 disparaging speeches in the non-public debate (out of 212)) and for the higher respect levels (explicit respect or agreeing with demands and counterarguments), the score is almost 70 percent in the public debate and 42 percent in the non-public debate. Compare this to the public debate on the polarized minimum wage debate in the competitive parliamentary and public arena of the British House of Commons: here the score of disrespectful speech acts amounts to 73 percent; there are no instances of speakers agreeing with the demands or counterarguments of their opponents, while instances of explicit respect are extremely rare (2 percent).

Even if we could identify a debate which had "ideal" features, the differences that we observed between institutional settings were not categorical, but rather subtle shifts along a continuum. But what is the use of subtle shifts, one might ask? Does it really matter if one setting is slightly more respectful than another or slightly better in the justification of demands? This brings us to the relationship between discourse and outcomes. Through a detailed study of the German Mediation Committee (VA), we analyzed how discourse influences both formal and substantive decision outcomes. With regard to the outcome dimension, we found that in the VA unanimous or nearly unanimous decisions were typically associated with a high level of discourse in the preceding debates.

Table 5.2 describes the relationship between a dichotomized version of a 3-component DQI (DQI-3) and a dichotomized version of vote outcomes. The DQI-3 is an index that combines the respect, level of justification, and constructive politics indicators. Here we used a median split to dichotomize this measure. The vote outcome measure contrasts (near) majoritarian with (near) unanimity decisions. As the table shows, of the ten (near) majoritarian decisions fully eight had DQI-3 values that were below the median. On the other hand, of the ten (near) unanimous decisions only one had a DQI-3 value below the median. Thus, there appears to be a strong relationship between the outcomes and discourse quality. This is borne out statistically: when we perform Fisher's exact test we obtain a test statistic of 9.404 with a probability value of .005, which means that we can soundly reject the null hypothesis that discourse quality and vote outcome are unassociated. Another way to look at the data is to use the DQI-3 to predict vote outcome. This yields a statistically significant (by an exact test) and substantively important value

Table 5.2 A cross-tabulation of discourse quality and decision margins

Decision margin	Discourse quality		Total
	Low	High	
Majoritarian	8	1	9
Unanimous	2	9	11
Total	10	10	20

Notes: Discourse quality is a median split of the 3-indicator DQI (DQI-3) described in the text. Decision margin groups majoritarian and nearly majoritarian decisions into one group and unanimous decisions and nearly unanimous decisions into another group. Fisher's exact *p*-value = .005; Goodman and Kruskal's tau = .495 (*p* = .005).

of .495 on Goodman and Kruskal's tau, which means that taking into consideration discourse quality helps us improve our predictions of the vote outcome by close to 50 percent. Thus, the results of the cross-tabulation suggest that there is a substantial relationship between vote outcomes and discourse quality, a relationship that is clearly statistically significant despite the small number of debates in the analysis. We also ran multivariate logistic regression models (see Steiner et al., 2004: 153) controlling for rival explanations such as initial polarization or majority distribution in the VA (which is measured here in terms of whether government and opposition have parity). Yet discourse quality continued to be an important and statistically significant factor. Rather than polarizing, discourse thus helped the different sides to find a commonly acceptable solution to an issue.

With regard to substantive outcomes, power trumped discourse. When considering our most comprehensive measure of discourse quality, combining level of justification, content of justification, respect, and constructive politics, we found no statistically significant effect on substantive outcomes.

In Table 5.3, we pitted a 3-point substantive outcome measure against a dichotomous version of a 4-component DQI (DQI-4). The DQI-4 is an index that combines the respect, level of justification, content of justification, and constructive politics indicators.[9] The dichotomization is based on a median split of the DQI-4 index. As Table 5.3 shows, egalitarian and neutral decisions are just as likely to follow after a low-quality discourse as after a high-quality discourse. Inegalitarian outcomes are actually more likely under a high-quality discourse than under a low-quality discourse. All in all, there is no evidence of a statistically significant relationship between discourse quality and the substance of outcomes: Fisher's exact test is .746 and not significant, while Goodman and Kruskal's tau is only .016, which is also not significant. The discourse quality only came into play in stalemate situations with no clear majorities on either side (see Steiner et al., 2004: 159). And even in such situations, the DQI-4 index had no effect; however, two of its elements,

Table 5.3 A cross-tabulation of discourse quality and substantive decision outcomes

| Decision margin | Discourse quality | | Total |
	Low	High	
Inegalitarian	2	4	6
Neutral	1	1	2
Egalitarian	6	6	12
Total	9	11	20

Notes: Discourse quality is a median split of the 4-indicator DQI (DQI-4) described in the text. Fisher's exact test = .746 (p = .811); Goodman and Kruskal's tau = .016 (p = .811).

content and level of justification had some effect. The more frequently egalitarian elements were made and the more they were justified, the higher the probability that the outcome corresponded to the notion of social justice in the sense of John Rawls.

In conclusion, we would like to stress two points. First, even though some debates achieved high scores on the DQI indicators, we should not overlook that the large majority of parliamentary debates that we analyzed are not really deliberative on all indicators – even if there were individual actors who followed deliberative standards. Thus, Keohane (2001) might be right that deliberation does not constitute a major logic of action informing many policy- making processes. Nonetheless, even if deliberation is a "rare event," our study clearly shows that it captures parts of political reality and matters for outcomes, too. Second, what we did not observe in our parliamentary debates were changes of their fundamental preferences. Taking into account that elected politicians cannot easily substitute their deliberatively gained opinions for those of their voters, such an expectation would be quite unrealistic anyway. But what we found is that actors revised positions through deliberation, because they learned about unforeseen consequences or because new alternatives were generated in discussion that resolved the dispute to their satisfaction. These findings match Vanberg and Buchanan's (1989) idea that preferences have both an "interest-component" and a "theory-component." While the former may be unaffected by deliberation, the latter can be affected when actors seek and share information about the likely effects of policies. Of course, this does not preclude that larger preference changes can occur over the longer run (see Goodin, 2005).

5.6 Conclusions

Our research project yields important results both for philosophers and institutional scholars. First, and very basically, we can demonstrate that deliberation can flourish within existing liberal and representative institutions. In particular, we can show that legislatures – which many political scientists consider to be not very likely cases for real deliberative action – do involve chances for open, respectful, and consensus-oriented deliberation, but that this is highly context-driven. This generates reasonable expectations that deliberation is alogic of action that can be found in other institutional contexts as well.

Second, our research project shows that certain types of institutions can build bridges between the normative concerns of political philosophy and the positive and realistic concerns of empirical-analytical political science. From this follows the idea of institutional engineering, in that normatively desired outcomes can be achieved through institutional manipulation. Of course, our study was limited to one organizational context – legislatures; but the analyzed institutional mechanisms refer to more general institutional design principles that might also come into play outside the realm of legislatures. Hence, some tentative advice to institutional designers can be given: if the goal is respectful deliberation that also entails argumentative change, then actor relationships should not be too competitive, actors should not have bound mandates, bodies should be small and explicitly geared toward rational discussion and reflection, and actors should have the opportunity of meeting in secret. This advice will certainly disappoint many deliberative democrats, as deliberation seems to be closely associated with a "pre-modern" and "gentlemen's club" model of politics rather than with modern mass democracies where disciplined parties compete for power.

Third, our results for the outcome dimension break some ties in the discussion on what deliberation is good for. On the procedural dimension of policy outcomes, advocates of deliberative democracy have frequently expressed the hope, if not the belief, that deliberation produces more consensual outcomes. Deliberative skeptics deemed this view overly optimistic and even expressed fears that deliberation might actually promote polarization (e.g. Sunstein, 2003). Our results show that the hopes and beliefs of deliberative advocates are not misled, as more unanimous decisions are typically associated with higher discourse levels. On the substantive dimensions of policy outcomes, however, optimism is less justified. With the power context being very strong with regard to egalitarian decisions, this is a strong hint that interests and power can neither by easily counteracted by deliberation, nor be lightly dismissed in the study of politics.[10]

5.A.1 Appendix : Indicators of discourse quality

1 Participation
0: interruption of a speaker: a speaker feels explicitly disturbed, or interruption occurs through a formal decision
1: normal participation is possible

2 Justification
2.1 Level
0: no justification
1: inferior justification: conclusion(s) embedded in (an) *in*complete inference(s)
2: qualified justification: one conclusion embedded in a *complete* inference; additional conclusions embedded in *in*complete inferences may be present
3: sophisticated justification (broad): more than one conclusion, each embedded in a complete inference
4: sophisticated justification (in depth): one or several conclusions, each embedded in several complete inferences

2.2 Content
0: explicit statement concerning constituency or group interests
1: neutral statement: either no reference to constituency or group interests or reference to several group interests
2: explicit statement in terms of a conception of the common good in utilitarian or collective terms
3: explicit statement in terms of the difference principle

3 Respect

3.1 toward group in general ("empathy")

0: no respect: explicitly negative statement concerning the group which would be helped

1: implicit respect: no explicitly negative statement concerning the group which would be helped

2: explicit respect: explicitly positive statement concerning the group which would be helped

3.2 toward demands

0: no respect: explicitly negative statement concerning the demand

1: implicit respect: no explicitly negative statement concerning the demand

2: explicit respect: explicitly positive statement concerning the demand

3: agreement with demands: speaker agrees with the demands of other actors and values them

3.3 toward counterarguments

0: counterarguments are explicitly degraded

1: counterarguments are ignored

2: counterarguments are neither explicitly degraded nor valued

3: counterarguments are explicitly valued

4: agreement with counterarguments

4 Constructive Politics

0: positional politics: speaker sits on his/her position

1: alternative proposal: proposal for a different agenda

2: consensus appeal: speakers make an unspecific appeal for compromise or consensus

3: mediating proposal: proposal within the same agenda

Notes

1. An exception is Lascher (1996: 502–503) who postulates that "it is important that researchers do not shirk from a more thorough assessment of how deliberation works in real-world legislatures." Similar to our research project, he developed a number of hypotheses under which conditions deliberation could play a role in legislative encounters. However, Lascher's study is only a "preface to empirical analysis" and the hypotheses were not put to an empirical test.

2. As Lijphart (2002: 49) correctly notes, the standard form of a presidential regime with a single president and presidential cabinet consisting merely of advisers might be difficult to reconcile with the grand coalition idea where all partners are co-decision-makers. Yet the real world involves more variety in this respect. In the Swiss cantons, for instance, we find directly elected collegial grand coalition executives, which are not in a confidence relationship with the respective legislatures.

3. One may legitimately ask why we focus on a Rawlsian view of justice. After all, in a truly deliberative world, even conceptions of justice should be open for debate, rather than being imposed from the outside. Our focus on Rawls is not gratuitous, however. First, as one of the premier critics of deliberative democracy, Rawls seriously wondered if deliberation was compatible with his view of justice, which in itself could be considered deliberative (the "veil of ignorance" presupposes a deliberation of individuals with themselves about justice). As an empirical matter, then, it is interesting to assess to what extent deliberation helps justice in the Rawlsian sense. Second, Gutmann and Thompson's (1996) emphasis on opportunity as an outcome of deliberation is entirely consistent with our current emphasis on equality.

4. This definition of participation is appropriate only for legislative contexts, which presuppose that several other barriers to participation, such as access to the debate, have been eliminated. In other contexts, the definition of participation should be expanded because certain individuals may be barred from the debate or not be given equal time.

5. We use the Swiss case to fill out the consensus-presidential cell in our design. Technically, Switzerland is not a presidential system, but it is quasi-presidential or at least non-parliamentary. Instead of having a single President, the Swiss system has a 7-headed executive branch. The key point, from the perspective of our theory, is that the Swiss executive cannot be voted out of power by the legislature. To our mind, that is the critical aspect of presidential systems and, in this sense, it is entirely appropriate to treat Switzerland as (quasi-) presidential.

6. The participation dimension was excluded from the analysis since this did not show sufficient variation.

7. Dichotomization does not affect the results. We ran all of the analyses using ordered logit models and obtained results consistent with those reported here. Furthermore, distributions on common good appeals and constructive politics were highly skewed. Therefore, we re-checked our logit analyses with gompit models. Results, however, did not change.

8. This analysis compares Swiss debates both with U.S. debates and German debates where party discipline was explicitly relaxed. Since we theoretically expected presidentialism and low party discipline to narrow the distance between consensus and competitive settings, this is the strictest test for this comparison.

9. We use a DQI-4 here because, according to our hypotheses, content of justification plays a critical role in shaping substantive outcomes.

10. Of course, one should keep in mind that the results about deliberative outcomes are based only on a consideration of the German Conference Committee. Future research will have to demonstrate if these results also hold in other institutional contexts.

6
How People Deliberate about Justice: Groups, Gender, and Decision Rules

Tali Mendelberg and Christopher Karpowitz

In recent years, theorists, observers and policy makers have increasingly promoted citizen deliberation. Yet little is known about how people deliberate about matters of politics. In this paper we ask how people deliberate about distributive justice, and in particular, about a guaranteed minimum income to the poor. If the proponents of deliberation are correct, deliberation is likely to enhance distributive justice and will lead people to grant a decent minimum income to the poor. But what actually happens when people deliberate about distributive justice? We make use of experimental data matched with discussion transcripts. The data were gathered for a somewhat different purpose but can shed light on the question of what deliberation actually does when people use it to decide a matter of justice. We find that deliberation can work as expected, enhancing distributive justice – and creating a long list of other positive outcomes – but only under certain conditions. Those conditions are structured by the decision rule (majority rule or unanimous vote) and by gender composition. Rules and gender interact to shape the group's social norms. When deliberation is not properly structured by rules and norms, it does not conform to the expectations of its proponents.

Political theorists and public figures have written and spoken a great deal recently about the promise of citizen deliberation. President Clinton's major initiative on race (the National Conversation of Race) and the National Endowment for the Humanities' local deliberations about American identity were designed to enhance consensus about the basic values of the nation (Merelman et al., 1998). Local dialogue groups have been spreading throughout the country (Walsh, 2003). As federal power devolved to states and localities, policy-makers have increasingly built opportunities for local discussion to allow citizens to influence the process of making and implementing policy (Crosby, 1995; Mendelberg and Oleske, 2000). The town meeting model of citizen participation is once again receiving notice, with calls for a "deliberation day" to be instituted as a national holiday (Fishkin, 1997; Ackerman and Fishkin, 2004). Like many political theorists, Dryzek urges democracies to engage in sweeping reform to allow for more deliberation: "discursive rationality should be expanded into ... social problems (especially complex ones), political and policy-making institutions, policy analysis, and empirical political science" (1990: 20).

Yet the more frequent, impassioned, and widespread these exhortations grow, the more striking becomes the dearth of knowledge about how people actually deliberate about matters of politics. In this paper we aim to contribute a bit of this knowledge by investigating how citizens deliberate about distributive justice, an issue among the core items on the agenda of any democracy.

We begin with two expectations. First, deliberation is not simply discussion; it is a more formal communication among people who often lack social ties to each other and who at times must come to some collective decision. The formal nature of deliberation leads us to expect that political institutions can influence the nature of deliberation. Those institutions include the decision rule: unanimous vote, majority rule, or some other rule. Our second assumption is that group norms matter. Not only does deliberation often occur within the context of politics and institutions; it occurs within the context of social interaction in a group setting, an interaction governed by group norms. We expect these structures of deliberation – political institutions, embodied here by the decision rule, and social interaction, embodied here by group norms – to matter to the process and the outcome of people's decisions about justice. We find support for these expectations, and urge the proponents of deliberation to more careful consideration of how politics and social forces may help or hinder good deliberation.

6.1   Deliberation and empathy

Deliberation means somewhat different things to different people, but generally it refers to a public discussion that is "reflective, open to a wide range of evidence, respectful of different views. It is a rational process of weighing the available data, considering alternative possibilities, arguing about relevance and worthiness, and then choosing the best policy or person" (Walzer, 1997: 1–2). Deliberation, ideally, is a process of communication in which people must address needs and perspectives quite different from their own. Those needs and perspectives are conveyed through reasoned arguments that are universal and generalizable, drawing on basic understandings with which other participants can agree (Chambers, 1996; Gutmann and Thompson, 1996).

Here we focus specifically on the expectation that deliberation can lead people to better empathize with the other, including with those who have less privilege. Empathy, defined as a willingness to adopt the perspective of another and to understand the reasons for the other's view, is a theme in the writings of a variety of deliberative theorists and practitioners (Yankelovich, 1991; Mathews, 1999: 241). The theorist James Bohman, for example, recommends deliberation in part because he believes it creates empathy for people with less privilege: "Citizens will then be more likely to overcome their myopia and ethnocentrism and to think of their democratic practices in an inclusive and future-oriented way" (1996: 184). Similarly, Mansbridge notes, "When people talk together, the discussion can sometimes lead the participants to see their own stake in the broader interests of the community. Indeed, at its best the democratic process resolves conflict not only by majority will, but by discovering answers that integrate the interests of minorities" (Mansbridge, 1991). Ackerman and Fishkin argue that deliberation in a New Haven Deliberative Poll increased participants' willingness to share their towns' tax revenues (Ackerman and Fishkin, 2004: 56). And according to Gutmann and Thompson, by really listening to the voices of the worst off, more privileged citizens deliberating about redistribution will not only promote the basic equality that democracy requires, but enhance their own civic capacities (Gutmann and Thompson, 1996: ch. 8).

We can interpret these writings to mean that deliberation is expected to enhance understanding about what it is like to be in the lower classes of society. If, for example, well-off people contemplate the possibility that they may end up among the worst off, their understandings of redistribution will converge on the understandings of the worst-off, and their preferences on the matter will come to resemble the preferences of the powerless or the poor. Those understandings, argue Gutmann and Thompson, should reflect the "basic opportunity principle" that guarantees citizens "that which is necessary to live a decent life according to the current standards of the society in question" (1996: 273). We know that deliberation about issues of redistribution is succeeding, Gutmann and Thompson assert, when deliberators acknowledge the need to prevent the worst off from utter destitution.

Thus, deliberation is expected to lead to empathy, and does so through a relatively egalitarian process of reasoned argumentation in which the worst off have an effective say. Deliberation should encourage people to empathize with the poor and thus to redistribute enough income from the best off so that the worst off can live in decency according to the standards of the time and place.

6.2   Will deliberation lead to empathy?

These prescriptions for more deliberation are hampered by the fact that we know little about how citizens deliberate in reality. The most thorough study of citizen deliberation remains Jane Mansbridge's *Beyond Adversary Democracy*, which is based on participant observation of New England town meetings and a participatory workplace. There have also been studies of deliberative polls, which assemble a representative sample for sessions of information-gathering and deliberation and then survey participants on their views, and of other types of citizen discussion groups (e.g., Merkle 1996;

1997; Luskin and Fishkin 1998; Merelman et al., 1998; Button and Mattson, 1999; Luskin, Fishkin and Jowell 2002; Ryfe 2002; Walsh 2003). Most studies of these deliberations have focused on aggregate changes in preferences and thus do not tell us much about deliberative dynamics (see Barabas, 2004 for a good critique; see Luskin et al., 2002 for a partial exception). Moreover, these analyses were done entirely or primarily at the individual level, despite the fact that in these forums people deliberate in small face-to-face groups (see Schkade, Sunstein and Kahneman, 2000 and Luskin et al., 2002 for a partial exception). By definition, deliberation occurs in groups. We miss an important part of the picture when we forego the deliberating group as the unit of analysis, overlook the nature of the discussion, and ignore group dynamics.

Getting an accurate picture of deliberation is particularly important when we consider that some studies of real-world deliberation suggest that deliberation does not always yield desirable outcomes. Mendelberg and Oleske (2000) studied the deliberation in two local meetings about school desegregation and concluded that people who already agreed with each other tended to agree even more, while those who disagreed with each other tended to disagree even more. There was little evidence of more open-mindedness, of a willingness to consider the perspective and needs of the other. The group with greater privilege and access to educational services showed no more generosity toward the disadvantaged group.

Laboratory studies confirm the conclusion that deliberation does not always lead people to empathy. Allowing people to communicate about social dilemmas, in which the optimal choice is to share resources but individuals are tempted away from cooperation by short-term personal gain, often yields powerful positive results and enhances cooperation (Ostrom, 1998). But subjects put into a severe conflict situation and instructed to communicate with each other may instead use communication as an opportunity to threaten each other rather than build cooperation (Deutsch, 1973; Pilisuk, Brandes, and van den Hove, 1976; Stech and McClintock, 1981; McClintock and Keil, 1983). Group discussion can also enhance the social or coercive power of a majority at the expense of the minority (Mendelberg, 2002: 161–165).

Do these discouraging findings mean that citizens are simply not equipped to make good use of deliberation? While possible, such a conclusion seems overly pessimistic and, given the lack of knowledge about actual deliberation, premature. Perhaps, instead, deliberation can succeed given the right conditions. The critical question is, what are these conditions?

6.3   Conditions for good deliberation: The social psychology of group discussion

Fortunately, the large literature in social psychology on group dynamics can point the way. Our perspective in this paper is grounded in this literature, whose maxim is that the group, to use Kurt Lewin's famous phrase, "is greater than the sum of the parts" (Lewin, 1951). An important aspect of group dynamics is group norms. Group norms work in at least four (often complementary) ways (Myers and Lamm, 1975; 1976; Weigold and Schlenker, 1991). First, norms reinforce consensual values. When members already share a value or attitude with each other, group discussion verifies their shared views (Myers and Lamm, 1976; Sanders and Baron, 1977; Myers, 1978; Goethals and Zanna, 1979). Second, norms are a route to social status. Individuals sometimes want to do what the group finds acceptable, including exaggerating their pre-existing preferences, in order to be liked or to obtain high prestige within the group (Myers and Lamm, 1976; Sanders and Baron, 1977; Myers, 1978; Goethals and Zanna, 1979). Third, norms are a route to reasoning. Norms help determine which arguments will be made more often, and more prevalent arguments often prove to be more persuasive (Burnstein and Vinokur, 1973; 1975; 1977; and Miller, 1983; Vinokur and Burnstein 1974; 1978). Fourth and finally, norms are a route to consensus about reality. Individuals rely on the group to obtain information about the state of the world. The more members who seem to view the world a certain way, the more influential that view becomes.

For example, in a classic study Muzafer Sherif used the "autokinetic effect" – the "illusory movement of a stationary pinpoint of light in a dark room" – to show how interaction between people creates stable group norms, which tell people how to perceive reality (Sherif, 1966; Forsyth 1999). In situations of uncertainty, as with the autokinetic effect, where no unambiguous reference point exists, Sherif found that the group generates the reference point because individuals assume that "the group must be right" (Cialdini and Trost, 1998). Sherif and others showed that the norm continued to operate even after the original members were replaced (Jacobs and Campbell, 1961; Pollis, Montgomery and Smith, 1975; MacNeil and Sherif, 1976). Group norms thus render groups into more than the simple aggregation of individual members.

Among the most consistent and powerful of group norm effects, and one of particular importance in studying deliberation, is group polarization, the tendency for group discussion to make individuals' pre-existing opinions more extreme (Myers and Lamm, 1976: 603). Groups can polarize many different kinds of opinion, across all types of individuals, and in laboratory as well as field situations (Pruitt, 1971; Lamm and Myers, 1978; Myers, 1982; Forsyth, 1999: 320). The most famous political examples of group polarization are the "groupthink" cases documented by Janis, in which foreign-policy decision-makers were led by their group norm to engage in blunders of judgment with a terrible cost in human life (Janis, 1982). More relevant to our study, civil juries appear to polarize as a result of deliberation, with some producing hugely inflated dollar awards to plaintiffs (Schkade et al., 2000).

Group norms, through such effects as polarization, can thus shape both the nature of deliberation and its outcome.

6.4   Deliberation meets group norms

These findings have a great deal to say to proponents of deliberation. Deliberativists may be correct in assuming that discussion matters, but it may matter not because people are exchanging arguments with dissenters, as deliberative theorists would like, but rather because of social factors. Rather than listening to and evaluating each other's diverse arguments, rather than broadening each other's perspective, deliberators may instead act based on the number of speakers in favor of a position, the social or political influence of a faction, the sheer frequency of an argument, their need to feel part of a consensus of values, or their desire to be accepted by the group. Perhaps deliberation functions as an opportunity for deliberators to present themselves as good exemplars of the group norm. If that is so, then deliberation serves a social purpose at odds with the goals of deliberative theorists. By the same token, perhaps deliberation functions not to air different perspectives but to bring minority views into line with majority views. The group dynamics literature challenges the expectation of deliberativists that when people adopt the other's perspective during deliberation they do so through reasoned, open-minded discussion (Mendelberg, 2002). Good deliberation can be undermined by group norms.

On the other hand, group dynamics research does provide some hope for deliberative expectations. That literature provides a general lesson of great use to deliberativists: the structural factors of group discussion matter, and they can be controlled. The question is, what structural factors lead to the kind of deliberation envisioned by theorists?

One structural factor of potential importance is the decision rule (see especially Gastil, 1993). The few deliberative theorists who attend to decision rules assume that the unanimity rule comes closer than majority rule to the ideal. In *Discursive Democracy*, Dryzek argues that a unanimity rule is best even when participants disagree on basic understandings (1990: 42). Consensus, or at least agreement, reached in the appropriate way, is an important value for many deliberative theorists (Habermas 1962; 1991; Chambers, 1995: 248–250, 255; Gutmann and Thompson, 1996). Thus, under ideal conditions, deliberative theorists may expect that a unanimous decision rule should produce better deliberation.

Unanimity may sound good, but in practice it may suppress conflict more than does majority rule (Mansbridge, 1980). When simulated juries are instructed to choose unanimously or with near unanimity, they almost always adopt an implicit norm that squashes the minority view (Davis, Bray, and Holt, 1977; Penrod and Hastie, 1980; Davis, Stasson, Ono, and Zimerman, 1988; Davis et al., 1989). Thus unanimous rule does not always produce a genuine, egalitarian, and empathetic exchange of views.

Unanimous and majority rules may differ in their consequences in part because the former may create stronger group norms than the latter. Unanimous rule appears to create the expectation that the group will behave as one, while majority rule implies that individuals are expected to disagree with one another (Mansbridge, 1980). One seminal study of mock juries, for example, reports that people told to decide with unanimous rule were more likely to shift their views during discussion than people assigned to majority rule juries (Hastie et al., 1983: 102). Deliberation may become more norm-driven with unanimous than majority rule.

The other structural factor that can shape norms and affect deliberation is the gender composition of the group. Because they are socialized to care for others and because of their distinctive economic experiences, women are more likely to empathize with the less well off in society. For example, women indicate more warm feelings than men toward "people on welfare" (Shapiro and Mahajan, 1986; Gilens, 1988; Sears and Huddy, 1990; Andersen, 1996). Women also tend to prefer equality (where every member of the group gets the same amount) over equity (where members receive only according to what they put in) even when they would be better off personally under a system of equity (Leventhal and Lane, 1970; Eagly, 1987: 111; Sidanius and Pratto, 1999; Scott et al., 2001). They also seem to be more sensitive to the principle of need in considering poverty (Scott et al., 2001). In studies of reward allocation between oneself and other group members, women tend to self-reward less than men do (Eagly, 1987: 111; Babcock and Laschever, 2003; Babcock, et al., 2003). In Western cultures, women tend to emphasize interdependence, to choose egalitarian solutions, and to use a democratic leadership style; men in turn tend to emphasize autonomy and to behave hierarchically (Knight and Dubro, 1984; Eagly, 1987; Eagly and Johnson, 1990; Josephs, Markus, and Tafarodi, 1992; Cross and Madson, 1997; Aries, 1998).

These differences among individuals are sometimes quite small and inconsistent (Sapiro, 2003) by comparison with other variables, and in contrast to the large variance within genders, differences between men and women are often insignificant (Aries, 1998). *However, small individual gender differences can become large and consequential when amplified by a group's gender composition.* Because of the norms it creates, a group's gender composition matters much more than does individual gender. In general, single-sex groups generate larger gender differences than do mixed-sex groups (Aries, 1996). In a meta-analytic study of how much people disclose about themselves, Dindia and Allen found that all-female groups display high levels of self-disclosure, all-male groups very low levels, and mixed groups fall in between these extremes (1992). A similar pattern of gendered group polarization emerges in studies of dominance behavior (Aries, 1976; Ellis, 1982; McCarrick, Manderscheid, and Silbergeld, 1981; Miller, 1985). Some gender differences in groups show up early in life, in girls' and boys' play patterns (Maccoby, 1998). For example, girls' play groups tend to avoid conflict within the group and to reach agreement more than boys' groups do (Miller, Danaher, and Forbes 1986).

Gender composition can polarize groups even when individual gender matters little because groups may develop gendered norms of discussion. When individuals meet face to face and are instructed to communicate their preference to other members, women conform to social pressures more than men (Cooper, 1979; Eagly and Carli, 1981; Bond and Smith, 1996). In a group situation women are often accorded a lower status than men; as a result, women may be less influential in group discussion and more susceptible to influence from men, not only because of what people say but also because of the way they speak (Eagly, 1987; Giles et al., 1987; Kathlene, 1994).[1] Women are also judged as less competent conversation partners specifically on the subject of politics (women do *not* in turn look down on men's expertise) (Huckfeldt and Sprague, 1995: ch. 10). Either because they face greater constraints on their ability to influence the group or their lesser desire to do so, we can expect women to have less influence over the discussion and over the decision in a group with many men than in a group of their own.

Let us summarize our expectations. In predominantly female groups, the average member is likely to begin with an inclination to relative generosity and cooperation. In these groups, a strong group norm will generate more group generosity than a weak norm would. Conversely, in the predominantly male groups, the average member is likely to begin with a lower inclination to generosity and a higher inclination toward competition. A strong group norm will generate less generosity and a more competitive atmosphere than would a weak group norm. Put differently, the impact of gender composition will vary with the strength of the group norm. When a group norm is strong, gender will have a polarizing effect on groups. When a group norm is weak, gender will have a smaller or no polarizing effect on groups.

The decision rule is likely to provide this difference in norm strength. The unanimous condition is likely to generate stronger group norms – whether of cooperation and generosity or of competition and stinginess – than the majority rule condition. Unanimity is thus more likely to polarize groups, sending predominantly female groups off toward an extreme of generosity and predominantly male groups off into their extreme of stinginess.

6.5 The distributive justice experiment

We analyzed individual-level and group-level data from an experiment conducted by Norman Frohlich, Joe Oppenheimer, and Cheryl Eavey (Frohlich, Oppenheimer, and Eavey, 1987; Frohlich and Oppenheimer, 1990; 1992). This experiment was designed to test Rawls's predictions about redistribution (Rawls, 1971; 1985). Rawls assumed that if people were to choose a principle of distribution without knowing whether they will be poor or rich,

Table 6.1 Number of groups (and individuals) in each condition

No deliberation imposed	Deliberation	
	Unanimous	Majority
10	9	5
(50)	(45)	(25)

they would rationally agree to maximize the welfare of the poorest member of the society, since that member may well be themselves. If people were to choose from this "original position" and behind a "veil of ignorance," reasoned Rawls, they would choose, unanimously and rationally, the "difference principle" according to which wealth is redistributed to the worst off.

Frohlich, Oppenheimer, Eavey, and their colleagues studied how people actually choose under a simulated veil of ignorance. The participants in their experiments were instructed to choose a principle that would simultaneously govern the income they earned during the experiment and apply (hypothetically) to the society at large. All individuals were first informed about several principles of distributive justice and tested on their understanding. Then groups were assigned to one of three conditions: *imposed, unanimous* and *majority rule* (see Table 6.1). In the *imposed* condition subjects were required by the experimenters to use the principle of maximizing the average with a floor constraint (chosen by most groups in previous experiments). In the *unanimous* and *majority rule* conditions subjects were told that they were to choose a principle by which they would distribute income earned later on in the experiment.[2] To achieve a "veil of ignorance" subjects were not told the nature of the work they would do, so they could not know how much income they could expect to earn or whether they may benefit from redistribution. Groups in the two deliberation conditions then discussed the distributive principles and decided collectively on a principle to govern their future distribution. The groups were told to engage in a "full and open" discussion, taking "whatever time you need, within reason" to talk. In order for the discussion period to end, the group had to agree unanimously that no further discussion was warranted. When it came to choosing a principle of distributive justice, the unanimous groups had to decide unanimously, the majority rule groups by majority rule. Subjects then performed their assigned work task – correcting spelling errors in a difficult text – and went through three rounds in which their productivity (the number of errors found) was recorded, their income calculated accordingly, and the taxation system they had chosen or been assigned applied to each person. The income was provided in yearly salary figures and was directly indexed to the financial rewards that subjects collected at the conclusion of the experiment. After each round the investigators asked each individual (in confidence) which distribution principle they preferred, how certain they felt about this preference, and their satisfaction with the principle (however, group discussion took place only once, before any rounds of work). After the last round of work and measurement the subjects answered a variety of questions about their attitudes and beliefs and provided relevant information about their background.

We go beyond Frohlich and Oppenheimer in several ways. First, in setting the floor amount – that is, the minimum income guaranteed to the poor – the groups varied a great deal in their generosity, something Frohlich and Oppenheimer did not explore but which relates directly to deliberative expectations. The participants seemed to understand the real implications of the dollar amounts with which they were dealing. Thus, the floor amount is probably a meaningful and valid summary measure of small group preferences regarding distributive justice, and the participants in the experiment did discuss it at length. According to deliberative expectations, the better the group's deliberation, the more empathetic the group's decisions will be, and the more the group will consider the adequacy of its floor guarantee. Following Gutmann and Thompson's definition, good deliberation should produce a floor amount that would provide for a "decent life."

Second, while Frohlich and Oppenheimer experimentally manipulated the decision rule, they conclude that it makes very little difference.[3] However, if group dynamics expectations are correct, the decision rule may influence the extent to which the discussion was empathetic and the level of group generosity toward the poor, measured as the floor amount – outcomes not examined by Frohlich and Oppenheimer. We analyze not only the floor amount but also the group discussion transcripts to find out whether the decision rule and the group's gender composition affect the process of deliberation.

Third, we treat as a measure of deliberative success several other variables used by Frohlich and Oppenheimer for other purposes: participants' productivity on the assigned task, certainty about their preferences, and satisfaction with the group's decision after they have experienced its effects personally.

We analyzed all deliberation groups for which both individual data and a discussion transcript were available, and all imposed groups – 24 groups and 120 individuals in total (see Table 6.1). All groups consisted of five individuals, people who according to Frohlich and Oppenheimer were "generally not close friends," recruited from large undergraduate classes at the University of Maryland.[4] The groups varied in their gender composition, with most consisting of three or four males and one or two females (two groups were all-male, no group was all-female).[5]

Before proceeding to the impact of decision rule and gender, we note two relevant results from Frohlich and Oppenheimer's analysis. First, the veil of ignorance does indeed lead people to converge on a principle of distribution.

That principle, however, is not Rawls's. Approximately 75 percent of the people chose not to maximize the income of the poorest, but to maximize the average income of the group while guaranteeing a floor below which the worst off member of the group would not be allowed to fall. In other words, they chose a system closely resembling reality – capitalism with a safety net. We can conclude from this that perhaps unsurprisingly, the deliberation seems to have altered people's commitments to their fundamental social, economic, and political reality very little.

The second simple fact we wish to highlight concerns the floor amount. Groups allowed to choose decided on a floor ranging from $3,600 to $19,000 (with an average floor income of $11,668; the "imposed" groups were assigned a floor of $9,900, the average provided by many groups averaged across several studies). These amounts were supposed to support a household, not an individual. To put these dollar amounts in perspective, the actual poverty threshold in the United States at the time of the study was $11,203 (for a family of four) (U.S. Bureau of Census, 1995: 474, 477, 481). People in the study thus chose, on average, a floor amount quite similar to the real world floor amount. It is significant from a deliberative perspective that the average floor amount subjects chose is approximately 2 standard deviations below both the mean salary that the participants reported they would find acceptable for themselves as fresh college graduates and the actual median income in the country (both at or near $24,000). That is, on average, people did not provide for a "decent life" for the worst off member of their society, but merely for survival. This is a striking result because the design of the experiment favors maximum generosity. The veil of ignorance is designed to prod people toward empathy as they consider the real possibility that they themselves may end up as the poorest, leading them to take into account the perspectives of everyone, not only of those who occupy the same current position in society as themselves. Yet on average, deliberation did not automatically yield the generosity deliberation advocates hope to see (though they would not expect to see it in every case).

6.6 The impact of decision rules on generosity to the poor

Perhaps because Frohlich and Oppenheimer paid little attention to the floor amount and to the nature of the deliberation, they concluded that the type of decision rule (unanimity or majority rule) had no impact (except on the change in individuals' certainty about their preferred principle of distribution).[6] But according to our analysis, whether the groups were required to decide on distributive justice by majority or by unanimity matters in a concrete and consequential way. The majority groups provided their worst off members with a median guaranteed income of $14,000. The unanimous groups provided $11,000, a difference of 27 percent. This

Table 6.2 The impact of decision rule and gender composition on generosity

	Coefficient	Standard error	T-ratio
Majority rule	2055	3238	0.54
Number of women	2433	1659	1.47
Group risk level	203	7121	0.03
Constant	6483	5079	0.23

N=13, Adj. R^2=.20. "Imposed" groups not included.

difference, however, could be due to the fact that the group's gender composition was not the same in the two conditions. To rule out the possibility that what seems to be a decision rule effect is really the effect of uneven gender composition we estimated the impact on the floor amount of the decision rule (a dummy variable coded 1 for majority and 0 for unanimous, entirely setting aside the imposed groups since they did not choose a floor amount) controlling on the gender composition of the group (coded from 0 to 5). Details of the variables and the models can be found in Appendix A, and explanations of the variables and their coding are in Appendix B.

As Table 6.2 shows, the majority rule groups seemed to have contributed more to the poor, though the effect is highly uncertain given its large standard error. In addition, the table suggests that the gender composition of the group may matter. The more women in the group, the more generous it is toward the worst off – its own worst off members (whose identity was yet unknown) and those in the larger society. The effect is significant only at a high threshold, unsurprising given the small number of groups, but it is sufficiently large to invite further thought: every additional woman produces an extra $2,433 for the poorest. So if a group was composed of five women, it would provide approximately $12,165 more than a group composed entirely of men; an amount well above a poor family's yearly government income. This is a hypothetical scenario since the data lack all-female groups, but clearly, the gender composition of the group may be an important structural feature of deliberation. It may change the outcome of deliberation, and in a direction lauded by deliberative theorists.

6.7 The interactive impact of gender composition and decision rule

Our hypothesis, however, is not simply that gender or decision rule will matter, but that gender will matter via the group's norm, which would be enhanced by the unanimous decision rule. Therefore, we turn to models that include an interaction term between the decision rule dummy variable and gender composition. We anticipate that unanimous groups with more women will generate more generous decisions than unanimous groups with more men – a gender polarization effect. The hypothesis predicts little or at least smaller gender polarization in the majority rule condition, and thus a small or nonexistent interaction between gender composition and majority rule.

Recall from our earlier results that the majority groups appear to have been more generous than the unanimous groups. The interactive results in Table 6.3, however, suggest that this effect may be contingent on gender composition (the effect is not statistically significant because of the small number of cases).[7] Now the majority rule groups no longer appear more generous than unanimous groups. Instead, the unanimous groups are the ones whose generosity stands out – *but only as long as they include several women.* As Figure 6.1 makes clear, if unanimous groups are composed entirely of

Table 6.3 The interactive impact of decision rule and gender composition on group generosity

	Coefficient	Standard error	T-ratio
Majority rule	1021	9102	0.11
Number of women	2354	1874	1.26
Majority*number of women	772	6290	0.12
Group risk level	−117	7984	−0.01
Constant	6784	5917	1.15

N=13, Adj. R^2=.19. "Imposed" groups not included.

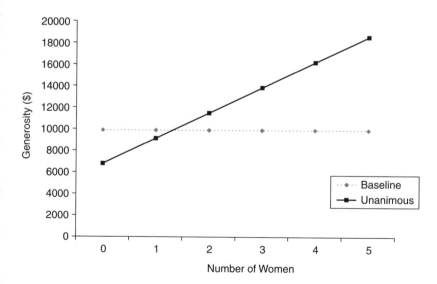

Figure 6.1 Impact of gender composition and decision rule on generosity

men, they behave quite stingily. In dollar amounts, unanimous groups with no women provide only $6,784, almost a third less than the multi-study average of $9,900 and nearly 40 percent lower than the actual poverty line in the United States. By Gutmann and Thompson's standard, that fails as a good deliberative decision because it does not guarantee an adequate level of basic support. Holding other variables constant, unanimous groups with four women are predicted to provide a total guaranteed income of $16,147, and unanimous groups with five women begin to approach the income amounts that deliberators indicated was fair and decent for themselves.[8]

This analysis is merely suggestive, since we do not have enough groups in general and specifically, data on gender composition in the majority rule condition (our later analyses will provide much better evidence). However, the important point for now is that the impact of unanimity may possibly differ considerably with gender composition in affecting the level of destitution people tolerate in their deliberating society.

6.8   Is it group gender or individual gender?

Does this gender polarization effect come from the group discussion and the dynamic it creates, or is it instead a simple matter of aggregating individual women? The group dynamics literature emphasizes the former over the latter, yet the literature on deliberation nearly uniformly assumes that people will be influenced only by individual factors and neglects group dynamics. To find out, we contrast the effects obtained with a group-level analysis to effects with an individual-level analysis, examining outcomes that are not produced by the group as a whole but by the individuals in it. We first regress the individual-level outcome on the interaction of gender composition and decision rule to measure the impact of group dynamics. Then we replace the interaction of rule and gender composition with the interaction of rule and individual gender. If deliberation is mere aggregation of individuals, then it will affect individuals as well as, or instead of, groups, and the interaction of *individual* gender and decision rule should yield the same pattern we found with *group* gender. In addition, this analysis of individual-level data allows us to perform more adequate statistical tests on the impact of gender and decision rule.

We begin with an analysis of the satisfaction individuals express with the group's decision. Each individual was asked how satisfied they were with the group's chosen principle of distribution. We regressed the individual's satisfaction with the group's decision, expressed just after discussion, on an interactive model, adding to the model a measure of individual gender (which we had been unable to do before due to collinearity with group gender at the group level of analysis). Unlike the models in Tables 6.2 and 6.3, these models also include all the groups who were forced by the experiment to accept imposed levels of generosity. Because the "imposed" groups are now

Table 6.4 The interactive impact of decision rule and gender composition on satisfaction with the principle after discussion

	Coefficient	Standard error	T-ratio
Unanimous rule	−0.45	0.55	−0.83
Majority rule	0.95	0.75	1.27
Unanimous*number of women	1.47	0.59**	2.48
Majority*number of women	0.64	0.70	0.92
Number of women	−1.37	0.56**	−2.45
Group risk aversion	1.10	0.56*	1.96
Female	−0.53	0.27*	−1.99
Constant	3.80	0.42****	9.01

N=70, Adj. R²=.15.
*p ⩽ .10, **p ⩽ .05, ***p ⩽ .01, ****p ⩽ .001

included, the model can now include dummy variables for both majority and unanimous conditions as well as interactions between both decision rules and gender composition. The results are displayed in Table 6.4.

Table 6.4 shows that unanimous rule generates more satisfaction than majority rule – *but only as long as the group has nontrivial numbers of women.* The number of women in the group actually has a negative effect in the imposed condition, but that negative effect is neutralized in the unanimous condition. What appears to be the effect of gender composition is *not* the spurious effect of risk aversion, which is controlled in the model. Thus, a similar pattern of results to what we found in our analysis of group generosity appears here, with groups polarizing by gender. But we can now be somewhat more confident that gender composition polarizes groups more under unanimity rather than under alternative rules. While we have too few groups with several women in the majority rule condition to say anything about that decision rule specifically, it is clear that gender creates group effects under unanimity that do not emerge under a regime of no deliberation and no choice.[9]

The question now is whether the interaction of decision rule and gender still influences satisfaction when we replace *group* gender composition with *individual* gender in the interaction with decision rule. Table 6.5 shows that the answer is no. Unanimity does not polarize *individuals* according to their gender. Rather, as Table 6.4 showed, it polarizes *groups* according to gender. We find this null result for individual gender in every subsequent assessment of satisfaction after successive rounds of work and redistribution, when individuals discover the position they occupy in the micro society they have constructed. Unanimity appears to set group norms, norms that vary by gender composition and that affect the satisfaction experienced by both men and women with the group decision.

Table 6.5   The interactive impact of decision rule and individual gender on satisfaction with the principle after discussion

	Coefficient	Standard error	T-ratio
Unanimous rule	0.61	0.36*	1.70
Majority rule	0.85	0.38**	2.22
Unanimous*female	0.60	0.82	0.73
Majority*female	0.39	0.89	0.44
Number of women	−0.10	0.16	−0.63
Group risk aversion	0.39	0.52	0.75
Female	−0.99	0.74	−1.34
Constant	3.35	0.36****	9.18

N=70, Adj. R^2=.06.
*$p \leqslant .10$, **$p \leqslant .05$, ***$p \leqslant .01$, ****$p \leqslant .001$

Table 6.6   The interactive impact of decision rule and gender composition on productivity

	Coefficient	Standard error	T-ratio
Unanimous rule	−4.25	1.38***	−3.08
Majority rule	−0.84	2.33	−0.36
Unanimous*number of women	2.24	0.69***	3.22
Majority*number of women	0.37	1.75	0.21
Number of women	−1.19	0.45***	−2.63
Group risk aversion	−0.53	1.25	−0.43
Female	1.18	0.74	1.59
Constant	7.47	1.01****	7.40

N=115, Adj. R^2=.06.
*$p \leqslant .10$, **$p \leqslant .05$, ***$p \leqslant .01$, ****$p \leqslant .001$

We now turn to our second individual measure, productivity. Table 6.6 and Figure 6.2 display the results of our analysis of the first round of the production task assigned to the participants, the task by which they earn their financial rewards. The pattern of effects on productivity reinforces our conclusion about the polarizing impact of unanimity on group norms. Table 6.6 and Figure 6.2 show that unanimous groups polarize their members' productivity relative to the baseline, with predominantly male groups producing significantly less and predominantly female groups significantly more. Under the no choice condition, on the other hand, polarization actually works in the opposite direction, with women-heavy groups producing far less than men-heavy groups there.[10] This is not due to the impact of *individual* gender; re-estimating the model by replacing the group gender interactions with individual gender interactions yields null results, as we found when we examined satisfaction.

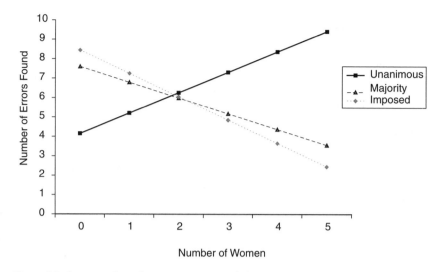

Figure 6.2 Impact of gender composition and decision rule on productivity

The final outcome we consider is the certainty individuals express about their individual preference for redistribution. The virtue of this measure is that it is the only one we have that was assessed both before and after discussion. When we apply the familiar interactive model to certainty we find that the divergence of male and female groups under unanimity really is the result of group discussion. *The interaction of gender composition and unanimity does not appear until after the discussion takes place;* before discussion, gender composition has no impact under unanimity ($b = -.11$, SE $= .21$, $p = .61$). As Table 6.7 and Figure 6.3 show, the impact of gender composition is clear after discussion, but again, only with unanimity (the only other significant predictor is the number of females, representing the impact of gender composition in the imposed condition). In this instance, the interactions are replicated to some extent when we replace gender composition in the interactions with individual gender ($b = 1.22$, SE $= .48$, $p = .01$). In other words, women – but not men – become much more certain of their own private preferences regarding redistribution after they deliberate and decide, but only if that deliberation happens under unanimous rule.

6.9 Polarization of pre-discussion preferences versus gendered discussion norms

We examined gender composition because we believe that it indexes the potential for group polarization. What can we make of our findings in light of the group polarization hypothesis? The hypothesis argues that polarization

Table 6.7   The interactive impact of decision rule and gender composition on certainty

	Coefficient	Standard error	T-ratio
Unanimous rule	−0.51	0.43	−1.18
Majority rule	0.21	0.71	0.29
Unanimous*number of women	0.61	0.22***	2.79
Majority*number of women	0.22	0.53	0.42
Number of women	−0.28	0.14**	−2.04
Group risk aversion	0.06	0.40	0.15
Female	−0.04	0.23	−0.18
Constant	3.89	0.31****	12.48

N=109, Adj. R^2=.08.
*$p \leqslant .10$, **$p \leqslant .05$, ***$p \leqslant .01$, ****$p \leqslant .001$

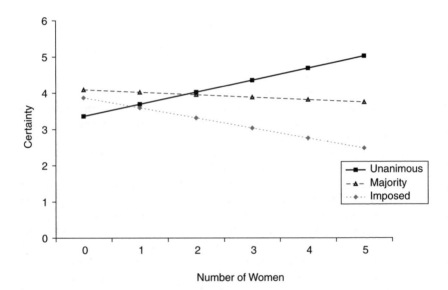

Figure 6.3   Impact of decision rule and gender composition on certainty

occurs in a group with many women because the average opinion before discussion favors generosity, with group discussion serving merely to reinforce this prior tendency. Conversely, in a group with few or no women, the pre-discussion average favors stinginess, and the group interaction moves the group decision in that direction. However, gender may matter not only in shaping pre-discussion preferences but also in shaping the nature of the discussion and of the norms that develop during it. Gender may drive the interaction toward more open-minded exchange in which the focus is on the collective needs of the group – or the opposite, in the case of predominantly-male groups.

To put to the test the standard polarization hypothesis against the gendered discussion hypothesis, we estimated the impact of group ideology on the group's generosity, satisfaction, and productivity. If the impact of gender simply reflects the fact that women tend to go into discussions with more liberal views and a greater concern for the poor, then replacing group gender with group ideology should yield a similar pattern of results. But that is not what we find. While in the unanimous condition having more women results in more generosity to the poor, having more liberals generates less generosity to the poor.[11] And while in the majority rule condition increasing the number of women has no statistically discernable effect, increasing the number of liberals does make the group more generous to the poor.

In a further test, we re-ran the analysis with class instead of ideology. Perhaps ideology misses an aspect of people's political preferences about economic redistribution, an aspect better captured by measures of class. Using different measures of socio-economic status, we find that the group's class composition mimics the effect of gender on the group's generosity to the poor in the unanimous condition, but the effect is smaller, and class does not mimic the effects of gender composition on the other dependent variables (nor does controlling on class decrease the impact of gender composition).[12]

Thus it is not merely the pre-existing tendency to sympathize with the poor, in the case of ideology, or to align one's choice about redistribution with one's interests, in the case of class, that determines whether the discussion will polarize the outcome. Rather, the strongest and most consistent findings point to the operation of gendered norms. Gender represents not only a set of political preferences, but a type of interaction. People appear to respond to institutional variables such as the decision rule, not simply because they are liberal or conservative but because they are in a group with men or women.

In sum, requiring a group to decide about justice with unanimity makes the group's initial tendency more extreme and creates dynamics that affect the group's decision-making, perceptions of legitimacy, and even individual performance on an unrelated task. If the group is composed primarily of women, it is more generous than it would be under majority rule, and subsequently generates greater productivity, more satisfaction with the group's decision, and a higher level of certainty about the group's decision. But if the group is composed primarily of men, it is less generous than it would be if it decided by majority rule, and its members subsequently show more alienation from the group's decisions and tasks. The more women in the group, the greater the initial tendency to be generous and to work with and for the group, and unanimity heightens that tendency. The more men in the group, the greater the initial tendency to be stingy and to work independently of the group, and unanimity heightens that tendency.

Thus, we find two structural variables that influence deliberation. One is the decision rule, the other is gender composition. These variables interact in a significant way. Majority rule leads to more generous guarantees of minimum income. But requiring a group to be unanimous may lead to still more generosity – so long as the group is composed primarily of women. Most importantly, we find that those gender differences are caused by the *dynamic of the groups*, not by the simple aggregation of the individuals in it. There is something about the group interaction that produces a *group* gender effect. We now turn to that "something": group discussion.

6.10   How discussion mediates the effects of gender composition and decision rule

How do the decision rule and the gender composition of the group affect the nature of discussion? We examine several aspects of the discussion: how certain, versus hesitant, the speakers are; how much the speakers focus on themselves versus on others; how competitive – even aggressive – versus cooperative is their speech; optimism versus pessimism; and satisfaction versus dissatisfaction.[13] We picked these characteristics because they index several aspects of group functioning relevant to deliberation, aspects relevant to inter-dependence and openness to others in the group. Our results so far suggest that unanimous female groups create a norm consonant with the deliberative ideal of cooperation and openness to other group members, particularly to the least advantaged members. We also found that these groups are more satisfied with the group and its actions. Therefore we should find echoes of these characteristics in the discussion itself. In addition, it may be that these groups are also working together effectively on the joint task, something that our productivity analysis demonstrated, and therefore we should find indicators of effectiveness and task-orientation in the discussions as well, although this dimension is not directly related to deliberative expectations. Finally, an important process variable highlighted by deliberativists is the extent to which the groups raise principles and reasons; good deliberation is defined in part as discussion that resorts to universal principles and to appropriate rationales.

For our analysis we rely on Roderick Hart's software program DICTION. The program includes a set of pre-defined variables, derived by Hart primarily from research in linguistics. Each variable consists of a unique list of words, and is standardized to control on differences in the length of the texts (for more information see Hart, 2000a; 2000b). We averaged the scores of each group's members to create group-level discussion scores. See Table 6.8 for the results and Appendix C for details on the language variables.

We find that the number of women in the group does in fact shape the nature of the discussion, largely in ways that reinforce our conclusions.

Table 6.8 Impact of gender composition, by decision rule, on the nature of group discussion

	Unanimous (n=9)			Majority (n=5)		
	Coefficient	Standard error	T-ratio	Coefficient	Standard error	T-ratio
Optimism and satisfaction						
Praise	−2.53	1.22	−2.08**	−1.51	2.58	−0.59
Blame	0.48	0.3	1.59*	−0.89	2.22	−0.4
Hardship	0.04	0.2	0.2	0.56	0.44	1.27
Satisfaction	0.75	1.03	0.73	−6.46	10.01	−0.65
Denial	−2.58	1.57	−1.64*	−6.58	10.07	−0.65
Task orientation						
Accomplishment	0.98	1.07	0.91	5.9	1.43	4.13**
Concreteness	2.02	1.43	1.41*	−10.69	9.58	−1.12
Embellishment	−0.18	0.13	−1.38	−1	1.85	−0.54
Cooperation and other orientation						
Self-reference	−1.37	1.7	−0.8	12.27	7.85	1.56*
Human Interest	0.62	3.12	0.2	−13.85	9.65	−1.44
Aggression	−0.18	0.13	−1.34	0.3	0.76	0.39
Rapport	−0.77	0.82	−0.93	−3.29	2.06	−1.6*
Cooperation	0	0.15	0.01	−1.3	1.71	−0.76
Expressions of certainty						
Ambivalence	−0.68	2.17	−0.31	10.81	5.37	2.01*
Tenacity	−6.43	1.70	−3.79***	−18.1	10.99	−1.65*
Overall certainty	−6.61	2.02	−3.27**	0.18	1.17	0.15
Reasons and principles						
Cognitive terms	−2.11	1.44	−1.46	13.41	3.31	4.05**
Inspiration	−0.19	0.44	−0.43	0.32	0.58	0.5

Cell entries are bivariate regression coefficients showing the impact of the number of women in the group.
*$p \leq .10$, **$p \leq .05$, ***$p \leq .01$, ****$p \leq .001$, one-tailed.

To some extent, gender shapes the discussion regardless of the decision rule. In particular, the "tenacity" of the speech decreases as the number of women rises, so that people speak less definitively and avoid the impression that they know all. This finding squares with the linguistic literature on gender differences which finds that women tend to speak less definitively than men, at least when speaking to men (Carli, 1990; Holmes, 1995). That, however, is where the clear and consistent effects of gender composition end. Gender's impact on discussion is not constant across situations but instead varies considerably depending on the decision rule, and in ways that largely confirm the implications we have drawn.

Under unanimous rule, the more women in the group, the less optimism its members express (less praise and more blame). The effect on blame, in particular, makes sense given that these are words "describing unfortunate circumstances or unplanned vicissitudes" (Hart, 2000b: 34), which corresponds to discussion of the poor. On the other hand, these groups also use fewer denial terms, which Hart takes as an indicator of satisfaction. So with unanimous rule, groups with more women discuss more thoroughly the problems of poverty (blame) yet express some form of satisfaction by avoiding negativity (denial terms). In addition, with unanimous rule, the more women in the group the more the group talks concretely. Hart classifies this as a category dealing with task orientation because it is about tangible and material matters. Among the words in this category are "sociological units" and "occupational groups." If these groups were engaged in more discussion about work and poverty, then they would also score higher on this measure since that would increase their mentions of "sociological units" and "occupational groups." In addition, groups with more women may produce fewer expressions of "aggression," which includes competition and social domination, although we offer this tentatively since the effect is just shy of significance. It seems that with unanimous rule, people in groups with many women avoid the words of destructive conflict. Under unanimous rule, people in groups with more women also use less certain language, especially avoiding expressions of tenacity which may correspond to arrogance.

This pattern of results stands in contrast with the majority rule condition. To be sure, there are similarities: majority rule groups with women show a strong effect on "accomplishment," the most direct measure we have of task-orientation, and majority groups with more women also tend toward less certainty in their language by avoiding expressions of tenacity and using more ambivalent language. These similarities are overshadowed by three differences, however. First, in contrast to the unanimous condition, majority rule groups with more women do not dissect the situation of the disadvantaged, reflected in the null effects on blame, and do not show increases in satisfaction, indexed by the null effect of denial, any more than male groups. Second and most relevant, majority rule weakens the communal dynamic in groups with women: with majority rule, adding women causes a group to engage in *more* self-references and *less* rapport (both under the over-arching category of cooperation and other-orientation). Third, and unexpectedly, majority rule groups with more women use more "cognitive" terms, an effect not found in the unanimous rule condition. This result is not consonant with any of the others and given the small number of groups and the large number of statistical analyses we do not put much weight on it, but we do note it.

Unanimous rule may thus render a group with more women a more unified, more cooperative, and less antagonistic unit than an all-male group; one that talks about its collective needs while trying to satisfy its individual members. Groups polarize in the quality of their discussion along lines of gender, with female groups producing a more deliberative discussion than male groups, but only under unanimous rule (noting the possible exception of the cognitive dimension). The majority rule groups show a fairly, though not completely, consistent pattern in which moving away from all-males groups does not lead to the processes or outcomes that deliberative theorists such as Gutmann and Thompson advocate. Norms and institutional structures matter to the quality as well as the outcome of deliberation.

6.11 Conclusion

The results of this study, while tentative because of data limitations, suggest that unanimous groups with female members, in contrast to their predominantly male counterparts, majority-rule groups, and groups with no discussion and no choice, make people: (i) more generous as a group, (ii) more productive individually, regardless of individual gender, (iii) more satisfied individually with the distribution scheme operating in the group, again regardless of individual gender, and (iv) more sure of their individual preference for distribution. These outcomes appear to be mediated by the nature of the discussion. Interestingly, while the people in these groups emerge more certain of their decisions, the discussion itself is characterized by more tentative words – a deliberatively desirable quality.

While requiring more definitive testing, these results support the hypothesis that norms generated during group discussion matter a great deal. They also support the hypothesis that norms are produced, in part, by gender composition working together with the decision rule. These two structural variables create norms that go far beyond the impact of aggregating individuals. This can be seen from the fairly consistent null results of individual gender, of group ideology and of group class composition, and from the evidence that gender and decision rule shape the nature of the discussion itself. The structural variables matter both on their own and, more powerfully, when they interact. This power is extremely wide-ranging, affecting not only the generosity of the decision but also the individual members' satisfaction, productivity, and certainty about their preferences. In other words, a group's composition and governing rules shape the meaning of the deliberation and its outcome. Deliberative theorists and practitioners want deliberation to produce a consensus on fundamental principles, and they want that consensus to emerge through empathy. We find that deliberation can certainly do so. But the structures of deliberation influence the degree to which people blur the line between themselves and the other and consider the needs of the least fortunate. These structures affect people's decision to raise the standard of living of the poor; their satisfaction with that decision; their certainty that their own view of redistribution is appropriate; and even their own productivity in a work regime governed by the group's decision.

Gender and deliberation. Attending to group norms has led us to better understand how gender shapes deliberation and political decisions. As Sapiro notes, gender differences are more than a matter of individual differences, of who one is (Sapiro, 2003). Gender is also "something one does, and does recurrently, in interaction with others" (West and Zimmerman, 1987: 140). It is not enough to "add women and stir" in our studies of politics (Silverberg, 1990). To capture gender effects in politics we must examine what happens when citizens interact with each other, as they do when they deliberate. We reported initial results suggesting that the effects we find are not caused merely by polarization based on the skew of pre-discussion preferences, but by the gendered discussion norms that emerge during discussion. More research is needed to explore how gender shapes deliberation, and how other social cleavages affect the nature of political discussion.[14]

Deliberation and the structure of choice. "The citizen," write Huckfeldt and Sprague, "is an information processor, but information is environmentally supplied, and individual choices are embedded within information settings that systematically vary in time and space" (1995: 292). We have taken a first pass at the impact of the systematic variation that Huckfeldt and Sprague conclude is so important to political choice. That variation is not only the composition of deliberating groups, but also the type of decision rule groups use. Of course, in the real world groups often control their own procedures (Mansbridge, 1980). Should a group, or an outside actor, wish to engineer the structure of deliberation, an experimental design that systematically varies the decision rule is of some help in suggesting how institutional rules that govern deliberation matter.

Future research should examine systematically how the institutional structures of deliberation affect the nature of the discussion. And those structures should be studied not only in mutual isolation but in interaction. For example, relative to unanimous groups with many women, we might expect to see that under other decision rules and with predominantly male groups: (i) women take fewer turns, (ii) women utter fewer sentences, (iii) women ask more questions, (iv) women are interrupted more often, and so on. Using such an analysis of the real world of legislative politics Lynn Kathlene has found that a legislature's committee hearings are highly gendered in these ways (Kathlene, 1994). We need more studies that examine how people actually interact in deliberative settings, and how institutional rules and social cleavages affect the quality of deliberation.[15] Such studies are critical because institutional rules and collective norms are likely to influence all types of situations in which people are invited to interact with others in an active way before reaching a decision; including legislative committees, local elected councils, town meetings, governing boards of organizations, work groups, church groups, and more. To the extent that empathy is expected or desired in these groups, then the people who influence them should consider the effects of the rules that govern their interaction.

The findings we report here serve as a caution against implementing deliberation without first thoroughly understanding when it will work for the desired end. Foundations such as Pew, Kettering, and the Jefferson Center, which have enthusiastically promoted citizen deliberation in the spirit of increasing democratic participation, should proceed in a more cautious fashion. Sponsoring these efforts is laudable if the efforts are evaluated systematically before they are recommended to the public. When citizens deliberate about matters of justice and public morality, they must contend with the powerful influence of gendered norms and decision rules. These influences can promote increased empathy under certain conditions, but they may also work against the kind of discussion that deliberativists wish to see. When they do, deliberation is likely to cause damage, leading to less empathy than before.

Deliberation is not necessarily a remedy for all the ills of politics. Social psychology (such as group norms and group effects) and politics (including institutions like the decision rule) do not disappear in the deliberative setting. Indeed, psychology and politics are deeply ingrained in deliberation, influencing the outcomes in subtle, but nonetheless powerful, ways. We must understand these influences before we rely on citizen deliberation to remedy the ills of democracy.

6.A.1 Appendix A

Models

1. Generosity, main effects (Table 6.2):

    Frange = majority + numfmale + g_rsk01x

    [Note: Groups with imposed decision rules are set aside, meaning that the regression includes only unanimous and majority groups. With respect to the dummy variable "majority," the unanimous groups are the excluded category.]
2. Generosity, with interactive effects included (Table 6.3):

    Frange = majority + numfmale + g_rsk01x + majority*numfmale

    [Note: As with Table 6.2, groups with imposed decision rules are set aside.]
3. Satisfaction, Productivity, Certainty, interactive model (Tables 6.4, 6.6, 6.7):

    Satisfaction [or Productivity or Certainty] = unan + majority + unan*numfmale + maj*numfmale + numfmale + g_rsk01x + female

    [Note: The imposed groups are the excluded category.]
4. The interactive model with individual gender (Table 6.5)

    Satisfaction = unan + majority + numfmale + g_rsk01x + unan*female + majority* female + female

    [Note: The imposed groups are the excluded category.]

6.A.2   Appendix B

Independent variables

> Unan = 1 if unanimous, 0 otherwise
> Majority = 1 if majority rule, 0 otherwise
> Numfmale = number of females in group (from 0 to 5, actual range is 0–4)

G_rsk01x = group's average risk aversion, measured continuously from 0 to 1, actual range from 0 to .58. Assessed with two questions, equally weighted. "Suppose someone offered to sell you a lottery ticket. In this lottery, one out of every four tickets will win $50. What is the most you would be willing to pay for it?" "Suppose you have a lottery ticket. In this lottery one out of three tickets will win $50. If someone asked you to sell them the ticket, what is the minimum price you would sell it for?"

> Female = 1 if participant is female, 0 if male.

Dependent variables

Frange = group's floor amount in dollars, imputed to the two groups choosing the range constraint according to the highest floor amount chosen in that group's condition (this method understates the actual floor amount). Results are robust across six versions of the floor amount variable.

Satisfaction = individual satisfaction with the distribution principle chosen by the group, 1 = very dissatisfied, 5 = very satisfied.

Productivity = individual productivity at each round of work, counting the number of errors found, from 0 to 13.

Certainty = individual certainty about the principle one prefers, 1 = very unsure, 2 = unsure, 3 = no opinion, 4 = sure, 5 = very sure. It is based on the question: "How do you feel about your ranking of these principles?"

Other variables

Expected starting salary: What minimum annual income (in thousands of today's dollars) do you think you will find satisfactory as your starting salary for your first job after graduation?

Ideology: Rate your ideological preference on a scale from 1 (most conservative) to 5 (most liberal).

6.A.3   Appendix C

Discussion variables (*Diction Manual* :. 33–37): Definitions (empirical descriptives available upon request)

Optimism and satisfaction

Praise: "Affirmations of some person, group or abstract entity. Included are terms isolating important social qualities ... physical qualities ... intellectual qualities ... entrepreneurial qualities ... and moral qualities."

Blame: "Terms designating social inappropriateness as well as downright evil ... adjectives describing unfortunate circumstances or unplanned vicissitudes."

Hardship: "Natural disasters, hostile actions, and censurable human behavior. It also includes unsavory political outcomes as well as normal human fears and incapacities."

Satisfaction: "Terms associated with positive affective states ... pleasurable diversion ... and words of nurturance."

Denial: "Standard negative contractions (aren't, shouldn't), negative-function words (nor, not, nay), and terms designating null sets (nothing, nobody, none)."

Task orientation

Accomplishment: "Words expressing task-completion and organized human behavior."

Concreteness: "Tangibility and materiality, including sociological units, occupational groups, political alignments, physical structures, modes of transportation, etc."

Embellishment: "A selective ratio of adjectives to verbs based on David Boder's (1940) conception that heavy modification slows down a verbal passage by de-emphasizing human and material action."

Cooperation and other orientation

Self-reference: "All first-person references, including I, I'd, I'll, I'm, I've, me, mine, my, myself."

Human Interest: "Standard personal pronouns (he, his, ourselves, them), family members and relations, and generic terms (friend, baby, human, persons)."

Aggression: "Human competition and forceful action, physical energy, social domination, goal-directedness."

Rapport: "Attitudinal similarities among groups of people, including terms of affinity, assent, deference, and identity."

Cooperation: "Behavioral interactions among people that often result in a group product, including designations of formal work relations, informal associations, more intimate interactions. Also includes self-denial."

Expressions of certainty

Ambivalence: "Words expressing hesitation or uncertainty, implying a speaker's inability or unwillingness to commit to the verbalization being made. Included are hedges (allegedly, perhaps, might), statements of inexactness ... and confusion ... Also included are words of restrained possibility ... and mystery."

Tenacity: "All uses of the verb to be (is, am, will, shall), three definitive verb forms (has, must, do) and their variants, as well as all associated contractions (he'll, they've, ain't)."

Overall Certainty: Constructed by DICTION : [Tenacity + Leveling Terms + Collectives + Insistence] − [Numerical + Ambivalence + Self-reference + Variety].

Reasons and principles

Cognitive Terms: "Words referring to cerebral processes, both functional and imaginative. Included are modes of discovery (learn, deliberate, consider, compare) and domains of study (biology, psychology, logic, economics). The dictionary includes mental challenges (question, forget, re-examine, paradoxes), institutional learning practices (graduation, teaching, classrooms), as well as three forms of intellection: intuitional (invent, perceive, speculate, interpret), rationalistic (estimate, examine, reasonable, strategies), and calculative (diagnose, analyze, software, fact-finding)."

Inspiration: "Abstract virtues deserving of universal respect. Most of the terms in this dictionary are nouns isolating desirable moral qualities (faith, honesty, self-sacrifice, virtue) as well as attractive personal qualities (courage, dedication, wisdom, mercy). Social and political ideals are also included: patriotism, success, education, justice."

Notes

Earlier versions of this chapter were presented at the 2000 ISPP and APSA meetings. We thank Dan Cassino for research assistance.

1. At least in the past, women participated less frequently in jury deliberations, and their statements tended to convey agreement and solidarity more often than men's (Strodtbeck and Mann, 1956; Strodtbeck et al., 1957; James, 1959; Nemeth, Endicott, and Wachtler 1976).
2. Subjects were told, "After the discussion, you will be asked to reach a group decision on which principle of justice you like best. Your 'take home' pay for Part III of the experiment will be partially based on the principle which the group chooses. In the third part you will be required to perform some tasks to earn some money. Your earned income will then be taxed or supplemented so that the final distribution of income in this part is in accordance with the principle adopted by the group. ... Upon completion of the third part you will receive the sum of your earnings from the earlier parts of the experiment by check. The money you receive will be yours alone. No discussion or agreement to share your final pay is permitted. Any such discussions may void the experiment and lead to your earning nothing!" (Frohlich and Oppenheimer, 1992: 228–235).
3. Allowing people to choose a principle for themselves rather than imposing a principle on them did create much greater satisfaction with and legitimacy for the principle, but regardless of the decision rule (1990).
4. Thus we avoid the high group cohesion caused by friendship and can better generalize to actual political situations.
5. The unanimous groups contained more females and the majority groups more males, but individual preferences regarding distributive justice, assessed before the groups were assigned to a decision rule, did not significantly differ across conditions. Liberal/conservative ideology was also randomly distributed across conditions (overall 35 percent conservative, 16 percent moderate, and 49 percent liberal), and every group but two had both conservative and liberal individuals. Party identification consisted of 39 percent Republican, 33 percent Democrat, 16 percent independent and 12 percent with no preference. Mean age was 21, ranging from 18 to 41. These variables were randomly distributed across conditions, as was a measure of self-support through college.
6. Caution is in order when interpreting the difference between majority rule and unanimity. Frohlich and Oppenheimer indicated in a correspondence with us that they did not use strict random assignment procedures when assigning groups to conditions.
7. Because all groups with imposed floor amounts are set aside, the model includes only majority and unanimous groups. This means that unanimous groups are the excluded category with respect to the "majority" dummy variable. In other words, the model controls for the majority condition and the interaction between the majority condition and gender composition. Thus, the coefficient attaching to the number of women in the group shows the impact of the gender composition in the unanimous condition.

8. The majority groups, by contrast, show no statistically significant increase with the number of women, though we note that this result stands on very weak data legs given the dearth of female groups in the majority rule condition.

9. The pattern in Table 6.4 holds when we examine satisfaction with the principle after the first round of production and redistribution. While the interactive effect of gender composition in the unanimous condition attenuates somewhat along with the rest of the effects in Table 6.4, it remains significant (in fact, it is the only statistically significant effect). This impact goes away after the second round of production and redistribution and stays away after the third and final round, but by then none of the variables in the model, including individual gender, matter either.

10. Figure 6.2 also shows predicted estimates for the majority condition, though the paucity of cases means we cannot say anything statistically definitive about those groups. Point estimates for Figures 6.2 and 6.3 were generated using CLARIFY software (Tomz, Wittenberg, and King, 2003), holding other variables in the model constant. Because standard errors for the majority groups were unusually large, we do not include confidence intervals in these graphs, but they are available from the authors upon request.

11. We estimated the impact of number of liberals separately for the unanimous and majority rule conditions, by itself and controlling on group risk. The unstandardized OLS coefficients for generosity are -3257, SE = 975 in the unanimous conditions, and 1997, SE = 375 in the majority rule condition. The effects are stronger still when we control on group risk level. Unlike with gender, we find no impact in the unanimous condition of group ideology on individual satisfaction and productivity.

12. First, we find that the higher the average group percentage of college expenses paid from the student's own income, the more generous is the group, in both decision rules, even after controlling on number of women. Second, we find that in the unanimous condition, the higher the average group number of hours worked, the more generous is the group, again even after controlling on the number of women. In the majority condition, however, the higher the group's average number of hours worked per week, the less generous the group becomes. Neither measure of class strongly affects the other dependent variables.

13. We set aside other categories that were irrelevant or too heterogenous in their meaning.

14. Gender composition may also produce threshold effects upon reaching a majority of women (Kathlene, 1994). We do not have the data to test this notion.

15. On group norms and decision-making in legislative politics see Eavey and Miller, 1984, and Loewenberg and Mans, 1988.

7
Types of Discourse and the Democracy of Deliberation

Shawn W. Rosenberg[1]

Despite this theoretical and practical interest in citizen deliberation, political scientists have only recently begun to go beyond the informal observation of particular cases to the conduct of more systematic studies of citizen's tendencies to engage in political talk (e.g., Delli Carpini et al., this volume), their views of deliberation (e.g., Walsh, 2004) and the impact of deliberation on participants' attitudes (e.g., Luskin, et al., 2002). However, little systematic research has focused on the quality of the exchange that occurs between citizens in deliberative settings. This is the case despite the fact that assumptions regarding the nature of that exchange are critical both to political theorists and practitioners.[2] According to the theory, political discussion can be considered deliberative only if it involves the reasoned consideration of participants' beliefs and preferences. It can be considered to be democratic only if it is conducted in a way that preserves the autonomy and equality of the participants. Failing to be deliberative or democratic, the ensuing discussion and the policy recommendations are less likely to be consensual, rational, fair, or legitimate.

My aim here is to examine the quality of citizen deliberations. I begin by offering a theoretically grounded description of how individuals actually engage one another when they are asked to deliberate. The intent is not to offer a more elaborated description of the reasoned discourse presumed by liberal democratic theorists, but rather to characterize the different forms of discursive practices that may emerge in deliberative settings. I then use this typology to guide the analysis of the of two different citizen deliberations that were convened under conditions highly favorable to deliberation. I conclude by considering the implications of the evidence of different forms of deliberative discourse for democratic practice.

7.1 Types of deliberative discourse

While briefly stipulating what a deliberative exchange should be like, most deliberative democratic theory focuses on the institutional context or social setting of the deliberation. The concern here is the circumstances that affect the persons who are included in the deliberation and, once included, the extent to which they participate in a free and equal fashion. Critical attention is paid to the ways in which institutional arrangements and social status operate to exclude people from the deliberation and then to distort the discussion of those involved by highlighting the concerns of the more powerful participants and by silencing the less powerful participants or forcing their conformity. The assumption here is that insofar as power can be neutralized and constraints on participation can be removed, individuals will engage one another in a more truly democratic deliberative fashion. Allowing for some variation among theorists, most argue that the result will be a collaborative consideration of a problem or issue through the assertions of fact or value (as personal narratives or explicit claims) that are actually or potentially backed by reasons or clarified by elaborations which may then be subject to challenge, defense, and revision. The assumption is that this presentation and interrogation of claims will involve the free and equal expression of personal views and a respectful consideration of others' perspectives, fairness, and the common good.

While instructive, this way of characterizing deliberative discourses is limited in two related ways. On the one hand, little reference is made to evidence on how people actually deliberate. This is justified insofar as ideal deliberation is realized or at least closely approximated in real deliberations. In her seminal study of town hall meetings, Mansbridge (1980) observed that deliberation was far from ideal. Insofar as this is generally the case, a separate analysis of how people actually engage one another in deliberative settings becomes necessary. On the other hand, the characterization of deliberative discourse focuses on a single kind of exchange, the kind that is both assumed and prescribed in deliberative democratic theory. If people engage one another in a different, non-normative fashion, the theory can therefore only offer a framework for negative description; it can only provide a way of describing what people are *not* doing. Consequently, deliberative democratic theory currently offers little direction for addressing the different ways in which people may deliberate or for considering the implications of these different forms of deliberation for democratic practice.

Here I adopt a structural pragmatic view of cognition and communication. Consequently I view meaning-making as a purposive, constructive activity that has both subjective and inter-subjective dimensions. I also assume this constructive activity may be realized in different ways, each of which produces its characteristic understandings and discourses (Rosenberg, 2002; 2003). This view yields a distinctive understanding of communication, one that suggests that communication may take qualitatively different forms thereby producing structurally different ways of coordinating the exchange between participants and different possibilities for the kinds of meanings they can inter-subjectively construct. Three types of communication or deliberation are described in Table 7.1: (i) concretely anchored, conventional discourse, (ii) cooperative discourse and (iii) collaborative, reconstructive discourse. While focusing on the different forms which discourse may take, it is important to note that I am not suggesting that a given deliberation will take a single form. To the contrary, I assume that at different moments in the

Table 7.1   Types of discourse

	Conventional	Cooperative	Collaborative
Aim of discourse	1. Choose correct course of action. 2. Maintain conventional social relationships	Reach agreement on the meaning and (conventional) claims in order to make effective and desirable decisions	1. Choose correct action 2. Use deliberation as an opportunity for a collaborative (re-)construction of meaning, selves and community
Mode of coordination	Shared experience and cultural conventions delimit the causal or categorical connections among *speech acts*	Cooperative expression of *perspectives* through reasoned argument involving reference to shared foundational assumptions	Complementary, caring engagement of *communicative strategies* to illuminate forms of subjectivity and inter-subjectivity
Rules of social interaction	Specific rules of polite and civil behavior as they pertain to particular social roles and status	Specific rules negotiated with reference to general principles of fair and effective participation	Self-reflective, negotiated management of the discourse to meet complementary needs of creating and sustaining (a) collaboration and
Rules of conversational relevance	Address specific topic of conversation or, secondarily, address remarks of prior speakers	Complementary, other oriented contribution to the definition/ explanation of the subject matter being addressed	the social reality of the group and (b) subjectivity and the personal reality of the self
Quality of meaning constructed	Shared representation based on common cultural definitions or exposure to similar objective experience	Common meaning based on agreement regarding place of propositional claims in their systemic context (objective, social, and personal)	A collaborative inter-action between different ways of constructing meaning without reducing their difference
Criteria of successful communication	1. Leads to effective and/or normatively appropriate action 2. Speech acts follow one another according to social convention and participants follow role prescriptions	1. Individual participants engage in critical self-reflection of specific beliefs 2. There is reasoned discussion of related claims with reference to a shared understanding of what is true, right, and authentic	1. Integrity of self is expressed and its limits engaged 2. Differences in how people construct meaning are recognized and engaged 3. Community sustained while fostering fragmentation

deliberation, different types of discourses are likely to emerge. The form of discourse may change over time with a shift in the subject matter or in the orientation of the participants. Additionally, different forms of discourse may be operative simultaneously when subsets of participants address the same topic in qualitatively different ways.

7.1.1 Conventional, concretely anchored discourse

The aims of discourse. Conventional discourse is oriented by two distinct goals. The first goal is to determine the nature of the problem and how to address it effectively. This involves identifying the defining attributes of the problem, establishing the operative causes and their concrete effects, considering possible interventions and determining the relative value of their different outcomes. The second goal is to regulate the social interaction between the participants according to prevailing social conventions of civility and politeness. The aim here is to insure that the discourse follows rather specific, concrete prescriptions regarding who speaks in what way when.

The formal qualities of the discourse. The basic unit of conventional discourse is a speech act. This consists of a commonly recognized use of an utterance for a commonly understood specific purpose (e.g., representing a particular objective experience to others or evoking a particular response from them). The relationship between speech acts is regulated by conventional rules of association that link particular speech acts causally, categorically or normatively in specific and concrete ways. Structured in this way, conventional discourse is organized around specific concrete topics. The topic may be a particular focal actor, object, action, or series of actions. To be relevant, a speech act must be linked to the concrete topic by expressing causal (e.g., refer to a prior cause or consequent effect of the topic) or categorical (e.g., refer to other concrete aspects of the topic) associations that conform to shared experience or accepted social conventions or definitions. The conversational result is a loosely related set of claims or elaborations that bear on a single topic. At the same time, conventional discourse is organized according to concrete rules of politeness and civility. They regulate the relationship between a particular actor, speech act, and the action that must follow from it. The concern here is who can make a particular speech act, and when and who must say or do what in response. Conventional discourse thus implicates the particulars of participants' normative values, their personal identities and their social connection to one another. As a result, a violation of these social rules of discourse may readily evoke the feelings, fears, commitments, and consequently the hostility of those involved.

The dynamic of the discourse. A conventional discourse is typically initiated in response to a particular problem. Something has gone wrong; an undesirable outcome has occurred or a social convention has been violated.

Alternatively the discourse may be initiated in response to the demands of civility. Social convention may require that individuals initiate conversation as part of sustaining conventionally defined relations among them, for example the way friends create opportunities to talk simply for the purpose of sustaining the friendship. When the conversation begins, routinized or privately directed behavior is typically suspended.

To begin, a topic is introduced by one of the participants. Constrained by rules of relevance, the discussion will consist of a succession of contributions that are intended, in part, to describe, to explain, or to evaluate the topic at hand. Often succeeding claims bear only indirectly on one another. Thus one speaker may offer a narrative or claim about an aspect of the anchoring topic and the next speaker may offer another narrative or claim that remains on topic but bears no direct concrete relationship to the prior narrative. Anchored in a common topic, but not addressing the linkages among different individuals' speech acts, the discourse produces a depiction of the topic that consists of a list of loosely associated claims and narratives.

In this context, one speaker may directly address a prior speaker's claim. Such a move may be a supportive one. This may consist of a simple affirmation of the validity of the first speaker's claim such as, "Yes, you are right." Alternatively the supportive move may involve making complementary assertions of concrete association. This may consist of providing a specific example of a general behavioral rule that has been asserted. Thus one speaker may follow another's claim that dull textbooks cause students to be bored by describing how her child had a bad textbook and subsequently became disinterested in the topic. Instead the second speaker can support the first by extending the causal chain the first asserted. Thus the second speaker may assert that textbooks bore students who then become disrespectful to their teachers. In either case, the second speaker makes a speech act that extends and thereby reinforces the claim made in the speech act of the first. In a conventional discourse, such supportive moves not only contribute to the analysis of the topic at hand, but they also reinforce shared beliefs and maintain a positive social connection between the participants.

A second speaker may also respond competitively. Here the causal or categorical link between actions and/or objects asserted by the first speaker is denied. This may involve a simple statement of rejection without an accompanying reason. Here there is simply a flat, "No." Alternatively, there may be a rejection of the first speaker's claim of causal, categorical, or evaluative relationship by suggesting a different relationship. For example, the second speaker may assert that textbooks are not boring or that students remain interested even if the textbook is boring. This competitive exchange may be extended with more assertions that bolster the claim of one side by offering supportive examples, citing supportive authoritative dictates, or emphasizing the authority of the supported speaker. In complementary fashion, one side may be diminished by offering contradictory examples of specific experience, citing contrary authoritative dictates or by pointing to the de-authorizing or de-legitimating qualities of the opposed speaker. Except where such competitive conversation is a matter of established social convention, the discussion becomes a competition between the belief, values,or identities that create or maintain social distance or distinction between the opposed participants.

The resulting quarrel may be resolved in one of several ways. One possibility is the claims of one side dominate as the opposing side acquiesces. There is a simple assertion of truth/power by one side over another. In a group discussion, this result may reflect the weight of numbers as participants not directly involved choose sides either because they share the same view or because they wish to reinforce their social connection to one side or distance themselves from the other. A second possibility is that a relevant civility rule is asserted and the claims of the two sides are peremptorily reconciled. This may be done by simply combining the two positions (without regard to existing incompatibilities). For example, there may be a joint recognition that both parties are right, or at least partially right. Alternatively the parties may agree to simply set their argument aside. Often this is accomplished indirectly through a form of conversational repair, for example, when one party makes a joke about the disagreement. In either case, conversation continues by turning to another aspect of the topic or to a different topic altogether. The third possibility is that the discourse is discontinued. Here the participants may choose to resolve the dispute by other means (e.g., a flip of the coin, recourse to an authoritative judge, or physical combat) or by simply withdrawing.

7.1.2 Cooperative discourse

Aim of the discourse. In cooperative discourse, the orienting aims of conventional discourse are reconstituted as objects of a second order discussion, one that has its own distinctive goals. One is to construct a *correct* understanding of the problem, both with regard to its elemental nature and dynamics. A critical approach is adopted toward participants' initial perceptions and specific cultural claims. The assumption is that these perceptions are likely to reflect a narrow and superficial focus. Consequently in the deliberation, an attempt is made to understand the problem better by considering both the relationship among its aspects and the relationship between the specific problem and the larger context in which it emerges. Similarly, in the discussion of cultural conventions, an attempt is made to insure that the invocation of any particular cultural definition or prescription is consistent with a broader understanding of the practical or social problem in question and with other possibly relevant cultural claims that might be made.

A second goal of cooperative discourse is to construct a *shared* understanding of the problem and how it is being addressed. A tentative approach is adopted toward what is regarded as the apparent meaning of the particular claims made by the individual participants. The presumption is that different individuals may be exposed to different experiences and different aspects of the broader culture and therefore may have different frames of reference for the claims they make. As a result different people may not understand a particular claim in the same way. The result will not be so much disagreement as misunderstanding. Recognizing this, a cooperative discourse involves a good deal of mutual interpretation in an effort to generate a shared understanding of the matter at hand.

The formal qualities of the discourse. The basic element of a cooperative discourse is the presentation of a perspective. This involves making a propositional claim of the relationship between concrete actions and then relating that claim to other propositional claims that constitute that system of meaning in which all the related claims are embedded. The cooperative exchange of these elemental perspectives is coordinated on three bases. The first are rules of argumentation. These rules regulate how claims may be related to each other and to the objective reality (physical, social, or personal) they are intended to represent. Included here is the demand that claims be elaborated, explained, justified, and challenged by presenting related claims (reasons) and evidence in a manner that follows the rules of logic and reliable observation. The second are fundamental assumptions regarding the general qualities of the world. These assumptions provide individuals with a common general ground to which they can refer when making specific arguments based on their different perspectives. Included here are assumptions regarding the basic organizational structure and dynamic qualities of the natural world of objects, the social world of human beings in groups, and the subjective world of the self. The third basis for the coordination of discourse rests on the foundations of the second. It involves a shared understanding of the social conditions required to maintain a cooperative exchange among individuals with potentially differing perspectives. This then suggests guidelines for determining who should be included in any particular discussion and how they should interact with one another.

Structured in this way, cooperative discourse is organized around a general subject rather than a particular concrete topic. The subject of the discourse is the systemic quality of the problem and the systemic context in which the problem is understood to be embedded. To be relevant, propositional claims must be related to the objective, social, or subjective context to which they refer. At any point in the discourse, only one of these contexts is likely to be emphasized while the other two are bracketed out. In this way dimensions of the discourse subject may be differentiated from one another and the discourse organized accordingly. For example, discussion may be structured so that the objective nature of the problem and the feasibility of different solutions may be considered first, and a consideration of the social value of different solutions be considered second. In addition, any given dimension of the problem may be internally organized by differentiating its constitutive aspects and then ordering them relative to one another. For example, the discussion of the objective dimension of the problem of education may include an attempt to differentiate different aspects of education according to administrative, teaching, or student management functions and then to organize the discourse to address each of these functions in turn. Organized in this way, the different turns in the discourse are related to one another as cooperative efforts to inform, to critique and to revise different perspectives with the aim of establishing a better and shared understanding of the problem at hand. This requires attention to both the subject of the discussion and to the views of individual speakers.

The dynamics of the discourse.   Cooperative discourse is initiated when conventional discourse fails (or is anticipated to fail). Irresolvable disagreement may emerge when participants do not refer to the same experiences, authorities or social conventions. At this point, conventional discourse may be suspended and a cooperative discourse may be initiated. Such a discourse typically begins with an attempt to sketch the basic contours of the subject to be considered. This may include a preliminary discussion of the bases of the initial disagreement and the dimensions or aspects of the problem addressed. This may lead to initial (and revisable) agreement as to how to organize the ensuing discussion.

In the discussion, any speaker may begin to present her perspective on the subject by making a propositional claim. In so doing, she recognizes that her understanding of the meaning and value of her claim is relative to her own subjective perspective and that the listeners' perspectives may differ from her own. Consequently the speaker will anticipate possible misunderstanding and the objections that will follow from it. This attitude will be reflected in her often unprompted attempts (i) to clarify the meaning of her claim by placing it in perspective, that is, relative to other claims she regards to be true or right, (ii) to explore possible specific differences of experience, knowledge, and preference that exist between her and the listeners, (iii) to explicate her claims with reference to the listener's perspective, and (iv) to validate her claims with reference to the fundamental assumptions that she and her audience share about the general nature of the objective world, social relations, and persons.

When disagreement arises, discussion will focus on the justifications for claims made. This may involve critical commentary on whether a justification violates commonly accepted rules of logic, coherence, and reliable observation. Alternatively the focus may be on the incompatibility of a claim or its justification with commonly accepted fundamental assumptions about the quality or dynamic of objective reality, society, or personality. In either case, an attempt is made to argue the incorrectness of another's claim in terms that she is likely to accept as binding. A disagreement may also be resolved by incorporating the differing positions under a common umbrella. Here reference is made to common rules and assumptions to demonstrate that the two positions are either complementary (perhaps illuminating different aspects of the same phenomena) or equally valid. In the latter instance, the two positions are defined as different results of drawing upon the same common basic assumptions and applying the same rules of logic and observation. The result is acceptable disagreement in which both the validity and distinctiveness of each position are acknowledged.[3]

Two kinds of circumstances prevent the engagement of cooperative discourse. In one case, one or more participants do not recognize or are incapable of using the basic rules of argument. In this case their contributions to the discourse will be devalued as substandard. Communication toward them may assume a pedagogical or care-taking character. Alternatively they will be excluded from the discourse or their contributions will be ignored. In the second case, one or more of the participants do not share the basic underlying assumptions of the others. This is likely when participants come from very different cultural backgrounds. Where discourse rules or foundational assumptions are not shared, the requisite common ground for cooperative discourse is lost and it reverts to a more conventional form. Given initial disagreement at this level, this may in turn lead to physical struggle to determine both the response to the present problem and the conditions of future discourse.

7.1.3   Collaborative discourse

Aims of the discourse.   While attempting to address particular problems, collaborative discourse aims to develop the psychological resources of the participants and the cultural resources available to them in the larger sociocultural environment. This involves reflecting on their discourse itself. In this vein, the discussion of a problem is used as an opportunity to focus on the processes whereby rules of argumentation are formulated, basic assumptions regarding nature, society, and individuals are defined, and the social conditions of the discourse are understood and institutionalized. Most important, this is done in a way that considers both (i) the current capacity and the developmental potential of the particular individuals involved and (ii) the current quality and transformative potential of the socio-cultural context that is structuring how those individuals are engaging one another. The objective is to foster modes of communication that not only enhance the subjective capacities and the integrity of the individuals involved, but also contribute to the flexibility and sustainability of the larger social context in which they are embedded. The goal is transformation, both personal and collective. At all times, this goal is defined and pursued relative to the particulars of the individuals involved and the socio-historical context of their discursive exchange.

Formal qualities of the discourse. The basic element of the discourse is a communicative strategy. It consists of an attempt to engage others in a collaborative effort to reconstruct (i) who each participant is (as a reflective subject and purposive agent), (ii) how the cultural context dictates how the participants interact with one another, and (iii) how these personal and cultural features of the discussion situation impact one another. This effort does not consist of a single contribution to a conversation, but a related series of contributions with a common goal. Such a communicative strategy is necessarily multifaceted. On the one hand it has a cognitive dimension. Addressing differences in perspective, it involves offering an interpretative reconstruction of the logic whereby the claims that constitute a given perspective are defined and related to one another. This includes giving an account of the formal qualities of both the rules used to relate claims to one another and the foundational assumptions in reference to which claims are validated. Given its transformative goals, this interpretative reconstruction also involves an attempt to explain how these structuring rules and assumptions reflect the subjective capacities of the individual speakers and the socio-culturally mediated relationship between them. On the other hand, a communicative strategy has an explicitly socio-emotional component. It seeks to lead participants to engage one another in a discussion of their personal reasoning, feelings, identities, and social connections that not only affirms these critical elements of their personal and collective being, but also seeks to transform them. Consequently, these participants are rendered unusually vulnerable. In order to promote the personal security, trust, and caring that a potentially transformative discourse requires, a communicative strategy necessarily includes initiatives that are intended to enhance the self-esteem, affective bonds, and commitments of the individuals involved.

As the interplay of communicative strategies, a collaborative discourse consists of a joint effort typically extending across a number of discussions. Such a collaborative discourse is not structured, at least not in any static or universal sense. It does not consist of one particular way of organizing how individuals communicate and therefore does not have specific formal properties. Instead it is characterized by a structuring dynamic, one that reflects the qualities of the subjectively structured discursive strategies of particular subject-participants and of the culturally structured manner in which these participants communicate with one another. In this light, the static formal qualities of a given collaborative discourse will be the particular product of the specific individuals involved and the socio-historical setting of their interaction. At the same time, this particular formal result is understood to be unstable. The capacity for individuals to reflect on their own subjectivity as they are engaged in communication with others and their ability to jointly consider the terms of their inter-subjective engagement gives collaborative discourse a developmental potential, one that may lead to a reconstruction of individuals, their community, and the discourse itself.

Dynamic of the discourse. When cooperative discourse fails, a collaborative discourse may be initiated. Given its reconstructive and critical qualities, collaborative discourse draws heavily both on the intellectual and emotional energies of its participants, and on the social and cultural resources of the larger social groups to which they belong. It therefore requires a special commitment. As a result, a collaborative discourse typically begins by establishing that it is in fact necessary. This may be done by referring to evidence in the prior discussion of the contested nature of basic rules of argument and foundational assumptions or the inadequacy of the social conditions of the exchange. The key here is the evident incommensurability of the ways in which different individuals are reasoning about or affectively responding to each other's contributions. This may be understood to reflect a difference in the cognitive and emotional capacities of the individuals involved or in the ways of understanding and discussing that is characteristic of the cultural groups to which those individuals belong. In either case, the conclusion drawn is that the current deliberation is being conducted in such a way that the individuality of the participants or the integrity of the group is being inadequately expressed or actively undermined. This may be confirmed by appealing to the sense of confusion, dissatisfaction, or alienation of the individual participants and to the apparent conflict among the ethnic, religious, or political groups to which they belong. On this basis, an explicit call will be made for the personal commitment and the open social space that collaborative discourse requires.

With its necessity and requirements established, a collaborative discussion or series of discussions may then begin. Initially this may focus on the failed attempt at cooperative discourse and thus on how the participants differ in their conception of how to arrive at a correct and shared understanding of the policy problem previously addressed. This will include both a consideration of how each participant is defining and explaining the problem and how each is responding to the other's attempt to communicate her point of view. This may include a consideration of both the cognitive and emotional dimensions of the interaction. Participants will not only attempt to expressly consider others' understandings, but also their feelings. At the same time, they will make an effort to express their own understandings and feelings to enhance their communicative and social relationship with their listeners. Following any one contribution, the interpretations offered and the emotions expressed may be addressed by other participants. This may include attempts to probe the meaning of what is being said by asking for clarifications, further elaborations, or extensions of the argument in new directions.

Explanations and justifications may be probed by a request to justify the account given. This attempt to assess the meaning of the views presented will eventually lead to attempts to characterize the formal or general quality of the inferential associations and foundational assumptions a given participant is making. Finally, the structure of the meanings expressed may be pragmatically linked to the cultural context of the discourse in order to show how it is shaped by and sustains social structuring forces. At issue here is the kind of interaction or discussion among participants that their broader context enables or prevents and its implications for who each participant can be in the discussion situation. This may provide the basis for cultural critique as well as personal reflection. Importantly, this collaborative effort may extend beyond boundaries of the formal deliberation by creating opportunities for participants to interact with one another in different social settings.

In the course of this collaborative discussion, differences in meaning-making will emerge more clearly and the ambiguity of apparently shared meanings will become apparent. The result will be a certain mutual lack of comprehension. Participants may recognize the relativity of their own way of understanding and the limits of their ability to properly understand or be understood by each other. This may lead to an attempt to construct an overarching frame of reference to facilitate mutual recognition and understanding of the different views being constructed and a means of purely collaborative exchange. This depends on people recognizing that while they may have different perspectives and capacities to construct perspectives, they are all sentient, thinking, feeling, social beings that act on the world and connect to one another. It also requires that the participants come to recognize their own interdependence. There must be some appreciation of how each person's way of thinking/feeling (and thus the kind of person she is) depends on how people engage one another. The resulting collaboration is a mixed attempt to forge commonalities and connections and to recognize differences and distance. This will include ongoing attempts to recognize and understand differences in how each of them is thinking, feeling, and talking about the issues being discussed by placing the varying ways in which different individuals are thinking in a complementary relationship with one another. These attempts may take different forms. One possibility is a pedagogical discourse predicated on a shared assumption that the individuals recognize that they share comparable potential, but that they differ in their current cognitive and emotional capacities to act and connect to one another. Another possibility is collaborative discourse predicated on a shared assumption that individuals reason and feel differently and yet are interdependent. The discourse here is oriented to creating mutually satisfying (if not fully comprehended) exchange that respects basic differences.

Collaborative discourses are realized in different ways depending on the capacities of the particular participants involved and the particular socio-cultural context in which they are interacting. Thus issues of the meaning or value of things, the nature of persons and cultural contexts and how these factors affect one another may be addressed at different levels of reflection, with different levels of inter-subjective collaboration and with differing degrees of comfort or safety. Any kind of collaborative discourse ends when new understandings of the problem, oneself, others, and the group emerge that resonate with the ways in which the individuals are thinking and how they are talking to one another. This may involve personal and social development or it may involve the construction of a complementarity that allows individuals to recognize their fundamental differences and communicate, even if only partially, across them. Alternatively, and perhaps more typically, a collaborative discourse will fail to achieve such a social integration. Instead the result is a dissensus in which the parties only achieve a clearer sense of the particularity of their own way of judging matters and a greater appreciation of the extent to which they do not understand and are not understood by others. But rather than being regarded as an anomalous or threatening state of affairs, this result is recognized to be normal and even desirable. In the latter case, the incommensurability of ways of understanding is understood as affirmation of the integrity of individuals and a resource for further creative engagement.

7.2   Methodology

The aim of the empirical research was to discover the nature of the discourse that takes place in actual citizen deliberations. To this end, two citizen groups were convened to deliberate about the quality of K-12 education in their neighborhood. The particulars of this study and its results are presented below.

Subject population.   The subject population includes 24 adults from Laguna Beach, California. (This is a subset of the 72 adults who volunteered to participate in the various stages of the study.) Laguna Beach is an upper middle-class, largely white community of about 30,000. Participants in the study were recruited by a mailing sent to the parents of 700 children in the grammar and middle schools. Approximately one in ten of the households receiving letters responded with an intention to participate. The subject population reflected the demographics of the larger community except for gender, two-thirds of the participants were female. Approximately 80 percent of the subjects were college educated (over three times the U.S. national average). Laguna Beach was selected as the site of the present study because it was believed to afford an environment that was unusually congenial to effective deliberation. Because of their relative wealth and education and their history of high levels of participation in community politics, it was assumed that residents of Laguna Beach would be unusually capable participants in a citizen deliberation.

Methods and procedures. The study combined an academic interest in analyzing the nature of citizen deliberation with a political interest in promoting citizen empowerment and practical action. Thus it was designed both to explore the nature of citizen deliberation and to encourage deliberative democracy practice in the local community. One result is that there are few issues of external validity – the deliberations included citizens who deliberated real issues of concern to them leading to policy recommendations forwarded to relevant policy makers.

Recognizing the potential mobilizing power of education as a political issue, a decision was made to initiate deliberations on the goals and conduct of K-12 education in the public schools of the City of Laguna Beach. Following preliminary discussions with school administrators, teachers, and some parents, parents were invited to participate in a deliberation about the delivery of public education in their community. (Laguna Beach constitutes its own school district and thus is self-governing in this respect.)

The volunteers were assigned to one of two groups, each of which consisted of twelve members (as in the citizen juries of England or Australia). Assignment was largely random, but also reflected the need to convene groups that reflected subjects' individual time constraints. In the initial design, each group was to meet six times every other week. However because the participants felt they needed extra time to complete their task, the groups met seven times. Each meeting lasted two hours. At the first meeting, the goals of the deliberation, to make policy recommendations and to encourage parental participation in school governance, were reiterated. The first four or five meetings were devoted largely to a discussion of current practices and a consideration of improvements or alternatives. The last two meetings were devoted to coming to consensus about recommendations to be communicated to the School Board and principals. All meetings were audio- and videotaped.

Each group was led by two facilitators. One had primary responsibility and the other played a support role. The facilitators were members of the research team (three advanced Ph.D. candidates in political psychology and me). Facilitators were given specific instructions regarding how to conduct themselves during the meeting. Throughout, the lead facilitator's role was to insure conversation was civil and when necessary (which was rare) to help coordinate participant turn-taking. During the first three-and-a-half meetings, the facilitators were instructed to actively intervene in a number of ways to encourage the participants to consider their specific concerns in broader contexts. This included beginning the first meeting by asking participants to postpone the consideration of specific issues and to begin by addressing two general questions: (i) What kind of people did they want their children to be when they reached the age of eighteen? (ii) What role might the schools play in reaching that goal? In addition, when the discussion provided an opening, facilitators were instructed to raise issues of justice and fairness (for example, when participants raised the possibility of greater support for either gifted or disadvantaged children) and the common good (how would this affect the neighborhood or the larger Laguna community). Facilitators were instructed to limit interventions of this kind to no more than twice a meeting. In the last three-and-a-half meetings, facilitators were told not to intervene in this fashion and thus leave the participants to address issues as they deemed appropriate.

The meetings typically began slowly as some members arrived late and initial exchanges were more social and less issue-focused. The quality of the deliberations declined somewhat as members tired during the last half hour of discussion. In the desire to explore the deliberations at their best, the analysis here focused on the middle hour of each deliberative session. These middle hours were transcribed, and were analyzed by two coders. The coders were unaware both of the analysis of the other coder and the identity of the group whose deliberations they were analyzing. Their task was to divide each one-hour session into its successive segments and determine the structure of each segment (conventional discourse, cooperative discourse, and collaborative discourse) and record its length (in minutes). A segment was defined as a portion of the deliberation that was structured in the same way (e.g., conventionally) and distinguished from the next segment by a shift in structure (e.g., from conventional to cooperative).

7.3   Results

In the initial task of distinguishing discrete segments of discourse, coders did agree on the identification of core segments 84 percent of the time. This allowed for slight variation (one or two conversational turns) in determining the specific point of initiation or determination of a segment. Where there was disagreement, coders met and common lines of demarcation were adopted. With regard to the analysis of the structure of each segment, intercoder reliability was 92 percent.

From the perspective of deliberative democratic theory, the most important result of the study was the relative prominence of different forms of discourse in the deliberations. Beginning with the most demanding type, the analysis suggests that no collaborative discourse emerged in either deliberative group at any point in their deliberations. This may come as no surprise given that cultural expectations regarding a policymaking discussion would leave little room for open discussion on such matters as how individual participants constructed their understandings or how their interaction with one another was regulated by conventional rules and foundational assumptions that might be inappropriate or inadequate. The initiation of a collaborative discourse requires an explicit recognition of the failure of cooperative discourse and explicit call for a different kind of conversation. This did not occur. This evidence of no collaborative discourse in the course of seven two-hour sessions suggests that typical citizen deliberations may not perform the critical or emancipatory role that some theorists might attribute to it.

The deliberations did include some cooperative discourse, but it was unexpectedly rare. In one deliberative group there were only two instances of a cooperative exchange and in the other there was none. The two instances mentioned combined for a total of approximately 14 minutes of the 14 hours of discourse that were coded. This was surprising for two reasons. First, the participants, by the standards of the American population as a whole, had unusually high levels of formal education and income. The presumption here (and certainly one that is made in most deliberative democratic theory) is that participants of this kind have the experience and capacity to engage in cooperative discourse. Second, the group facilitators actively attempted to encourage more cooperative discourse by (a) beginning the deliberation by shifting the focus away from some specific complaints or desires to a consideration of the basic goals of education, and (b) by occasionally (twice in each of the second, third, and fourth meetings) posing questions that raised broader issues of justice as fairness and the common good. Despite the presumed capacities of the participants and the encouragement of the facilitators, the deliberation about educational policy and practice was rarely cooperative.

It should be noted that certain participants did, on occasion, respond to the facilitator's initiatives or spontaneously try to steer the deliberations in the direction of a more cooperative discourse. Interestingly these initiatives were typically met with resistance. Some was overt. Other participants explicitly rejected the cooperative initiative suggesting that the conversation avoid abstract or hypothetical issues in favor of a focus on the specific concrete concerns currently being addressed. More often the resistance was more subtle. In this case, participants responded by ignoring the attempt to move to a more cooperative discourse and simply continued as they had been doing previously.

The vast majority of the deliberative discussions analyzed were clearly conventional. This was true when deciding on topics to address, discussing the nature of the problem or addressing differences in opinion. At times, discussion would shift to a more proto-discourse, particularly when a particular group meeting was first beginning or ending. Here talk became more routinized and less clearly other-oriented. However during the active policy discussion in the middle hour of each deliberation, conversational moves in this direction were infrequent. When such a move was made, its inappropriateness or irrelevance (when placed in the context of a conventional discourse) was not addressed directly. Instead other participants simply ignored the initiative and continued the discourse at the conventional level.

Examples of types of discourse. Here several excerpts from the deliberations are presented to illustrate the different types of discourse. The first is extracted from a longer discussion of one of the goals of education, to teach children to become competent economic actors. The excerpted exchange is conventional in several respects. First, conversational relevance requires remarks be directed toward the topic and thus produces a discussion that is organized as list of the attributes of the topic. There is no attempt to relate these aspects to one another, either conceptually or conversationally (i.e., by introducing a new attribute by reference to an earlier one). In this brief excerpt, the following attributes are mentioned: being able to learn, to communicate, to handle money by investing, to consider retirement, to understand health insurance, and to balance a checkbook. Second, remarks are also relevant, if only in a secondary way, if they are addressed to a particular comment of an earlier speaker. This typically consists of a simple statement of support (e.g., turns 2, 9, beginning 10) a simple counterclaim (e.g., turn 7, 11, 15), or an implicitly critical questioning (e.g., turn 5). These usually receive a minimal response or are simply passed by in the discussion. Third, questions of meaning are not raised. Participants do not ask one another what they mean by what they are asserting. Fourth, when reasons are offered, they are typically not addressed directly and then subjected to critical consideration.

1. Ri   The thing is as an economic actor, you're also faced with a rapidly changing environment. And you have to be able not only to use the skills you've acquired and the knowledge you've acquired; you also have to be learn new things quickly.
2. Lza   Right.
3. Ri   Because today if the school doesn't teach you how to learn, how to process information, and how to evolve, you would be very quickly out of work basically.
4. Lza   Well isn't one of the skills that's going to separate a winner from a loser in life, the ability to communicate? And I think that's something that's overlooked in education. Because they have to come out with all these facts, and they have to take these tests tests tests based on facts. But they really can't sit around a table like this and explain themselves at all. They can't articulate their opinions, their classes are too big to have a discussion ... And whether it's verbally or on paper, with emails, I can't believe my kid's emails, sometimes I think, aren't you embarrassed to send that out?
5. Da   Did you have that in your education?
6. Lza   No, but that's why I'm even ... no because I had to learn this the hard way. I was always playing catch up because I didn't have basic grammar. I wasn't asked to write essays. And a lot of it, it's class size, 'cause work load, you know a teacher has five periods with twenty-five kids, but if we don't get these kids to be able to [think], if they're gonna vote, they gotta know why. Or be able to have an intelligent conversation to express their point of view. And then back it up with something ...

7. Liz   But now what they need to know is science and math.
8. Lza   Yeah. But if they can't write a letter, write an email, write a proposal, you know if you could be the most brilliant scientist, but you're going to have to write a grant, and give it to the government and say, you should support my research because x, y, and z. But if they can't write that down in a clear way, so I think that [what] should be, [to Ri] on this journey, is to be able to communicate.
9. Ri   It's definitely a critical point.
10. Fr   I think that's an important point. Before we get off the economic actor, I want to remind you that there are lots and lots of high school investment clubs, where kids are reading the stock market reports every day. And they have a pool of money and they're being taught how to read the market reports and how to invest. And its very feasible. And so part of being an economic actor is to understand how money works in the culture ... Every kid has to handle money, they all do.
11. Th   Talk about retirement. You know how you're going to live when you're not working.
12. Fr   Oh gosh, it's hard for them to even think about how they're going to spend their allowance.
13. Di   Well even what you were saying about health insurance. I wish that people would sit down with kids and talk about how far does money really go in the real world? I don't think they have any sense of, you know, so now say you get sick and have to go to the doctor and if you don't have insurance how do you pay for it?
14. Ci   But did you know all of that?
15. Di   No but, I wish I had.
16. Ci   I think experiencing life in general is an education itself. It's just a process.
17. Th   We had to learn how to balance a checkbook, we had to keep ...

The following two excerpts illustrate the limits of conventional discourse and the difficulties that consequently may arise. In the first excerpt, Di and Ci are both interested in introducing media education into the schools. However Di is interested in the consumption of mass media and Ci is interested in the use of media technology. The exchange proceeds as though they are discussing the same thing and even when they begin to discover they are not, the disparity is not really addressed. Instead conversation at turn 9 shifts to another topic.

1. Di: To me, it's huge, the way our children receive information through the consumerism, from the time they're two years old, what their expectations are, versus what reality is. And I really think it would be worthwhile to teach the kids to filter the information

they're receiving, because I think it sets them up to have anxiety, to fail, you know they don't really know how to identify what they like. ... We pour all this stuff from the outside world into them and I think then they ...

2. Ci   So you're saying media awareness taught in public education that's kind of what I'm trying to get to, because when the media's in the schools, it's like they don't use it.

3. Di   I'm just saying when a child gets, I don't know if you ever, they had a great woman for Thurston, and she kind of gets the kids to understand about who's selling them this, what does that really mean. What does that really do to the world when you buy all this stuff, where does it go, all this junk you're buying, and how long do you keep it? And what does that, just you know responsibility as a citizen of the planet, and what are we supposed to do as a consequence of our lifestyle.

4. Ci   So what I hear you saying is that you want to bring it into the curriculum.

5. Di   I don't know if it could be something, maybe, that parents get kids to do on the side. I don't know, but just, I don't think it would be a bad idea to have some little block where the kids ...

6. Ci   Yeah because if we had real librarians then they would teach the kids about media, as far as internet. It's just that California chooses not to have librarians in their schools.

7. Di   No I mean beyond that, I mean if you could get the (inaudible)

8. Ci   But I'm trying to figure out how it integrates into the education system ...

In the second excerpt, after Ma questions the value of fostering independent thinking, the facilitator (FC) raises the problem of the meaning directly and introduces it as a subject for group discussion (turn 5). After a little unease (reflected by the laughter), the group begins. Even in this context, discussion consists of a listing of attributes with no elaboration or cooperative probing or developing of the meaning of the particular claims individual participants are making.

1. Ma   I think it is really important to get these kids motivated. I think that maybe it is important that it is goal oriented, freedom of choice oriented, see the results of your choices. I think there is a difference between critical thinking, which I think is really good, and independent thinking which at too early an age or even in junior high, they start thinking that they are too smart for this school. They start not going to school. And the whole thing compounds itself and it's just not a good situation.

2. Cra   Well you got to learn before ...

3. Chr   Right.
4. [Brief cross talk]
5. FC   It depends on what we mean by independent thinking.
6. [Everyone laughs, a number of participants say, "yah, yah."]
7. Ang   You can have independent thinking without being arrogant.
8. Chr   I think you can be quite responsible and be socially aware in an independent way but it is not spoon fed. It is not ...
9. Ang   That is the difference.
10. Eliz What comes in is your responsibility as a parent at home. What kinds of independent thinking are you fostering? I mean how independent are you trying to get your six-year-old to what kind of decisions she should be making ...
11. Chr   It depends how far you think they are going to go.
12. Eliz Exactly.
13. Sha   Well that is where the values come in. Do you do your homework after school or do you do it after dinner. That is an important choice to make, but you can make it. So you can have some independence.
14. The   Sure.
15. [A momentary lull and the topic shifts to teachers posing questions during class.]

The next excerpt provides an example of cooperative discourse. The exchange between To and Ri is exemplary in several respects. First, To attempts to articulate a general understanding of the current educational enterprise and the alternative strategy he is proposing (turns 1, 3, 10). He does so in a way that recognizes the perspectives of others, both by trying to incorporate their concerns (turn 3) and by elaborating his distinct perspective so that they may understand. Second, Ri engages To's effort. At several points, Ri offers his understanding or a clarification of what To is trying to communicate (e.g., turns 2, 9, 11, 13, 15). Third, To responds directly to Ri's inquiries and concerns (12, 14). Fourth, Ri then places the immediate discussion in the broader context of how the subject matter has been organized. In turn 17, Ri provides a general interpretation of the meaning of To's perspective. In so doing, he reminds To that the current focus is on goals and that strategies have been bracketed out for the moment. The exchange ends because To nods agreement and the discussion returns to elaborating the goal of educating citizenship.

1. To   This kind of hits the core of what I was thinking about after we got out last time. ... what you want for [from] academics. I kind of realized when I was thinking about it that we're so outcome based in our teaching. All we teach is the outcome. We don't really let you see the process or development of anything that's come [inaudible] that we miss out on a lot of history.

I was just thinking about like, well you know, the calendar. How do we have this calendar? All we learn about is the months and days and stuff, and then we're done. But if you go back to learn how the heck that calendar came about, you learn a lot of things about the math that you learn and how it's used, and the world ...

2. Ri   Are you saying ...

3. To   ... [inaudible] that process being taught, than the outcome. So that the students are going through and learning history. I wouldn't teach history as history, I would teach history as a part of whatever it is I'm teaching. Just kind of development. And we could do this with all the different subjects you all have talked about as being important ...

4. Ci   Tom you are radical.

5. [General laughter]

6. Ri   So basically you teach it not as an objective ...

7. Ci   I'm kidding.

8. [crosstalk]

9. Ri   Okay education is not a place where you want to be, it's not an objective you're trying to reach, it's a journey.

10. To   Right. You know, I got to thinking, my mission basically, I got to thinking what is it you want to achieve in your education. I tried to simplify it as much as possible. And I said to myself, ... what I want [is] a basic curriculum that just touches on how to teach the media. Which would be arts and games and things, but media, from day one. I would teach commerce, the law, health and medicine and technology. And that would be my basic program throughout your years.

11. Ri   No history?

12. To   Well history, that's what I'm saying. History is taught ... through that. So if you teach commerce, you go back to when you start valuing money. So you get to the point of math, where you understand money, then you can start to learn about commerce and work your way through well, how did that happen. Then you get into exploration, you get into wars, you get into all these aspects to talk about. But you start with basic, simplified knowledge, when you're young, instead of trying to remember the fifty states, you journey through the states and pick it up as you go, through history. There's all these different things, same with health, when you learn about ...

13. Ri   What you were saying basically ... you were taking some objectives, and you were looking at a different way of getting there.

14. To   Right.

15. Ri   Almost devising a new strategy ... teaching strategy. Which has a lot of implications, you know, how you teach. ...

16. To   That's what I was wondering, what do you teach in order to get –
17. Ri   Exactly, so you're already defining solutions basically on how to reach the objectives, and I think we haven't really cleared all the objectives and we haven't agreed on all the objectives.
18. [To nods agreement and the topic shifts]

The foregoing excerpt is also interesting in two other respects, both of which relate to the conversational move made by Ci, with some support from the larger group, early in the exchange. To begin, this is interesting as an example of conventional resistance to the initiation of cooperative discourse. Ci's move in turn 4 and the supportive group laughter that follows constitute an attempt to resist To's initiation of a cooperative exchange. Ci engages To in a more conventional discourse, both by implicitly rejecting his effort to present a whole perspective (his educational alternative) and in doing so by simply labeling him in a negative and alienating way. Although the move fails, attempts to resist cooperative discourse through conventional responses typically succeeded in this group's deliberation.

In addition, this exchange revolving around Ci and To is interesting for its failure to take advantage of an opening for a more collaborative exchange. The group discussion could have focused on this resistance to a shift in type of discourse. Questions could have been raised regarding what Ci understood To's effort to involve, how she felt about it and why other group members responded by laughing. In this context, To's response to Ci's initiative and their differing understandings of the topic could also have been explored. This may have led to a more collaborative consideration of the group members' differing logics and ways of constructing meaning as well as the nature of the social relationships among them. In addition, questions could have been raised regarding the way the group felt constrained in the kinds of issues, both political and socio-emotional, it could address and why it was constrained in this way.

7.4   Forms of discourse, deliberative democratic practice and constituting citizenship

The two deliberations observed in this study were assumed to occur under conditions that were unusually favorable to the conduct of democratic deliberation. The participants were highly educated, relatively wealthy individuals who volunteered to meet seven times to discuss a topic that was of serious concern to both of them. Their background and evident motivation suggest that they would be unusually good deliberators. In addition, the topic they were addressing, the education of their children, was rich with the potential for a critical consideration of social dynamics and orienting cultural values. This potential was occasionally evident in their disagreements. Some participants advocated challenging students with a more demanding curriculum that would prepare them to be competitive in the economic marketplace.

Others were more concerned with pedagogy that focused on students' emotional well-being and was geared toward producing young adults who were more socially responsible to each other and their community. Despite the capacities of the deliberators and the richness of the problem they addressed, the group deliberations generally did not rise either to the level of cooperative discourse expected in more liberal democratic conceptions of deliberation or to the level of collaborative discourse expected by more critical and emancipatory democratic conceptions. This raises questions about the political implications of the different kinds of discourse. A central issue here is the democratic quality of the different discourses. To address this, I briefly consider the nature of the personal autonomy, political relationships, and critical reflection fostered by conventional, cooperative, and collaborative discourse (see Table 7.2). In so doing, I view communicative

Table 7.2   Political implications of types of discourse[a]

	Conventional	Cooperative	Collaborative
Construction of self as actor	Selfish pursuit of externally dictated interests and/or selfless conformity to social conventions	Self as author of belief and preference. Is a self-regulating system, a personality, and a thinker	Self as active, socially embedded actor who constructs meaning and value in collaboration with others
Socio-political definition of individual	Individual defined by specific behavior and by social role, status or group membership	Abstract concept of the individual as self-directing system that has inherent integrity	Self as a construction produced both by the individual and through his interaction with others
Political relationship fostered	Rigid set of role and situation specific relationships based on social convention and cultural definition	General relationship of equals that may be variously realized in specific social situations	A productive relationship of complementarity among individuals that may be manifestly unequal
Impact of deliberation	Coordinates behavior in a way that reinforces existing conventional practices and cultural prescriptions	Allows for critique of specific cultural beliefs or conventional practices. Operates to sustain dominant ways of thinking and foundational assumptions	Allows for critique of dominant ways of thinking, rules of argument, and foundational assumptions. Creates complementary, rather than shared understandings and values. Facilitates personal and community development
Limits of deliberation	Cannot address differences in belief or behavior produced by differing personal experience or cultural exposure	Cannot address different ways in which meaning is constructed. Cannot address differences in foundational assumptions and values	

Notes: [a] The first two rows, "construction of the self" and "socio-political definition of the individual," address the kind of autonomy different discourse enables. The third row, "political relationship fostered" addresses the kind of political relationship between participants that is created by different discourses. The last two rows speak to the kinds of political outcomes the different courses allow.

interaction as a constructive activity that enables certain forms of meaning, personhood, and interpersonal relationship to be realized in a given social interaction.

7.4.1 The democratic potential of conventional discourse

Conventional discourse has only limited democratic potential. Participants in such a discourse are constituted as autonomous, but their autonomy is a shallow one. In the discourse, the individual participant is constituted as having a set of wants and desires that are expressed as preferences and orient her action. Participants recognize themselves and each other in these terms. The individual is thus accorded a degree of self-determination. But this capacity for self-determination is significantly constrained. It is not the individual participants in a conventional discourse who freely define themselves and their preferences and thus determine how they may interact with others. Instead it is forces external to the participating individuals and their interaction that regulate how individuals may engage one another and therefore who each of them can be in the context of their exchange. Sociocultural definitions and rules (and to a certain extent objective realities) determine what claims may be made, how they may be related to one another and who can make which claims. As result, speech acts (and consequently the speakers who make them) are judged relative to objective realities, conventional practices, and social norms. Authority and value is located there and not in the individual speakers or listeners. In this context, there is little consideration of the personal integrity and contribution of the individual speaker. Speakers have socially defined roles to play and politeness rituals to enact. They must conform to these. Insofar as they do not, their value and place in the discourse will be diminished.

There is also little room for equality in conventional discourse. Speakers enter the discourse with their social status defined and their possibilities to speak and be heard thus determined. This prior allocation of communicative possibilities may extend to formal exclusion if the speakers belong to relevant out-groups. Even in democratic societies where there are abstract norms pertaining to equality of participation, these norms enter into conventional discourse only as ritual prescriptions of specific ways in which people are allowed to act in particular circumstances. Moreover these prescriptions are typically readily overridden by conventions regarding social practice, status, and power. Consequently, invitations to equal participation typically lead to the rejection of socially inappropriate contributions and to the diminution of those individuals who make them.

A final issue is the potential for critique in conventional discourse. Again space is provided, but only of a very restrictive kind. In discourse of this kind, discussion focuses on specific behaviors and beliefs. Claims will be made and defended by relating the behavior or belief in question to the particulars of an objective state or to specific conventional practices or cultural imperatives. The process consists of identifying, highlighting, and collecting what it is the participants already know. Because participants perceive the same reality and accept the cultural dictates, these kinds of justifications will compel agreement. The social meaning thus constructed is concrete, fragmentary (not internally coherent or coordinated), rigid, and culturally specific. Here direct experience and cultural dictates constitute the medium of meaning-making, not its object. They are not themselves subject to critical consideration. When their meaning or value of conventional beliefs or behaviors is questioned, the claims made will be rejected and those who make them will be denigrated.

7.4.2   The democratic potential of cooperative discourse

In many respects, cooperative discourse is well suited to democratic deliberation, particularly in its liberal conceptualization by theorists such as Rawls (1993), Cohen (1996), and Gutmann and Thompson (1996). Cooperative discourse constructs individual participants in a manner that is consistent with these theorists' assumptions of autonomy and equality. In the discourse, participants are constituted as individuals who observe, reason and reflect in a rational, integrative manner. In this context, individuals view themselves and others as subjects who construct their own beliefs and preferences and direct their actions accordingly. They are not only the pursuers of their preferences, but also the authors of their own understandings and generators of the personalities that give rise to those preferences. In this sense, they are regarded as fully self-determining and are in this sense autonomous.

At the same time, individuals are constituted as equal by virtue of their common and comparable capacities to be reasonable, reflective, self-directing subjects. In a cooperative discourse, this equal capacity for autonomous thought and action translates into a demand for equality of participation. Given their equal capacities and their varying experience, individuals are accorded equal opportunity, at least at the outset, to introduce their points of view freely into the discussion and have those points heard with respect. Similarly it is the agreed quality of the arguments made (an agreement voluntarily accepted by equals) rather than the status or power of the individual who makes them that will determine the relative impact different speakers have on the agreements finally reached. As a result, cooperative discourse typically carries with it normative demands of freedom and equality of opportunity for expression and will operate to protect individual participants accordingly.

Cooperative discourse opens up greater possibilities for social critique. Specific cultural claims or action prescriptions may be targeted for consideration and then judged with reference either to a systematic observation of the facts or in light of other related cultural definitions of fact or value. In the process, inter-subjective agreement may be reached on the falsehood or wrongness of the particular claim or convention and thereby produce effective critique of specific commonly accepted practices or beliefs. On the other hand, individuals may come to critically reflect on the adequacy of particular beliefs they hold or practices they engage in. Through reflection induced by a cooperative discourse with others, individuals may come to change some of their own particular beliefs and practices in a way that is not only more consistent with inter-subjectively agreed upon understandings, but also with their own subjective understandings and personality. Insofar as this involves reconsidering specific practices and beliefs that were learned or imposed by others, this frees the individual to uncover her own point of view and discover herself. This then enables her to direct her actions in a way that is more independent of particular circumstances or social influences.

Despite its advantages, there are significant limits to the social critique that cooperative discourse fosters. The problem is that argument based on reasons oriented to establishing inter-subjective agreement is limited to the use of rules of argument and foundational assumptions about the general nature of reality, human nature, discourse, and society that are already established and commonly accepted. These rules and assumptions may be clarified, but are not themselves subject to critical reflection. The basis rather than the object of discursive consideration, they are understood to be the invariable means for producing meaning and not a product of social, psychological, and political forces which may themselves vary. Consequently there is a tendency to regard these foundational rules and assumptions as universal. When an alternative set of rules and assumptions are detected, the alternative is typically denigrated or excluded from the discourse (e.g., Rawls's (1993) exclusion of comprehensive doctrines from the arena of political debate about fairness).

7.4.3   The deliberative democratic potential of collaborative discourse

Democratic potential.   Collaborative discourse is predicated on a conception of individuals and social relationship that suggests an understanding of basic political principles and governance, which differs from most liberal democratic thought. In collaborative discourse, individuals are defined by how they think and engage others. This is reflected in their capacity to construct the logics, meanings, and values that will determine what they can identify, understand, and value. Constituted in these terms, not only are individuals recognized to be the authors of their beliefs and preferences, they are also understood to be engaged in activity which structures the quality of their authorship. In this context, political autonomy is itself understood to be a construction, one which reflects the efforts of an individual to define, understand, and judge her own individuality and her relations to others. Collaborative discourse fosters the recognition that this constructive activity and the autonomy it engenders may take a variety of forms. As a result, some people may be more self-consciously constructive and thus more self-directing in the meanings and definitions they construct. They will therefore be able to exercise a greater level of autonomy. However these differences are not considered to be absolute or immutable. Instead, differences in the capacity for autonomous thought and action are regarded as differences in actual development achieved by individuals who share the same potential. Thus significant differences among individuals are recognized, but at the same time all individuals are regarded as potentially equal in their capacity to be autonomous and as essentially equal in their right to the respect and caring consideration of others.[4]

Complementing this view of individuals is a democratic, if not liberal democratic, conception of the political relationship between individuals. On the one hand, it recognizes that, in their autonomy, all individuals have a basic integrity, but at the same time they are fundamentally dependent on one another. The construction of meaning is not only an activity of a reflective subject, but also the activity of a group coordinating the exchange among its members. Indeed the two activities are intertwined in such a way that each requires the other. As a result, individuals depend on one another for their own personal development. Thus not only does a collaborative discourse require mutual respect, but it also requires mutual caring and support. On the other hand, a collaborative discourse recognizes that all individuals are not equally able to define their own meanings and purposes nor are they equally able to engage one another in discourse. This evident inequality does not, however, suggest disempowerment or the need for authority. Rather it creates a demand for complementarity – a coordination of perspectives and pursuits that both realizes the limits and enhances the capacities of the individuals involved. This complementarity is understood to depend on the collaborative, self-reflective efforts of individuals and the appropriate social structuring of the terms of their discursive engagement. The latter requires social regulation that facilitates interpersonal coordination, while recognizing the integrity and limits of individuals' autonomy.

Of the three types of discourse considered here, collaborative discourse encourages the broadest and deepest form of social and political critique. In its presumption of the psycho-social and dynamic qualities of how meaning and value are constructed, collaborative discourse fosters personal and collective criticism that is structural or systemic rather than substantive or particular. At the same time, it makes that critical activity the centerpiece of discussion. Discussion is thus understood as the medium both for the expression and the construction of personal autonomy and cooperative social exchange. It is here that citizens can express the quality as well as the substance of their point of view and who they are. It is also in the play of the differences between individuals that citizens can also develop and reconstruct how they think and therefore who they can be. It is thus an explicit vehicle for deepening autonomy and thus for emancipation. At the same time, collaborative discourse allows for the expression and transformation of the conditions of communicative exchange. In the discourse, there is an exploration of the fragmentation of cultural meanings and the social divisions among the participants. At the same time, there is an attempt to establish a means for communicating these distinctions and thus creating at least thin communitarian bonds among otherwise different groups. Thus the limits of current ways of communicating and interacting are recognized and alternative means are explored.

7.5 Conclusion

I have attempted to offer a more differentiated understanding of the nature of discourse and democratic deliberation. Applying this theoretical understanding of deliberative discourses to the empirical study of actual citizen deliberations led to several conclusions. First, the quality of the discourse varies in the course of a deliberation. Second, even in what might be considered the favorable case of highly educated, empowered adults raised in a liberal democratic polity, the deliberation very rarely was rational, reasonable, or critically reflective in the ways assumed by deliberative democrats. That said the deliberations rarely manifested the egocentric quality typically assumed by the rational choice or materialist critics of deliberative democracy. Some narrowly self-interested claims were made by several of the participants early in each of the deliberations. However these were typically ignored. The lack of response quickly extinguished these kinds of initiatives.

In the terms of deliberative democratic theory, these empirical findings raise serious issues about the normative and practical value of deliberation as a form of democratic engagement. Even if deliberation is not openly conflictual and dominated by narrow self-interest, the fact that deliberative discourse among educated, empowered adults is largely conventional is problematic because this kind of discourse typically: (i) engenders a conformity to prevalent norms that enables only the most limited forms of self-reflection or social critique, (ii) maintains existing social divisions and hierarchies, and (iii) is unable to address differences in social norms and the ensuing value conflicts that are typical of multicultural societies. Consequently this kind of democratic deliberation cannot offer the normative or practical benefits claimed by either its liberal or more developmental democratic advocates.

In my view, the foregoing results do not reflect on the nature of citizen deliberation per se, but only how deliberation is theorized and how it occurs in particular socio-political contexts. The suggestion here is that we adopt a new approach to democratic deliberation. Rather than developing a context-independent, ahistorical understanding of what deliberation is, the focus shifts to further exploring the different forms which deliberative exchanges may take. This includes a consideration of the conditions that foster different types of deliberative exchanges. The present research suggests that creating a context that "frees" individuals to speak their mind under conditions of civility, openness, and equality does not guarantee the quality of the discussion that will follow. Clearly substantial intervention will be necessary in order to create the conditions that are likely to foster deliberations that are more cooperative or possibly collaborative and transformative. This sets the agenda for future theory and research. On the one hand, there is the theoretical problem of assessing the analytical and normative implications of the claim that individuals' capacities are discursively constructed and therefore that their ability to engage one another in an autonomous and equal way may require substantial intervention in order to foster desired democratic practice. On the other hand, there is the empirical problem of discovering (i) which conditions foster more adequate forms of deliberation and (ii) how those conditions may be most effectively instituted in particular deliberative settings.

Notes

1. Much of the inspiration for this project reported here came from two discussion groups to which I belonged and from which I greatly benefited. The first has continued intermittently for three years and included a number of doctoral students including Scott Winterstein, Mark Sellick, and Ted Wrigley. The second was a very stimulating faculty discussion group that met weekly at UC Irvine in the winter of 2003. It included Janusz Reykowksi (Warsaw School of Social Psychology, Poland), Molly Patterson (Aquinas College, Michigan), and Lisa Garcia Bedolla (UC Irvine).

2. For an early observation on the discourse that occurs in a town meeting, see the innovative work of Jane Mansbridge (1980). For a recent example of a more systematic attempt to evaluate discourse in a parliamentary setting, see the work of Jurg Steiner and his colleagues (e.g., Steiner et al., 2005).

3. As the foregoing comments suggest, the bases of cooperative discourse (unlike the rules of conventional discourse) are constituted in general and abstract terms. Cooperative discourse therefore tends to be less affectively charged than conventional discourse. There are several reasons for this. First, individual participants are defined abstractly and proscriptions of how they relate to one another are quite general. This tends to have the effect of distancing the discussion from the particulars of an individual's personal identity or preferences and the specifics of her socio-emotional connection to particular other people. Second, differences and disagreements that emerge are considered with reference to shared rules of argumentation, common beliefs, and a shared understanding of the discourse. Thus, while specific and immediate differences are acknowledged, this is done with reference to shared general assumptions of truth and right and a shared understanding of appropriate conversational behavior. Divisions between those who disagree are thus not reciprocally denying or mutually alienating as they are in conventional or proto-discourse.

4. For an interesting theoretical argument that takes a more developmental approach to democratic citizenship, see Warren, 1992.

8
Minipublics: Deliberative Designs and Their Consequences

Archon Fung[1]

8.1 Introduction

Activists, foundations, and even some scholars interested in improving the quality of the public sphere have pursued an array of modest projects that attempt to create more perfect public spheres. They convene citizens, in the dozens or hundreds or thousands, but certainly not in the millions or tens of millions, in self-consciously organized public deliberations. Following Robert Dahl, I will call these efforts *minipublics*.[2] Sometimes they resemble town meetings, and sometimes they function as purposeful associations. They look like, because they are, exercises in "reformist tinkering" rather than "revolutionary reform."[3]

Perhaps for these reasons, or because of their modest scale, these efforts have occurred mostly under the radar of democratic and social theorists. Nevertheless, those interested in improving the public sphere should pay more attention to minipublics for at least three reasons. Though small, they are among the most promising constructive efforts for civic engagement and public deliberation in contemporary politics. Second, given the fragmentation of cultural and political life, effective large-scale public sphere reforms may consist largely in the proliferation of better minipublics rather than improving the one big public.[4] Finally, even those who subscribe to visions of tectonic, macroscopic improvement will need to know something about the details of institutional design for effective public deliberation. A close examination of these minipublics will help generate that knowledge.

Like minipublics themselves, my aims in this chapter are modest. Many democratic activists use the very same words – words like participation, deliberation, and civic engagement – to describe their projects, yet they utilize very different designs and strategies. They can't all be right. Even if each is effective in its own way, each also stands to gain from comparing the logics of other approaches. I aim to accelerate conversations among these practitioners and theorists of citizen deliberation. Such conversations may be the best way to advance knowledge and practice in this arena of democratic innovation.

Toward that end, the next section makes the most important of these design choices explicit. Laying out the range of institutional design options illuminates the diversity of these projects, guides reflection upon the wisdom of particular choices, and helps to spur a conversation among similarly situated actors pursuing divergent strategies. Furthermore, the public sphere has many functions. A healthy public sphere might, for example, foster deliberation, increase civic engagement, make citizens more wise or sociable, educate elites, make government more accountable, make policy more just, and mobilize citizens for political action. The third section develops several hypotheses about how institutional design choices make minipublics more or less likely to advance such objectives. The fourth section illustrates how design choices relate to public sphere goals by reviewing the experiences of five contemporary minipublics – James Fishkin's Deliberative Polls, the Citizen Summits in Washington, D.C., public deliberation under the Oregon Health Plan, Chicago's community policing program, and the Participatory Budgeting system of Porto Alegre, Brazil.

8.2   Institutional design choices

Suppose that you want to improve the quality of civic engagement and public deliberation and that you are in a position – through your access to a modicum of financing or state power – to carry out a project toward this end. You decide to create a minipublic that will convene citizens and perhaps officials to deliberate on some important public concern. This minipublic will contribute to the democratic project of reinvigorating the broader public sphere not just by modeling the ideal, but also by improving the quality of participation and deliberation in a significant area of public life. As with any project of political construction, you face many critical questions in the course of planning your minipublic.

8.2.1   Visions and types of minipublics

The first important choice, informing all of the others that follow, concerns your ideal of the public sphere. Beyond simply convening citizens to deliberate with one another and participate in public life, what should a minipublic do?

In one vision, the minipublic is an *educative forum* that aims to create nearly ideal conditions for citizens to form, articulate, and refine opinions about particular public issues through conversations with one another. The conditions of deliberation in this minipublic would differ from those in the actually existing public sphere in at least three ways. Whereas inclusion in actual public debate reflects many kinds of background inequalities – wealth, gender, education, position, control over the means of communication and production – the minipublic would attempt to fairly include all of these diverse voices. Second, actual public debate frequently falls short of the ideal of deliberation and public reason. Under more ideal conditions, participants would take each others' claims, explanations, reasons, proposals, and arguments seriously. Third, citizens often form ill-considered opinions because information is costly. A minipublic might therefore inform citizens by training them and by making briefing materials and expertise easily available. In a minipublic that addresses these problems of representation, reasonableness, and information, conversations between citizens would dramatically improve the quality of their public opinion. Of the explicitly "deliberative" programs sponsored by foundations and community organizations, educative forums are the most common.[5] They include the deliberative polls invented by James Fishkin, the National Issues Forums begun by the Kettering Foundation,[6] the study circles initiatives supported by the Topsfield Foundation,[7] and the 1998 Americans Discuss Social Security town-meetings organized by AmericaSpeaks and supported by the Pew Charitable Trusts.

A second type of minipublic might be called the *participatory advisory panel*. It aims not only to improve the quality of opinion, but also to align public policies with considered preferences. Participatory advisory panels do not stop after creating the ideal deliberative conditions of the first vision. They also develop linkages to economic or state decision-makers to transmit preferences after they have been appropriately articulated and combined into a social choice. Participatory advisory panels have often resulted from partnerships between non-profit organizations devoted to public discourse and government offices seeking to solicit citizen input and enhance their own legitimacy.[8]

A third type of minipublic might be called *participatory problem-solving collaboration*. This type envisions a continuous and symbiotic relationship between the state and public sphere aimed at solving particular collective problems such as environmental degradation, failing schools, or unsafe streets.[9] Two broad justifications support this intimate relationship between public and state. First, some public problems are so wicked that they defy even the best expert solutions. For some of these problems, citizens may invent novel solutions that leverage resources and ingenuity from both the civic and state spheres; the central contribution of this kind of minipublic is creativity. Second, often the state cannot be trusted. Some democratic skeptics locate the central contribution of an improved public sphere in its ability to tether state action and make it publicly accountable.

A fourth vision, call it *participatory democratic governance*, is more ambitious than the other three. This flavor of minipublic seeks to incorporate direct citizen voices into the determination of policy agendas. Proponents of such minipublics often view structures of representative legislation and insular administration as easily captured, or at least biased, toward wealthy and socially advantaged sections of the polity. Injecting direct, mobilized, deliberative citizen participation into democratic governance might favor the voices of the least-advantaged and so offer a procedural antidote that enhances the equity of legislation and policy-making.

8.2.2   Who? Participant selection and recruitment

How should individuals come to participate in a minipublic? The most common mechanism is voluntary self-selection. Public meetings and activities are often open to all who wish to attend. Sometimes they are required by law to be open in this way. Those who hear about the opportunity and have the resources, interests, and time participate. One difficulty with voluntarism is that those who show up are typically better-off – more wealthy, educated, and professional – than the population from which they come. Nearly all forms of political participation exhibit participation patterns favoring high status persons, and more demanding forms tend to exacerbate that bias.[10] As Chapter 6 of this volume shows, the outcomes of deliberation depend critically upon who it is that deliberates.

One solution is to choose specific participants who demographically mirror the general population. Deliberative polling efforts pursue this tact by selecting participants through random select methods. A second option is affirmative action through recruitment. Selection in the Citizen Summits (discussed in Section 4.2) was voluntary, but program organizers achieved demographic representation by publicizing the event in communities that would otherwise be under-represented.

A third option is to create structural incentives for low status and low income citizens to participate.[11] Participation patterns are determined not only by the resources constraints on citizens (favoring the better-off), but also by the goods that participatory institutions deliver.[12] In particular, if a minipublic addresses poor peoples' concerns, and if they expect that participation will yield results, then the poor may participate more than the rich. As we shall see, voluntary selection mechanisms for minipublics that address urban crime and basic urban infrastructure result in disproportionately high participation by poor and less educated citizens.

8.2.3   What? Subject and scope of deliberation

Presuming that problems of participant selection and bias can be solved satisfactorily, the next large question concerns the subject of deliberation. What public issue will participants consider? Public deliberation is often general in the sense that its rules, structures, and benefits are not thought to depend upon particular topics. All issues are thought to be fair game for debate in the broad public sphere, not least because excluding some subjects would improperly restrict liberty of expression and political freedom.

At the less abstract level of institutional design, however, the choice of subject importantly shapes the subsequent operation and impact of a minipublic. It determines what, if anything, citizens are likely to contribute in terms of insight, information, or resources in the course of participatory deliberation. Some areas would benefit very little from deliberation because they require highly specialized kinds of knowledge or training or because citizens have no distinctive insight or information.[13] On the other hand, many areas of public concern stand to benefit from increased public deliberation. To identify them, institutional designers should consider whether citizens possess a comparative advantage over other actors such as politicians, administrators, and organized interests. In some areas, citizens can contribute information about their preferences and values that is unavailable to policy-makers. In others, they may be better positioned to assess the impacts of policies and deliver this feedback to officials. In still other contexts, citizens enhance public accountability when civic engagement allows them to monitor potentially corrupt or irresponsible officials.

8.2.4 How? Deliberative mode

A fourth institutional design choice concerns the organization and style of discussions in a minipublic. In a simple formulation consistent with many of those in recent democratic theory, deliberation is a process of public discussion in which participants offer proposals and justifications to support collective decisions.[14] These proposals are backed by justifications that appeal to other participants and by reasons that others can accept. These reasons, for example, may appeal to some common good (e.g., "This is the best way to improve our school because ...") or common norms of fairness (e.g., "You do for me this time, and I do for you next time around"). When each participant decides what the social choice should be, she should choose the proposal backed by the most compelling reasons. When it generates social choices, deliberation is distinctive because, as Habermas put it, there is no force "except the force of the better argument."[15] Other decision methods, by contrast, rely on authority, status, numbers, money, or muscle. Decisions resulting from deliberation may be more *fair* and *legitimate* because they result from reasons rather than arbitrary advantages. They may be *wiser* because they allow a broad range of perspectives and information to be pooled together.[16] Discussion may *help individual participants* to clarify their own views.

At this level of generality, the theory of deliberation offers justifications for the institutional designer of a minipublic, but not much guidance. Any particular deliberative process will have more specific aims and obstacles that it must address through training, facilitation, and the structure of discussion.

One aim of the public sphere, for example, is to provide space in which individuals can reach their own considered views and gain confidence in their own perspectives; it is a space where the weak should be able to find their own voice. Some critics have objected that deliberative processes disadvantage those who speak less well, or who speak in ways that are devalued by the dominant culture.[17] The best response to this important criticism contends that public spheres should be constructed in ways that, first and foremost, allow those without voice and will to find and form it. Processes of reason giving and taking cannot be fair absent this prior process of will formation and development that moves individuals from silence to self-expression. For example, the most important contribution of the public sphere in a Latin American city may be to allow a favela dweller to realize and effectively assert her rational self-interests in basic sanitation, water, and education. Developing reasonable capacities to limit these demands according to the property rights of the middle and upper classes, needs of other favelas, and limits of state financing comes later. When a minipublic aims centrally to foster the formation of individual will and preference in this way, appropriate interventions include testimony, story-telling, relating needs, principled advocacy, and the airing of conflicts and tensions.[18] Facilitation will seek to assure that the weak, and not necessarily those with the best ideas or arguments, have ample time to speak and express themselves.

In contrast with this approach, some kinds of deliberation aim to generate consensus or to solve concrete problems. Such deliberations might follow the rules of proposal, justification, and planning just outlined . Deliberative institutions in this mode should offer training and education to create informed participants. A facilitator might level the field to allow participants to engage and guide the conversation toward emergent consensus. Deeply divisive issues and positions are sometimes simply ruled out of order. The premium on reaching a fair and good decision may favor the most articulate or popular (rather than the most needy). Indeed, Mansbridge reports that such "unitary" decision processes work to exclude those who reside on the margins.[19]

8.2.5   When? Recurrence and iteration

A fifth design characteristic is the frequency with which a minipublic convenes. The participatory democratic impulse is that more is better. But this intuition is incorrect, for the frequency of minipublic meetings should follow from their purpose. If a minipublic is convened to deliberatively form or ascertain public opinion on a nearly static issue, as in some educative forums or participatory advisory panels, then one conclusive round of deliberation may be enough. Further rounds would be justified if new information surfaced or relevant conditions changed. Minipublics devoted to participatory problem-solving or democratic governance should be convened more frequently, perhaps many times per year, because their decisions must be frequently updated and because monitoring officials should be an ongoing endeavor.

8.2.6   Why? Stakes

Since engagement depends upon interest, a designer should have a clear account of the stakes that participants have in a minipublic's deliberations. Does the discussion concern some issue that affects participants' welfare or deeply held beliefs? Are participants interested because the issue has become a public controversy? On one view, deliberation should be *cold*. Individuals with low stakes in a discussion will be open-minded, begin without fixed positions, and will be dispassionate. I tend to the opposite view; *hot* deliberations with participants who have much at stake make for better deliberation. More participants will be drawn to hot deliberations. Participants will invest more of their psychic energy and resources into the process and so make it more thorough and creative. The results of deliberation are more likely to be forcefully supported and implemented. So far as I know, we have no empirical evidence regarding the relative merits, and appropriate circumstances, of hot versus cold deliberation.

8.2.7 Empowerment

A minipublic is empowered just in case its results influence public decisions. In her recognition of this distinction, Nancy Fraser contrasts *strong* publics – those that exercise authority – with *weak* ones.[20] Many minipublics should not be empowered or strong. If the participants lack any claim to exercise voice in a decision, empowerment amounts to private capture or an illegitimate delegation of state power. Even when participants have some legitimate claim, the quality of their deliberations may be so poor, or the issue so important, that empowering them would degrade the wisdom or justice of public decisions. Since empowerment usually increases individual stakes in public deliberations, the reasons to favor cold deliberation also weigh against empowerment, and in favor of weak minipublics.

But there are good reasons to empower some minipublics. When a democratic deficit manifests itself as lack of state accountability, or when the minipublic is a component of a governance or problem-solving scheme, then empowerment follows from the purpose of public deliberation. As with hot high-stakes deliberation, an empowered, or strong, minipublic can create powerful incentives by offering influence over a slice of state power in exchange for participation. Individuals may take deliberations in empowered minipublics more seriously than in forums where discussions are severed from tangible consequences.

8.2.8 Monitoring

Most minipublics are front-loaded in the sense that they aim, like an opinion poll or election, to generate public discussion and refine opinion about a candidate, issue, or policy choice. The expectation and hope is that politicians and officials will take these public deliberations into account in their subsequent decisions. Some minipublics, however, also incorporate back-loaded participation that reviews the quality of ongoing action and implementation. If a minipublic generates sufficient interest to sustain the ongoing participation necessary for monitoring, important benefits can redound to participants.

Public learning is the first of these. In minipublics that convene frequently to observe and consider the consequences of various policy decisions or problem-solving strategies, participants also acquire experientially based knowledge – learning by doing – about what sorts of decisions are likely to work and which are not in various contexts. Accountability is a second important benefit. In environments where official actions depart from public interests, an important function of a minipublic might be to pressure officials to serve public ends or plans. The transparency made possible by monitoring can enhance legitimacy and good faith. A minipublic that does not monitor official action cannot contribute to public accountability in these ways.

8.3   Consequences of minipublic design

A healthy minipublic contributes to the quality of democratic governance in several ways. One cluster of contributions concerns the character of participation in a minipublic: the quantity of participation, its bias, and the quality of deliberation. A second group concerns informing officials, informing citizens, and fostering the dispositions and skills of citizenship. A third cluster connects public deliberation to state action: official accountability, the justice of policy, and its efficacy and wisdom. A final function of public deliberation and participation is explicitly political: popular mobilization. Consider several rough, *ceteris paribus*, working hypotheses about how the design choices described above affect a minipublic's capacity to advance these functions. These hypotheses connect design to democratic consequence and so serve to guide the empirical examination of minipublics.

8.3.1   Civic engagement as quantity of participation

By definition, all minipublics aim to increase civic engagement by drawing citizens to deliberate. For many of them, the quantity of participation is an important measure of success.

Obvious design features – the capacity of meetings and their frequency (8.2.5) – set an upper limit on participants. Typically, however, those who organize minipublics do not approach this ceiling. Public apathy and malaise pose more substantial obstacles. Thus, the quantity of participation also depends heavily on the ability of organizers to mobilize individuals. Successful mobilization in turn depends on the presence of supportive community associations and their own recruitment capacity (8.2.2). Minipublics can also draw participants by creating the structural incentives that make engagement worthwhile. As discussed earlier, the subject of deliberation (8.2.3), the stakes that participants have in it (8.2.6), and the extent to which the minipublic is empowered or strong (8.2.7) all create incentives for participation.

8.3.2   Participation bias

Another important dimension of civic engagement concerns the profile of those who participate. Are they disproportionately wealthy, educated, and professional, as they are in nearly all varieties of political participation? Are they drawn evenly and representatively from all sections of the population? Or, as in two of the minipublics described below, are disadvantaged citizens *over*-represented?

The factors governing the quantity of participation also affect the direction and magnitude of participation bias. One way to mitigate natural tendencies toward over representation of the advantaged is for those who operate minipublics to concentrate their outreach and recruitment (8.2.2.) efforts on disadvantaged communities. A second strategy is to create structural incentives that make a minipublic especially attractive to less well-off citizens because it addresses their particular concerns (8.2.3, 8.2.6) and empowers them to act (8.2.7).

8.3.3 Quality of deliberation

Minipublics also aim to foster high quality deliberation. Good deliberation should be rational in the instrumental sense that individuals advance their own individual and collective ends through discussion, brain-storming, information-pooling, planning, and problem-solving. It should also be reasonable in the sense that participants respect the claims of others and constrain the pursuit of their own self-interest according to the norms of justification. Reasonableness may require participants to restrain themselves when others offer compelling reasons based on common group interests or commonly held norms such as respect, reciprocity, and fairness. For example, reasonableness may require someone to withdraw his support from a proposal that would best advance his own self-interest because others are more needy. Good deliberation is also equal and inclusive. Participants should be roughly equal in their opportunities and capabilities to propose ideas and make claims.[21] When they are highly unequal, discourse aimed mainly toward will-formation, discussed in section 8.2.4 , may be a necessary precursor to a fuller deliberation.

Whether the aim of deliberation is will-formation or reasoned social choice, several design features are likely to enhance the degree of instrumental rationality in the process. Minipublics will exhibit greater rationality when their topics are ones in which participants have epistemic advantages (8.2.3). For example, citizens have privileged access to their own preferences and values. They may also possess local knowledge that officials and outsiders lack. Recurrence (8.2.5) and monitoring (8.2.8) also increase the rationality of deliberations by making additional information available and by making experiential learning possible. Finally, hot deliberation – discussions in which participants have high stakes (8.2.6) and affect the exercise of public power (8.2.7) – tends to increase the rationality of processes; participants have greater motivations to correctly align their ideas and views with their interests and values.

Some of the same factors that increase rationality may inhibit reasonableness. Discussions aimed at fostering and clarifying individual preferences, for example, by airing conflicts and advocating conflicting principles, may advance individual rationality while rendering participants less flexible and more self-interested.[22] Similarly, participants may be more inclined to restrain the pursuit of their own self-interests reasonably in cold deliberations – in which there are low stakes (8.2.6) and few implications for policy change (8.2.7). On the other hand, hot deliberation may drive participants to be reasonable when collective action depends on agreement and consent.

8.3.4   Informing officials

Another important contribution of public deliberation, then, is that politicians, administrators, or other officials gain information from the process. When these officials, from internal motivation or external incentive, aim to act as responsible agents for the public, the information they gain may improve the quality of policy and public action.

Educative forums and participatory advisory panels (8.2.1) appraise officials of the considered interests, values, and preferences of citizens. Beyond the design considerations favoring good deliberation generally, the subject of deliberation (8.2.3) largely determines whether officials can learn from discussion in a minipublic. Officials are more likely to reap informational benefits when the subject is one in which citizens' possess special knowledge, or in which their views are divided, opaque, or especially likely to change in the course of deliberative consideration.

Problem-solving and participatory governance minipublics have more ambitious informational goals.[23] In these efforts, citizens enter into detailed and sustained deliberations with officials about the content, design, and effects of particular projects, strategies, or programs. Here, officials may hope to learn not only about the preferences and values of citizens, but also about their own operations and strategies: about what's working and what's not in their problem-solving and policy-implementation efforts. The institutional design considerations conducive to generating this higher-resolution information are just those necessary for a minipublic to consider the details of public action as it unfolds over time: recurrence (8.2.5) and monitoring (8.2.8).

8.3.5   Informing citizens

Most of those who champion minipublics see citizens, not officials, as their principal beneficiaries. In one survey of organizations that sponsor citizen dialogues, "45% reported that one of their major goals was simply to provide information."[24] Compared to public professionals, citizens typically have more limited access to information, less time and training, and are asked to spread their attention over a larger range of public issues. Most citizens are likely to clarify their views and preferences and learn about substantive policy issues in any effective minipublic. The factors contributing to good deliberation (8.3.3) also produce information for citizens. Factors that create participant interest – such as stakes and empowerment – also enhance the incentives for citizens to pay attention and exert the energies necessary to become informed.

8.3.6 Democratic skills and socialization

Beyond learning about policies and public affairs, participatory democrats have long claimed that deliberative arenas function as schools of democracy where individuals acquire the skills of citizenship and come to consider public interests more highly in their own preferences and dispositions.[25] The extent to which participation imbues democratic skills and habits has received far more conceptual attention than empirical scrutiny. Absent the empirical basis from which to formulate firm hypothesis about the institutional design of minipublics, two working hypothesis should be tested.

First, citizens are more likely to gain democratic skills and dispositions where deliberations have tangible consequences for them. In empowered (8.2.7) minipublics where citizens have high stakes (8.2.6), they also have incentives to conduct structured and purposeful deliberations. They will, furthermore, be inclined to engage in the give-and-take process of reason giving and settlement that requires, and so fosters, the skills of proposal formulation, justification, listening, cooperation, and compromise. Minipublics with recurring deliberation (8.2.5) are more likely to contribute to the development of democratic skills and dispositions than those that convene once or only infrequently. Iterated interaction increases both incentives and opportunities for cooperation.[26]

8.3.7 Official accountability

Increasing the accountability of public officials and organizations is another potential contribution of minipublics. Through organized public deliberation, citizens can collectively examine the actions and policies of officials, assess the alignment of this state behavior with their own wishes and values, and attempt to bring the two into conformity. For example, the public generally has an interest in integrity that departs from the corrupt practices found in the governments of many developing, and some developed, countries. Similarly, officials may be accustomed to shirking their jobs or responsibilities in ways that can be corrected through appropriate participatory-democratic supervision.

This function is especially important, and likely to be exercised, where the gap between public interest and state action is large. So, minipublics that focus on issues or problems (8.2.3) where there is an accountability deficit, or where reflective public opinion differs substantially from official practice, will be more likely to contribute in this way. Appropriate focus is a necessary, but not sufficient, design condition for advancing accountability. Citizens participating in a minipublic must also be able to identify accountability gaps and develop solutions to them. Those in a minipublic cannot increase accountability unless they can press for changes in policy or action that tighten the tether between public and state. These capacities depend in turn on the quality of deliberation (8.3.3), whether the minipublic is empowered (8.2.7), and its ability to monitor (8.2.8) official activities.

8.3.8 Justice

Minipublics also contribute to ensuring justice from public policy and action when they allow those who are politically weak or excluded to form, express, and press for their preferences and values. Straightforwardly, minipublics that treat subject areas (8.2.3) in which there is substantial inequity and that enjoy sufficient scope – for example, authority over allocative decisions – are more likely to advance social justice. Enhancing the voice of the disadvantaged also requires their presence (8.2.2) and accessible modes of deliberation (8.2.4). Furthermore, a minipublic cannot advance justice without power (8.2.8).

8.3.9 Effectiveness

Deliberation can contribute to the efficacy of public policy in at least three ways. Public deliberation creates opportunities for those who will be subjected to a policy to criticize it, consider its justifications, and perhaps modify it. This discussion may enhance the legitimacy of a policy or agency, and so may make citizens inside and outside a minipublic more disposed to cooperate and comply. Minipublics that have high quality deliberation (8.3.3) and affect official action (8.2.7) are more likely to boost efficacy by generating legitimacy. Second, some minipublics address policy areas (8.2.3) where citizens possess comparative advantages – in terms of relevant resources or information – over officials. Third, minipublics can help to improve the details of implementation – its strategies and methods – over time by incorporating popular deliberation into the ongoing governance or problem-solving efforts of public bodies (8.2.4). The activities of these minipublics may be more likely to be sustained over time (8.2.5) and devoted in some measure to monitoring and evaluating official action (8.2.8).

8.3.10 Popular mobilization

Turning from policy to politics, deliberations inside minipublics can contribute to the mobilization of citizens outside of it, especially when they are related to the more encompassing agendas of secondary associations or political actors. For example, citizens may come to support the substantive policy findings of a minipublic because that position is the product of reasoned discussion and open participation. These policy positions may also receive heightened media attention as a result of having been considered in a minipublic. In addition to supporting substantive policy positions, citizens may also be drawn to support the institution of a minipublic itself. A novel institution that effectively addresses some urgent public problem or creates channels of voice for those who were excluded may mobilize support for its continued existence. Similarly, political actors who sponsor successful minipublics may thereby attract popular support for themselves or their parties.

Several design factors are likely to contribute to the capacity of a minipublic to mobilize these varieties of popular support. First, a minipublic may mobilize political activity if it addresses a salient problem or need (8.2.3, 8.2.6). For example, crime and public safety is such an issue in many inner-city neighborhoods, but less so in safe suburban ones. Second, a minipublic is likely to mobilize political activity only if it makes a difference with respect to some salient problem. This, in turn, requires the minipublic to establish a high quality of deliberation (8.2.4) and that it be empowered to act upon the results of that deliberation (8.2.7).

The discussion above has ranged over many dimensions of design choices and their potential effects. Figure 8.1 below summarizes these relationships.

	8.2.2 Recruitment and selection	8.2.3 Subject of deliberation	8.2.4 Deliberative mode	8.2.5 Recurrence	8.2.6 Stakes	8.2.7 Empowerment	8.2.8 Monitoring
Character of participation and deliberation							
8.3.1 Quantity	X	X		X	X	X	
8.3.2 Bias	X	X			X	X	
8.3.3 Deliberative quality	X	X	X	X	X	X	X
Information pooling and individual transformation							
8.3.4 Informing officials	X			X			X
8.3.5 Informing citizens	X	X	X		X	X	X
8.3.6 Democratic skills and socialization				X	X	X	
Popular control and state capacity							
8.3.7 Official accountability	X					X	X
8.3.8 Justice of policy	X	X	X			X	
8.3.9 Efficacy of policy		X	X	X		X	X
Political effects							
8.3.10 Popular mobilization?	X	X			X	X	

Figure 8.1   Consequences of minipublic design choices (more important factors in bold face)

The columns list institutional design choices and their functional consequences appear in the rows. The important design features for each function are marked with an "X" and the crucial choices are indicated with a bold-face "X."

8.4   Five applications

This discussion of minipublic designs and their consequences has been thus far abstract for the sake of generality. To render these concepts and hypotheses more concrete, and perhaps more believable, this section describes the designs and achievements of five actual minipublics. These examples are in no way a representative sample, much less a comprehensive catalog. Rather, they have been chosen to illustrate the great variation in the institutional designs of projects that aim to improve the public sphere. They also show how particular design choices inevitably advance some desirable qualities of the public sphere while sacrificing others.

8.4.1   Deliberative polling

The deliberative poll, invented by James Fishkin and his colleagues, attempts to create educative forums that model citizen deliberation under ideal conditions.[27] As Fishkin puts it,

> The idea is simple. Take a random sample of the electorate and transport those people from all over the country to a single place. Immerse the sample in the issues, with carefully balanced briefing materials, with intensive discussion in small groups, and with the chance to question competing experts and politicians. At the end of several days of working through the issues face to face, poll the participants in detail. The resulting survey offers a representation of the considered judgments of the public – the views the entire country would come to if it had the same experience.[28]

In each event, organizers select several hundred participants through a random process similar to those used in ordinary opinion polling (8.2.2). This method overcomes the obstacle of participation bias (8.3.2) and guarantees that the actual participants will mirror the underlying population demographically. Deliberative poll designers have also concentrated on creating highly informed deliberation (8.2.5) by distributing balanced briefing materials to participants prior to the event, facilitating small group discussions between participants, and making experts available to answer participants' questions. These efforts seem to have fostered open and searching discussions (8.3.2) in which participants become more informed about policies and consistently alter their views upon fuller reflection.

On other dimensions, however, the design of deliberative polling seems to yield only moderate impacts. Because participants have very low stakes (8.2.6) in discussions and because they are one-shot affairs (8.2.7), deliberative polling is unlikely to substantially foster the skills or dispositions of citizenship (8.3.6) in participants. As described in two of Fishkin's books, the subjects of deliberative polls have been general public policy questions such as economic policy, criminal justice, the European Union, and energy policy.[29] Citizens enjoy little comparative advantage compared to experts in answering these complex policy questions. At most, they can appraise politicians and administrators about their values and preferences in general terms, but they are unlikely to provide information that improves policy. We therefore judge that deliberative polls have a relatively low potential to inform officials (8.3.4).

Deliberative polls are not designed to substantially advance popular control over state action or to improve policy. Because they are neither empowered nor well connected to the levers of state power and policy-making, the activities within deliberative polls are unlikely to increase the accountability of public officials (8.3.7), the justice of policies (8.3.8), or their efficacy (8.3.9). These events are typically connected to civil society and the broader public through media broadcasts and other news coverage.[30] In some cases, officials have adopted specific policy recommendations from deliberative polling, but this is not the norm nor is it integral to the design of this minipublic. Deliberative polls thus seem to have weak mobilizing capacities (8.3.10) and they are not highly empowered (8.2.7).

8.4.2 America speaks citizen summit

Anyone who has been persuaded by the arithmetic case against participatory democracy – that the mode cannot possibly accommodate more than a few dozen participants if each is to be able to speak for more than a minute or two in a meeting of several hours – should attend one of the town halls organized by AmericaSpeaks.[31] On October 6, 2001, for example, some 3500 residents gathered in the Washington D.C. Convention Center to deliberate about Mayor Anthony Williams's Strategic Plan.[32] The event was called the second Citizen Summit; the first was held in November 1999 and drew almost 3000 residents.[33] Though both meetings were open to all residents, organizers had targeted their outreach and recruitment (8.2.3) energies to low-income and minority communities to mitigate natural tendencies toward upper-class participation bias (8.3.2). These efforts were successful; the demographic profile of participants in both meetings was largely representative of the larger Washington, D.C. population.

The 2001 meeting featured an impressive use of technology to facilitate large group discussion. The group was organized into approximately 350 tables of 10 seats. At each, a trained facilitator led discussions and a volunteer recorded the major points of conversation on a laptop computer. The computers were networked together to instantaneously relay small group discussions to meeting facilitators, who compiled the views from the tables to present them back to the large group. Each participant was also given a polling keypad, resembling a television remote control, which allowed meeting facilitators to conduct straw polls, collect demographic surveys, and solicit quick reactions throughout the meeting. These wireless devices allowed organizers to instantaneously aggregate participant responses and display them for everyone to review.

Citizen Summits are participatory advisory panels that construct spaces for residents to reflect upon city priorities and communicate their views to the Mayor. The subjects of deliberation (8.2.4), then, are citywide issues such as economic development, education, government responsiveness, and the quality of neighborhoods. The discursive mode (8.2.5) among citizens is preference clarification; by talking with others residents and reflecting on official strategic plans, they clarify their own values and views about what city government should be doing. Citizens are likely to invest themselves in these discussions more than in deliberative polling because they have substantial stakes (8.2.6) in the disposition of public resources and behavior of city agencies. They need not reach a consensus with one another. Citizens are likely to gain substantial knowledge about city government, its plans, and its objectives through these discussions (8.3.5). In the second Citizen Summit, for example, discussions were organized around a detailed draft strategic plan for the city that laid out major goals and action plans for several dozen city agencies and offices. Conversely, the Mayor and his staff evidently analyze this feedback quite closely (8.3.4). The feedback provides focused, and otherwise unavailable, information about citizen values, preferences, and perspectives on the details of urban policy. Because these deliberations address the goals of city policy rather than details of implementation, officials are unlikely to gain substantial insight into their operational successes and failures. On the goal of fostering the skills and dispositions of citizenship (8.3.6), the Citizen Summits by themselves are unlikely to have substantial impact because they recur (2.5) infrequently.[34]

In its design, this program empowers (8.2.7) citizens to steer city government by issuing advice regarding broad objectives. Ideally, they would utilize this feedback to align the city budget with popular priorities, re-task municipal departments, and create new programs or agencies where deliberation has revealed gaps and silences. One of the major findings of the first Citizen Summit was that citizens wanted greater voice in neighborhood-level planning and service decisions. The Mayor responded by creating a Neighborhood Services Initiative that devolved the coordination of agency services to the neighborhood level. More broadly and perhaps extravagantly, the Mayor claimed that, "You helped design the City's budget. Since the first Citizen Summit, more than $700 million has been invested to improve the delivery of services that you said were more important."[35] Skeptics might charge that these investments would have occurred without the Citizen Summit and that the Summit merely creates support for a pre-set agenda. This dispute between proponents and skeptics concerning the extent of empowerment cannot be settled without a close examination of administrative decisions following each Citizen Summit.

8.4.3 Oregon Health Plan

In early 1990, Oregon Health Decisions held a series of 46 community meetings throughout the state in which 1003 residents gathered to "build consensus on the values to be used to guide health service allocation decisions."[36] This public participation process was one result of the health care reform movement in Oregon that began in the early 1980s. At a time when many other states were retrenching, activists and policymakers sought to expand Medicaid coverage to include all of those in the state whose earnings fell below the poverty line.[37] In order achieve this expansion but keep it financially feasible, policy makers foresaw difficult and controversial choices regarding the categories of medical conditions and treatments that would be covered by public health insurance. An eleven member panel of health policy experts called the Health Services Commission was to determine which health conditions would be publicly insured and which excluded. The Oregon Basic Health Care Act required the Commission to make these decisions based upon values established in a participatory community process. The Commission engaged Oregon Health Decisions to organize that process. Oregon Health Decisions, in turn, created a decentralized participatory advisory panel to solicit public input.

Two institutional design features – selection (8.2.3) and subject (8.2.4) – of the subsequent assemblies predictably skewed participation toward a narrow band of professionals and citizens of high socio-economic status (SES). Because meetings were voluntary and little effort seems to have been expended to recruit from disadvantaged communities, participants were typically wealthy and highly educated; 67 percent were college graduates and 34 percent had household incomes greater than $50,000. This minipublic addressed health care, and 70 percent (!) of participants were healthcare and mental health workers. The medically uninsured composed just 9.4 percent of participants.[38]

Despite these serious defects in the character of participation, actual deliberations were well structured (8.2.4). The careful attention to organization, facilitation, and the relatively high stakes of the subject for participants formed the foundation for engaging discussions. Deliberations were designed to elicit the values that participants, upon reflection, felt should guide health care priorities. Meetings typically lasted two hours. Participants received informational materials, watched a slide show to orient them, and received individual questionnaires concerning health care priorities. Participants then discussed their individual rankings of health care priorities with one another and attempted to reach group consensus on the relative importance of various health care values. Oregon Health Decisions staff generated a summary ranking of priorities by aggregating the results of these community meetings. All of the community meetings ranked prevention and quality of life very highly. These priorities were followed by cost-effectiveness, ability to function, and equity. Somewhat lower in importance were mental health and chemical dependency, personal choice, community compassion, impact on society, length of life, and personal responsibility.[39]

It is difficult to evaluate the degree to which participants learned about health care policy (8.3.4) or gained democratic skills and dispositions (8.3.6) in the absence of appropriate survey evidence. However, the process was moderately empowered (8.2.7). Health Services Commissioners attempted to combine their own expertise and judgments with the results of the participatory process. They developed a list of 709 Condition–Treatment pairs and ranked them into seventeen categories that roughly corresponded to values expressed at community meetings. Their eventual rankings reflected the values identified by Oregon Health Decisions as most important – prevention and quality of life.[40] This outcome is consistent with the interpretation that officials learned and respected (8.3.4, 8.3.7) what was important to the public as approximated by these highly imperfect community meetings.

According to close observers of Oregon health care reform, however, these details about deliberative quality and technocratic interpretation miss the crucial, and somewhat unanticipated, contribution of the participatory process.[41] By the mid-1990s, Medicaid coverage in Oregon had been successfully extended to cover everyone below the poverty line, and partial coverage – for children and pregnant women – for many above the poverty line. Between 1993 and 1996, the number of uninsured Oregonians fell from 17 percent to 11 percent. However, treatment had not been rationed. The funded portion of the condition–treatment pair list provided a substantially *more* generous coverage than the pre-Oregon Health Plan Medicaid package. Political mobilization (8.3.10) in favor of this more generous and just (8.3.8) health care policy distinguished Oregon from many other states where health care reform collapsed over this same period. Jacobs and his colleagues write that the Oregon Health Plan has become the "third rail" of state politics – you touch it and you die. Media coverage and attention, the close connection of this minipublic to health care reform organizations, combined with the legitimacy of a decentralized and open community process likely contributed to the deep public support for the Oregon Health Plan.[42]

8.4.4　Chicago community policing

While these three minipublics use deliberation primarily to clarify and revise the preferences and values of participants and to communicate those preferences to policy makers, the fourth minipublic invites citizens to join police and other public agencies in the work-a-day activities of solving public problems. In 1994, the Chicago Police Department unveiled its community-policing program. Chicago's program emphasized direct citizen participation much more than analogous programs in other American cities. The Department divides the city into 280 neighborhood-sized beats. Since 1995, open meetings have been held monthly in each beat.[43] In these community beat meetings, police officers and citizens deliberate about how to improve public safety in their neighborhood. They set priority problems (e.g., a dangerous park or crack house), develop strategies to address those problems, agree to division of labor between police and citizens, review the success of prior strategies, and revise accordingly.

These meetings draw substantial levels of participation. On average, 17 persons attend each meeting, cumulating to a citywide attendance of approximately 5000 people per month. In surveys, 12 percent of adults in Chicago report that they have attended at least one community-policing meeting. Though these meetings are completely open and voluntary, there is an obvious structural incentive (8.2.2) that makes participation particularly attractive to disadvantaged participants: well-off neighborhoods have very little crime, and so there is not much to discuss there. Reversing the ordinary participation bias, residents from poor and less well-educated neighborhoods turn out at much higher rates than those from wealthy ones (8.3.2) because they have high stakes – increasing their own physical security – in the subject at hand (8.2.3).[44]

The quality of problem-solving deliberation varies greatly across beats. Community organizations and central-office police personnel support the deliberations of residents and beat officers by providing training, organizing, and facilitation, but the coverage and quality of these services is uneven. Where support is strong, deliberation is frequently quite good (8.3.3). Participants (both citizens and police) follow the problem-solving process of identifying problems, prioritizing them, developing strategies, implementing them, assessing outcomes, and revising approaches. Discussions are empowered (8.2.7) when police heed (as Departmental policy directs them to do) citizens' reflective opinions about which neighborhood problems are most urgent in the neighborhood and how those problems should be addressed. These strategies frequently employ novel methods that lie outside, far outside, the repertoire of traditional police methods. For example, citizens form subcommittees that negotiate with problematic private parties such as landlords or business owners and they form court advocacy and watch groups. Some of the most effective strategies focus and coordinate services from a number of different agencies – such as sanitation, buildings inspection, and traffic in addition to police – to tackle persistent problems such as an open-air drug markets. When deliberation is effective and creative, both citizens and officials learn (8.3.4, 8.3.5) in ways that increase the efficacy of their public safety efforts (8.3.9).

The iterated design of Chicago community policing also distinguishes it from the three minipublics already discussed earlier. The repeated interactions between police and citizens and the problem-solving focus of their deliberations creates opportunities for citizens to monitor (8.2.8) the activities of police over time. The poor quality of police performance and their shirking is a frequent topic of beat meeting discussions. This deliberative design thus increases the accountability of street-level police officers (8.3.7). Because the central goal of these meetings is to develop common agendas and strategies, citizens (and police) are likely to gain deliberative and cooperative skills over the course of community policing deliberations (8.3.6).

8.4.5 Participatory budgeting in Porto Alegre, Brazil

Nowhere in the United States is there a political entity that possesses both a deep commitment to participatory deliberative democracy and sufficient power to make good on that commitment institutionally. Not so in Latin America. Therefore, our final minipublic examination considers the participatory budgeting system in Porto Alegre, Brazil as example of participatory democratic governance. Porto Alegre is the capital city of the state of Rio Grande do Sul and home to 1.3 million inhabitants. In 1989, a left-wing party called the Worker's Party (the Partido dos Trabalhadores, or PT) won the Mayoralty on a platform of advancing social justice through participatory democracy. These vague commitments were institutionalized into arrangements under which control over the capital portion of the municipal budget shifted from the city council to a bottom-up decision-making process called the Participatory Budget (Orçamento Participativo or OP) that combines direct and representative mechanisms.[45]

It works roughly like this. In March of every year, large assemblies are held in each of the city's 16 districts. Often drawing more than a thousand participants and attended by city hall staff, citizens in each assembly review the extent and quality of implementation of the projects in last year's budget (8.2.4, 8.2.8). The projects under the OP's scope concern basic urban infrastructure in areas such as sewage, housing, pavement, education, social assistance, health, and transportation (8.2.3). Participants in these meetings also elect delegates to represent specific neighborhoods in subsequent rounds of the OP process. This formula for representation creates incentives for mobilization; the number of delegates allocated to each district increases as a diminishing marginal function[46] of the total participants in that district's assembly. In subsequent rounds, representatives from each district and neighborhood meet to deliberate about the schedule of priority themes in their areas (e.g., (1) street, (2) education, (3) housing) and the priorities within each theme ((1) street A, (2) street B). These reflective preferences are aggregated into a single city budget (8.2.7), detailed with particular works and projects, according to a weighted formula that incorporates the schedule of expressed preferences, the population of each district, and the relative deprivation of each district.

Since its inception, the OP has drawn steadily increasing participation as citizens have gained confidence in the institution (8.3.1). In the 1999 and

2000 cycles, more than 14,000 residents participated in the first round of plenary assemblies. Observers estimate that some 10 percent of the adult population participates in the process annually, though precise estimates are difficult because much participation occurs in numerous informal neighborhood meetings and committee sessions. As with the Chicago community policing reforms, the design of open meetings combined with strong structural incentives for participation by disadvantaged participants has inverted the ordinary high-SES participation bias observed in most political arenas. Poor people are substantially over-represented in OP meetings (8.3.1).[47]

This process generates a wealth of detailed knowledge for officials (8.3.4). Some of this knowledge concerns the values and priorities of residents, such as the difficult trade-offs between issues such as clean water and schools. Officials also gain very specific knowledge about where particular works and projects should be located, and whether they operate successfully or fail. Conversely, residents also gain substantial knowledge (8.3.5) about where, and whether, public monies are appropriately spent, and about the detailed operations, successes, and failures of city agencies. Through participation in these discussions, citizens likely gain democratic skills of compromise and cooperation (8.3.6). However, because deliberations focus upon very local goods and needs, the institution has not disposed citizens to think about the greater good of the city, the just trade-offs between jurisdictions, or the good of the city through the long arc of time.

The OP has reduced corruption and eroded traditional patronage relationships between city councilors, legislators, businesses, and local notables by making the financial decisions of city government more transparent. One result of this increase in official accountability (8.3.7) is that many fiscal leaks have been plugged and the actual revenues available for public investment have grown. Good government (through participatory democracy) has in turn increased the legitimacy of the municipal state and increased tax compliance. Advancing both justice (8.3.8) and efficacy (8.3.9), city agencies charged with building and operating public works have become much more productive and the lion's share of new activity has occurred in poor areas:

> Of the hundreds of projects approved, investment in the poorer residential districts of the city has exceeded investment in wealthier areas … Each year, the majority of the 20–25 kilometers of new pavement has gone to the city's poorer peripheries. Today, 98 percent of all residences in the city have running water, up from 75 percent in 1988; sewage coverage has risen to 98 percent from 46 percent. In the years between 1992 and 1995, the housing department offered housing assistance to 28,862 families, against 1,714 for the comparable period of 1986–1988; and the number of functioning public municipal schools today is 86 against 29 in 1988.[48]

	8.4.1 Deliberative polling	8.4.2 Citizen summits	8.4.3 Oregon Health Plan	8.4.4 Chicago community policing	8.4.5 Participatory budgeting
8.2.1 Purpose and vision	Simulate ideal deliberative conditions	Align public policy with considered citizen preferences		Improve problem-solving through participation	Participatory democratic governance
Design features of the public space					
8.2.2 Who? Recruitment and selection	Representative sample	Voluntary + targeted recruitment	Voluntary	Voluntary + institutional incentive	Voluntary + institutional incentive
8.2.3 What? Subject of deliberation	Large scale public policy questions	Citywide strategic plan	Health care rationing	Neighborhood public safety	Capital infrastructure investments
8.2.4 How? Deliberative mode	Clarify principles and positions	Clarify priorities / feedback	Assert and clarify priorities	Problem-solving	Assert and reconcile priorities
8.2.5 When? Recurrence	One-shot, centralized	Infrequent, centralized	One-shot, decentralized	**Frequent, decentralized**	**Frequent, decentralized**
8.2.6 Why? Stakes	Low	**Moderate**	Low–moderate	**Moderate–high**	**High**
Connections from public space to state					
8.2.7 Empowerment	Low	**Moderate**	**Moderate**	**Moderate–high**	**High**
8.2.8 Monitoring	None	Low	Low	**Strong**	Moderate

Figure 8.2 Institutional design features of five minipublics (distinctive design features in bold-face)

	8.4.1 Deliberative polling	8.4.2 Citizen summits	8.4.3 Oregon Health Plan	8.4.4 Chicago community policing	8.4.5 Participatory budgeting
Shape of participation					
8.3.1 Quantity	Low	**Moderate**	Moderate	**High**	**High**
8.3.2 Bias	**Representative**	**Representative**	Positive SES bias	**Inverse SES bias**	**Inverse SES bias**
8.3.3 Deliberative quality	**High**	Moderate	Moderate	Moderate	Moderate
Information pooling and individual transformation					
8.3.4 Informing officials	Low	**Moderate**	**Moderate**	**High**	High
8.3.5 Informing citizens	**Moderate**	**Moderate**	Moderate	High	High
8.3.6 Democratic skills and dispositions	Low	Low	Low	Moderate	Moderate
Popular control and state capacity					
8.3.7 Official accountability	None	**Moderate**	**Moderate**	**Moderate**	High
8.3.8 Justice of policy	No	**Moderate**	**Moderate**	Low	High
8.3.9 Efficacy of policy	No	Low	Low	**High**	High
Political effects					
8.3.10 Popular mobilization	Low	Low	**Moderate**	Low	**High**

Figure 8.3 Outcomes in five minipublics (strengths of each design displayed in bold-face)

The treatment discussed of these complex minipublics has been necessarily quite compressed and omits many important details. Two tables below summarize these variations and comparisons. Figure 8.2 summarizes the institutional design features of the five exemplary minipublics. Figure 8.3 summarizes the practical consequences of these design choices. In each table, the most distinctive design features and those discussed in the text are displayed in bold face.

8.5 Conclusion

Many public leaders and organizations are now engaged in the important work of constructing spaces for civic engagement and public deliberation. They describe their efforts and motivations in strikingly similar terms: enhancing participation, creating deliberative democracy, improving civic engagement, making government more accountable, and increasing social justice. This homogeneity is perhaps unsurprising; public intellectuals and political theorists have described their own projects and ideals in similarly uniform terms. That uniformity – for example the understanding of deliberation as decision-making through the giving and taking of reasons – is appropriate at a high level of abstraction.

More concretely, however, initiatives created by proponents of participatory and deliberative democracy – projects that I call minipublics – display rich multidimensional variation. Because practitioners are inclined to invest their limited energies in improving their own projects rather than exploring details of like-minded ones, there has been surprisingly little discussion in either the scholarly or practical literature on these variations and their implications. I have tried to describe the most important dimensions of difference from the perspective of institutional design. Both ordinary reasoning and concrete illustrations show that these design choices have important implications for the capacity of minipublics to accomplish their many laudable goals. Bringing this variation to light and imposing a conceptual structure on it will, I hope, contribute to comparative conceptual and practical discussions of the role of such efforts in contemporary democracies and how they might be improved.

I have focused on the details of the design and operation of actual minipublics. In important ways, this discussion lacks a beginning that justifies the existence of minipublics by describing their role within the array of contemporary democratic institutions and the range of political ailments that they might address. It also lacks an appropriate end that would describe the objections to robust participation in minipublics, offer guidance among the described design choices, and address the unsolved problems that minipublics face. No minipublic that I know of, for example, has successfully developed mechanisms to integrate centralized deliberation over macroscopic priorities with decentralized local problem-solving deliberations. All empowered minipublics also raise questions of legitimacy, for they entail a delegation or transfer of authority from conventional institutions (e.g., from agencies in the case of the Oregon Health Plan and Chicago community policing, and from the city council in the case of Porto Alegre). The answers to those questions may come more easily with frequent conversations between the practitioners of democratic innovations and its theoreticians. One way to move that conversation forward, and so to spur the energy for further investigation, is to address a concern that sits squarely at the intersection of both camps: the question of institutional design.

Notes

1. I thank Joshua Cohen, Stephen Elkin, James Fishkin, Joseph Goldman, Robert Goodin, Jennifer Hochschild, Sanjeev Khagram, Jane Mansbridge, Nancy Rosenblum, Charles Sabel, Lars Torres, and the participants of the Democracy Collaborative's "State of Democratic Practice" workshop for illuminating suggestions on previous drafts of this chapter. An earlier version of this chapter appeared in the *Journal of Political Philosophy*.
2. This terminology follows Robert Dahl's notion of a minipopulus (1989) and Jack Nagel's (1992) notion of Deliberative Assemblies on a Random Basis – DARBs. As explained below, my notion of a minipublic is both more inclusive and more connected to both civil society and the state than either Dahl's or Nagel's proposals.
3. Unger, 1987.
4. Fraser, 1992.
5. See, for example, Button and Mattson, 1999.
6. See Matthews, 1999.
7. See, for example, Gastil 2000: 113–116 and the URL:http://www.studycircles.org/ (last visited on May 1, 2002).
8. See Gastil, 2000 for a discussion of existing participatory advisory panels, including the citizen's jury, and his proposal for one kind of powerful minipublic of this type: citizen panels.
9. Cohen and Sabel, 1997; Fung and Wright, 2003; Weber, 2003.
10. Verba and Nie, 1972; Nagel, 1987.
11. This mechanism is similar to the notion of selective incentives that help overcome collective action problems. Structural incentives differ from selective incentives in that benefits from the former inhere in the structure of minipublics and in particular in the subjects they address. Benefits for participants come from their potential collective and social effects rather than in ancillary "positive inducements" (Olson, 1971: 133).
12. Cohen and Rogers, 1983.
13. Perhaps public education in wealthy suburban school districts offers an example of a policy area in which there is sufficient participation and public deliberation.
14. Cohen, 1989; Gutmann and Thompson, 1996.
15. Habermas, 1984: 25.
16. Fearon, 1998.
17 Sanders, 1997; Fraser, 1992; Mansbridge, 1980.
18. Sanders, 1997; Jacobs, Cook, and Carpini, 2000.
19. Mansbridge, 1980.
20. Fraser, 1992: 132–136.
21. This discussion utilizes Rawls' coordinates of rationality, reasonableness, and equality.

22. Jacobs, Cook, and Carpini, 2000.
23. See Section 8.2.1 for a discussion of distinctions between these three varieties of minipublics.
24. Jacobs, Cook, and Carpini, 2000: 22.
25. Pateman, 1970; Verba, Schlozman, and Brady 1995.
26. This line of reasoning suggests that participation in consequential and ongoing minipublics such as school governance committees will have more salutary consequences for citizenship than participation in the juries (few consequences for the deliberators and one-shot) that Tocqueville famously lauded: "Juries are wonderfully effective in shaping a nation's judgment and increasing its natural lights ... It should be regarded as a free school which is always open. The main reason for the practical intelligence and the political good sense of the Americans is their long experience with juries" (Tocqueville, 1969: 275).
27. Fishkin, 1991: 93.
28. Fishkin, 1995: 162.
29. Fishkin, 1991, 1995.
30. Fishkin, 1995: 190.
31. They have also organized discussions on the future of U.S. Social Security, regional planning in Chicago and Cincinnati, and the redevelopment of lower Manhattan after the attacks of September 11, 2001.
32. Chan, 2001.
33. Cottman, 1999.
34. It should be noted that Citizen Summits are one mechanism among others for popular participation in Washington, D.C. Another major component is the Neighborhood Planning Initiative, which allows residents to participate in strategic planning at the neighborhood level and is better described as a participatory problem-solving minipublic. The further development and integration of participation at these two levels–citywide advice and neighborhood problem-solving, may yield a compelling hybrid.
35. Government of the District of Columbia, 2001.
36. Hasnain and Garland, 1990. See also Sirianni and Friedland, 2001.
37. Jacobs, Marmor, and Oberlander, 1998: 2.
38. Hasnain and Garland, 1990; see also Nagel, 1992 for criticism and discussion.
39. Hasnain and Garland, 1990: 5–6.
40. Nagel, 1987, 1992.
41. This account follows Jacobs, Marmor, and Oberlander, 1998.
42. Jacobs, Marmor, and Oberlander, 1998: 9.
43. The account in this section is drawn from Fung 2004; see also Skogan and Hartnett, 1997.
44. Within neighborhoods, wealthier residents and homeowners participate at higher rates than poor residents and renters.
45. This account is drawn from Baiocchi (2001) and Santos (1998).
46. See Baiocchi (2001): The number of delegates for a district is determined as follows: for the first 100 persons, one delegate for every 10 persons; for the next 150 persons, one for 20; for the next 150, one for 30; for each additional 40 persons after that, one delegate. To cite an example, a district that had 520 persons in attendance would have 26 delegates.
47. Baiocci, 2001.
48. Ibid.

9
Deliberation with a Purpose: Reconnecting Communities and Schools

M. Stephen Weatherford and Lorraine M. McDonnell

9.1 Introduction

This chapter examines a trio of deliberative experiments, alternative realizations of a general template that aspired, as its title proclaimed, to "Reconnect Communities and Schools" in South Carolina. Reconnecting sought not only to foster citizen deliberation but also to influence the decisions of school and community elites. In the end, Reconnecting succeeded in mobilizing parents of students along with community residents who had no direct connection to the schools, and in fostering a series of penetrating discussions whose civility and equality surprised seasoned local observers. These South Carolina forums take their place among the steadily cumulating body of cases showing the constructive potential of citizen deliberation over significant, contested public issues. But unlike other deliberative assemblies, the citizens who participated in Reconnecting were not content simply to discuss the current state of their public schools; their intention was to develop an action plan, and to see that their recommendations received a hearing and visibly moved school policy and community practice. Neither the rich theoretical literature nor empirical research on deliberative democracy yields much insight about the conditions under which a citizen deliberative forum can preserve its autonomy and yet influence policymaking in a political context typified by adversarial bargaining.

This chapter addresses that question, drawing on a multi-year study of the Reconnecting process. Because the initial organization of the Reconnecting initiative included no formal statement of the relationship between the deliberative forum and the established school and community governing bodies, the relationships that emerged were shaped by local history and political culture. The resulting variation across the three districts offers useful insights into the conditions under which grass roots deliberative forums might have an effect on local institutions and might be able to take root as a sustained source of citizen input in a political environment more attuned to confrontation. The next section gives a brief overview of the two streams of ideas from which Reconnecting drew inspiration: selective borrowings from each tradition fed into a model that gained in political practicality what it gave up in theoretical neatness. The following section describes the South Carolina deliberative experiment, depicting the three communities in which it was implemented and summarizing our methods and data. We then present a framework for explaining variation in deliberative outcomes and analyze the South Carolina results. The final section discusses the implications of the Reconnecting initiative for how public schools function as civic institutions and for how they structure their relations with local citizens.

9.2 Two models for strengthening democratic citizenship

Concerns about the health of American democracy are widespread: too few people participate in the political process; too many feel that government is unresponsive to the preferences of ordinary citizens. The decline in voting is the most prominent symptom, but nonvoting masks a more troubling trend toward a thin and even antipolitical conception of citizenship, in which many Americans appear to conceive of citizenship as limited to voting and perhaps occasionally volunteering in some nonpolitical context (Hibbing and Theiss-Morse, 2002a; Schudson, 2003). Although some reforms have focused on motivating Americans to vote, more thoughtful critics have stressed the meager character of the solitary, episodic, and unreflective act of voting: they have advocated a more robust form of citizenship. Among many proposed remedies, two broad themes can be perceived. Each school emphasizes one aspect of American democracy's ills, the one focusing on the level of participation, the other on its quality.

Increasing the number of meaningful participatory opportunities might, for instance, involve decentralizing governmental power and turning policymaking authority in local areas over to neighborhood residents. Attempts to foster greater community involvement in public school governance partake of this theme. After a rather checkered history in the 1960s, the idea of neighborhood associations in urban areas as "structures of strong democracy" has seen a revival over the last decade or so.[1] The supposition is that multiplying participatory opportunities will elicit greater citizen involvement, and that over time it will lead to gains in relevant knowledge and political skills such as public speaking and negotiating, not to mention increasing the government's responsiveness to ordinary people. Local democratic institutions do appear to fulfill many of these expectations, but effective neighborhood associations require nurturance, for they threaten powerful, established interests. A critical aspect of the success of neighborhood associations is the commitment of the city government not only to support the costs of organizing and maintaining them, but also to institutionalize their authority over issues in their local juris-dictions and as a legitimate input into citywide policy (Berry et al., 1993). Not all proposals for increasing participation are as explicitly tied to government. A wide array of recent local initiatives share an image of citi-zenship that Boyte titles "civic populism ... a conception of politics as the interaction among citizens who have roughly equal, horizontal relationships with one another in many settings, not simply in vertical relation with the state." These organizations are most effectively participatory when their purpose centers on "public work ... the sustained effort (paid or unpaid) by a mix of citizens to create goods (material or cultural) of lasting civic value."[2] Two characteristic traits contribute to explaining effectiveness in these orga-nizations: they are focused on some visible local problem that people realize cannot be solved without cooperative collective action; and they have no (or very little) connection to formal governmental bodies. They are not devoid of politics, but it is the politics of negotiating across differences to create social capital out of diverse individual interests, not partisan position-taking or expert-dominated bureaucratic encounters.

Initiatives directed toward expanding meaningful citizen participation – whether in formally authorized structures or nongovernmental community groups – have several important strengths. First, they focus on concrete, identifiable problems; these are not vague "good government" groups, nor is their intention to make people better citizens. The problem orientation strengthens the incentive for participating; constitutes a visible common interest that spans individual differences; and provides a route for finessing value conflicts that would otherwise stymie action if it required prior agree-ment on abstract social or ideological beliefs.[3] Second, their local character situates the actions of these organizations within the shared sense of place that links neighborhood residents, heightening the salience of common concerns and cueing neighbors' shared images of the history and future of the place.[4] Third, by distancing their efforts from conventional politics, the focus on local issues responds directly to the public's cynicism about politi-cians and the disproportionate influence of moneyed elites. Finally, even modest short-term policy successes appear to generate changes in individu-als' knowledge and political skills that will strengthen their capacities and confidence to take on a more assertive citizenship role.[5]

These strengths, however, go along with two significant weaknesses:

- *Representativeness.* Because these organizations tend to be led (if not constituted) solely by traditional activists, less assertive residents or less popular concerns are often not effectively addressed.
- *Narrow interest politics.* Neighborhood mobilization not infrequently takes the tone of "us versus the downtown elite," thus framing partici-pation competitively and heightening the salience of subgroup identities at the expense of citywide interests. Within the organizations, the dominance of established activists exacerbates this effect.

These weaknesses are the central concern of the other theme in the literature addressing the thinness of contemporary democratic citizenship. This
school holds that more participation should not come at the expense of procedures that "are more likely to lead to an enlightened demos – and thus to
better decisions" (Dahl, 1989: 111).[6] The idea of deliberative democracy
emphasizes the quality of citizens' participation, focusing on the process of
discussion and decision-making, and structuring participation that goes
beyond simply advocating one's own interests and holding incumbents
accountable after the fact. Gutmann (2000: 75) summarizes the ideal as "public discussion and decision making that aim to reach a justifiable resolution,
where possible, and to live respectfully with those reasonable disagreements
that remain unresolvable." Young (2000: 7) emphasizes reciprocity and
equality as defining traits of "a process in which differentiated social groups
should ... be willing to work out just solutions to their conflicts and collective
problems from across their situated positions." Four deliberative democratic
criteria were central to defining the Reconnecting process:

- *Inclusiveness*: open participatory opportunities, plus purposive recruitment of the sorts of local residents who might not otherwise take part;
- *Political equality*: equal standing in discussion, including the expectation
  that interests would not be represented vicariously but that individuals
  would speak about their own concerns;
- *Open-mindedness*: acknowledgement that preferences may be changed
  by participation in the deliberative process, and that better reasons
  rather than resources or bargaining strategies should determine outcomes; and
- *Transparency* in the process for bringing issues onto the agenda and
  recognizing speakers.[7]

As with the reforms intended to expand participation, so also do deliberative democratic reforms have their own characteristic strengths and weaknesses. Strengths include deepening the quality of individual participation –
via provisions for disseminating information, actively discussing claims,
and publicly presenting and defending the reasons for one's preferences;
enhancing the representativeness and legitimacy of collective decisions –
via the focus on inclusiveness, equality, and reciprocity; and (potentially)
producing better decisions – because choices are less likely to be driven by a
partial view of the situation, and because framing arguments in terms of
public reasons cues participants toward considering more distant as well as
proximate consequences.[8] The weaknesses of deliberative reforms are the
complements of these strengths, and two lines of criticism are especially
telling:

- *Deliberation is too rationalistic.* The emphasis on reasoned argumentation
  to the exclusion of emotion, personal experience, and less assertive

conversational styles, excludes some interests and individuals (Young, 1997; 2000).

- *Deliberation is too abstract and divorced from practical concerns.* Gutmann and Thompson (1996), for example, hold that deliberation should be employed primarily for the resolution of fundamental conflicts over values,[9] and virtually no deliberative theorists take up the issue of how a deliberative forum can influence the actions of government authorities.[10]

The complementarity of these two lines of thinking – the one focusing on the level of participation, the other on its quality – points toward a synthesis, and the Reconnecting initiatives did indeed draw on both traditions. But these models center on mobilizing and structuring deliberation; they still leave open the problem of how deliberative citizen participation can be sustained and effectively influence public policy. The notion of "practical deliberation"[11] focuses on the problem of translating theory into practice, in response to two closely related challenges: engaging citizen participation and securing authoritative influence over policy. We concentrate not on the deliberative aspects, which have been treated at length in the literature, but on implementation. Getting a deliberative discussion started is often surprisingly easy: if asked, citizens are willing to participate in an organized discussion of political issues.[12] There are good reasons for this: the ideal of democratic participation is an attractive one, and deliberation approximates the ideal much more closely than voting, appearing at a public hearing, or almost any other citizen involvement; moreover, such a discussion is likely to be interesting. But few political issues can be resolved with one discussion, and continuing participation cannot be sustained without some promise of accomplishment: ultimately what matters is the opportunity to influence outcomes.

The efficacy of democratic deliberation typically hinges on the dilemma of resolving two distinct but equally legitimate claims to authority: that of the deliberative forum, based on the inclusive and egalitarian character of the process; and that of incumbent officials, based on a formal authorizing procedure such as election or appointment. The success of the deliberative assembly in securing a share of real influence in an ongoing policy system depends on relaxing the exclusive claims of established authorities, including elected school board members and expert administrators. Some situations may provide an opening for direct citizen input, for instance where an intransigent policy problem leads rational officials to a new appreciation of the attractions of sharing responsibility (or deflecting blame). In other contexts, however, incumbent politicians will vigorously resist opening up the decision process. For example, the experience of the Community Action Program shows that citizen groups that seek meaningful influence – even when their input is formally authorized – often provoke tension with established authorities, and usually find their influence fragile.

"Reconnecting Communities and Schools" melded some of the best components of the neighborhood organizing model and the theory of deliberative democracy. As such, it provided an illuminating lens on the potential and pitfalls of moving toward practical deliberation. In many ways typical of deliberative experiments taking place across the country, "Reconnecting" included several unusual aspects. Like neighborhood associations, Reconnecting was strongly localistic and focused on a specific problem: it drew much of its impetus from grass roots dissatisfaction with how the schools were being run and how effectively they were educating students. As with many civic populist organizations, participants initially envisioned working on problems independently of established institutions and officials, although as the discussion progressed participants came to realize that improving conditions required inserting their ideas into the policy stream. Unlike many neighborhood associations, however, procedures for recruiting participants and organizing discussions sought explicitly to adhere to norms of inclusiveness, equality, and mutual respect. The outline of the Reconnecting initiative was, however, largely silent on the sort of linkage that was expected to be established between the deliberative forum and school or community governing bodies.[13] Consequently, the relationships that emerged varied significantly, shaped by local history and political culture in addition to the immediate interaction between the citizen deliberative forum and elected political bodies or administrative agencies. Our analysis charts the origins and effects of this variation.

9.3   An overview of reconnecting

South Carolina's students had scored near the bottom of national rankings for decades, but in the mid-1990s, the public seemed at last to have lost patience with the assurances of administrators and school boards that improvement was just around the corner. Disengagement and even denunciation were becoming the defining features of school politics.[14] The new State Superintendent of Education, the executive director of the South Carolina School Boards Association (SCSBA), and the executive editor of the largest newspaper (*The State*)[15] shared the concern over declining public involvement with the schools, and they came together in a series of conversations, discussing David Matthews's *Is There a Public for the Public Schools?* and Robert Putnam's "Bowling Alone," and eventually raising the money for a statewide survey by Public Agenda. Sampling both public and elite opinion, the research tapped overall evaluation of the public schools, perceptions of major problems and potential solutions, and prospects for change. The surveys sharpened the diffuse impression of public dissatisfaction, with only 37 percent of the general public rating the schools as doing an excellent or good job. Business and civic leaders were even more critical than the general public, voicing similar concerns about the lack of accountability for student performance, the inequitable distribution of resources across schools, and the schools' inability to enforce discipline and ensure safety. Although the survey showed that the public was willing to pay more for schools if there were greater accountability, it also indicated that many felt that the schools were not receptive or responsive to input from parents and the community (Immerwahr, 1997).

This survey stimulated several initiatives, including a workshop the State Department of Education held with business and education leaders, and strategic planning exercises organized by the School Boards Association. The Reconnecting project sprang from these. Intentionally designed to be deliberative, Reconnecting represented a self-consciously innovative approach to public engagement. In each community, a series of neighborhood public meetings would be held under the auspices of a steering committee comprising citizens selected by the school district as broadly representative of the community, but who would operate independently of the school district. At the meetings, participants would be asked to discuss their aspirations for the community, what keeps people apart and what brings them together in the community; and what role the schools should play in the community. After completion of the neighborhood meetings, the steering committee would select 50 citizens reflecting the demographics of the school district in terms of ethnicity, age, social class, residence, and parental status to come together in a "community conversation" to forge an agreement that would outline hopes and expectations for the actions different segments of the community would do to rebuild the connection. The process would be structured, but open-ended in terms of its outcomes.

Three aspects of Reconnecting distinguish it from other attempts to engage the public in local schools. First, the process was controlled by the citizen members of the steering committee, not by the school district. It was, in effect, an opportunity for the public to specify the terms of their engagement with the schools, rather than following the traditional pattern in which educators define the nature of that relationship. Second, Reconnecting's initiators were clear that it should focus on all the schools in the district and their relation to the community. Neighborhood meetings and community conversations were to be structured in such a way that participants would be encouraged to look beyond their local schools to the larger community. Third, news of the local meetings and community conversations would be disseminated throughout the school district in coverage by the local newspaper. The norms of civic journalism influenced this expectation, and it was hoped that media coverage would focus on the substance of discussions and minimize the use of conventional adversarial story lines.[16]

The SCSBA initially asked 10 school districts to participate, and four agreed to do so. Districts were required to meet two conditions: the majority of the school board had to agree to the district's participation, and the local newspaper had to agree to chronicle the entire process. Each district was expected to back its participation with a financial contribution, and although the amount was small (about $15,000 for mailings, facility rentals, and other steering committee expenses) it signaled the school boards' commitment to take the initiative seriously. Media participation was important not only to disseminate news about the process but also to frame information in a way that avoided the usual image of adversarial politics. The newspaper would not be a sponsor of the initiative, but would rather act as a "committed observer," reporting on the process from beginning to end, whether or not it generated any news in the traditional sense. In districts that decided not to participate, school boards offered a variety of reasons, including ambiguity about the outcome of the process, a belief that the board was already adequately responsive to the public, or a concern that the newspaper would not participate in the way expected.

The four districts that agreed to participate were Greenville County in the northern part of the state, Richland 2 and Lexington 5 located in the Columbia metropolitan area, and Horry County in the southeastern corner of the state. Lexington 5, an affluent suburban district that prides itself on having the highest student test scores in the state, subsequently suspended the process after low attendance at neighborhood meetings.[17] The districts share some important characteristics. Each is located in a growing area, where newcomers are contributing to changes in traditional community boundaries and relations among races and classes.[18] As Table 9.1 indicates, they are among the largest districts in the state, and each has a staff person in the central office responsible for community relations who could serve as a liaison to the Reconnecting steering committee. The participating communities themselves are also large and diverse, at least by South Carolina standards. For example, Horry County includes the affluent communities around Myrtle Beach, but it also includes the tobacco farms in Aynor and Green Sea-Floyds. Similarly, the Greenville area is home to a large BMW plant and the North American headquarters of Michelin, but it also includes rural communities at the southern end of the county and up near the North Carolina border. Richland 2 is an urban-suburban district with a few rural pockets.

Its creators hoped that the Reconnecting process would engage "new voices, people who don't usually get involved [with the schools]." By creating a forum that bracketed competition and emphasized community, Reconnecting would provide a route for participants to "cross the threshold into public life," and thus involve more than just the "frequent fliers" who routinely attend school board meetings to press their own agendas. The organizers were less clear about what they expected in the agreements, although they hoped that they would provide some kind of blueprint for citizen action as well as input to school district and local civic officials.

Alongside these similarities, important differences in their politics and school-community relations distinguish the three districts that completed

Table 9.1   Characteristics of reconnecting districts, as compared with South Carolina and national averages*

	Greenville	Horry	Richland 2	South Carolina	U.S.
Enrollment	59,768	28,416	17,045	4,334 (median district) 59,763 (largest) 727 (smallest)	**
Racial composition					
Percent Black	28	28	51	42	17
White	72	70	44	56	63
Other		2	5	2	20
Percent free or reduced price lunch	31	54	32	49	***
Palmetto Achievement Challenge Test (PACT) percent of 4th graders scoring advanced or proficient in:					
English Language Arts	44.6	41.6	51.5	36.9	NA
Math	27.2	25.5	36.1	23.6	NA

* District-level data on student enrollment and background characteristics are for 2000–2001; the state and district PACT scores are from spring 2000; and the national and state-level student data are for 1998–1999.
** Only 6 percent of all the school districts in the U.S. have enrollments similar to the three South Carolina districts (i.e., with > 10,000 and < 100,000 students). However, 39 percent of all students are enrolled in districts of this size.
*** Seven states did not report free lunch eligibility data for at least 70 percent of their schools, so national totals could not be calculated. Within those states and schools that did provide this information, the proportion of students who were reported as eligible to receive a free lunch ranged from a low of 11.2 percent in New Hampshire to a high of 63.4 percent in Mississippi. (Education Statistics Quarterly, Overview of Public Elementary and Secondary Schools and Districts: School Year, 1998–1999. Report available at: http://nces.ed.gov/pubs2000/quarterly/summer/2feat/q2–5.html#Table-7).

the process. Despite having started with the same template, for instance, the steering committees organized the Reconnecting process quite differently. As Table 9.2 indicates, the time frame for reaching an agreement, the number of public meetings and community conversations, and the level of newspaper coverage differed significantly.

In addition, the relationship between the steering committee and school district leaders, and the role of the district in the process also varied. In Horry and Richland 2, the relationship was mutually supportive, and respondents talked about sharing in a common initiative. School board members and district officials attended Reconnecting meetings, although they were careful to serve as "resource people," speaking out only in response to specific requests for information. In contrast, the steering committee in Greenville operated quite independently of the school district. Because the first of the public meetings was held just prior to a school board election, the steering committee

Table 9.2 Variation in the reconnecting process

	Greenville	Horry	Richland 2
Time Frame*	10 months	6 months	3 months
Number of public meetings	12	25	5
Attendance at public meetings**	250–300	400–450	150–300
Number of community conversation sessions	3–4 held in each of 3 regions of the county; 2 county-wide	5	5
Number of newspaper articles	12 – *Greenville News*	34 – *Myrtle Beach Sun News*	15 – *The State*

* Elapsed time from the first public meeting to completion of the agreement.
** Estimates obtained from the steering committees and the newspapers.

recommended that board members not attend, in order to avoid the meeting becoming a platform for political candidates. The steering committee maintained this stance throughout the process, believing that a visible symbol of their autonomy from the school district was important to the success of Reconnecting deliberations, and neither the superintendent nor school board members attended any of the neighborhood meetings or community conversations.

In other work, we have examined the extent to which Reconnecting met the process standards articulated by normative theories of deliberative democracy (McDonnell and Weatherford, 1999), and we can briefly summarize those conclusions here. Reconnecting was inclusive in that the public meetings were widely publicized and held in natural, well-defined communities. For instance, meetings were held in church basements, senior citizen centers, a hospital, and even in the food court of a local mall – all easily accessible places where people naturally congregate. The citizens attending the neighborhood meetings were diverse with regard to race, social class, gender, age, and parental status. When the process moved to the community-wide conversations, however, participants were somewhat more likely to be educated and middle class and hence slightly less representative of the entire spectrum of the community. Nevertheless, Reconnecting was more inclusive than conventional venues for citizen participation in education politics, for instance at public hearings or compared with the profile of turnout in school board elections.

Organizers were sensitive to the principle of equal standing, and there was no indication that any participants felt they had been denied the right to speak. It is worth noting, however, that while the discussion raised a wide range of difficult issues, including class-related disparities in school resources and the community's commitment to funding special programs for disadvantaged students, other issues – notably those dealing with race (which had been aired with striking frankness in the first round of neighborhood public meetings) – tended to be skirted when they arose in the Community Conversations. Participants found that the processes for placing topics on the agenda and recognizing speakers were transparent and straightforward, but the newness of the approach, coupled with the amateur composition of the grassroots steering committees, meant that plans and schedules were frequently modified (e.g., to allow more time for a given topic or to set up an additional meeting in order to reach consensus on an agreement). Finally, Reconnecting measured up most successfully on the standard of open-mindedness: norms of civil discussion were widely accepted, and even initial skeptics were surprised at the tone and level of the conversation.[19]

Before turning to a discussion of deliberative outcomes, we describe our research methods and data sources.

9.4   Data sources and case selection

Our analysis is based on multiple data sources: face-to-face interviews with 57 Reconnecting participants, including the SCSBA and Harwood organizers, steering committee members, community conversation participants, school district officials, and newspaper staff; attendance at two public meetings, four community conversations, and two steering committee debriefings; and a review of all relevant documentary sources (e.g., the materials prepared by Harwood, the local publicity materials, all the newspaper articles on Reconnecting, and the final agreements). These data were collected during seven trips to South Carolina between May 1998 and March 2001.

Even though we have a substantial collection of rich and detailed data – especially the interviews with participants, many of whom we talked with several times – the data are most complete for Greenville and Horry County. The major barrier to collecting fully comparable data on all four of the initial sites is simply that the development of the Reconnecting process was highly responsive to the quality and pace of the evolving deliberation. For instance, the local steering committees all modified their initial schedules, sometimes changing the dates of meetings on very short notice.[20] In addition, we had originally planned to study the Greenville and Lexington 5 districts in greatest detail, and when the steering committee in Lexington 5 suspended the process there, we replaced it with Horry County as a site for intensive data collection. As differences in the evolution of the process across the sites became clearer, we also decided to collect limited data on Richland 2 after it had produced an agreement.

Case study methods, of course, purposely trade detailed observation of processes and interactions for the statistical representativeness that would be enabled by a large sample. Although relatively small, South Carolina is typical of many other jurisdictions in the centrality of race and class as public concerns. Other issues such as language and culture that shape public life in larger, more heterogeneous states are, however, only beginning to appear on educational and political agendas. As in many southern states, religion plays a much stronger role in South Carolina as a form of "civic glue" than it does in more secular states,[21] but on broader measures of social capital South Carolina ranks very low among the fifty states. To the extent that social capital is a key facilitating condition for public deliberation to flourish, in other words, South Carolina is an especially demanding test of its prospects.[22] If a process such as Reconnecting worked well there, the potential should be quite good for similar deliberative forums in states with greater stores of social capital. As for the communities and school districts that participated in Reconnecting, the districts are larger and more heterogeneous than most school districts in South Carolina and in the United States generally, but they are smaller and less diverse than the largest urban districts in the United States. Nevertheless, they face challenges common to many others across the country: managing enrollment growth, responding to increasing student diversity, closing the black-white achievement gap, and coping with an inadequate and unpredictable resource base. In this sense, their experience with Reconnecting may be quite informative for other districts seeking to develop community-sanctioned solutions to these and similar problems.

9.5 Deliberating with a purpose: From process to outcomes

Just as the designers of Reconnecting lacked clear expectations about outcomes, political philosophers have also been vague about this dimension. Theorists have tended to focus on the process, and specifically on the interactions among individuals in deliberative settings, and the empirical literature has pursued similar themes, focusing on the mechanisms and rules for deliberative forums (Fishkin, 1995), charting individual-level changes in knowledge or opinion (Cook and Jacobs, 1998; Luskin and Fishkin, 1999), but generally not attempting to track changes in individual behavior or collective outcomes. Research on other sorts of deliberative arrangements, for instance advisory boards, citizen juries and the like, assumes that elected and appointed officials will seriously consider such input. But the mandate to do so is often a loose one, and the assurance lacks credibility since the process of citizen consultation is typically initiated and its parameters circumscribed by the agency receiving the advice. There is, in fact, little research on deliberative forums in which ordinary citizens set the agenda and where an important motivation is the promise of an independent opportunity for criticizing rather than simply supporting the agency or organization. Nor has extant research followed the operation of citizen deliberative forums over time, with an eye to analyzing the conditions under which the "soft power" of deliberation can influence outcomes in a political environment peopled by competitive politicians and expert administrators who have their own strong conceptions of the sources of legitimate authority.

In the case of Reconnecting, the designers assumed that the school district would value and give serious consideration to the eventual agreement, both because the initiative originated as a response to an acknowledged problem in school–community relations and because of the inclusive and democratic character of the deliberative process. Moreover, the emphasis of Reconnecting's architects on the role of schools within the larger community and on joint citizen–government responsibility meant that any long-term outcomes would need to be organized across governmental agencies, voluntary associations, and individual citizens. In this sense, Reconnecting was charting a course not covered by deliberative theories or by most attempts to instill practical deliberation in local communities.

Although deliberative theory has devoted less attention to outcomes than to process, it is possible to draw out several inferences about potential impacts. First, if deliberation has the potential to shape participants' views, it should also have behavioral effects. Whether the results were to mobilize a potential electoral coalition or merely to surface formerly latent opinion, the change in the political climate should elicit a response from governmental bodies that are the targets of new demands or expectations. Second, since deliberation is a collective endeavor, a visible, successful community deliberation might foster collaborative approaches to other public issues. Finally, to the extent that deliberative participation yields positive experience with a novel process for resolving differences and addressing common problems, it might serve as a model for the evolution of civic engagement toward more deliberative norms in other institutions. Three sorts of outcomes might be expected following the Reconnecting process:

- *Citizens take action on their own.* Actions might range from volunteering at a school, to lobbying policymakers, to helping establish or run a civic organization, and future civic activity might show improved representation of previously excluded people and interests.[23]
- *Governmental bodies change their policies or administrative routines.* Deliberative procedures lend outputs sufficient legitimacy to command serious consideration by policymakers. Yet deliberative norms are fundamentally at odds with conventional politics, where decisions are often made through adversarial bargaining.
- *Deliberative forums are institutionalized.* Lasting changes might range from informal shifts in social norms, such as people acting more civilly in public spaces, or via the dissemination of the deliberative model to other venues or issue areas.[24]

Three aspects of the institutional context are critical to explaining the extent to which citizen deliberation moves from civil conversation to instrumental outcomes. The first is *how the deliberative process is organized*, particularly its relationship with individuals and agencies empowered to make policy decisions: whether the impetus and leadership flow downward from those in positions of formal authority, or upward from grassroots citizens. Are elected and appointed officials active participants or collaborators in the process, and if so does their status give them disproportionate influence? Or do they absent themselves from the process, and if so is it out of neutral respect for the autonomy of the citizen forum or a more adversarial intention to inhibit the forum's access to information or the symbols of legitimacy? Is there a clear expectation that relevant governmental agencies will strive to implement the deliberative agreement? A second factor is the *quality of the deliberative output*. Have the conclusions and recommendations of a deliberative exercise developed from a process that visibly meets the normative standards of democratic deliberation, and that is, in addition, informed by a realistic appreciation of the problem and constraints on possible solutions? Finally, deliberative forums such as Reconnecting come into existing communities with well-established citizen attitudes about government, norms of civic engagement, and patterns of relations among citizens and between citizens and governmental agencies. *Local history and political culture*, particularly as these are reflected in a tradition of citizen involvement and a characteristic level of trust in governmental institutions, constitute the third factor.

9.6 Reconnecting's deliberative outcomes

In this section we focus on outcomes of the Reconnecting process. In order to be attributable to Reconnecting, outcomes had to meet two tests: we can trace their inception to specific Reconnecting discussions or to the community agreement; and there is consensus among Reconnecting leaders and the targets of the activity that the specific outcomes were wholly or partly due to Reconnecting.[25] All three of the agreements proposed mechanisms for increasing civic volunteerism to support the schools, including calling on business and encouraging participation from citizens who did not have children in the schools; and all outlined what the schools should do to be more responsive to the community, for example, "using schools as a focal point for community programs" and "expanding and redefining the roles of school improvement councils and advisory boards to make them more inclusive of the community." In Horry County, the agreement was critical, but it took an overall tone of collaboration between Reconnecting and incumbent officials. The Greenville agreement, on the other hand, was much more politically bold, calling for consideration of restructuring the school district, establishing at least one at-large school board member, including the school district in county planning decisions, and "reinvigorate[ing] Greenville's political base where politicians are held accountable." This last point reflects a distinctive theme running throughout the agreement, which cites "poor management of the school system" and "a lack of trust," and implies that the school district has not been entirely forthcoming about how it spends its tax money. Richland 2 was the most modest of the three: it emphasizes building greater support for the schools by increasing citizen and business involvement, but, in contrast to Greenville's reformist tone, it neither identifies problems nor proposes administrative or political changes. Table 9.3 provides a summary overview of outcomes. Several of these amounted to quite substantial policy initiatives or institutional changes that would not have occurred without Reconnecting. The next section discusses commonalities and differences in detail.

9.6.1   Outcomes

9.6.1.1   Greenville

The most ambitious, the Greenville agreement was detailed and specific in calling for major structural changes in the school district and county government. The theme of the deliberative agreement was that the school district was not well connected to parents and the public and that it needed to make its budgetary decisions more transparent. The district responded by moving to decentralize administrative operations and to establish new processes for communicating with the public, including holding community meetings throughout the district. The Reconnecting agreement called for a district-wide code of student conduct, and the district formulated and implemented one. The county's rapid growth had, in the eyes of the Reconnecting participants, led to sidelining the school district when the planning commission approved new housing tracts and economic development projects. The county responded to this concern by increasing and formalizing consultation between the planning commission and a district staff member, following a meeting of the planning commission with members of the Reconnecting steering committee and a subsequent gathering of all the public and private sector entities affected by county growth.

These changes in the district's stance toward the public coincided with the appointment of a new superintendent, selected in part because of his commitment to strengthening the schools' ties with the local community. Although the search for the new superintendent was independent of Reconnecting, virtually all observers, including a board member initially opposed to the district's involvement in Reconnecting, agreed that that while Reconnecting had not "gone out and discovered problems that we had not thought about or come up with brand new solutions ... it helped turn our attention to some problems. One of the most important of these areas is communication." This board member went on to say that "Reconnecting had a major role" in prompting administrative decentralization. A steering

Table 9.3 Reconnecting outcomes

	Greenville	Horry	Richland 2
Citizen action		• Impetus for Loris Family Learning Center • Some Reconnecting participants worked to pass school bond measure • Training in customer relations for district and school staff provided by local businesses	• Facilitated machine tool academy at one high school • Some Reconnecting participants worked to pass school bond measure • Increased school volunteerism, but already a district focus independent of Reconnecting
Policy or administrative changes	• District paying greater attention to communication with the public • Administrative decentralization • Policies on student discipline and dress codes made more consistent across schools • Increased attention to coordination between the school district and county planning commission	• Changes in school advisory structures • Formation of superintendent's cabinets • Shift to "policy governance" by the school board • Board holding "linkage" meetings • Schools more open to community use of facilities	• Strengthened coordination between Reconnecting participants and school district personnel re school / community issues
Changes in norms of citizen engagement/ deliberative forum institutionalized	• Reconnecting model now being used in one high school and its feeder schools • Reconnecting procedures being used by school improvement councils	• Community coalition dealing with health issues using the same neighborhoods and deliberative model as Reconnecting, for carrying out community meetings	• Not clear whether Reconnecting will continue as an ongoing organization, but expects and attempts to do so

committee member summarized Reconnecting's effect in this way:

> It's not so much that the district was unaware of the issues [we] empha-
> sized, more that these issues had been ignored, downplayed, or given
> only a rhetorical or symbolic response – now the district has a reliable
> inventory and a more accurate measure of what these issues mean to the
> community.

In addition, Reconnecting's deliberative model was adapted to other arenas
and problems. For instance, one member of the steering committee convinced
the high school, middle school, and three elementary schools in his area to
come together to discuss community needs and how the schools' programs
could address those needs:

> [W]e held a community meeting, and we tried to structure this along the
> lines of Reconnecting. Each of the principals did a short presentation to
> the community, then I moderated, and we focused the discussion on
> themes and looking toward the future. We have had similar community
> meetings in the past: they have turned into gripe sessions, and neither the
> community people nor the school people came away with any construc-
> tive ideas for what to do next. For me, this was the first time that we have
> had a civil, constructive discussion. The people in the room kept on the
> theme and discouraged potential grandstanders from just grousing.

This same model has been used by the school improvement councils in
other schools to deal with potentially divisive issues such as how the school
day should be organized.

Some of the agreement's most ambitious proposals, however, were not
fulfilled. These included creating an at-large seat on the school board, developing plans for re-structuring school district governance, and supporting the
devolution of authority for school level problem-solving. What is perhaps
most surprising, given the assertive tone of the Greenville agreement, is that
the Steering Committee did not press its case vigorously, after the initial presentations to the school board and the planning commission. Members of
the Steering Committee offered several reflections on the decision. Most
concurred that Reconnecting had had a visible impact, on district processes
and on the new superintendent's initial actions, and that stepping back to
monitor the official response did not amount to ending the quest. As steering
committee members put it: "We've ... gotten an initial hearing from all the
main parties and we're willing to leave the ball in their court for right now. ...
participating in Reconnecting was worth it. During our fifteen minutes, we
made the school board listen. The school district heard Reconnecting –
heard different ... concerns, expressed in a new, more constructive way."
Some noted that Reconnecting's closer engagement with the policy process

had revealed that problems identified with the school board and district administration were not as bad as citizen participants had assumed when viewed from outside. The district had already recognized some of the most prominent problems – financial management, for example – and was addressing them.

Others emphasized the organizational difficulties of keeping such a process going. Over a two-year period, steering committee members focused nearly all their free time on the process, and – although they had begun to recruit new leadership from Community Conversation participants – there were no resources for mailings or other tasks required to maintain the organization. Core participants kept in touch and in general increased their involvement in civic activities throughout the county, but no successor group emerged as a continuing entity. In short, although it is unlikely that the issues highlighted by Reconnecting will be ignored, the responses will be designed by incumbent officials rather than in consultation with an ongoing citizen forum.

9.6.1.2 Horry County

Of the three communities, Horry County's agreement generated the most extensive outcomes. Significant grassroots action by Reconnecting participants in the rural part of the county resulted in the establishment of the Loris Family Learning Center,[26] and the school district's response to Reconnecting led to major changes in procedures for relating to the community. The school district also enjoys strong public support that district officials, citizen activists, and the local media attribute largely to Reconnecting.

The Family Learning Center is a direct outgrowth of Reconnecting, from the initial impetus to the negotiations for active school district participation. As one participant summarized it:

> The Family Learning Center is just the sort of thing Reconnecting envisioned, as I understand it. Through this program, parents are becoming more productive citizens, working together with other members of the community, and moving into the schools – learning how the schools can be helpful to them and the community, and in turn becoming willing to speak and participate in support of the schools. I don't think the Family Learning Center would have happened without Reconnecting. The community wouldn't have been supportive of it; the school district wouldn't have given up so much space.

The school district also moved quickly to implement most of its recommendations related to governance and operations. Over time, for instance, the district had created a number of parent advisory groups, seeing these bodies as evidence of responsiveness. But in practice, the groups were poorly coordinated and their multiplicity dissipated parent and community involvement over narrowly defined issues, their work overlapped, and their connections with policymakers were ambiguous. The district consolidated these, formalized parent and educator representation, and clarified connections among school-level bodies and new "cluster boards" spanning several schools in the same community and designed to deal with special issues such as appeals of student conduct cases.

Other mechanisms for obtaining public input have also been improved. Prior to Reconnecting, the superintendent had formed issue-specific "cabinets" including a teacher and a parent from each school in the district and one student from each middle and high school, that met with her monthly. After Reconnecting, she formed two additional cabinets representing the business community and the public, structuring all of them so that school district presentations took up no more than half the meeting time, with the rest devoted to listening and discussing with community participants. In addition, the school board president initiated "linkage meetings" in neighborhoods. Modeled after Reconnecting's meetings, these have involved residents in solving pressing issues such as the redrawing of school attendance areas[27] as county growth continues. Others have been organized around specific groups such as the clergy who speak for segments of the population that the school board might not have heard from in the past.

Reconnecting also spurred a fundamental change in the relationship between the school board and the superintendent, with a clearer distinction between the board's role in setting policy goals, holding the superintendent accountable, and acting as a link to the community, as distinguished from the superintendent's role in implementing policy and managing day-to-day operations. A member of the school board explained the impetus for the change:

> One of the clearest sentiments that came out of the Reconnecting conversation for me was that the community did not want a school board that was deeply enmeshed in micro-managing the district. The board had been thinking about this before; we had met with consultants more than three years ago, but there was some resistance on the board and we were not really on top of it. This change was unlikely to have gone forward without Reconnecting.

Finally, one effect of Reconnecting in Horry County has the potential to alter significantly the balance of power between South Carolina school districts and other local government agencies. To foster economic growth, South Carolina had historically allowed local governments to grant tax exemptions to particular kinds of business park developments. In Horry County, the school district determined that a tax exemption to be granted to a large developer, Burroughs and Chapin, would result in substantial lost revenue for the school district. When negotiations with the Horry County

Council and the City of Myrtle Beach failed to reach an acceptable settlement, the school district filed suit against the city and county. Although the South Carolina Supreme Court eventually decided against the district,[28] the lawsuit was unprecedented, and represented an assertion that schools districts should have equal standing in local development decisions from which they have traditionally been omitted. School district officials were clear in saying that they could not have filed this lawsuit without Reconnecting:

> The Burroughs-Chapin issue seems to take us a little far afield, but in fact it has an important link to Reconnecting, and the history of this fight would be completely different without it. Reconnecting has disseminated information about the schools and the district; it has generated interest and stimulated public involvement in making the schools, and through them the community, stronger. A few years ago, the school district would have had no choice but to take what Burroughs-Chapin and the county planning commission gave them, but Reconnecting has shown the Superintendent and the board what the community wants us to do, and it has given the community a reason to support the district's decision to stand up and fight (member of the school board).

The community support that we received over the lawsuit in the Burroughs-Chapin matter has been a real eye-opener, and it would be hard for anyone to argue that the same thing would have happened without Reconnecting. When we had to go out and make our case to the people, they were listening with "new ears," and they could see that it just didn't make sense to go on diverting tax money from education to subsidize developers at the same time that the community wants to make itself a center of growth for high tech R&D (school district official).

9.6.1.3 Richland 2

The initial effects of Reconnecting in Richland 2 were modest. After the Reconnecting agreement was completed, the steering committee had planned to work through homeowners' associations, school improvement councils, and other neighborhood groups to establish "civic brigades" throughout the district to get people talking about the agreement and motivate individual involvement. But attendance was low at the initial meetings, and the unanticipated variety of concerns made coordination difficult. Consequently, the steering committee sought to initiate several projects that would impact the entire district. Reconnecting shares the credit for increasing the participation of community volunteers, especially senior citizens, in the schools, and also for strengthening ties between schools and the business community. For instance, the steering committee worked with a teacher in one of the high schools to enlist local businesses in upgrading the school's vocational training facilities so that graduates would be competitive for state-of-the-art jobs. According to a steering committee member,

> The upshot has been that the businesses have gotten together to re-equip the school, and they will send trainers who are expert on the new generation of machines. If it had not been for Reconnecting ... this idea would have died like previous contacts. Reconnecting opened a door between the community and the district, and it then just needs a few people with good ideas and willingness to network to get the flow of support going.

In contrast to Greenville and Horry counties, several members of the Richland 2 school board noted that Reconnecting participants had not recommended any policy changes to the board, although it would likely have been open to them. Rather, the school board saw Reconnecting's contribution as less tangible than in the other two communities.

> [T]he Reconnecting organization and process gave the public a better mechanism for being heard. The fact that it was independent of the district, and that it was oriented toward moving beyond merely griping and emphasized thinking together about solutions, set a constructive tone that we in the district probably could not have accomplished on our own. ... I envision Reconnecting continuing to integrate ordinary people from the community into an active, thoughtful part in school politics. (Board member)

Before turning to an explanation of the differences in Reconnecting outcomes, it is important to note several indications of Reconnecting's effect at increasing public support for the schools, as the designers of the process expected. Greater support for the incumbent regime is not an outcome expected of all deliberative forums, and in fact the encouragement of engaged and discerning citizenship might well multiply criticism and opposition. The pattern of election results before and after Reconnecting is, however, quite clear. Horry and Richland 2 held school bond elections after Reconnecting, and Greenville had an advisory election on a millage (school tax) increase in May 2001. In Horry County, several Reconnecting participants were visible advocates of the bond measure, and it passed by a large margin, with 77 percent voting in favor.[29] Coupled with support for the district's lawsuit, the evidence is that Reconnecting increased and solidified public support for the schools. In Richland 2, there were two bond elections after the Reconnecting agreement: the first failed by a three percent margin, but the second, following an energetic campaign that included several prominent Reconnecting participants, passed by 36 percent with voter turnout six times higher than it had been in the earlier election. A school board member was typical in crediting Reconnecting with contributing to the strong positive vote:

> In the end, we got around 70 percent of the vote, and I'm convinced this is because the district had good relations with the community. This was partly due to the Reconnecting people on the bond committee, but I believe that the ties that had been established over the last couple of years, by way of the Reconnecting local meetings and community conversations, were very important.

In Greenville, school district supporters of the millage increase hoped that Reconnecting's committed concern for the schools would lead to an endorsement by steering committee members, but the issue of past school board spending practices and Reconnecting's role in crystallizing the issue appears to have weighed in on the opposite side. The proposed increase was defeated with a 69 percent negative vote.

9.6.2 Explaining the outcomes

In this section we compare the outcomes in Greenville and Horry County. We hypothesized that three factors – the organization of the deliberative process, the quality of the deliberative output, and local history and political culture – are likely to be significant in explaining differences in the extent to which citizen deliberation results in visible outcomes. The quality of the deliberative output does not distinguish these two communities. Reconnecting was equally inclusive in Greenville and Horry; the agreements were reached through a generally transparent process; norms of political equality were respected; and in both communities the process was notable for its civility and open-mindedness.

There was, however, considerable variation on the other two factors. The organization of the deliberative process revealed distinctions along two dimensions: the relationship between Reconnecting and the school district, and the quality and extent of media coverage. The collegial character of the connection in Horry County registered in several ways: the steering committee set the agenda but looked to district officials for background briefings on issues. Both sides felt comfortable with citizens discussing public expectations and criticisms in the presence of the superintendent and school board members. The superintendent's constructive posture sprang from her confidence that Reconnecting could serve as a useful component in an overall leadership strategy aimed at strengthening the links between the public and individual schools, and that the process would generate information about public concerns and preferences that could not be obtained as effectively in any other venue. Moreover, in a county where the overwhelming majority of adults have no direct contact with the schools because many are retired "empty nesters," Reconnecting offered the potential for expanding citizen involvement. Finally, Reconnecting was a source of leverage for the superintendent over the district's 43 principals, some of whom were less open to public engagement than she, but who were key to the success of her reform agenda. All the principals attended at least one Community Conversation and subsequently met with key participants. The result was that they clearly heard the public's criticisms, but they also felt less threatened once they could see that the public's involvement was motivated by supportive concern.

In contrast, the Greenville steering committee operated largely independently of the school district, receiving minimal logistical support for informing or mobilizing the public, and taking the position that district officials should not attend any of the meetings. The upshot was that the school board felt no special connection to Reconnecting and accorded it less weight than other community groups such as the Chamber of Commerce: "many board members are still smarting from being excluded from Reconnecting ... We were not 'reconnected' with them; we were not part of the process." Still, even on reflection almost a year after the process had ended and Reconnecting's limited impact in Greenville was evident, a steering committee member argued that:

> We've been very conscious to keep the establishment at arms-length through this process. The Greenville community has been one where the movers and shakers have been very good at manipulating people, splitting the opposition, discouraging people from getting involved by telling them that it's too complicated or by withholding information – and we did not want Reconnecting to be hijacked by their smooth operation.

A second difference between the two communities was the quantity and quality of the newspaper coverage. The *Myrtle Beach Sun News* published twice as many articles about Reconnecting as the *Greenville News* and the articles were longer and more in-depth. This variation reflects both differing approaches to civic journalism by the chains that owned the two newspapers (Gannett, then owner of the *Greenville News*, took a less comprehensive approach to civic journalism than Knight-Ridder, then owner of the *Myrtle Beach Sun News*), and differences in the editorial policies of the local papers themselves. The *Greenville News*, for instance, had four different reporters covering education in just 18 months, while the *Sun News* had the same reporter through the process. Like the *Greenville News*, the *Sun News* had young, inexperienced reporters, but the editors saw Reconnecting as a training opportunity for them. As one editor noted, "internally, we hope that Reconnecting will help develop different listening and reporting skills among our reporters, and that they will interact differently with citizens."[30]

These differences in how Reconnecting was organized reflect larger and more enduring differences in the history and political culture of the two communities. Despite their similar population growth and in-migration in recent years, Greenville and Horry are very different communities with sharply contrasting patterns of political development. Greenville has made a seamless transition from a mill town to a modern manufacturing hub. Yet its growing cosmopolitanism has not eradicated a long tradition of divisive politics that dates back to its racially segregated past, and that is reflected more recently in tensions between a traditionally powerful conservative business elite and newly mobilized Christian fundamentalists (Huff, 1995). The rancorous tradition of Greenville's politics is reflected in alternative newspapers and local talk radio, which have provided venues for a variety of groups, including anti-tax organizations and religious conservatives, to mount a chorus of nay-saying about government actions, and respondents of every political stripe commented on how this had increased cynicism about government and undermined support for promising private–public collaboration. A small sampling of comments by Reconnecting participants illustrates these sentiments:

> The negative voice in Greenville County started with the anti-tax people, but it goes deeper than that. You never read what these people are for, only what they are against. They have no answers for what should be done. A big segment of the community listens to them, and will believe what they say before they believe what the authorities say are the facts
>
> [...]
>
> the county council and authorities are clever at baiting the extremists so they fight and there's no coherent public position. Then they go on and do what they want. The school board is not trusted much more – they don't listen or else they manipulate the agenda so the testimony at public hearings gives them what they want. It's because the political authorities around here aren't trustworthy that the Greenville agreement focused on politics and policy.
>
> [...]
>
> local politicians seem to cater to special interest groups even more than they do in national politics. This is especially obvious when you look at the development of new housing subdivisions – which seems to be the main thing government does here in the Greenville area. Going to the public hearings about this kind of thing is a waste of time. ... We had a situation here where they wanted to build a hotel out on the road. People on our block wanted to go down to the county planning commission. I told them it would be a waste of time unless we had someone who was president or vice-president of a large company. You can't expect people to participate in government when they know they are not going to have any effect. The developers and the bankers are always there at those meetings, and they're probably also talking to the politicians and planning commis-

sion people in private. Politicians need them to finance their campaigns, so the bankers and developers have access that ordinary people don't.

In contrast to Greenville, Horry County has a tradition of more open, populist politics, which developed largely because of its geographical isolation well into the twentieth century. Its historical reputation of being the "independent republic of Horry" is still celebrated, even as the county has grown with the influx of newcomers. Part of that rural populist tradition emphasizes "self-help as a way of life" (Lewis, 1998: 140). Throughout Horry's history, ordinary citizens in the small towns throughout the county have come together in civic endeavors to build schools, libraries, and hospitals with local, grassroots contributions (Lewis, 1998). Because people generally feel closer to government in Horry, they are more trusting, but they also take a more differentiated view of political authorities. Reconnecting, for instance, revealed a variety of views of local government, with some characterizing county government much as their counterparts in Greenville do, while others were more trusting and positive. When it came to the school district, however, the consensus among Reconnecting participants was that the school district could be trusted. People noted that the administration and the board occasionally made mistakes and didn't always accomplish their goals, but they were seen as consistently "trying to do what's right." Participants wanted the school district to do a better job of improving student achievement, and some, particularly African-Americans and parents of students with disabilities, expressed concern about inequitable treatment. But throughout the process, it was clear that there was a strong reservoir of trust: participants believed that the school district leadership was sincere and working in the public interest, and several specifically mentioned that the current board was the best in recent memory.

Differences in history and political culture also influenced the strategies the steering committees followed in seeking to involve the public. The steering committee in Greenville understood its community, and in organizing Reconnecting it acted on the belief that the process would have little credibility if it did not distance itself from the district. Its aspiration – to bring a representative group of citizens together in a sustained deliberative process and to get a hearing for their agreement – stopped short of expecting that the school district would be highly responsive. In contrast, the steering committee in Horry looked to a more trustful and self-confident citizenry, especially in the rural parts of the county that are relatively untouched by developers and where local politicians live in circumstances quite similar to their constituents. Corresponding differences distinguish how citizens expected officials to respond. In Horry, Reconnecting participants had high expectations that school district officials would give sincere and positive consideration to the recommendations of ordinary citizens, even if they pointed to the need for fundamental changes. School officials in Greenville found this level of openness an unauthorized intrusion, but it provided the Horry County district a reservoir of active public support when the school district's fiscal autonomy was threatened. The legacy of local history is prominently reflected in the story of the Loris Family Learning Center, perhaps the most exemplary citizen action effort to come out of Reconnecting. The deliberative forum was a critical influence, but Reconnecting did not so much create the needed social capital as provide the impetus for acting on a long history of citizen involvement.

9.7 Conclusions and implications

With its normative requirements for inclusiveness, political equality, open-mindedness, and transparency, democratic deliberation represents an appealing alternative to how public participation and policymaking are currently structured in a number of policy domains, including education. As an ideal, deliberation holds great promise for reengaging the public in public education, and providing a more effective way to settle inevitable value-laden disputes. But deliberative ideals need to be translated into practical forms that take into account citizens' incentives to participate in public life and the barriers to that participation. The Reconnecting initiative in South Carolina sought to cross the boundary between deliberative conversation and policy impact by melding salient aspects of neighborhood associations and civic populism on the one hand with the normative canons of deliberative democracy on the other. By focusing citizen participation on specific problems in school–community relations, but grounding criticism in a wide-ranging conversation that highlighted past community achievements and hopes for the school district as a whole, the initiative moved beyond formulaic complaints to engage citizens in a critical but constructive dialogue.

Deliberative democracy has been criticized for being excessively rationalistic and animated by an implicit image of public choice without conflict. The Reconnecting process, marked by vigorous conversation at every level, squarely contradicts this depiction. By virtue of the public and deliberative quality of its proceedings, Reconnecting achieved a strong claim to constitute a legitimate input to the local political process. But other factors also conditioned its eventual impact on policy, most important among them the degree to which Reconnecting organizers and established political elites were able to converge in seeing the enterprise as potentially supportive rather than competitive, the extent to which media coverage of the deliberations fostered a sense of common enterprise in the community beyond the immediate participants, and the ability of the deliberative agreement to tap into embedded stores of local social capital.

9.7.1   Reconnecting's lessons

When we focus not on the differences across constituencies but on the commonalities, five lessons are indicative of the opportunities and challenges that a deliberative forum like Reconnecting presents to local school districts. The first, perhaps obvious in retrospect but worth stating for its difference from conventional shibboleths that hamper civic engagement, is that it is possible to have a civil discourse about the schools, even in communities with a history of divisiveness. As a member of the Greenville steering committee said in summing-up its accomplishment:

> Reconnecting really did work to do something that had never been done around here. It developed a structured but open environment that encouraged conversation rather than a gripe session. It was a method that worked successfully against domination, especially against the backdrop of local politics where the public always seems to be excluded unless the politicians want support for something. ... Through the process, community members learned to sit and have a civil conversation with people they disagreed with.

It was not by any means obvious at the beginning of the process that, if given the opportunity, ordinary citizens would be willing to engage in serious discussions about issues that directly impact their lives and to abide by norms of public civility.

A second lesson is that citizens representing a much broader spectrum of the community are willing and capable of engaging in discussions of education issues than has traditionally been assumed or encouraged by school districts. Although only a small proportion of the total population (less than one percent) participated in Reconnecting, the diversity of participants brought a wider range of backgrounds and interests than is typically represented at school activities, public meetings, or elections. Estimates of the proportion of "new participants" varied across the three communities, ranging from about ten to thirty percent of the total attendees, with all of them attracting unusual numbers of senior citizens and younger people without children.

A third lesson is that the success of a citizen forum in framing a realistic diagnosis of current problems and articulating their ideas for improvement as feasible proposals will often hinge on professionals' providing information, but without using their expertise and status to dominate the discussion. In places like Horry where the education establishment is trusted and accustomed to providing information in ways that preserve the equal standing of the public, incumbent officials can serve this function. In communities where public trust is lower and where there is little tradition of reciprocity between officials and the public, the role may need to be performed by third parties such as the League of Women Voters, other community groups, or local academics.

Fourth, Reconnecting highlights the challenge of mobilizing citizen action and institutionalizing a process of deliberative consultation. Reconnecting worked well in prompting the school districts to be more responsive to citizen concerns, but less well as a way to rally citizens to take responsibility for their schools. To some extent, this shortfall may be inevitable: the conventional image of American citizenship emphasizes monitoring and evaluating elected representatives' actions, not participating directly in governing (cf. Schudson, 1998; Pangle and Pangle, 2000: 27). Reconnecting shows that, if the purpose of a deliberative forum is to promote ongoing citizen participation, then it will be necessary to pay particular attention to building an infrastructure to sustain involvement. Creating a deliberative process is only the first part of the job. The next stage, implementation – pressuring political officials to take up the deliberative message – will require equally skilled leadership perhaps of a different sort, and at least as much commitment of time and resources. In the case of Reconnecting, the steering committee in each community devoted an extraordinary amount of time and effort to the deliberative process over more than a year; it was probably unrealistic to expect that this core group would also spearhead implementation of the agreement. Deliberation is widely acknowledged to be a costly decision mechanism; our research on *practical deliberation* shows that implementation costs need to be factored into the calculus that now focuses on decision costs.

The final lesson reflects on Reconnecting's mixed success as a public engagement effort aiming at getting citizens to look beyond their own schools and neighborhoods to the broader community. In all three communities, Reconnecting gave practical shape to deliberative theory's emphasis on political equality and inclusiveness, by beginning a process of building political identities and public understandings that extended beyond individual schools and neighborhoods. Yet the perspective was difficult for participants to sustain, and several of the most notable outcomes of Reconnecting were aimed below the level of the entire county or district. Moreover, the trade-off between expanding participation and conceptualizing interests at the level of the larger community was more difficult the larger and more heterogeneous the community was. As one school official noted, "geography doesn't create community, [and] this county is too big to have real 'community' in the true sense of the word." But an African American activist who wanted Reconnecting to concentrate more of its attention at the neighborhood level recognized in the same breath the importance of encouraging participants to think more broadly:

Even though there was no county-wide community change that came out of Reconnecting, the schools needed to hear the concerns, and it was important for people in the county to see that it was possible to think about the whole district in concrete terms. The large group meetings gave people a sense of what it was like in the rest of the county. And particularly questions of diversity and equity can only be seen and – ultimately – resolved at the level of the whole district.

The tension between the greater ease of mobilizing participation at the neighborhood level and the need for citizens to relate to wider jurisdictions is not easily resolved. One could, however, imagine a deliberative process that starts with decentralized public meetings, moves to the larger community level so participants understand the circumstances of their fellow citizens and can consider solutions that may require redistribution across local areas, but then returns to individual neighborhoods for some types of collective action.

In analyzing the Reconnecting experience, we have tried to be as balanced as possible in our assessment of it as an example of practical deliberation, and not to portray it as yet another "silver bullet" that will solve the problems of public education. We have seen that practical deliberation poses significant challenges for citizens: it demands participation from people not used to taking part; it admonishes thinking beyond immediate self-interest and acting on the principle of mutual respect; and it rewards articulate reflection more than status and material resources. But it is arguably the case that "deliberating with a purpose" demands even more of incumbent politicians, professional educators, and established bureaucrats: like their fellow citizens, they will need to defend their policies and practices publicly and be open to considering the merits of alternatives to their favored approaches. The pay-off, if practical deliberation is effective, is a broadening of the citizenry that trusts the schools as civic institutions and is willing to criticize when necessary and to help when needed. Like democracy itself, practical deliberation offers no guarantees, only possibilities.

Notes

1. On the history of citizen organizations in urban politics, see Peterson, 1981; on the Community Action Program, see Kramer, 1969; Altshuler, 1970; Lemann, 1989; on neighborhood groups see Yin and Yates, 1975; and especially Berry et al., 1993; Fung, 2004: ch. 1 is a concise overview.
2. Boyte, 2003: 738, 739; cf. Boyte and Kari, 1996; Sirianni and Friedland, 2001; Boyte, 2002.
3. On the practical value of "incompletely theorized agreements," see Sunstein (1996); Graham (2002).
4. The shared identification that springs from the "sense of place" not only recalls the history of experiences residents have in common but also points to a shared future. The "shadow of the future" makes the promise of long-run gains a realistic reason for participating or otherwise contributing to a collective effort in the short run.
5. Warren (2001).

6. Among the criteria of democratic processes, "enlightened understanding" is inevitably imprecise. Dahl (1989: 112) elaborates this standard: "This criterion implies, then, that alternative procedures for making decisions ought to be evaluated according to the opportunities they furnish citizens for acquiring an understanding of means and ends, of one's interests and the expected consequences of policies for interests, not only for oneself but for all other relevant persons as well. Insofar as a citizen's good or interests requires attention to a public good or general interest, then citizens ought to have the opportunity to acquire an understanding of these matters."

7. Gutmann and Thompson, 1996; Bohman, 1996; Benhabib, 1996; Cohen, 1997; Macedo, 1999; for an insightful overview, see Rosenberg, 2004.

8. On "public reason" in deliberation, see Rawls (1997); Cohen (1997); Bohman (1996: ch. 1); Gargarella (1998). On inclusiveness and legitimacy, see Young (2000); cf. Gunderson (1995); Goodin (2000). Relevant recent empirical studies include Druckman and Nelson (2003); McClurg (2003); Mutz (2006).

9. Moscovici (1985); Mendelberg (2002) reviews the literature in social psychology.

10. It should be noted that researchers' (and proponents') interest in deliberative polls and similar forums such as Americans Discuss Social Security has tended to be in gauging the effect of deliberation on participants' knowledge and opinions, rather than influencing policy (Price and Neijens, 1998; Lindeman, 2002 provide excellent reviews). Citizen juries, on the other hand, typically include a link to policymakers, but it is one that undermines the legitimacy of the deliberative forum as an autonomous expression of grass roots opinion, since citizen juries (like the "thin" public hearing mechanism they supplant) are organized by and are creatures of the administrative agencies that bring them into being (Rosenbaum, 1978; Crosby, 1995; Gastil and Levine 2005).

11. McDonnell and Weatherford, 1999; 2000.

12. For instance, although the organizers of deliberative polls have nearly always offered some remuneration, it has typically been minimal and the reasons given for nonparticipants seldom have to do with inadequate compensation (Fishkin, 1995; Cook and Jacobs, 1998).

13. This was due in part to the fact that the idea was novel and not completely worked out, but it is also the case that the organizers were aware that school and community leaders were sensitive about their prerogatives. Berry et al. (1993: 301–303) find very few cities in which neighborhood organizations have an established voice and administrators and elected politicians have formal incentives to respond, but this appears to be a necessary condition for sustaining neighborhood associations; cf. Fung, 2001.

14. In our interviews, school officials and parent leaders noted that conservative talk radio commentators had taken on the public schools as a regular topic, and they expressed concern that this medium was becoming an influential channel for the spread of highly negative – and often inaccurate – information and opinion.

15. All have since left those positions.

16. On "civic journalism," see Black (1997); Merritt (1998). The State Department of Education funded the project, with the Schools Boards Association taking responsibility for organizing it. The SCSBA was assisted by the Harwood Group, a national consulting firm that specializes in a variety of public engagement projects. Harwood worked with SCSBA and other school and media leaders to develop the overall template for Reconnecting and the materials to be used in the

public meetings and community conversations. Its staff also trained the steering committee members and, along with staff from the SCSBA, were available to consult with and assist the local steering committees.

17. Observers and participants identified a number of different factors for the low attendance, including public involvement in a district-wide strategic planning effort and several task forces that diverted participation away from Reconnecting; strong parental identity with a particular school, but not with the larger community or school district; the steering committee's lack of experience in mobilizing public participation; the neutrality of the school board about Reconnecting; and spotty newspaper coverage.

18. Greenville County is the largest of the 86 school districts in South Carolina, and over the past decade the county population grew by 18.6 percent to 379,616. Horry County's population grew between the 1990 and 2000 census by 36.5 percent to 196,629. Richland Two is one of two school districts in Richland County that has a total population of 320,677. Richland County's growth rate of 12 percent was slightly below the statewide rate of 15.1 percent.

19. "Ground Rules for Staying on Track" were posted at each meeting, and were honored by all participants. They included:

   • Everyone participates; no one dominates.
   • There are no "right" answers.
   • Keep an open mind.
   • It's okay to disagree – everyone has a right to their own views.
   • Focus on finding constructive solutions – not on complaining or placing blame.
   • Help keep the discussion on track.

20. For example, at the fourth and "final" Community Conversation in Horry County, the participants decided that they could not finish the agreement that night, and asked for an additional meeting several weeks later. During the interim, participants gathered more information on what the school district was already doing and refined their own recommendations for action. Consequently, we had to arrange to send another member of the research team to observe the final meeting and interview participants.

21. The role of religion in civic life and in the Reconnecting process merits a separate discussion, but it was present in every site in a variety of forms – e.g., in who was included in the Community Conversations, in where public meetings were held and how participants were recruited, in what topics were discussed, and in how participants viewed the role of the churches in shaping and supporting the schools.

22. Our composite measure includes rates of volunteer activity, number of club meetings attended in a year, number of nonprofit organizations per 1000 inhabitants, voter turnout in presidential elections, along with individual-level measures of informal sociability and social trust (cf. Putnam, 2000).

23. Such actions need not be in support of status quo policies or institutions; indeed given that deliberation is designed to foster reflective discussion of conventional arrangements, it is perhaps likely that participation would stimulate criticism and greater openness to change.

24. Public authorities might decide, for instance, to reconvene the original forum on a regular basis or to recur to deliberative procedures as an "institutional safety net" for especially demanding public choices (e.g., when a new initiative is being considered, or a crisis occurs).

25. Our fieldwork continued through the completion of the Reconnecting process in Greenville and Horry counties, and thus we can discuss outcomes there with some finality. In contrast, we were not able to observe in detail how the process came to closure in Richland 2, so that our discussion of that district is more tentative and less complete than for the other two.

26. The Loris Family Learning Center is located in a town of 4000 residents but serves adults throughout the rural communities in the northern part of the county. It is designed to teach adults computer skills and was primarily intended to train single parents as a way of moving them off welfare, but senior citizens and working adults are also taking advantage of the self-paced classes that are open to any adult county resident. In addition to the 52-hour computer class (four hours/week for 13 weeks), students must attend nine hours of parenting seminars and volunteer six hours either at the Learning Center or a school; non-parents volunteer 15 hours instead of attending the parenting seminars. Largely drawing on volunteer labor, the Center provides child care while parents are in class. When participants successfully complete the program, they receive a reconditioned computer. The county school district staffs the Center with the funding coming from the County Department of Social Services.

27. The "attendance area" for a school is the geographical boundary that circumscribes the area (e.g., neighborhoods) whose children are assigned to attend that school. When new housing subdivisions are built on the periphery of a town, this raises questions about which school the added children will attend. The issue becomes politically contentious when, for instance, nearby schools are already crowded, the social class composition of the new neighborhood is very different from nearby older neighborhoods, etc.

28. Horry County School District v. Horry County and the City of Myrtle Beach, opinion no. 25355, 4 September 2001.

29. With a requirement for a two-thirds majority, the prior school bond had failed at 61 percent approving.

30. One of the ways the *Sun News* used Reconnecting as a training opportunity was to have the entire staff, including the sports reporter, cover the 25 public meetings and report on them not in traditional news articles, but rather through verbatim transcripts of an entire meeting so readers would know exactly what was said by everyone who spoke.

Part II

Theoretical Reflections on the Empirical Research

10
Deliberative Democracy
Joshua Cohen

Before getting to the matter at hand, I want to say how moving it is to read a set of papers that are committed so deeply to both democratic hopes and rational inquiry. Democratic commitments have not led the contributors to back off from the implications of their research, and commitments to rational inquiry have not provoked cynicism about political values. Putting aside the important lessons about deliberative democracy, there is much to be learned from this volume about the marriage of rational inquiry and moral-political conviction.

10.1 Deliberative democracy

Carl Schmitt said that deliberation belongs to the world of parliamentarism, where legislators reason together about how to address public problems, not to the world of mass democracy, where ethno-culturally homogeneous peoples find leaders who instruct about who the enemy is. According to Schmitt (1985: 6), "the development of mass democracy has made argumentative public discussion an empty formality." Rejecting Schmitt's view, deliberative democrats explore possibilities of combining deliberation with mass democracy, and are hopeful about the possibilities of fostering a more deliberative democracy.[1]

Deliberation, generically understood, is about weighing the reasons relevant to a decision with a view to making a decision on the basis of that weighing. So an individual can make decisions deliberatively; a jury has a responsibility to deliberate; and a committee of oligarchs can deliberate: deliberation is not an intrinsically democratic matter. Democracy is a way of making binding, collective decisions that connects those decisions to the interests and judgments of those whose conduct is regulated by the decisions. The essential idea is that those subject to the decisions are treated as equals by the processes of making the decisions, including agenda-setting and preference formation, as well as collective decision-making. Democracy also is a kind of society – a society of equals – but because this volume focuses largely on formal decision-making bodies at different levels of government, I will confine myself to the more specifically political understanding of democracy. I should add that even if we think of democracy politically, as a way to make binding collective decisions, constructing a more deliberative democracy is not an exclusively political project: deliberative democracy requires attention to encouraging deliberative capacities, which is, inter alia, a matter of education, information, and organization (the comments in Chapter 9 by Weatherford and McDonnell on the importance of media in successful local school reform are instructive on this point). But, once more, I will put these issues (largely) to the side because of the focus of the volume.

Deliberative democracy, then, combines these two elements, neither reducible to the other. It is about making collective decisions and exercising power in ways that trace to the reasoning of the equals who are subject to the decisions: not only to their preferences, interests, and choices, but to their reasoning.[2] Essentially, the point of deliberative democracy is to subject the exercise of collective power to reason's discipline, to what Habermas famously described as "the force of the better argument," not the advantage of the better situated. The point of deliberative democracy is not to do away with power, whatever that might mean; it is not simply to subject power to the discipline of talking, because talking is not the same as reasoning (consider verbal assaults, threats, insults, racial slurs, lies, blowing smoke, cheering, exchanging pleasantries, exploring common experiences); nor is it simply to reason together, because reasoning together may have no effect on the exercise of collective power.

Moreover, not just any subjection of power to reason's discipline is a form of deliberative democracy: Plato's philosopher-guardians subject power to reason's discipline – that, at any rate, is what they say they are doing. But deliberative democracy is a kind of democracy, so the reasoning must in some recognizable way be the reasoning of the equal persons who are subject to the decisions. And not just the process of reasoning, but the content of the reasons themselves must have a connection to the democratic conception of people as equals. Deliberative democracy is about reasoning together among equals, and that means not simply advancing considerations that one judges to be reasons, but finding considerations that others also can reasonably be expected to acknowledge as reasons. In short, the ideal of deliberative democracy is to discipline collective power through the common reason of a democratic public: democracy's public reason.

Deliberative democracy, thus understood, is a distinctive interpretation of democracy: democracy, no matter how fair and no matter how participatory, is not deliberative unless actual reasoning is central to the process of collective decision-making. Nor is democracy deliberative simply because the process and its results are reasonable: capable of being given a rational defense, even a rational defense that would be recognized as such on reflection by those subject to the decisions. The concern that the results be reasonable must play a role in the process itself. Thus the contrast between deliberative and aggregative democracy. In an aggregative democracy, citizens aim to advance their individual and group interests. If the process is fair, the results may be reasonable (depending on the content of the interests). But unless the reasonableness is aimed at by participants in the process, we do not have deliberation. Of course, it might be argued that reasonable results must be aimed at to be achieved, and that democracy must therefore be deliberative to be reasonable. So, for example, if we have a hypothetical test for the reasonableness of decisions, where the hypothetical process involves reasoning under idealized conditions about what is best to do, then it might be said that the actual process must look something like the hypothetical to provide a basis for confidence in the reasonableness of results. Still, it is best to see this connection between reasonableness and deliberation as a broadly empirical claim, and to keep deliberation as a way of deciding – a way that comprises both the nature of the process and the content of the reasons – distinct from reasonableness as a property of decisions.

Aggregative and deliberative democracy do not exhaust the space of interpretations of democracy. Consider a community of politically principled citizens, each of whom endorses a conception of justice. The conceptions they endorse differ, but each person accepts a conception of justice as setting bounds on acceptable policy and decent institutions. Assume further that they do not see much point in arguing about what justice requires, though each conscientiously uses his or her own conception in deciding what to support and in setting limits on what is permissible. No one in this political community thinks that politics is simply about advancing interests, much less a struggle between friends and enemies. But reasoning together plays a very restricted role in public political life: the members accept that they owe one another an exercise of conscientious judgment, but not that they owe a justification by references to reasons that others might reasonably be expected to accept. I will not develop this distinction further here, but mention it to underscore that the case for deliberative democracy needs to be made not simply in contrast with accounts of democracy that focus on interests and power but also in contrast with views that assume an exercise of moral-political judgment by individual citizens, but not deliberation.

This emphasis on subjecting power to reason's discipline is a thread that runs through much of the literature on deliberative democracy. Thus, Amy Gutmann and Dennis Thompson (2004:.3) say that "deliberative democracy's basic requirement is 'reason-giving'." Jon Elster (1998: 8) also emphasizes that deliberation is about argument, in fact arguments addressed to people committed to rationality and impartiality. John Dryzek (2000: 31) says that a "defining feature of deliberative democracy is that individuals participating in democratic processes are amenable to changing their minds and their preferences as a result of the reflection induced by deliberation."

Elsewhere he (2000: 8) emphasizes "communication that encourages reflection upon preferences without coercion." But these characterizations of deliberative democracy are not literally *defining*: they follow from the more fundamental characteristics of deliberative democracy. The *point* of deliberative democracy is not for people to reflect on their preferences, but to decide, in light of reasons, what to do. Deciding what to do in light of reasons requires, of course, a willingness to change your mind, since you might begin the deliberative task with a view about what to do that is not supported by good reasons. But the crucial point is that Dryzek (2000:167) emphasizes that deliberation is basically about reasoning – about rational argument – and that other kinds of communication need to be "held to rational standards."

This very abstract statement of what deliberative democracy is raises large questions: about what more precisely deliberation is, about how to make democracies more deliberative, about the consequences of deliberation for political outcomes, and why deliberative democracy is a good thing. The chapters in this book all throw new light on these issues. Given the constraints on space, I have focused my comments on two questions: in the first section, I explore the connections between several of the arguments and the deliberative-democratic ideal, at least as I have described it. I have emphasized the essential role of reasoning, and want to consider whether the arguments in the chapters here are really about reasoning as distinct from other forms of communication and participation. In the second section, I explore the implications of the studies reported here for whether deliberative democracy is a good thing: in particular, whether it has the kinds of outcome-improving effects that have been attributed to it.

10.2   Deliberation?

I have emphasized that deliberation is about reasoning, not simply discussing: the connection to reasoning, I believe, lies at the roots of the normative distinctiveness and force of the deliberative democratic idea. Rosenberg's distinctions between different kinds of discourse points in this direction, as does the Mendelberg-Karpowitz distinction between social-norm-guided and reason-guided discussion. But several of the papers collected here have a very uncertain bearing on the deliberative-democratic idea because they are not in any straightforward way about reasoning.

Cook, Delli Carpini, and Jacobs (CDCJ) tell a hopeful story about political participation. Large numbers of citizens, their survey indicates, are discursive political participants: contrary to common complaints about citizen disconnection from politics, CDCJ find that a large majority (74 percent) talk about political issues in public settings, though the principal public setting seems to be conversational, rather than at formal political meetings. Moreover, CDCJ argue, socio-economic status is not a big predictor of discursive participation, but political interest and organizational membership are: as with so much else in politics, discursive participation – and therefore democracy itself – is fostered by a vibrant world of organizations intermediate between family and polity. With discursive participation, as with most forms of participation (except campaign contributions), interest and opportunity are the big players, not resources.[3] They observe that a large predictor of attendance at meetings, as one location for discursive participation, is whether you have been invited by an organization. Of course, and as ever, worries about endogeneity loom large: invitations are not randomly distributed, and discursive attendees may be invited by organizations because of a prior record of attendance. But however the causation works, the findings about the organizational roots of discursive participation are important.

But while the findings about discursive participation are hopeful and important, I am uncertain about their bearing on deliberative democracy. Participation, even discursive participation, is not the same as deliberation. So we need to know whether discursive participants are reasoning and whether that reasoning has any impact on the exercise of power: intuitively, we need to know whether the discussion aims at persuasion by appeal to evidence, or principles, or analogies, or arguably illustrative stories, or other considerations that aim to show why one decision is the right one or the best one. (I am not trying to define deliberation here: we all have a decent grasp of what a relevant reason is, and of the plurality of forms of reasoning.) To be sure, if citizens were not especially discursive the news would be very bad for deliberative democracy, because deliberation is a subset of discourse. But CDCJ do not tell us anything about the substance of the discursive communication, which could consist not in reasoning but in reports on or discussions of political news or bare expressions of political attitude, with no particularly deliberative thrust, or the kind of egocentric discourse described in Rosenberg's contribution, or communication substantially guided by social norms. Moreover, much of the discursive participation they describe – both in informal conversation and at meetings – might consist largely of discussion among the like-minded, which arguably is not a form of deliberation.

Katherine Cramer Walsh's paper raises similar questions. Walsh distinguishes civic dialogue from deliberation: one especially important difference is that, whereas deliberation aims at decision, dialogue does not. Walsh suggests that discussion of the kind that we find in programs of civic dialogue – for example, efforts at civic dialogue on race – may have distinctive virtues in enabling people to explore differences in outlook, precisely because such discourse does not aim at decision, is therefore not competitive, and parties may therefore be more willing to open up. Moreover, it may be that until people have explored their differences in experience, attitude, and belief they may lack the mutual understanding that is needed to deliberate together in real time. So discourse may be a helpful precursor to deliberation, especially under conditions of racial or ethnic division. If, for example, we want to reason together to address issues about the allocation of resources to schools or the design of programs in a racially diverse community, our efforts may be aided by arriving at some prior mutual understanding about attitudes toward race and education, understanding that may be difficult to achieve in the more focused setting of collective decision-making, no matter how deliberative.

Walsh's claims on this issue are interesting and suggestive. But the findings would be more persuasive if we had some studies of deliberation by comparably diverse groups with and without prior discourse. After all, the idea that open-ended discourse is a helpful precursor to deliberation is not at all obvious, in part for reasons that Walsh mentions. It might be that the discipline of arriving at a consequential, practical decision – the discipline associated with deliberation rather than dialogue – helps to make differences in attitude and belief seem less germane, whereas dialogue that provides for and encourages a more free-floating exploration of differences may serve precisely to "exacerbate divides" (24). Rather than examining differences as a way to better appreciate common ground, discursive participants may use the occasion to reaffirm them, or may simply be unwilling to invest the effort in what strikes them as a low-return activity. This last possibility is suggested by Walsh's observation that the willingness to invest in a discursive exploration of differences may be limited by the fact that discourse does not aim at decision. In civic dialogues about race, a large burden is placed on black participants, and "Without the incentive of a potential impact on policy, why, indeed, would angry brothers and sisters choose to be involved?" (12). Moreover, and on the other side, it might be that deliberation about policy issues might work well, even without prior discourse, if the deliberation is properly mediated and parties are well informed.

Without, then, disputing the importance of discourse, I do not think we yet have a compelling case for the interesting idea, suggested in Walsh's contribution, that discourse helps to set the stage for a more fruitful deliberation. Discourse might break down because it is too open-ended, and deliberation may be able to work without discourse if it is well structured.

Christian List explores the role of deliberation in addressing a fundamental issue of social choice theory: how, he asks, can we restrict the scope of disagreement among individuals so that attractive methods of collective choice – say, majority rule – will result in collective decisions that satisfy minimal rationality conditions? Arrow showed that collective choice rules cannot, over an unrestricted domain of individual orderings, generate collective rankings that are both responsive to individuals – thus express an idea of voter sovereignty – and are rational. List proposes that deliberation may work to restrict the domain of individual rankings in ways that make collective rationality consistent with voter sovereignty. Unlike the other contributions in this volume, List's argument is largely analytical, not empirical. And his case for the disagreement-limiting effects of deliberation – particularly in the judgment-aggregation setting – is correspondingly speculative. The speculation is interesting, but its force is limited, I believe, by the absence of an explicit account of deliberation.

List emphasizes that deliberation need not produce consensus in order to reduce disagreement in ways that make rational collective choices possible. He distinguishes preference aggregation from judgment aggregation, and offers some suggestive evidence – from Fishkin-Luskin deliberative polls – that deliberation induces the property of single-peakedness in individual preference orderings that makes rational collective decisions possible. The result is important because, as List observes, people with single-peaked preferences need not agree on what is best to do, but do have a kind of meta-agreement about how to locate alternatives in a single dimension. So with single-peakedness, some people may prefer the left, some may prefer the right, and some may prefer the center, but no one puts the center at the bottom of their list.

List proposes an analogous condition to single-peaked preferences for judgment aggregation: he calls it unidimensional alignment (U). List shows that if U is satisfied, then we can have consistent group judgments (and thus avoid the "discursive dilemma"), and he suggests – this is the speculative part – that deliberation may encourage judgments that satisfy U.

I find this speculation very puzzling. To see why, let's consider List's example. We have three judgments:

P: A deficit is affordable
Q: Spending on education should be increased
If P, then Q: If a budget deficit is affordable, then spending on education should be increased.

I will observe in passing that List interprets the conditional in the third judgment as a material conditional, rather than a subjunctive conditional: this keeps the semantics simple, but it seems otherwise implausible. This interpretation implies that someone who judges that a deficit is not affordable must also accept the conditional: *if a deficit is affordable, then spending on education should be increased* (because the antecedent is false, the conditional is true). This interpretation substantially restricts the arrays of individual judgments that judgment aggregation needs to address: we do not have the case of the person who thinks that a deficit is not in fact affordable, thinks (perhaps for libertarian reasons) that spending on education should not be increased, and rejects the claim that *if a deficit is affordable, spending should be increased*.

Putting this concern aside, let's consider the problem of judgment aggregation under majority rule in a three-person group. Suppose two people judge that *P*; two others judge that *If P, then Q*; and that two also judge that *not-Q*. If we accept the requirement of "systematicity," then the group judgment on any proposition is fixed by aggregating individual judgment on that proposition (whether atomic or not). So we have the group judging that P, that *If P, then Q*, and *not-Q*. But if the group is rational, and judges that P and that *If P, then Q*, then it is committed to judging that Q. The problem is that we have two ways to fix the group judgment about Q: by aggregating individual judgments on Q and by treating the group judgments as closed under (known) logical consequence, and these two ways can come apart.

Enter condition U: if individual judgments satisfy U, this group-level inconsistency cannot arise. Notice now that a collection of three rational individuals faced with judging whether P, whether $P \rightarrow Q$, and whether Q can satisfy U in two ways (assuming that no two share the same judgments):

Case 1: (P, $P \rightarrow Q$, Q), (not-P, $P \rightarrow Q$, Q), (not-P, $P \rightarrow Q$, not-Q)
Case 2: (not-P, $P \rightarrow Q$, Q), (not-P, $P \rightarrow Q$, not-Q), (P, not-[$P \rightarrow Q$], not-Q)

But we have a violation of U in the following case:

Case 3: (P, $P \rightarrow Q$, Q), (not-P, $P \rightarrow Q$, not-Q), (P, not-[$P \rightarrow Q$], not-Q)

List mentions Case 2, not Case 1, perhaps because Case 1 avoids the dilemma through agreement on a proposition ($P \rightarrow Q$), rather than through meta-agreement, and he wants to show that something weaker than substantive agreement on a proposition suffices to avoid the dilemma.

Deliberation now enters because, List speculates, it may induce satisfaction of U. But what model of deliberation could support the conclusion that Cases 1 and 2 might result from deliberation, but Case 3 could not? To see the difficulty, notice first that there is nothing intrinsically unreasonable about (P, $P \rightarrow Q$, Q): that is the ordering of person 1 in Case 1. Now notice, too, that Case 3 – which violates U – differs from Case 2 – which does not – only in that person 1 judges (not-P, $P \rightarrow Q$, Q) in Case 2 and (P, $P \rightarrow Q$, Q) in Case 3. Suppose that person 1 changes judgments because he is persuaded through further argument that a deficit is affordable: factual considerations advanced by the third person may suffice to convince him. The other two parties remain fixed. This means that we have produced Case 3 from Case 2 by an apparently reasonable change of opinion. We have already said that there is nothing intrinsically unreasonable about judging that P or that (P, $P \rightarrow Q$, and Q). How could we exclude the possibility that this shift of individual judgments, from a reasonable position to a reasonable position, might result from deliberation?

In answer to this question, someone might object that U comes into play in an entirely different way than I have been supposing, and that this different way will link it to deliberation: that U plays a more constitutive role in deliberation. In particular, suppose we think of deliberation as aimed at deciding *what we judge best*, not simply what each of us individually judges best (this appears to be what Rosenberg has in mind by rational as distinct from conventional discourse), and that we see U as a necessary condition on there being we-judgments rather than merely I-judgments. Then, since we only have we-judgments if minimal rationality conditions are fulfilled at the group level, and those conditions can be fulfilled only if U is satisfied, individual deliberators need to take U into account in deciding what their own judgments should be. If we are deliberating, thus looking to arrive at we-judgments, then the fact that the separate judgments do not satisfy U would provide a reason for modifying our judgments.

But this will not do. While we-judgments (like any other judgments) need to meet minimal rationality conditions and, assuming systematicity, this requires individual judgments to satisfy U, the deliberators can nevertheless resist U: that is, form their own judgments without thinking of violations of U as providing reasons for changing judgments. All they need suppose is that not every collection of individuals constitutes a personifiable *we* with its own judgments: the basis for a distinctively group deliberation, focused on what *we* ought to do, may be absent. This response is available, even if the collection of individuals needs to make a decision: even then, it is open to members of the group to say that while each person has his or her own judgments and the process must issue in a result, that it would nevertheless be wrong to treat that result as expressing the judgment of a personifiable group: individual judgments lack sufficient coherence to provide the basis for a we with its own judgments.

This is not the place for a more detailed discussion of the discursive dilemma: in a larger discussion, it would be important to ask about systematicity as well. But however the dilemma is to be handled, the connection between deliberation and U strikes me as unconvincing.

10.3   Why deliberative democracy?

I want to shift attention now, from comments focused on the issue of what deliberation is to a discussion of why deliberation is a good thing and what the contributions to this volume say about this question.

10.3.1   Reasons for deliberative democracy

There is no single story about why deliberative democracy is a good thing. To be sure, it seems hard to deny that the exercise of collective power should be supported by appropriate reasons: that it should have, in the jargon of the constitutional lawyer, a rational basis. But as I have emphasized, deliberative democracy is not simply the indisputable thesis that the exercise of power should be rationally defensible, even rationally defensible by reference to some restricted class of reasons suited to democracy. The question is why it is important to discipline the exercise of power by actually reasoning together. I will mention three kinds of considerations.

One argument has to do with promoting justice. Thus suppose we think that requirements of justice are worked out by reasoning under ideal conditions of information and equal standing. It might be said that agreement under idealized conditions *determines* what justice requires, or, alternatively, that such agreement provides good evidence about what the independently fixed demands of justice are. In either case, whether idealized agreement has a constitutive or an epistemic role, the argument for deliberative democracy is that we need actual deliberation if collective decisions are to meet the standards of justice that would be accepted under idealized conditions of information and equality, because actual deliberation is our best way to figure out what the results of ideal deliberation could be (I say "what the results could be" rather than "what the result would be" because it might be that ideal deliberation imposes constraints, but does not – as Rawls argues – fix a determinate set of principles).

A second argument in support of deliberative democracy is about desirable consequences of deliberation, apart from promoting justice. The central intuitive idea behind these outcome-improving arguments is that reason-giving is a distinctive form of communication. One way that this might matter is that the requirement that I defend my proposals with reasons that are capable of being acknowledged as such by others, will – whatever my own preferences – constrain the proposals I advance and defend in ways that promote the common good. Of course if every proposal can be rationalized in an acceptable way, then the requirement of defending proposals with acceptable reasons will not have the desired effect. A second way that the need to give reasons acceptable to others might produce desirable consequences is if reason-giving of itself changes preferences. So while I start preferring most what is best for me or my group, the practice of defending proposals with reasons may change my preferences, dampening the tension between my beliefs about what is right or politically legitimate and what I prefer. The third way it might work is for deliberation to elicit information: this depends on a commitment to truthfulness or sincerity in communication, which may itself be reinforced through deliberation, but is hard to construct from nothing. But that is true about the entire account of deliberation: though deliberation may reinforce a prior commitment to argue on terms that others can acknowledge as reasons, some such prior commitment must be in place if the enterprise of mutual reason-giving is to get off the ground and be sustained. No amount of uncertainty and mutual dependence, and no amount of care in crafting decision rules, will turn strategic reasoners into deliberators.

A third case for deliberative democracy is not about its consequences, but its intrinsic virtues as a way to make collective decisions. Making decisions by reasoning together on common ground arguably has attractions on grounds of legitimacy, mutual respect, and community, and also provides a plausible foundation for the authority of coercively enforced law.

The concern of papers in this volume is principally with the second of these arguments, with some attention to the first. So I will put the third aside here, but it is important to bear in mind that the intuitive attractions of deliberative democracy derive substantially from arguments of the third type. Indeed, one way to think about the relationship between the intrinsic case and the first two lines of argument is that the intrinsic case shows why deliberative democracy is a compelling political ideal. But then arguments along the first two lines help to strengthen the case by showing the fit with justice and with effectiveness of policy.

10.3.2 Some empirics

Archon Fung offers one argument about deliberative democracy and policy outcomes. Fung describes a range of efforts – community policing in Chicago, deliberative polling, the Oregon health plan, Porto Alegre's participatory budgeting, and citizen summits – to promote a more deliberative democracy by creating "minipublics." He offers an analytical framework for understanding these efforts by setting out their "design features," and then explores what kinds of results we can expect from each in virtue of the design features: Fung has five cases, eight design features, and eight dimensions of outcomes. The analysis of design features is original and important: it is of great help to have a way to draw analytical distinctions between efforts as different as participatory budgeting and deliberative polling, even as we see them as different ways to make democracy more deliberative by getting citizens to reason together about the substance of public policy. Moreover, Fung is right to see that a wide range of outcome measures may be relevant to assessing the virtues of minipublics with different fundamental features. Thus it matters whether the participants get new information as a result of reasoning together, and it also matters whether deliberation shapes the substance of policy. The capaciousness in the argument is especially attractive.

That said, the results linking design features to outcomes are very preliminary and largely speculative. Of course it is hard to pin down the effects of eight distinct design features on eight outcome dimensions, all qualitatively described, with five cases. But I do not mean simply to be making an obvious point about small-N studies. We face a familiar and generic difficulty in showing, either through case studies or large-N studies that changes in processes of collective decision-making lead to differences in outcomes. Putting aside the issue of deliberative democracy, it is difficult to make the case because whatever is producing the process changes may also account for the changes in outcome: as when a party with a redistributive project politically mobilizes the less advantaged (as in the Porto Alegre case) and also promotes a shift in economic resources to them, thus suggesting (incorrectly) that the mobilization explains the outcome.

A few studies, though not of deliberative democracy, have addressed these problems of spuriousness. Ansolabehere, Gerber, and Snyder (2002) have shown that court-ordered reapportionment in the 1960s shifted public goods spending in the states in the direction of previously underrepresented districts: a compelling argument about process changes (equal votes) leading to changes of result (equal spending), but a special case because reapportionment – and the increased equality of representation – was arguably a court-ordered exogenous shock, not the product of something that might itself have caused the changes in public goods expenditures. Similarly, Chattopadhyay and Duflo (2004) have shown that reserved seats for women on Indian village councils have led to shifts in public goods spending, with greater spending on goods that are preferred by women when the head of the village council is a woman. Here the methodological problem is solved by randomness in the process that determines which village councils will be headed by women. These two studies are exceptional, and we have no equally compelling case in the analysis of deliberative democracy for the conclusion that changing how decisions get made – in particular, making them more deliberatively – leads to changes in the content of the decisions.

Still, we do have some suggestive evidence. Thus, participatory budgeting in Porto Alegre – one of Fung's cases – appears to have produced substantial shifts in the allocation of public resources to the poor: In Porto Alegre, for example, access to water doubled between 1989 and 1996, growing from 49 percent to 98 percent. It should be said, however, that these results may come not from deliberation, but – even putting aside the dominance of a left party – from the sheer fact of broader participation. To be sure, deliberation may be part of the story: it may shift preferences and collective decisions by excluding proposals that cannot be defended on the basis of acceptable reasons.[4] And we do have a good case for policy-preference-shifting deliberation in the case of deliberative polling, where the random sampling provides a good case that deliberation is doing the work.[5] But as Fung observes, deliberative polling is pretty far upstream from policy, so we do not have much evidence of effects on the exercise of collective power, and do not know about the persistence of political beliefs acquired in the deliberative polling set-up. What we may need to make headway on these issues of spuriousness is a mix of findings drawn from deliberative polls and group-decision experiments, with comparative studies of institutional innovation of the kind that Fung reports.

Like Fung, Weatherford and McDonnell are concerned about the effects of deliberative democracy on outcomes, and they complain – rightly in my view – that deliberative democrats have not focused sufficient attention on this issue. They compare efforts in three places to incorporate community input into decisions on school reform, and find that efforts are most successful in the community (Horry) in which background levels of trust are greater and the media play a more constructive role. The results on media effects are not surprising, but they are of great importance. The discussion of deliberative democracy has not given enough attention to the media either in helping to make it possible for citizens to deliberate in the first place or in helping to channel the results of deliberation into effective policy: indeed, much of the literature has barely paid attention to the media (Habermas is an important exception, and Ackerman and Fishkin's *Deliberation Day* makes some suggestive speculations). Weatherford and McDonnell (Chapter 9 in this book) remind us that moving deliberative democracy from theory to practice will require closer attention to the political role of old and new media.

A second important finding is that the process of community deliberation works better when the school board cooperates closely with the steering committee that is responsible for devising programs to reconnect community and schools. We find such cooperation in Horry, where the level of trust is higher, rather than in Greenville, where fears of cooptation (against a background of lower trust) led to less cooperative and less productive relations between school board and steering committee. This conclusion may seem intuitive: of course you get more effectiveness when the recommending body and the policy-making body are in a cooperative relationship. But it runs counter to the concern that close collaboration between citizen deliberators and elected officials will lead to insufficient independence of the citizen deliberators and, in the limit, to cooptation: yet more colonization of civil society by the state, and short-circuiting of independent reflection on what is right by administrative concerns about practicality.[6]

The findings by Weatherford and McDonnell do not show that the concern about cooptation is wrong, but they do qualify it. They suggest that we need to be attentive to both the conditions required for good deliberation and the conditions required for real impact on outcomes. In some cases, as was arguably the case in Horry, there may be no tension: if a policy-making body is genuinely interested in policy innovation, and if there is a high degree of trust between citizens and policy makers, then close connections between deliberative citizens and elected officials may be the key to success. When that background is absent, as in the case of Greenville, we may face trade-offs between deliberativeness (which requires independence) and effectiveness, which requires collaboration.

Mendelberg and Karpowitz (Chapter 6 in this book) look more closely at deliberation in experimental settings (focused on income distribution) and suggest that deliberative democrats have been naïve in their expectations about the results of deliberation. Deliberative democrats expect people who discuss issues to reason about them, to increase their level of empathetic concern, and arrive at substantively just decisions. According to Mendelberg and Karpowitz, two factors intervene to disrupt such expectations. First, discussions have a social side, and much that happens is a matter of compliance with group norms, not advancing reasons. Second, discussions have a political structure: in particular, deliberation issues in decision, decisions require decision rules, and decision rules shape outcomes. So it turns out that in the experiments they study, groups with large numbers of women deciding under a unanimity rule fix a more generous income floor than other groups. Deliberative democrats expect reasoning to result in a generous floor. But they are, Mendelberg and Karpowitz argue, insufficiently attentive to social psychology and politics. The generous results depend not so much on the pure structure of reasoning, but are highly sensitive to group composition and decision rules.

A different way to describe the results is to return to the distinction between deliberation and discussion. It could be that group composition and decision rules are important to transforming mere discussion into reasoning of the right kind: the point is not that genuine deliberation sometimes generates mean-spirited results, but that not every discussion is deliberative. As Mendelberg and Karpowitz observe, "good deliberation can be undermined by group norms" (p. 10). Once we attend to the discussion/ deliberation distinction (or to the distinctions between form of discourse that Rosenberg explores), we should not expect deliberation – certainly not good deliberation, attentive to diverse arguments – to be the automatic product of group communication.

Thus consider the concern, noted here and emphasized by Cass Sunstein, that deliberation may make things worse by producing group polarization. Three sources of such pressure have been suggested: that group discussion imposes normative pressure on group members (in particular, pressure not to be less extreme than the group mean, so that those who are less extreme move closer to the predeliberative mean, thus shifting the mean); that group discussion in a relative homogenous group is dominated by arguments embraced by the majority; and that participants tend to express shared information in group discussion not private information (Mendelberg, 2002). Wide-ranging evidence, from both experimental and real group-decision-making settings, underscores the seriousness of these concerns. But at least in general terms, the remedies seem straightforward, whatever the likelihood of their adoption. Thus, polarization of group opinions is driven in part by homogeneity. So it is important to be sure that deliberative settings include an expression of diverse views: in some deliberative settings, the competitive quality of the decision – when the issue at stake is the allocation of scarce resources – engenders such expression. In other settings, ensuring diversity of opinion may be a matter of institutional principle or the responsibility of a moderator. It may be important as well to ensure that some time is devoted, as part of the design of discussion, to expressing beliefs or judgments that are assumed not to be shared by others in the group: ensuring that this happens seems to be well within the reach of moderators or participants themselves.

The point generalizes beyond the case of polarization: deliberative democracy, like any form of democracy, depends for its success on a variety of particulars, including institutional particulars, and its deficiencies may be remediable by modifying those particulars. For this reason, studies of pathologies of deliberative decision-making need to be treated with some care. Typically, as in the results reported here by Mendelberg and Karpowitz, the pathologies may emerge from group decision-making conducted without efforts to avoid the pathological results. Such studies are of great importance, but they often can be interpreted as a source of cautionary notes and recommendations for improvement rather than as undermining the importance of deliberation.[7]

That said, I do not want to underestimate the significance of the concerns expressed in Mendelberg and Karpowitz, which, I believe, go to the heart of the ideal of deliberative democracy. The more fragile deliberation is, the more structure that needs to be in place to move from discussion to good deliberation, the less confidence we can reside in the project of building a more deliberative democracy. A naïve version of the deliberative ideal supposes that people are waiting to deliberate, and only need to get divisive, competitive, political structures out of the way. Deliberation, as Mendelberg and Karpowitz underscore, seems to be a more fragile accomplishment.

This issue of fragility also emerges in Rosenberg's essay (which is why I have reserved discussion of his contribution until now, though it could have been discussed in the previous section, since it is not principally about the effects of deliberation on outcomes). Rosenberg's essay offers a rich and complex conceptual account of four kinds of discourse – egocentric, conventional, rational, and transformative. He studies the relative prevalence of these distinct forms of discourse in conversations among Laguna Beach parents about issues of education policy in the local school district. Though the distinctions between the four types of discourse are not original to Rosenberg, he has made impressive steps not only in clarifying them, but in making them empirically tractable. An intercoder reliability of 92 percent in classifying the forms of discourse is encouraging, though it would be even more encouraging if there were more variations in the kinds of discourse. Rosenberg finds that there is very little rational or transformative discourse. Instead, the discussions are largely conventional: that is, each person says what he or she thinks the policies should be, rather than making strategic moves (egocentric), or seeking common ground and aiming to articulate we-judgments (rational), or critically analyzing his or her own views (transformative).

Rosenberg suggests that this setting – largely white, largely wealthy and well-educated, highly participatory – might be thought especially well suited to "effective deliberation." But he also observes that the largely conventional quality of the discussion may not be all that surprising: if you take a group of people and ask them to formulate some policy ideas for a relatively homogeneous school district, and to do so under circumstances in which the results of their discussion will be of uncertain effect, and without specific instruction to reflect on the fundamentals on their views about education or to devise a common perspective, most of us would expect the discussion to be conducted in what Rosenberg describes as conventional terms.

But I am not inclined to find the outcome as disappointing as Rosenberg does, for two reasons. First, it is not clear to me why we should want or expect deliberation in a setting of the kind described – focused on educational policy in a particular jurisdiction – to be more reflectively rational or transformative. To see whether the "failure" to take the conversation in a more rational direction is troubling, we would need to know more about the resistance to rational discourse that Rosenberg describes. He mentions two kinds of resistance: active expressions of hostility to moving in a more "abstract or hypothetical" direction, and more subtle resistance, in the form of simply declining the invitation to go reflective. The participants may have felt that these more abstract concerns simply were not of any real practical relevance.

Second, Rosenberg worries that "deliberation may not perform the critical or emancipatory role that some theorists might attribute to it". I am inclined to think – here echoing my comments on Mendelberg and Karpowitz – that whether we expect a conversation to be deliberative at all, and what we expect the deliberation to result in very much depends: and what it depends on includes the role of facilitators in encouraging broad participation, focused discussion, dispersion of information, and defense of positions with reasons, especially when those positions are challenged. It may also depend on a sense of the urgency of the discussion – that it has the possibility of making a real practical difference (recall the comments on Walsh) and that the arguments matter to the practical effects. That said, the same point that emerged at the end of my discussion of KM applies here: if deliberative democracy is a possible but highly fragile acccomplishment, then we need to reconsider whether it is a compelling political ideal.

The ways that deliberation depends on circumstance are forcefully underscored by the results in Baechtiger, Spoerndli, Steenbergen and Steiner (BSSS). They find that the institutional setting of legislatures makes a large difference to the quality of debate – in particular to whether it is deliberative or not. Thus presidential systems, second chambers, and a lack of publicity, for example, are all good for fostering mutual respect in discussion, and a concern for rational justification. Unfortunately for deliberative democrats – and in keeping with the traditional criticism of parliaments as mere talkshops – BSSS also find that deliberativeness in legislatures does not matter much for the outcomes: when it comes to substantive results, they conclude, interests and power matter and deliberativeness does not.

But this result – like the arguments in Mendelberg and Karpowitz – depend on the assumption, expressed by BSSS, that deliberation is equality enhancing. While this issue transcends the immediate concerns here, the connections between deliberation and equality are worth further exploration. Deliberative democrats often hold that a more deliberative democracy would be a more egalitarian democracy, not only because deliberation assumes as a precondition a greater equality of political capacity than we commonly observe, but also because much of the inequality we see – and the kinds of policies observed by BSSS – cannot be given a rational defense and must be the product of interest and power, not reason. But if we find that people are sometimes pre-deliberatively more egalitarian than they are post-deliberation, and we are confident that they are genuinely deliberating, maybe we need to revise our judgments about the relationship between deliberation and equality. Suppose for example we find that deliberators, asked to decide on an income floor, reduce the floor after deliberation, and suppose, too, that they appear to have been moved in their decisions by concerns about negative incentive effects of a high floor. We may disagree with their reasoning, and think they arrived at the wrong conclusion – perhaps that they have not given due attention to all the relevant reasons. But we should not be so quick to conclude – with BSSS – that the decision is really driven by interests and power rather by reasons.

Conclusion

The first generation of theories of deliberative democracy focused on the intrinsic virtues of deliberation as a mode of collective decision-making and speculated about both the preconditions of successful deliberation and its beneficial effects. After nearly two decades of theorizing and a growing body of empirical research about both preconditions and outcomes, the intrinsic attractions remain clear (so it seems to me), and we have a better appreciation of the complexities of achieving a more deliberative democracy. My own assessment, reinforced by reading the impressive essays collected here, is that a more deliberative democracy is possible for us, and remains an attractive direction of political reform.

At the same time, a concern that runs through these essays, and that I have returned to several times, is whether the conditions for achieving deliberative democracy are so highly specific that it is always on a knife-edge, always about to degenerate into decision-making dominated by the articulate, or controlled by interests and power, or governed by social norms rather than reasons, or controlled by the unguarded guardians of deliberation who decide on the relevant information and fix the agenda. I do not think we have a strong case for the truth of that unhappy proposition, but I wish we had a more compelling case for its rejection.

Notes

1. In writing this response, I have not tried to survey the now-massive literature on deliberative democracy, but have responded in light of my own earlier discussions of deliberative democracy, which have emphasized the idea of a shared basis of public reasoning. See "Deliberation and Democratic Legitimacy," in Alan Hamlin and Phillip Petit, eds., *The Good Polity* (Oxford: Blackwell, 1989)," "Procedure and Substance in Deliberative Democracy," in *Democracy and Difference: Changing*

Boundaries of the Political, ed. Seyla Benhabib (Princeton, NJ: Princeton University Press, 1996), "Directly-Deliberative Polyarchy" (with Charles Sabel), *European Law Journal*, 3 (4) (December 1997): 313–342, "Democracy and Liberty," in *Deliberative Democracy*, ed. Jon Elster (Cambridge University Press, 1998), "Habermas on Democracy," *Ratio Juris*, 1999, "Power and Reason" (with Joel Rogers), in Archon Fung and Erik Olin Wright, eds., *Deepening Democracy: Institutional Innovations in Empowered Participatory Governance* (New York and London: Verso, 2003); "Deliberation and Participation" (with Archon Fung), *Swiss Journal of Political Science* (forthcoming).

2. Mansbridge (1999: 211–239) offers an account of what she calls the "deliberative system" that puts less weight on reason-giving.
3. See Sidney Verba, Kay Schlozman, and Henry Brady, *Voice and Equality* (Cambridge, MA: Harvard University Press, 1995).
4. See Abers (2003:206).
5. See Ackerman and Fishkin, 2004: 52–58.
6. This problem is expressed with great force in an excellent paper on policies of "deliberative public administration" in South Africa by Lucio Baccaro and Konstantinos Papadakis "The Downside of Deliberative Public Administration" (unpublished paper on file with the author).
7. For a survey of the relevant literature on small group decision-making, see Mendelberg, 2002 and Sunstein, "Group Judgments." Both Mendelberg and Sunstein are too quick to see large implications in the experimental literature, without giving sufficient attention to the possibilities of institutional remedy. See Ackerman and Fishkin, *Deliberation Day*, pp. 61–73, on the importance of institutional issues in the deliberative polling context.

11
Theory, Evidence, and the Tasks of Deliberation

John S. Dryzek

Deliberative democracy now constitutes the most active area of political theory in its entirety (not just democratic theory). There is also widespread interest in making real-world politics more deliberative, be it by introducing novel sorts of institutions, improving existing institutions, or enhancing the quality of public debate. Enthusiasts and critics alike have often made their arguments with no empirical warrants at all; when they do introduce empirical evidence it has often been in the form of casual assertions or stylized facts; and only recently has more careful and systematic evidence been brought to bear.

In this chapter I will begin by discussing the role of empirical evidence in informing the theory and practice of deliberative democracy. I shall distinguish between approaches that use, respectively, no facts, stylized facts, bad facts, and better facts. The empirical studies reported in earlier in this volume mostly report "better facts," and that is all to the good. But that does not mean we currently have enough facts when it comes to the project of deliberative democratization. I develop a list of qualities, grounded in democratic theory, that deliberation ought to be able to achieve or promote. I show which of these are spoken to by the empirical studies, and to what effect, as well as identifying some important gaps in the current empirical coverage.

11.1 Approaches to the use of evidence concerning deliberative democracy

11.1.1 No facts, just assumptions

Normative political theory is sometimes characterized, generally unfairly, as being an evidence-free zone. Sometimes, however, theorizing does proceed on the basis of the way the world or entities within it are assumed to be. Consider, for example, the seminal work of Rawls's theory of justice. Rawls is sometimes treated as one of the ancestors of deliberative democracy, though his own explicit conversion did not come until the 1990s (Rawls, 1997: 771–772;

1999: 139), and as Chambers (2003: 307) points out, Rawls is not a *democratic* theorist. Still, in Rawls there is indeed a kind of deliberation – though it is deliberation in the sense of a solitary person's cogitation. In *A Theory of Justice* Rawls imagines what kinds of political arrangements a rational individual would support if he/she were ignorant of his/her place in those arrangements.

Habermas is often seen as another foundational theorist of deliberative democracy. His approach is grounded in his theory of communicative action (1984, 1987). In this theory Habermas appeals to empirical work in developmental psychology, but in the end communicative rationality is a theoretical ideal grounded in the logical presuppositions of speech, not in empirical evidence. The legitimacy of political arrangements – such as deliberative democracy – then rests on how they can stand up in the light of this ideal.

Habermas and Rawls have fairly elaborate accounts concerning the dispositions and capacities of individuals who enter their theories. But it is possible to assume no more than that individuals simply have the disposition and capacity to deliberate – and to have this as an explicit rather than implicit assumption. Some of the early statements of the normative theory of deliberative democracy take this form – especially when they proceed in abstract terms, silent on who exactly is to deliberate, where, when, and how (for example, Cohen, 1989). The requirements of participants in a deliberative democracy can be quite demanding in these theoretical treatments. For example, Cohen (1989) requires them to subscribe to the idea that deliberation is the basis of legitimacy, to favor institutions in which deliberation transparently affects outcomes, to recognize the deliberative capacities of other participants, to be capable and willing to give reasons for their positions, and to seek reasons that are acceptable to all in the forum.

The absence of empirical evidence of any sort in these sorts of treatments is not a fatal weakness, for these studies are generally concerned mainly to present an ideal, from which real world practices and possibilities can be expected to diverge to greater or lesser degree. Only if we actually want to think about ways to make the real world more deliberative do the limitations of such ideal theory become apparent.

11.1.2   Stylized facts

Stylized facts play a large role in political theory of all sorts. If it is a fault, this reliance on stylized facts should not be blamed on theorists themselves, but rather on the failure of empirical social scientists to deliver anything in their place. Among the more prominent stylized facts is Rawls's (1993) "fact of reasonable pluralism." In his *Political Liberalism*, Rawls attempts to come to grips with the reality of contemporary societies that he so studiously ignored in *A Theory of Justice*. He does not actually investigate this reality, but instead stipulates several facts about it – notably, that it is pluralistic, featuring a number of "comprehensive doctrines." Yet despite their incommensurable fundamental beliefs, individuals subscribing to these doctrines all have some less fundamental beliefs that can be drawn upon to constitute an "overlapping consensus." As Rawls's critics have noted, these doctrines must have a substantial liberal component to begin with if they are to converge on the liberal principles that Rawls still seeks.

Critics of deliberation deploy their own stylized facts. For example, Young (1996) asserts that deliberation is essentially argument, and as such conducive to the communicative style of well-educated white males. These facts are both probably wrong: real-world deliberative forums feature many kinds of communication alongside argument. Moreover, those who have observed designed deliberative forums are typically impressed by the degree to which communication can be entered equally by individuals from all sorts of social backgrounds. Young argues for the alternative communicative styles of greeting, rhetoric, and storytelling. Implicitly she assumes that the capacity to engage in such alternative communication is more equally distributed than the capacity to argue; or that hierarchies of ability in the four forms of communication cancel each other out, rather than reinforce one another. But she has no evidence to offer on any of these points.

11.1.3 Bad facts

Theorists' reliance on assumptions or stylized facts is understandable in light of the problem that many of the facts provided by empirical researchers turn out on closer inspection to be highly suspect. In part, this is a function of the limitation of social scientific instruments through which facts are produced. Many such instruments, in particular the opinion survey, embody presumptions that are antithetical to deliberative democracy. The survey encounter is not a deliberative one, and it puts the subject in a straitjacket that precludes creativity and reflection. The urge to generalize to a larger unreflective population means that unreflective responses are sought in the survey (Dryzek, 2005a).

Even when investigators take care to move beyond the limitations of single instruments, they can produce misleading information. Take, for example, the critique of participatory democracy and deliberative democracy allegedly based on empirical results from focus groups and surveys about the desires and capacities of ordinary citizens contained in Hibbing and Theiss-Morse (2002a). Hibbing and Theiss-Morse believe that citizens generally want elites to govern without being beholden to special interests, and certainly not to become involved themselves. Their survey results at first seem to show that people want a system that is more participatory – but they deploy focus group results to show that people do not really want to participate more themselves, only to remove power from selfish elites (130). The focus group results that back this conclusion are actually just unconstrained interpretations of transcripts, a few snatches of conversation about the undesirability of direct democracy. Thus they interpret their very limited survey results through reference to a selective interpretation of focus group transcripts; their evidence is actually soaked in two sorts of dubious interpretations.

The focus group transcripts are not parsed using any theoretical classification. The snatches reported in the book actually admit interpretations different from those Hibbing and Theiss-Morse choose to place upon them. Consider their interpretation of a conversation between three individuals in a focus group. One woman initially expresses support for direct democracy, but "quickly reversed her position" after some counterarguments (93). Yet the reported comments suggest to me not a reversal, just a qualification of the initial support for direct democracy. A feminist reading would be that a woman supporting participatory democracy was silenced by two men. Which of these three interpretations of the transcript is correct? There is no way to tell.

Hibbing and Theiss-Morse claim from their interpretation of focus group transcripts that people generally find conflict unpleasant and do not enjoy being confronted with opposing views (202–203). Thus most people are unwilling deliberators. Yet the focus group is itself a discussion, thus these sorts of obstacles to deliberation should appear in the focus group itself, and so negate the inferences they draw from the focus group. For example, if "people clam up when they sense that their interlocutor is not a kindred spirit," or if "disagreement creates a negative psychological tension" (202), there is every reason to suppose this effect will occur in their focus groups (see Dryzek, 2005a for a more extended discussion of the deficiencies of Hibbing and Theiss-Morse). In short, their results shed no light at all on the prospects for deliberative democracy.

There are many other sorts of bad facts. These include facts at a distance – for example, extrapolations from jury studies to the very different setting of deliberative democracy (see, e.g., Sanders, 1997). Facts gathered for other purposes should be used with care; this also applies to any attempt to extrapolate standard findings from the literature on political participation to *deliberative* participation, which may introduce quite different considerations (for better or for worse) into individual decisions about whether or not to deliberate.

11.1.4   Better facts

The purpose of this volume, along with a flurry of recent empirical studies of deliberative democracy, is to produce better facts. This production can help in the refinement of deliberative democratic theory, making it more sensitive to real-world constraints and opportunities. It can also benefit designers of deliberative institutions, giving a sense of what may work, how, when, and why – and what may be difficult. The benefits extend to the practice of empirical political science. Speaking from his position as a leading practitioner of comparative politics, Bo Rothstein (2005) has worried that the discipline is producing "technically competent barbarians" with no moral compass. He sees the solution in terms of engagement with political theory. "The good news is that, unlike other disciplines, I think we have the solution within our own field of research. The solution, I believe, lies in reconnecting the normative side of the discipline – that is, political philosophy – with the positive/empirical side" (Rothstein, 2005: 10). The project of this volume is surely exactly the kind of political science that Rothstein argues for.

Before we can assess the degree to which empirical studies are actually producing better facts, we need to ask exactly what those facts need to be good for. What, then, do theorists want deliberation to produce or promote? I will now try to generate a reasonably comprehensive list of items gleaned from the theory of deliberative democracy (though the field is now so large and complex that I allow the list may be incomplete). After generating this list, I will go through its nine items and summarize the state of play in terms of generation of empirical evidence, and what it says about the task in question.

11.2 The tasks of deliberation

To begin, a deliberative forum should produce *a particular kind of communication*. The precise content is a matter of dispute. To those who follow Rawls, arguments should be made in terms of "public reason" – carried out by citizens, whose substance is the good of all, and whose procedure is open. To Gutmann and Thompson (1996) the key principle is "reciprocity," the making of arguments in terms that others with different points of view can accept. Those following Habermas (1984) would instead rely on his theory of communicative action. Communicative rationality would rule out coercion, deception, self-deception, strategizing, and manipulation. A "philosophy seminar" model of deliberation would privilege rational argument. A more expansive view of deliberation would allow any kind of communication (rhetoric, storytelling, gossip, jokes) provided it is noncoercive, capable of inducing reflection, and capable of connecting particular points and experiences to more general questions and principles (Dryzek, 2000: 167).

Still at the basic level, deliberative theorists want this kind of communication to produce something rather than nothing. This might seem so obvious as not to be worth stating. Yet there is a point of view grounded in rational choice theory that sees political communication, including that found in deliberative forums, as nothing more than 'cheap talk' (Austen-Smith, 1990, 1992). Talk is treated as signaling; it cannot change the underlying preferences of a listener, but it might influence the listener's perception of how actions connect to consequences. Speakers disseminate information selectively in order to further enhance their own strategic position. If necessary, they will distort or withhold information, if that is expedient. Thus political talk is unreliable. Discussion will not produce collective outcomes more sensitive to individual preferences because deception may induce false beliefs in listeners about what action is in their own interest (Przeworski, 1998).

However, rational listeners will not trust speakers but instead be aware of these possibilities, making calculations of their own whether or not to believe speakers. In this light, deliberation might change collective actions, but not through changing individual preferences, only by influencing strategic assessments of participants. Deliberative theorists do of course have a very different expectation: that the reflection central to deliberation enables (though it does not always require) *preference change*, and this is how the 'something rather than nothing' task can be operationalized.

The theory of deliberative democracy was first articulated as a theory of democratic *legitimacy*. That is, decisions are seen as legitimate to the degree the individuals subject to them (or their representatives) have the right, capacity, or opportunity to participate in deliberation about their content, and as a result grant their reflective assent to the outcome (Manin, 1987: 352; Cohen, 1989: 22; Benhabib 1996: 68). Deliberative legitimacy is going to be hard to measure directly. There is a conceptual problem that needs solving first, relating to scale. In a polity of any size, it is impossible for everyone affected to deliberate directly. While solutions to this problem are available (Parkinson, 2003a), none commands universal assent, and all require commitment to a particular version of deliberative democracy. Given theoretical indeterminacy, it is perhaps no surprise that nobody has yet tried to measure the legitimacy produced by deliberation directly, at least not in any real-world setting.

One of the necessary conditions for legitimacy is that deliberation has some *impact*. The most obvious way to seek impact would be for the results of deliberation to somehow be embodied in public policy. Once impact is achieved, the result ideally ought to be better policy, judged not only in terms of its legitimacy, but also in terms of its quality when it comes to solving public problems. Such problem solving concerns are likely to engage institutional designers and practitioners. But theorists too should be attracted by the *problem-solving rationality* of deliberation – especially those who assert an epistemic case for deliberation (Estlund, 1997), or those who believe deliberation across those concerned with the multiple facets of a complex problem ought to improve the quality of solutions to that problem (e.g., Dryzek, 1990: 57–76).

Even if it cannot demonstrably contribute to demonstrably better solutions to public problems, deliberation should be capable of *making collective choice more tractable*. In particular, deliberative democracy should be able to answer the charges of some social choice theorists that all democratic procedures are unstable and vulnerable to manipulation (Riker, 1982). Van Mill (1996) argues that the conditions of open dialogue that deliberative democrats favor make this problem worse; because these conditions are unstructured, they render collective decision still more vulnerable to arbitrariness and instability. Theoretical replies to this kind of charge have been developed (Dryzek and List, 2003), but they need to be demonstrated empirically.

Because deliberative democracy is about democracy as well as deliberation, it should also be capable of producing two of the standard central desiderata of democracy: popular control and political equality. If we have policy impact, then control is taken care of, though political equality across those who exercise control is desirable from a democratic point of view. Thus *political equality* in the right, capacity, and opportunity to participate in deliberation should be added to the list.

Deliberation does not have to be tied closely to policy decision. For deliberation can also involve *social learning*. That is, deliberation across different kinds of individuals and groups can be productive in restructuring social relationships in a more respectful direction and producing mutual understanding. This is an especially pressing problem in societies divided by deep identity conflicts related to nationality, ethnicity, or religion (Dryzek, 2005b; Kanra, 2005). What such societies may need first and foremost is communication across difference, rather than better public policies (though of course these are not mutually exclusive).

In addition to its effects on public policies and social learning, the impact of deliberation can also be sought in making *better citizens* of those who engage in it. This effect is consistent with the educative effects of political participation postulated long ago in John Stuart Mill's model of developmental democracy. More recently, the hoped-for impact on citizen competence and engagement is one reason for the upsurge of interest in deliberation in the United States. Making the polity more deliberative might be one to revive civic commitments in a balkanizing and individualist society (see Shawn Rosenberg's introduction).

11.3 Empirical evidence speaks to the tasks of deliberation

We are now in a position to ascertain the degree to which empirical evidence can or does speak to these specifications of the tasks of deliberation. I will focus on the contributions of the studies reported in earlier chapters of this collection. Occasionally I will point to other studies, but I make no claim to any more systematic survey of empirical studies of deliberative democracy.

11.3.1 A particular kind of communication

The discourse quality index deployed by Bachtiger et al. is grounded theoretically in Habermas's theory of communication (which does have its critics as a source of standards). Bachtiger et al. look at the quality of debate in a number of existing parliamentary institutions, finding that discourse quality tends to be higher in consensual institutions and presidential regimes, in the presence of a second chamber, when it is out of the public eye, and when issue polarization is low. The penultimate finding will disappoint deliberative theorists such as Gutmann and Thompson (1996), for whom publicity is one of the defining features of deliberation, and those who value Rawlsian public reason, one characteristic of which is that it is carried out in public. The last finding will worry deliberative theorists who believe that the toughest conflicts of morality and identity should be amenable to deliberative treatment. In applying the discourse quality index, it is hard to say whether the deliberation in any of the cases analyzed is actually good enough by any theoretical standards. The index is just a comparative measure.

This emphasis on the determinants of deliberative quality is shared by the Mendelberg chapter, though the answer is sought in controlled experiment rather than observation of real world interaction, and the criterion for good deliberation is far more controversial (degree of support for distributive justice). Mendelberg finds that a decision rule of unanimity is conducive to good deliberation in small groups – though only if those groups are predominantly female. The institutional design implications are murky, because presumably it is going to be hard actually to require a female preponderance in any real world setting. Mendelberg's conclusion is striking in light of feminist critiques of deliberative democracy (Young, 1996), because it seems that given the right circumstances, the presence of women makes for good deliberation – and certainly not the marginalization of women by deliberative norms.

When it comes to institutional design, the moral of Bachtiger et al. presumably points to a presidency, consensual institutions that work mostly in secret, and bicameral legislatures. None of their cases concern institutions that have actually been designed with deliberation in mind – the discursive designs that now litter the political landscape, or the 'recipes for public spheres' described in Fung's chapter. It would be straightforward to apply the discourse quality index to these sorts of institutions. It would be very hard to apply the analysis to diffuse deliberation in the broader public sphere, as stressed in the theories of Benhabib (1996), Habermas (1996), and Dryzek (2000).

The question of deliberative adequacy about which Bachtiger et al. are silent is answered in the chapter by Rosenberg, who finds that even when provided with conducive settings, ordinary people do not generally engage in deliberation of a very high quality. In contrast to Bachtiger et al., the participants are ordinary people rather than professional politicians and public officials. But this is of scarce comfort to the deliberative theorists, for the relative non-partisanship of lay participants ought to make them more amenable to reflection and persuasion than political partisans. Thus the news is on the face of it pretty bad, though Rosenberg does try to soften the blow by pointing to the importance of institutional design in promoting better deliberation, and possibilities for civic education to produce better deliberators. His results are also inconsistent with 'cheap talk' rational choice critics of deliberation who see talk as the instrument of strategy, even if the talk observed does not go very far in the transformative direction that deliberative theorists would like.

Theorists might question the conclusiveness of Rosenberg's results on three grounds. The first is that any inadequacies of deliberative quality in a particular forum may be made up elsewhere in what Mansbridge (1999) calls the "deliberative system" of society. Again, theorists who emphasize diffuse communication in the public sphere would not be especially dismayed by any lapses in particular locations. The second is that the kind of communication theory that informs Rosenberg's expectations may be unnecessarily restrictive, if all that is required is that communication be uncoerced, capable of inducing reflection, and connecting the particular to the general. A third is that what Goodin (2002) calls "deliberation within" cannot easily be captured by coding speech acts. Still, there is plenty in Rosenberg's results to give pause to the deliberative enthusiast.

Setting the bar a little lower, it may be the case that deliberation can dispel some of the worst features of symbolic politics (Edelman, 1964), even if it cannot produce quite the quality of interchange that Rosenberg sought but could not find. Niemeyer (2004) shows that before their participation in a deliberative citizen's jury, there is no connection between individuals' subjective positions (values and beliefs) relevant to the policy issue at hand, and their preferences on this issue. He argues that this lack is due to the power of widely held symbolic beliefs disseminated by elites on both sides of the issue affecting preferences. After deliberation, there is a strong relationship between subjectivity and preference – evidence that deliberation successfully dispelled the distortions of symbolic politics.

11.3.2 Preference change

Good deliberation requires that individuals be open to changing their preferences across policy alternatives as a result of reflecting on them and concluding that they merit adjustment. However, the absence of preference change is not a sign of bad deliberation, for individuals may upon reflection stick with the preferences with which they began. Still, the possibility of preference change is crucial. Mackie (2002) calls this effect of deliberation into question. He asks the question "Does Democratic Deliberation Change Minds?" and answers "No" after surveying the available evidence. Or, rather, it is very rare for individuals to admit to changing their minds in a particular forum.

In contrast, studies of deliberative forums such as Fishkin's deliberative polls reveal in most cases that there is a substantial preference shift, toward some policy options and away from others. Fishkin charts such shifts in questionnaires administered to individuals before and after their participation in deliberation.

These results can be reconciled by the fact that Mackie and Fishkin are talking about two different kinds of deliberative participants. Mackie is talking about partisans, who cannot readily admit to changing their minds even if privately persuaded; for they will lose face in the eyes of both their adversaries and their own side. Fishkin is talking about lay citizens recruited using random (or stratified) sampling from the general population. Given that lay citizens are not stakeholders and have nothing to lose by changing their minds, it is much easier for them to behave in the fashion required by deliberative theory than it is for partisans. This is a crucial matter because abstract theoretical presentations of deliberative democracy normally assume that deliberators are partisans, so there is a lack of fit between theory and practice. The fit is made slightly easier by Mackie's recognition that even if partisans will not admit to changing their minds in the confines of one forum, it is much easier for them to adopt a new position after time has elapsed and they find themselves in different company. Still, one very large institutional design question concerns the balance of, and roles for, partisan and non-partisan deliberators.

11.3.3   Democratic legitimacy

While democratic legitimacy is at the heart of the theory of deliberative democracy, it is very hard to test empirically. The ideal test might involve comparing the perceived legitimacy of policies that did and did not receive deliberative treatment. But this is fraught with difficulty. No good measure exists for the perceived legitimacy of a policy; legitimacy is not the same as agreement. Survey results on this score could not be trusted, given that most people out there would have minimal awareness of the existence of any policy decisions, let alone the degree to which they have been deliberated.

Hibbing and Theiss-Morse (2002b; discussed in Delli Carpini, Cook, and Jacobs 2004: 333) report on an experiment designed to test the effects of deliberation on perceived legitimacy, finding that the willingness of individuals to accept the decision of a judge against them did not depend on the degree to which they were allowed to express their opinions to the judge beforehand. Such adjudication is not of course deliberative *democracy*, nor for that matter is it very deliberative (because participants could only give voice to the judge, not to each other). The attraction of the experimental approach is understandable, given the difficulty in measuring legitimacy in the real world.

Parkinson (2005b) carries out a detailed study of legitimacy issues in health policy in the United Kingdom, in light of the deliberative innovations that have been pursued therein. A contemplation of legitimacy issues in particular cases shows that legitimacy can be promoted through combining different institutional designs at different stages of the policy process.

11.3.4   Impact

Communication is of course woven into the fabric of all politics, and it can meet greater or lesser standards of deliberative adequacy. The discourse quality index of Bachtiger et al. may capture the quality of deliberation in ostensibly central institutions such as parliament, but it is silent on the policy impact of deliberation. It is quite conceivable that parliamentary deliberation has no policy impact – if, for example, parliamentary votes are determined by party instruction; or if rational choice theorists are right that legislatures can best be modeled in terms of strategic as opposed to communicative interaction; or if post-Marxists are right that important issues of public policy are determined by the requirements of the capitalist economy. To prove otherwise, it would be necessary to present cases where minds were changed by the quality of an argument (or of a story, or of rhetoric), and that as a result a policy decision was changed. So for example Risse (2000) shows that the outcome of negotiations over German reunification involving the Soviet Union, United States, Germany, and North Atlantic Treaty Organization (NATO) turn on President Gorbachev of the Soviet Union being persuaded by American arguments at a key point. Of course that particular case is at most a matter of deliberation, not deliberative democracy.

In a deliberative democracy, we would want to be able to trace some causal connection between citizen deliberation and public policy content. That is extraordinarily hard to do. Even sponsors of exercises in citizen deliberation (recipes for public spheres) rarely claim such impact; they are likely to fall back on the idea that the exercise in question was an input into the policy process. Even in Denmark, where there is a legal requirement that parliament must respond to the recommendations of government-sponsored consensus conferences, in only a few of these cases is the recommendation actually embodied in policy.

The results reported in the chapter by Weatherford and McDonnell do manage to trace a direct connection between deliberative forum and policy impact. Given that their South Carolina case featured local variations within a common program, and some instances where impact was not achieved, they can also look at the determinants of impact. It would be instructive to gather success stories of when impact is achieved – while bearing in mind that this is no substitute for comparative research that also looks at the far more numerous cases of failure to achieve direct policy impact. Several of the cases discussed by Fung – notably the Oregon Health Plan, community policing in Chicago, and participatory budgeting in Porto Alegre – do appear to feature such impact. But it is not entirely clear how generalizable the conditions for this impact would be.

11.3.5 Problem-solving rationality

If impact is achieved, is the result for better or for worse? Fung's Porto Alegre case points to improvements in the social justice of public policies that have resulted since participatory budgeting was adopted in 1989. Porto Alegre has become a case that is now widely referenced in the literature by participatory and deliberative enthusiasts. It joins other celebrated cases such as the Berger Inquiry from mid-1970s Canada. But the fact that the literature comes back time and again to one or two celebrated cases is a cause for worry. They show that problem solving rationality in complex and highly politicized situations *can* be promoted by deliberative means. But they also suggest that these cases are quite rare (unless researchers in this field are extraordinarily bad at picking up on more cases). It should also be noted that exemplary cases can turn bad. In the early 1990s, the participatory process employed by the province of Alberta to identify and construct a toxic waste treatment facility was widely hailed in the literature (see, e.g., Fischer, 1993). This process eventually led to the construction and operation of a facility at Swan Hills. What happened subsequently was that the site proved just as messy and contentious in its operation as most other toxic waste facilities, prone to accidental release of toxics into the environment, and the subject of lawsuits and the kind of adversarial stalemate the process was initially praised for overcoming.

11.3.6 Making collective choice more tractable

From social choice theory, Arrow's theorem is deployed by anti-democrats such as Riker (1982) to suggest the arbitrariness and manipulability of collective choices. However, if Arrow's unrestricted domain condition is relaxed, then a preponderance of single-peaked preference profiles in the decision-making group solves the problem. List describes this condition as meta-consensus: individuals may not agree on what is to be done, but they do agree on the dimension on which preferences are structured. Results from deliberative polls show that in general deliberation does increase the degree of preference meta-consensus, and so the problems that social choice theory presents to democracy are ameliorated. There is a school of thought in deliberative theory that sees simple consensus as the proper aim of deliberation (Elster, 1986; Habermas, 1996) – and simple consensus if achieved would solve a host of problems, not least the social choice theoretic critique. But the less demanding idea of meta-consensus should attract deliberative theorists. List describes only one kind of meta-consensus, which can be called preference meta-consensus. However, meta-consensus can also refer to values and beliefs (Dryzek and Niemeyer, 2003). Normative meta-consensus exists to the extent of recognition of the legitimacy of disputed values. This condition is sought by proponents of deliberative mediation and "consensus-building" approaches (Susskind, 1999), for it facilitates cooperative search for outcomes that can respond to the values of all sides. (Susskind would call such agreements 'consensus', but theorists would not, on the grounds that people support the agreed outcome for very different reasons.) Epistemic meta-consensus exists to the degree of recognition of the validity of disputed beliefs. It may be desirable on the grounds of deliberative economy (because it provides a common factual frame of reference), and also because it is instrumental to the generation of both normative and preference meta-consensus. At any rate, these three sorts of meta-consensus can be measured empirically, and so can the impact of different kinds of deliberation upon them.

11.3.7 Political equality

Some leftist critics of deliberation charge it with exacerbating inequality, on the grounds that well-educated white males are more likely to be at home in the kind of argumentative forum that deliberation constitutes (e.g., Young, 1996). Rosenberg's finding that little in the way of high-level argument actually occurs in deliberative forums, even when the participants are very well educated, ought to ameliorate this kind of worry. This amelioration does of course come at substantial cost in terms of deliberative quality and the hopes of those with faith in the transformative power of deliberation. Chapter 2 by Cook, Delli Carpini, and Jacobs shows that though inequalities in deliberative participation do exist, they are actually less pronounced in terms of income than other sorts of participation. With a relatively expansive definition of deliberation, the number of people who actually deliberate in the United States is actually quite large. The good news for deliberative democracy from the study of Cook, Delli Carpini, and Jacobs is that deliberative participation is not that hard to achieve once individuals are mobilized into organizations of some sort. Of course, institutional designers need not rest there; there is plenty of evidence that how organizational contexts are structured and facilitated makes a big difference in terms of the kind of communication that individuals are likely to engage.

11.3.8 Social learning

Walsh concludes her chapter by suggesting we rethink "the types of bonds citizens are attempting to create in the context of difference." She points out that dialogue is not the same as debate. Clearly an expansive conception of deliberative democracy is capable of accommodating both, which should be treated as subcategories of deliberation. Walsh demonstrates the prevalence and importance of civic dialogue that is not directly connected to decision making, but is nevertheless crucial in producing mutual understanding and respect across difference. This social learning aspect of deliberation is still more crucial when it comes to the identity conflicts besetting deeply divided societies. Kanra (2005) shows that in the case of Turkey, some surprising points of contact are emerging across the secular-Islamist divide. It took a lot of empirical digging to uncover these points – such as the common interest of left-liberals and Islamists in freedom of expression and association in the shadow of a secular Kemalist regime that has in the past lapsed into military dictatorship. Kanra also demonstrates the commitment of Islamist members of the public to principles of dialogue across the divide – partly a lesson of bitter experience of what happens when more confrontational political strategies are pursued. At any rate, the empirical study of dialogue in the public sphere as a crucial aspect of deliberative democracy has now begun.

11.3.9   Better citizens

Do individuals become better citizens as a result of deliberative experience? Mansbridge (1995: 1) asserts that "Participation does make better citizens. I believe it, but can't prove it. And neither can anybody else." Mansbridge believes that any effects are likely to be too subtle, the available social science instruments too blunt. A more severe problem is that it is likely to be more engaged citizens who choose to participate in deliberative forums of any sort to begin with. What this suggests is that we should look at the effects of deliberation on individuals who do not choose to deliberate, but are nonetheless chosen. The nearest forums to this ideal are deliberative polls, citizens juries, consensus conferences, and planning cells, all of which select individuals from the population at large via either random sampling or stratified sampling. (There is still an unavoidable element of self-selection, as individuals do not have to accept the invitation to deliberate.) The limited evidence from deliberative polls indicates that participation "increases political efficacy (and thus potentially and indirectly strengthens other aspects of citizenship that are positively related to efficacy, such as political interests and civic and political participation)" (Delli Carpini, Cook, and Jacobs, 2004: 334). These findings come in the reports of the sponsors of the polls.

11.4   Conclusion

Most PhD dissertations typically conclude with a plea for further research, and so does this chapter. The nine tasks I have identified have generated empirical research that ranges from non-existent to limited. Yet this is a major advance over the situation of just a few years ago, when writing on deliberative democracy was overwhelmingly theoretical, with at most an occasional illustrative case thrown in. Today, research on deliberative democracy is at the cutting edge of the integration of political theory and empirical social science. The empirical findings are quite capable of discomforting theorists, just as theorists are quite capable of discomforting empirical researchers. Deliberative democracy is not a hypothesis that can be falsified, nor is it a model, but rather a project, to which theorists, researchers, citizens, and activists alike can contribute.

12
"Deliberative Democracy" or "Democratic Deliberation"?

Jane Mansbridge[1]

12.1 "Deliberative democracy" and "democratic deliberation"

Two traditions have grown up, side by side and intertwining, in the disciplines of philosophy and political science – the classic tradition of "deliberative democracy" and the more pluralist tradition of "democratic deliberation."

In the classic tradition, adopted more by philosophers and perhaps also Europeans, "deliberative democracy" is the only legitimate form of democracy. In addition to its other legitimating features such as equality and liberty, deliberative democracy must, crucially, rest on reason and be aimed at the common good. This ideal derives from a deep critique of modern democracy for incorporating the pursuit of self-interest in contrast to reasoning about the common good.

In what I will call the "neo-pluralist" tradition, more characteristic of political science and perhaps also Americans, "democratic deliberation" means deliberation within democracies that have mixed sources of legitimation through both good deliberation and fair aggregation. Deliberative democrats in this tradition promote deliberation without claiming that deliberation is the only source of legitimate law. From this perspective, the better the quality of deliberation in legislatures and throughout civil society, the more legitimate the eventual laws; in addition, the better the quality of aggregative processes, the more legitimate the eventual laws.[2]

In a book devoted to the empirical study of deliberation and originating in the United States, it is not surprising that the chapters hew far more closely to the neo-pluralist ideal of democratic deliberation, which makes deliberation part of a democracy that derives legitimacy from more than one source, than to the classic ideal of deliberative democracy, which derives legitimacy only from reasoned deliberation on the common good. Many of the chapters do touch in one way or another on two central features of the classic ideal: reason and the common good. Shawn Rosenberg's chapter

251

explores the concept of "rational" deliberation in detail. Other chapters explore aspects of "common ground" and "meta-agreement." Stephen Weatherford and Lorraine McDonnell argue, at least implicitly, that the quality of deliberation in their citizen groups legitimates the conclusions of those groups. André Bächtiger and his colleagues explicitly investigate both reason and the common good in deliberation. They also base their work on the philosophy of Jürgen Habermas, who insisted that legitimate laws must derive only from reasoning on the common good. Yet not one of the writers in this volume suggests that whenever the democratic process moves from reasoning on the common good to exercising political power, that move delegitimates the resulting law. Not one makes rational deliberation on the common good alone the only mechanism for legitimating the coercive apparatus of the state. Instead, all take stances compatible with a neo-pluralist position that recognizes as legitimate, along with deliberation, the use of power to aggregate conflicting interests.

12.2   The tradition of "deliberative democracy"

The early work of Jürgen Habermas illuminates most clearly the roots of the classic philosophical tradition that I am calling "deliberative democracy." That tradition, visible also in the work of Carl Schmitt and Hannah Arendt, insists that the source of law should never be merely the people's will in matters of conflicting interest but always only the exercise of reason on matters of the common good. Democracies take their legitimacy – and should make "law" – only from this exercise of reason.

In 1962 Jürgen Habermas argued in a work later translated into English as *The Structural Transformation of the Public Sphere* that "the bourgeois public sphere" in the eighteenth century was characterized by the "people's public use of their reason" ([1962] 1991: 27) in "rational-critical debate." That process, he believed, renounced any "form of a claim to rule" and thus opposed "domination" (28); it rested only on "the standards of 'reason'" (28) and "the authority of the better argument" (36) on matters of "common concern" (37).[3]

In this analysis Habermas did not differ from many German theorists of the nineteenth and early twentieth centuries, including Carl Schmitt, whom he approvingly quoted as saying, "Law is not the will of one or of many people, but something rational-universal; not *voluntas*, but *ratio*."[4] As Habermas described it, in the golden era before the negative "transformation" of the public sphere, public opinion was ideally thought to work as a refining mechanism that allowed reason instead of will to emerge. Before that transformation, the model of "a public sphere in the political realm" supposed it to be "objectively possible," by orienting society strictly to "the general interest," to "keep conflicts of interest … to a minimum" (130–131). Yet once "the public was expanded" by the press and presumably by an extended franchise, its presupposed "shared class interest" crumbled (131), the public sphere became an arena of conflicting interests, and laws began to result not from a reasonable consensus on the common good but from a "compromise between competing private interests" (132).

In this new situation, political thinkers had to resign themselves to "the inability to resolve rationally the competition of interests in the public sphere" (135) and society was "forced to relinquish even the flimsiest pretense of being a sphere in which the influence of power was suspended" (144). The resulting compromises could "no longer be vindicated as regards their elements of 'truth'" (179), but were instead "haggled out, produced temporarily through pressure and counterpressure and supported only through the unstable equilibrium of power constellations between state apparatus and interest groups" (198). Once irreconcilable conflict emerges, Habermas concluded, "public opinion" in the strict sense (i.e., public rationality exercised on a general interest) becomes almost impossible. Thus today, "the unresolved plurality of competing interests … makes it doubtful whether there can ever emerge a general interest of the kind to which a public opinion could refer as a criterion" (234).

Habermas's thought has evolved considerably in the 43 years since he wrote this work. He has moved toward some acceptance of "strategic" action (aimed at winning) rather than only "communicative" action (aimed at understanding) in democratic politics. Yet he has never in that time allowed any legitimacy to the aggregative aspect of democracy, which rests to some degree on coercive power (e.g., in theory, on the equal power of every voter). In *Between Facts and Norms*, his most recent major work, Habermas continues to claim that "only those statutes may claim legitimacy that can meet with the *assent (Zustimmung)* of *all* citizens in a discursive process of legislation that in turn has been legally constituted" ([1992] 1996: 110, emphasis mine).[5] The justificatory apparatus of "adversary democracy" that in a more plurally based democratic system legitimizes the exercise of political power by some citizens over others when they disagree has no value in itself.[6] In 1989 Joshua Cohen adopted a similar view, arguing that the outcomes of deliberation are democratically legitimate only when the deliberation aims to arrive at "a rational consensus" (1989: 19).

The classic formulations of Habermas and Cohen, both philosophers, contrast with the neo-pluralist approach of the deliberative democrats in the political science tradition who, while wanting to rehabilitate deliberation, virtue, and the common good in the face of atomizing and aggregative strands in democratic practice and theory, also believe that aggregative procedures and the negotiation of conflicting interests produce democratically legitimate results.

12.3   The tradition of "democratic deliberation"

The empirical studies in this volume all fall squarely in the tradition of plural legitimation. Although five of the seven authors cite Jürgen Habermas, not one subscribes to his underlying argument that legitimate legislation can derive only from reason producing consensus about what is "in the interest of all." They study not "deliberative democracy," which can be legitimated only by reasoning on the common good, but rather "democratic deliberation."

The problem of legitimacy in the law is not a major theme in this volume, because most of the studies collected here deal with groups that do not make law. Yet because the quality of citizen deliberation before a law is enacted affects that law's legitimacy, a concern with legitimacy undergirds all of the studies. The following analysis arrays the instances of deliberation studied on the dimension of empowerment, with the question of legitimate power being least overtly relevant for the groups with least power to impose their decisions on either themselves or others.[7] As part of the comparison with the "deliberative democracy" tradition, the analysis also examines the role of the common good and reason in each of the studies.

The least empowered group in this volume is the "civic dialogue" group reported by Kathy Cramer Walsh. Communications theorists, Walsh tells us, distinguish "dialogue" from "deliberation," limiting dialogue to the "pre-deliberative" act of sharing information about perspectives, while deliberation involves decision. Unlike deliberation, dialogue is explicitly disempowered, presumably in the hope that with little at stake participants will be more able to create "shared understandings" across different cultural perspectives, "actively create connections with one another," and craft a "new 'language' jointly understood by all parties."[8] (As Walsh points out, this feature of disempowerment dramatically reduces African American participation. It probably also reduces the participation of the poor. Archon Fung in this volume provides data indicating that the best way to eliminate the usual class gap in participation is to give policy-making power on issues important to their daily lives to those who are usually marginalized in the political system.[9]) In the light of their radical disempowerment, we should not be surprised that the goals of the civic dialogue groups reported here never mention legitimacy.

As for the common good, this goal appears among the stated goals of dialogue groups without the classic links to either rationality or aiming at consensus on the common good. First, instead of the more unitary phrase, "the common good" or Habermas's "the general interest," we hear the more pluralist and pragmatic "common goal," "common concerns" (also a frequent phrase in Habermas's work), or "common ground." "Working toward a common goal," psychologists conclude, helps reduce prejudice (Peltigrew and Tropp, 2000, cited in Walsh, this volume). But that kind of work differs from converging rationally on the general interest. The "Tips for study circle participants" that Walsh cites advise that "when disagreement occurs," participants should have two aims: "Try to identify the ideas that are in conflict," and "Search for the common concerns beneath the surface." This "tip" does not suggest that with the application of reason the conflicts could be reconciled, but only that with the application of good will and mutual understanding groups can often productively identify *some* "common concerns." Walsh points out that practitioners in the dialogue field differ strongly on whether or not to aim at consensus, with one set of instructions to facilitators explicitly saying, "Help participants identify 'common ground,' but don't force consensus."[10]

Second, certain dialogue practices "privilege the expression of emotion" in contrast to reason. One guide to dialogue tells participants that in an "honest" conversation "you say things to *reveal* your feelings" (emphasis in original). Another such guide specifies that "dialogue is not ... a logical process using reflective reasoning. ... [R]easoned argument ... is not always an effective tool, since positions are usually formed by historical circumstances, emotions and experiences as much as reason." Thus neither in its aims nor in its methods is civic dialogue designed to meet the classic philosophical requirements for legitimate democratic decision.

Tali Mendelberg and Christopher Karpowitz study student experimental groups that come one small step closer to empowerment. Unlike Walsh's dialogue groups, these experimental groups do come to a "collective decision" (which Mendelberg and Karpowitz, along with Walsh, consider part of the definition of "deliberation" in contrast to "dialogue"). But the decisions are binding only on the participants. In discussing these decisions, the authors stay firmly within the "democratic deliberation" perspective of plural legitimacy by assuming that these deliberations may legitimately end not in consensus but in "majority rule, or some other rule."

As for the role of reason and emotion, although Mendelberg and Karpowitz cite theorists who define deliberation as "a rational process of weighing the available data" (Walzer, 1999: 58) and making "reasoned arguments that are universal and generalizable" (paraphrasing Chambers, 1996 and Gutmann and Thompson, 1996), they themselves focus instead on "the expectation that deliberation can lead people to better empathize with each other" (4). In their analysis, empathy seems to include emotional connection. In the settings they investigate, they find that a slightly greater inclination to generosity and cooperation on the part of individual women translated, after discussion in unanimous groups with high percentages of women, into greater generosity and cooperation than emerged in groups of men. Although Mendelberg and Karpowitz do not have intermediate measures that capture expressions of compassion or empathy per se, the groups with high percentages of women probably include more such expressions.[11] Mendelberg and Karopowitz's analysis implies that the empathy prompted by deliberation joins reason in the process as one of the bases for legitimate decision.

The groups that Shawn Rosenberg studied were more empowered externally than those of Walsh or Mendelberg and Karpowitz. In his study, two 12-person groups deliberated and then made recommendations to local governmental institutions and to the local community at large about current practices and possible improvements in their neighborhood schools. Although their decisions did not directly produce laws binding on the participants or others, the explicit goal of the exercise was "practical action." If and when the School Board and school principals acted upon their recommendations, the participants themselves would have to live with the policies they had recommended.

Rosenberg does not discuss the legitimacy of these deliberations, their decision rule, or their use of emotions. Yet he is, like the classic theorists, highly concerned with their "rational" and "transformative" quality. He draws his understanding of the "rational" in part explicitly from Habermas, but adds to it and is perhaps even more demanding in his meaning. In Rosenberg's view, a "collaborative, rational" discourse begins with "a critical attitude toward initial perceptions and specific culturally accepted definitions, actions and outcomes." It aims to uncover the broader context or underlying nature of the problem to see how it is related to larger systems, in order to redefine the problem and understand it in its systemic context. Recognizing the likelihood of initial disagreement, the process addresses the disagreement by "uncovering commonalities of human experience and cultural norms that underlie the variation." Participants explain any causal claim or assertion of truth by indicating how it is produced. They justify any moral claim by relating it to other commonly accepted definitions and norms, so that it may be challenged and revised by giving reasons. The bases of this discourse are "general and abstract," applied to specific circumstances, and speakers "will tend to speak paragraphs rather than sentences." In moments of disagreement, speakers will "focus on underlying justifications and elaborations and the bases on which relevant linkages are made," so as to understand "why differences in the perception of the same experience emerge and how they may be reconciled," and "why cultural prescriptions may contradict one another and how this contradiction may be resolved." This definition makes reason central. It does not mention empathy or other emotional skills.

Rosenberg finds little of his stringent form of rationality in the groups he studied. He concludes that even in their most deliberative sessions, these two groups of highly qualified citizens rarely proceeded beyond what he calls "cooperative conventional" interaction – oriented by concerns of efficiency and effectiveness, focusing on particular concrete causes and tangible effects, and guided by what is normally the case or what legitimate authorities have mandated. In conventional interaction of this sort the discourse is regulated by social conventions of politeness that sustain existing conventionally defined relations among the participants, each assuming that others see the topic of their discussion in the same way.[12] Only twice, briefly, did Rosenberg find instances of his "collaborative, rational" discourse, in which the goal is "coming to a correct and common understanding" of the task – an understanding that becomes common precisely because it is the "correct" or "best" understanding.

Rosenberg found it a "surprise" that only two instances of this rational discourse appeared in one group and none in the other, in the entire 12 hours of discourse coded. He found no instances at all of his even more demanding ideal of "transformative discourse," which shifts the focus of discourse to how the very "rules of argument, foundational claims or social conditions of a discourse ... are formed" and so develops the capacities of the individuals in the group.

Observers of citizen deliberations in settings like town meetings, where the participants must make binding decisions, will not be surprised at the paucity of collaborative rational discourse and the complete absence of transformative discourse. Even explicitly deliberative groups, where more time has been allocated for discussion than is usual when citizens have to make binding decisions, rarely adopt the aims or procedures that Rosenberg proposes for collaborative rational or transformative discourse.[13] Nor, probably, would these groups want to adopt these aims and procedures. The members of these highly practically oriented groups often do not want to uncover broader contexts or explain their causal claims. They may prefer to speak not in paragraphs but in shorter, more staccato, comments. In building understanding they might prefer to rely more heavily on emotional skills such as empathy rather than on Rosenberg's version of rationality. They might "give reasons," a looser descriptor than "rationality," by beginning with a simple declaration of emotional discomfort ("I don't feel comfortable with that")[14] and proceed disjunctively and interstitially, cumulatively, and collectively, until out of a host of disjoint statements and even parenthetical phrases a pattern emerges that encompasses causal relation and reasons.

Is "rational discourse," as Rosenberg defines it, the right metric for legitimacy? Or, as I would argue, are plural criteria more appropriate? This is not Rosenberg's question. Because his groups do not make binding decisions, he need not relate the quality of discourse in his groups to the eventual legitimacy of their recommendations.

The two deliberations on which Stephen Weatherford and Lorraine McDonnell report come closer to a point where the question of legitimacy becomes relevant. These groups were specifically designed, as the authors say in their title, to have "a purpose." On paper the intent of those who organized these groups may have differed little from the intent of those who organized Rosenberg's groups. Their intent "was to develop an action plan, and to see that their recommendations received a hearing and visibly moved school policy and community practice" (1), while Rosenberg's groups had a similar goal of "citizen empowerment and practical action" with specific recommendations. Yet the organizers of Weatherford and McDonnell's groups seemed to have been more seriously concerned with the outcome. Those organizers not only intended their groups to strengthen the connections between citizens and schools; they also had an implicit goal of activating the public's potentially greater willingness (revealed in an earlier survey) "to pay more for schools" in the face of assaults by "anti-tax" forces and "conservative talk radio commentators." Because the legal initiative establishing these citizen forums was "largely silent on the sort of advisory or representational linkage that was expected to be established between the deliberative forum and school or governing bodies," much hung on the inherent legitimacy of the process.

This is the only chapter in the volume to make the issue of legitimacy a focus. Weatherford and McDonnell argue implicitly that because the larger political system they study did not authorize any forum for public deliberation on these issues, only the quality of deliberation in their citizen groups legitimated the groups' conclusions. Those conclusions, however, then formed only "legitimate input" (30) to a later process; they were not the sole basis for the legitimacy of the laws. Weather ford and McDonnell imply here that aggregative processes such as majority rule in the legislature also create "legitimate input."

Weatherford and McDonnell argue explicitly that the two cases they studied in depth managed to have a noticeable effect on their school systems not only because of the intrinsic reasonableness of some of the deliberators' suggestions but also because of the legitimacy of the process. They state that the three characteristics of "inclusiveness, equal standing and mutual respect" give deliberative agreements "a strong claim to legitimacy," although that claim will be ineffective if the relevant elected officials and bureaucrats do not find it in their interests to act. The inherent qualities of the process do the legitimating work: "Deliberative procedures seek to strengthen ... [the] legitimacy of collective decisions – via the focus on inclusivity, equality, and reciprocity" (6).

Weatherford and McDonnell take their criteria for legitimacy from a normative literature that stresses equality more than reason or the general interest. Thus, although their chapter is the only one to focus on legitimacy, it is, ironically, one of the only two in the volume that never mentions Habermas (List's chapter being the other). Weatherford and McDonnell's first two criteria for legitimation (inclusivity and equality) measure equality in the process. The third criterion, which they call variously "mutual respect," "reciprocity," and "open-mindedness," comes closest to the classic philosophical understanding of "rationality," as it incorporates the straightforward Habermasian idea that "better reasons rather than resources or bargaining strategies should determine outcomes" (5). Yet the authors explicitly adopt the normative criticisms of past standards of deliberation for being too rationalistic and abstract and thus marginalizing or excluding emotion, personal experience, and mundane concerns. Accordingly, none of the names they give this criterion ("mutual respect," "reciprocity," and "open-mindedness") exclude emotional communication. They interpret "better reasons" loosely. In sum, the only chapter to treat deliberative processes in the context of legitimation seems to employ both (unspoken) criteria beyond deliberation for legitimacy in the making of the laws and criteria beyond reason for legitimacy in the deliberation.

Christian List never uses the word "legitimacy." His entire argument, however, assumes that if a group cannot achieve genuine consensus on substance, it is perfectly legitimate to switch to another decision procedure such as majority rule. List shows that deliberation can generate another kind of consensus – a meta-agreement on what issues should be decided by some procedure other than consensus – and argues persuasively that when democratic theorists think about agreement and citizens seek agreement in practice, they should place more emphasis on such meta-agreement (2). List also demonstrates that deliberation is likely to produce "structuration" – that is, the identification of a common issue dimension, agreement on how options fall along that dimension, and individual identification of where each participant's preferences fall on that dimension (6).[15] Structuration makes aggregative democracy through majority vote more legitimate by preventing meaningless cycles in the results. Democratic deliberation in List's view functions as part of a mixture of legitimate decision mechanisms. In practice, he points out, when issues are contested sufficiently to suggest creating a deliberative experiment, group deliberation rarely leads to unanimity.[16] He concludes in a neo-pluralist vein that "democracy needs to have alternative resources for dealing with conflicts of preferences in those plausible and numerous cases in which deliberation fails to produce unanimity."

André Bächtiger, Markus Spörndli, Marco Steenbergen, and Jürg Steiner study actual legislatures, which, as the primary sources of coercion in democracy, require legitimacy. It is not quite true, as these authors claim, that "In the study of deliberation ... legislatures have been largely neglected" (1). Joseph Bessette (1982, 1994) coined the term "deliberative democracy" to describe actions in the U.S. Congress. The most prominent recent book on deliberation, by Amy Gutmann and Dennis Thompson (1996), dealt almost exclusively with legislative behavior.[17] It is true, however, that the authors of this chapter have produced the first quantitative empirical study of deliberation in legislatures, and it is both conceptually and empirically rich. It also provides us with an important measure, the Discourse Quality Index.

In an earlier article on the measures that compose the Discourse Quality Index, the authors write that this index is "rooted in Habermas' discourse ethics."[18] They thus begin with Habermas's "principle of universalism, which holds that a norm is valid only when everyone who is potentially affected by the norm accepts its consequences, including any anticipated negative side-effects" (2003: 25). The consent that individuals give to those norms must arise through a process in which "individuals give and criticize reasons for holding or rejecting particular validity claims, so that universally valid norms can be discovered through reason" (25). Of the six ideal "rules" of discourse ethics they enumerate both in the earlier article and in this volume, three involve points that I associate with the classic philosophical concept of "deliberative democracy": (1) justification through reason (which they measure by "logical coherence. ... The tighter the connection between premises and conclusions, the more coherent the justification" [idem]); (2) that "the participants in the discourse should consider the *common good*" (idem, emphasis in original); and (3) that "ideal deliberation aims to arrive at a rationally motivated consensus" (26, citing Cohen, 1989: 23). The other three rules require congruent values such as respect, open participation, and authenticity (although authenticity is not included in their index because of measurement difficulty).

Bächtiger et al. make a compelling case that five empirical factors – (1) "consensus systems" (such as the Swiss), (2) presidential regimes, (3) second chambers (such as the U.S. Senate), (4) non-public arenas (such as closed committee hearings), and (5) non-polarized issues (characterized by a consensus among elites) – when combined, predict most of their five measurable features of high-quality deliberation. They also point out that in the German conference committee that they studied in depth these features of high-quality deliberation were associated with unanimity. In the causal direction that they postulate, those features would help "the different sides to find a commonly acceptable solution to an issue" and "produce more consensual outcomes." In the other causal direction, however, participants might first judge the likelihood of consensus, then move toward more high-quality discourse when consensus seemed possible and toward polarization and aggregation when consensus seemed impossible. The causal arrow could also run in both directions, with high-quality discourse causing unanimity and the greater potential for unanimity causing high-quality discourse.

Although the work of Bächtiger et al. could be framed as measuring the preconditions for legitimate legislation, the authors in fact raise the question of legitimacy only briefly, to introduce the question of substantive outcomes like justice (6). I find it helpful analytically to judge the justice of outcomes separately from the legitimacy of process. Sometimes a process that is normatively relatively legitimate can produce laws that are nevertheless unjust. In the cases that Bächtiger et al. studied, high-quality discourse did not seem to produce more just (defined as more egalitarian) outcomes. We may conclude, however, that these outcomes were nevertheless more legitimate than those produced by low-quality discourse. If we think of legitimacy as a spectrum rather than a dichotomy, then a process with high-quality discourse should produce laws with a greater claim to legitimacy than a process based on discourse of a lower quality. This is the only chapter in the volume to investigate deliberation in legislatures. More clearly than any other, it makes the classic theory of rationality and the common good (in this case Habermas's theory) the explicit foundation of its investigation. Although it does not explore the issue of legitimacy as deriving from process, it provides a significant tool by which we can think more concretely about, and measure, features of the deliberative process that arguably contribute to legitimacy.

12.4 Deliberative neo-pluralism

More than forty years have elapsed since the publication in 1962 of Habermas's *Structural Transformation of the Public Sphere*. In that time, Habermas's own thinking has evolved, as have the thoughts of many others in the field. But, as we have seen, Habermas and some other political philosophers continue to promote the classic contention that only reasoning on the common good can generate legitimate law. By contrast, I argue here for a more plural approach to reason, the common good, legitimacy, and deliberation itself. If most thinkers in the field have also moved on to a plural understanding of these concepts, it is time to make that new position explicit.

"Reason" has a unitary implication, with only one outcome that can meet its demands. As Habermas put it in his early work, the "rationality" that ought to govern "strove to discover what was at once just and right." By contrast, "giving reasons" employs the plural. One can give reasons for many sides of a question, and opposing reasons may be both right. Giving reasons thus fits better in deliberative settings where participants expect not only to come to consensus on some matters, but also to conclude on other matters that after reason-giving these issues must be negotiated or decided with a decision-rule on which there has been, in List's terminology, a "meta-agreement."

In the neo-pluralist approach, "reason-giving" can include any statement that sincerely answers the "why" question. A "reason" in this usage can include an emotional state ("I feel blue," "I feel alienated from this meeting"). Amelie Rorty (1985) and Martha Nussbaum (1995, 1996, and other works), the first philosophers to address the subject in detail, also point out that reason requires emotion and emotion reason, and that the line between the two categories is not bright.[19] Recent work in neuroscience provides strong substantiation for their claims, showing that emotion is required for attention and commitment to any issue. Moreover, the emotional pathways in the brain pick up sources of discomfort before the conscious mind can analyze them (Marcus 2002 and sources therein). Thus the emotionally based interjection, "I don't feel comfortable with that," lets a participant articulate a sense of unease even before fully understanding that sense cognitively. That articulation in turn gives the person addressed a reason to slow down and reexamine his or her line of thought before developing it more fully. Just as emotions often intertwine inextricably with cognition, so emotional discourse intertwines inextricably with rational discourse in deliberation.

Because the stakes are higher, binding decisions usually unleash stronger emotions than pre-deliberative dialogues. The guides that urge participants to reveal their feelings (Walsh, this volume) derive from dialogue groups that are explicitly disempowered in order to facilitate such revelations. Public hearings with high stakes, by contrast, often reveal high levels of negative emotion and relatively few of the cooperative dynamics that dialogue groups hope to encourage (Mendelsberg and Oleske, 2000, Karpowitz and Mansbridge, 2005; also Mansbridge, 1980). Yet in this volume, Archon Fung hypothesizes that *"hot* deliberations, with participants who have much at stake" (emphasis in original) will in some ways produce better deliberation, because when the stakes are high more participants will be drawn to the deliberations, participants will "invest more of their psychic energy and resources into the process and so make it more thorough and creative," and results will tend to be more "forcefully supported and implemented." Fung's research supports the point that low-income participants often turn out more for high-stakes decisions. As he points out, we need more evidence on the effects of empowerment and stakes on the quality of deliberation in different contexts.

As our criteria for good deliberation become more plural, encompassing emotion as well as cognition in "reason-giving," we will also need more evidence on how other contexts affect deliberative quality. We will need evidence on how different contexts – especially the larger structures in which the decision is embedded,[20] specific decision rules,[21] deliberative traditions, the amount of time available for deliberation, and perhaps most importantly, the payoff to cooperation – interact with different kinds of emotion and the best ways to engage emotions constructively in deliberation. We now know, however, that emotions help us, among other functions, to think, weigh the importance of alternatives, feel empathy, and decide. So "giving reasons" must be an emotional as well as purely cognitive process, plural in its very nature.

The "common good" can also be plural, functioning adequately for many philosophical and practical purposes in spite of having several noncongruent, contested meanings. We can praise people for being oriented toward the common good without specifying whether we understand the common good as the good of a functional or organic whole, the correct result of reasoning on a problem, an aggregative entity that includes every individual but for different individual reasons, an aggregative entity that need include only more than a majority (or a supermajority), the good of each in his or her role as member of the public, or other meanings.[22] Yet different understandings of the common good fit different understandings of the role of deliberation. The classic tradition that I have labeled "deliberative democracy" depends on an understanding of the common good as based on reason. When Habermas wrote of "a *ratio* that … came into being as the consensus about what was practically necessary in the interest of all" ([1962] 1989: 82–83) or a "final unanimity wrought by a time-consuming process of mutual enlightenment" (195), he undoubtedly did not mean a common good produced through consensus on side-payments. Nor, almost certainly, did he mean what Bächtiger et al. propose as one version of the common good: the "utilitarian" concept of "the best solution for the greatest number of people."[23] Both of these versions of the common good are more compatible with bargaining and aggregration than the concept of *ratio* implies. A plural understanding of democratic deliberation, however, can adopt any of these versions of the common good.

"Legitimacy" can be plural as well. Depending on the context, it can have both aggregative and deliberative sources. Moreover, the criteria for aggregative legitimacy can have sources that are normatively independent of deliberation. That is, if deliberating citizens choose a non-consensual decision rule, they may do so for reasons that depend on ideals intrinsic to aggregative legitimacy – such as that in the decision each member of the polity be free and have equal power over the outcome. The legitimacy of the decision rule then comes not only from the deliberative choice (or hypothetical deliberative choice) but also from those intrinsic ideals.

The aggregative criterion of equal power must, of course, be a "regulative" ideal, in the sense that it cannot be fully achieved in practice. No actual democracy, no matter how small and egalitarian, ever reaches fully equal power in aggregation. In an exact parallel, the deliberative criterion of no power other than the force of the better argument is also a regulative ideal. No actual democracy, no matter how small and egalitarian, ever achieves a deliberative speech situation free from power. Thus no law, whether made by aggregation, by deliberation to consensus, or by a mixture of the two, is ever fully legitimate. Legitimacy is a spectrum, not a dichotomy. The question is whether aggregatively derived laws, based on "political will" rather than "rational agreement" and which correspond "more or less overtly to the compromise between competing private interests" in Habermas's words, can nevertheless be relatively legitimate when the decision rules prescribe equal power for each participant. A plural approach to legitimacy answers in the affirmative.[24]

Finally, "deliberation" can be plural in both ends and means. If one admits the possibility of relatively legitimate aggregate decisions, then the goal of deliberation becomes not only building bridges between individuals, as in the dialogue model, or aiming at a rationally motivated consensus, as in the classic "deliberative democracy" model, but also illuminating conflicts that might previously have been obscured. If the ends are plural and clarification of interests is one of the goals (as Archon Fung argues in this volume), then deliberation must also become plural in its means, incorporating not only the rational search for the common good but also other forms of communication that clarify both common and conflicting interests.

Seen in this light, the core concept of "weighing" in deliberation (from the Latin root *libra*, a balance or scales) could include negotiation and even bargaining. Both bargaining and negotiation can help all parties understand their own and others' interests better, allowing them to weigh their options more realistically.[25] Moreover, if we admit as a form of common good "the best solution for the greatest number" (Bächtiger et al., this volume), then bargaining and negotiation must figure as important parts of the mutual communication for forging and discovering that good. Bargaining in this view would be part of genuine deliberation, not its antonym. Empirically, Jon Elster (1998) has found more bargaining in the non-public than in the public arenas of his constitutional conventions, while Bächtiger and his colleagues (this volume) have found more mutual respect in the non-public than in the public arenas of their legislatures. The association of bargaining and expressions of mutual respect in non-public areas may have emerged because bargaining and negotiation promote genuine listening.[26]

Habermas and many others in the classic philosophical tradition of democratic deliberation have considered not only bargaining but also self-interest antithetical to the common good. Again, however, if clarification is a function of deliberation, expressing self-interest becomes more legitimate. Archon Fung (this volume) suggests a fruitful two stage analysis.[27] In the first stage – of public opinion and will-formation – deliberation allows individuals, among other things, "to realize and effectively assert [their] rational self-interests." In this stage deliberation appropriately encompasses both the kind of instrumental approach in which "individuals advance their own ... ends" along with collective ends."[28] In the second stage of "reasoned social choice," however, participants should "constrain the pursuit of their own self-interest according to the norms of justification."[29]

Thus at the moment of decision the common good should prevail over self-interest: "[W]hen each participant decides what the social choice should be, she should choose the proposal backed by the most compelling reasons" (344). Or as Fung wrote earlier (with Erik Wright), at the moment of decision each participant should vote "not for the option that best advances his self-interest, but rather for the choice that seems most reasonable" (Fung and Wright, 2003: 17–18).[30]

Practical and theoretical problems emerge from this two-stage solution. First, as Fung points out, in practice it is not easy to combine in one deliberation the instrumental "rationality" of self-interest and the "reasonableness" that constrains self-interest. In Fung's words,

> Some of the factors that increase rationality may inhibit reasonableness. Discussions aimed at fostering and clarifying individual preferences, for example, by airing conflicts and advocating conflicting principles, may advance individual rationality while rendering participants less flexible and more self-interested.

These practical tensions can be addressed only by experimenting with different formats that try to promote both ends without each destroying the other.

Second, on a more theoretical plane, the decision to cordon off the investigation and expression of self-interest to a separate sphere temporally prior to the deliberation over social choice (in the equivalent of Habermas's 1996 "two track" process of deliberation in the public sphere and the legislature) fails to acknowledge fully the importance of interest clarification up to the very moment of choice. As Mary Parker Follett's example of negotiation over opening the window in the next room rather trivially demonstrates, it is sometimes only in the act of social choice that one realizes what one really wants and what are in one's real interests.[31]

If we assume that interest clarification can go on up to the very instant of social choice and that legitimate social choice includes bargains based on a combination of self-interest and a principle of fairness, then, after deliberation clarifies common and conflicting interests, we might apply the following tripartite normative principle for citizen duty: "In choice, vote first for the substantive common good. If this is not available, vote second for the outcome of a fair bargain or negotiation. If these are not available, vote third for your self-interest in a voting scheme that aggregates interests fairly."[32] This formula makes it clear both that deliberation must include the exploration of self-interest and that choice itself can, in the right circumstances, legitimately include self-interest.

In addition to expanding the definition of deliberation to include the exploration of self-interest, we may helpfully expand that definition also in the direction of informality. Walsh (this volume) recommends to empiricists who want to explore deliberative democracy that they consider including in the larger "deliberative system" (Mansbridge, 1999) not only forms of public talk such as testimony (Sanders, 1997), storytelling, greeting, and rhetoric (Young, 1996), but also more generally discursive communication (Dryzek, 2000, 2001), which would include "everyday talk" (Mansbridge, 1999, Harris-Lacewell, 2004). All these forms relax some of Bächtiger et al.'s (and Habermas's) "rules" of deliberation. John Drysek and Mark Warren (this volume) similarly recommend, in Warren's words, "multiple kinds, modes, and levels of deliberation," complementary with one another and matched to the appropriate and justified differing purposes and goals.

Cook, Delli Carpini, and Jacobs (this volume) open the door to such a more relaxed, plural, and informal definition of deliberation with the activities they call "discursive participation." They include in discursive participation all those who answer affirmatively when asked if they had had "informal face-to-face or phone conversations or exchanges with people you know about public issues that are local, national, or international concerns" at least "a few times a month." This group comprises 68 percent of the respondents in their survey, with an additional 6 percent engaging at least a few times a month in interactions regarding local, national, or international concerns through meetings or the internet (but not, incongruously, reporting talking with others about such things often either face-to-face or on the phone).

The use of the term "discursive participation" allows Cook, Delli Carpini, and Jacobs to avoid the question of whether or not to call the informal conversations and exchanges they are measuring "deliberation." Another category, which they do call "deliberative," covers interactions that are not simply *about* public matters but that also take place *in* public, in the meetings they categorize as "formal face to face deliberation." Of their respondents 25 percent had attended such a "formal or informal [organized] meeting" to discuss a local, national, or international issue in the last year or so.[33] These are precisely the sorts of groups that Walsh, Weatherford and McDonnell, Rosenberg, and Fung investigate in this volume. With their category of discursive participation, Cook and her colleagues direct us beyond these meetings to the far greater number of people who talk with one another about public matters in a discourse that cuts across (although it is not equally dispersed across) class, race, and other boundaries.

Yet deliberation can be conceived as even more inclusive than the "discursive participation" on public issues on which Cook, Delli Carpini, and Jacobs report. Some issues of common concern involve "the authoritative allocation of values" (David Easton's 1953 definition of the political), but do not involve what many think of as, in the words of the survey, "public issues that are local, national, or international concerns." When two friends discuss sexual harassment, trying to understand and decide what behavior ought to be grounds for firing the president of their university, or when they discuss the threat to their jobs from their company's decision to outsource several of its departments, they might not think to themselves, or report on a survey, that they have discussed "public issues that are local, national, or international concerns." Nevertheless, sexual harassment and outsourcing are issues of general concern, matters the public ought to discuss, consider, and weigh. These issues affect the authoritative allocation of values.

When society functions as the relevant authority, even informal norms can be the subject of the authoritative allocation of values. Social authority often settles what is appropriate behavior for men and women – what counts as the rightful behavior of a male head of family, for example, or what counts as "male chauvinism." When matters involving the authoritative allocation of values become open for discussion, criticism, and consideration, then the "everyday talk" (Mansbridge, 1999) in which people weigh these issues becomes a form of deliberation broadly defined – although usually a patchwork, interrupted, sometimes staccato form.

In everyday talk, people both weigh issues and make decisions on them. They decide that their next-door neighbor is wrong in her stance on abortion, that Oprah's latest guest is right, or that what they themselves thought yesterday did not take some new fact or insight into consideration. When many individuals engage in everyday talk, update their earlier ideas, and coordinate on a new, temporarily settled conviction, the society itself may be said to have "decided," and a new "authoritative allocation of values" is born.[34]

If we extend the meaning of "deliberation" in these various ways, it helps to modify the noun with adjectives in order to retain a clear analytic meaning. We must distinguish between more "cognitively-based" and more "emotionally-based" reason-giving, a "unitary" and "utilitarian" common good, "deliberative" and "aggregative" legitimacy, and "formal" and "everyday" deliberation, as well as "high" versus "low" quality deliberation. These adjectives improve the analysis by encouraging fine-grained distinctions. They also help avoid the confusion that ensues when different analysts use a general word in different ways without modifying adjectives.

I suggest the term "neo-pluralist" to describe an approach to deliberation that, unlike the original version of pluralism, values and promotes the common good, seeking ways to advance that good within democratic processes, while at the same time valuing the expression of self-interest and legitimating aggregative procedures that rest on coercive power, such as majority rule. Deliberative neo-pluralism builds on the classic tradition of deliberative democracy and on the republican tradition of deliberation on the common good, keeping central the ideals of equal respect and non-domination, but adding to these values a positive valuing of self-interest, an acceptance of frequent conflict in material interest as well as of opinion, and a legitimation of democratic aggregation through some version of equal power.

The study of deliberation has been expanding over time from what I have called the classic philosophical model of "deliberative democracy" based only on reasoning on the common good, with restricted meanings for both "reasoning" and "common good," toward a neo-pluralist model of "democratic deliberation" based on relatively expansive definitions of "democratic," "deliberation," "reasoning," "the common good," and "legitimacy."[35] This chapter recognizes and begins to explore the implications of this expansion. If "reason-giving," the "common good," "legitimacy," and "deliberation" itself have all acquired more expansive meanings, and if we are therefore all neo-pluralist "democratic deliberators" now, it is time to recognize this fact and its analytic implications.

Notes

1. I thank the Radcliffe Institute for a fellowship that allowed me time to work on this paper, parts of which have been drawn from my "Deliberation and Self-Interest" (Mansbridge, 2006).
2. I have adopted the labels "deliberative democracy" and "democratic deliberation" to highlight the differences between the traditions, without meaning to suggest that others who use the terms intend the distinction I draw here. By "legitimate law" (or "legitimacy") I mean not law that is *believed* to be legitimate (sociological legitimacy), but law that has *justifiable grounds* for being considered legitimate (philosophical or "normative" legitimacy).
3. For more on this line of thought in *The Structural Transformation of the Public Sphere*, see Mansbridge 2006.
4. Schmitt *Verfassungslehre* (1928), quoted in Habermas ([1962] 1991: 81). Ellen Kennedy's (1988) introduction to Schmitt [1923] 1988 reveals how widely held this view was among certain German philosophers.
5. Estlund (2006) interprets Habermas's criterion for legitimacy as hypothetical, that only those statutes may claim legitimacy that *could* meet with the assent of all the citizens *if* they *were* able to engage in a process that met the criteria for an ideal discursive process. Although in this passage Habermas's verb *können* is not *könnten* ("could"), it admits of a hypothetical, as does the English "can." (I thank Isaac Nakhimov for help in translating this passage.) Rosen (1999) suggests that an ambiguity regarding hypothetical versus actual speech characterizes Habermas's more general stance.
6. See Mansbridge, 1980 for the legitimating criteria of adversary democracy; see Fraser (1990) on Habermas not admitting private interests to the public sphere (59) and restricting discourse in public spheres to deliberation about the common good (62, 70 ff).
7. On empowerment, see Fung, this volume. Any democracy is by definition a system of rule, a system by which to make binding decisions. Thus, of Gutmann and Thompson's four characteristics of deliberative democracy, the third is that the "process aims at producing a decision that is *binding*" (2004: 5). In this volume, only the legislatures studied by Bächtiger et al. produce decisions that are binding on a polity.
8. Walsh notes in another context, however, that for "some respondents" even the dialogue process produces "signs of heightened group conflict" (Walsh 2003: 26), cited in Delli Carpini, Cook, and Jacobs 2004: 331.
9. One of Weatherford and McDonnell's respondents makes this point forcefully: "You can't expect people to participate ... when they know they are not going to have any effect" (28).
10. For Walsh, civic dialogue represents the stance that community connections are best improved "when conflict is addressed, rather than obscured with the demand of politeness or assumptions of underlying harmony." No one in the classic philosophical tradition of deliberative democracy would deny this, as all endorse the creative role of conflicting opinions. In this tradition the proper subject of deliberation is conflicting opinions on the common interest, not conflicting interests. It is unclear whether Walsh's dialogue groups address conflicting interests or only conflicting opinions about the common interest.
11. Such a gender difference would be congruent with gender stereotypes – particularly the gendered stereotypes regarding reason and emotion that have

permeated the European philosophical tradition – although it would not be fully congruent with past individual-level measurements of male and female behavior. Mansbridge, 1993 points out that although the language in most countries of the world (particularly English and German-speaking countries) associates men with reason and women with emotion, and although philosophers such as Kant and Hegel do the same, psychological research on empathy at the individual level indicates that the more the subject is aware of what is being measured (e.g., through a questionnaire specifically asking, "How empathetic are you?"), the greater the gender differences in measured empathy, particularly among individuals who subscribed strongly to traditional gender roles. The less aware the subject (e.g., in studies of galvanic skin response to the cries of a newborn), the more miniscule the gender differences, in the least aware cases amounting to zero. Mendelberg and Karpowitz's innovation is to show that in a group setting, gender differences, presumably activated by implicit gender roles, can influence group norms and thereby magnify any individual differences. (Sunstein, 2000 on group polarization reports a similar effect.)

12. In this dynamic, causal claims are reinforced or rejected through loosely linked personal narratives (rather than, as in collaborative, rational discourse, through "the rules of logic, coherence and reliable observation" and "referring to commonly accepted underlying assumptions"). The group reaches its conclusions by implicit consensus, by the implicit weight of the majority, by a polite "joint recognition that both parties are right, or at least partially right," or by simply stopping talking.

13. These claims derive from observing a score of town meetings, participating in hundreds of academic department and voluntary association meetings, and analyzing closely the tapes of citizen deliberations in 10 different groups (Mansbridge et al., 2006).

14. I thank Matthew Amengual for directing me to the significance of this statement, which rests on a mixed emotional and cognitive base and in an open-ended manner allows change in both self and others.

15. David Miller (1992) had also suggested that deliberation could both structure participation by helping to make preferences single-peaked and enable participants to choose a voting mechanism to aggregrate preferences when deliberation fails to achieve consensus. List's work with Luskin, Fishkin, and Mclean ([2000] 2005) demonstrates that deliberation actually fills this structuring function.

16. In practicing direct assembly democracies, where citizens must decide a host of issues that come before them, many decisions are unanimous. So are many decisions in the U.S. Congress. Contested decisions, however, make the news – and generate deliberative experiments. Thus it is not surprising that "experiments on group deliberation have produced little evidence of post-deliberation unity" (List, this volume).

17. See also Mansbridge, 1988 and works cited therein.

18. Steenbergen, et al., 2003: 21; see also 22–24, discussing Habermas's discourse ethics as "the foundation of the DQI" (23). Habermas has himself praised this index (2005: 391).

19. For more on emotion in deliberation, see Hall, 2005 and Krause, forthcoming.

20. For example, the structures of consensus politics, non-public venues, small groups, and groups with lasting interactions (Bächtiger et al., this volume).

21. For example, a unanimity rule has different effects in the different contexts of relatively conflicting interests and relatively common interests; see Delli Carpini, Cook, and Jacobs, 2004: 327, Mendelberg, 2002: and Mansbridge, 1980.

Communication itself has different effects in different contexts. When groups are in competition, communication tends to increase cooperation within a group but decrease cooperation with the out-group (cf. Mendelberg, 2002 and Delli Carpini, Cook, and Jacobs, 2004: 325).

22. Held, 1970 reports and analyzes these and other theories of the common good. When several choices have individually a zero-sum character, an agreement with sub-payments (Buchanan and Tullock, 1965) can produce an aggregate or composite "common good" that includes everyone but is not a unitary common good on which everyone can substantively agree. See Mansbridge, 1998 for more on the different meanings of the common good and for a fuller argument that the essentially contested meaning of the common good does not vitiate its philosophical or practical usefulness.

23. Held, 1970, in ch. 3 discusses theories in which the common good means the good of the "preponderance" of the public.

24. Some theorists have confronted this issue without taking the full neo-pluralist position that I propound here. Simone Chambers advances the view that "the more the issue under public discussion involves deep foundational issues of justice the more important rational consensus becomes" (1996: 187). "But," she continues, "fair compromises and majority decisions are legitimate to the extent that citizens believe there are good reasons to settle for these decisions rules" (188). Later she also argues that a legitimate political order could include voting (308, 311) and bargaining (309) so long as citizens have been able "to deliberate and decide when and where bargaining is a fair and appropriate method of dispute resolution" (idem). Compare also Bernard Manin and Seyla Benhabib, who have similar definitions of legitimacy (Manin, 1987: 352; Benhabib, 1996: 68) and of the deliberative basis of majority rule (Manin, 1987: 359; Benhabib, 1996: 72). Manin, however, is more pluralist, giving the majority principle equal status with deliberation and arguing that it is the "conjunction" of the two elements of deliberation and the majority principle that "creates legitimacy" (360).

25. See Mansbridge, 2006 for an extended argument that deliberation can include both bargaining and negotiation.

26. One could test this hypothesis by re-coding the speeches analyzed by Bächtiger et al. for the presence of bargaining and negotiation.

27. The separate stages may not require separate spheres. Moreover, the stages may be highly contiguous or perhaps overlapping space and time.

28. These functions of advancing one's own ends and airing conflicts may fit into deliberation simply "as ways to present *information*" (Cohen and Rogers, 2003: 247, emphasis in original), but Fung's analysis also seems to allow the active pursuit of self-interest in the deliberative process.

29. Fung writes, "Reasonableness may require participants to restrain themselves when others offer compelling reasons based on common group interests or commonly held norms such as respect, reciprocity, and fairness. For example, reasonableness may require someone to withdraw his support from a proposal that would best advance his own self-interest because others are more needy." The use of "may" in this passage suggests that even in this second, social choice stage, reasonableness need not require the restraint of self-interest for the common good.

30. Note that even in Fung's second stage a fair bargain, based on both self-interest and political equality, is also legitimate: "You do for me this time, and I do for you the next time around." Thus when the choices are inherently zero-sum (or in other contexts of fundamental conflict), the "compelling reasons" that mandate

one's vote could include aggregative formulae that balance self-interests. See Guinier, 1994 on taking turns, Lijphart, 1999 on consociational democracy, and Mansbridge, 1980 on proportional outcomes.

31. Mary Parker Follett [1925] 1942, on "integrated solutions" (later dubbed "win-win solutions,"cf. Fisher and Ury, [1981]1983). In Follett's classic example one party wants the window open to make the room cooler, the other does not want a draft, and the solution is to open the window in the next room, giving both parties what they really want.

32. When there is no obvious common good other than aggregation, voting for one's self-interest furthers the fair aggregative process. ("How many people for baseball? How many for football?") If no substantive good is available and the alternatives have been fairly produced, choosing the option that wins the most hands produces "the best solution for the greatest number" (Bächtiger et al., this volume) that time around. Of course, as Guinier, 1994, Lijphart, 1999, Mansbridge, 1980, and others have pointed out, if those who favor football win and those who favor baseball lose all the time, some form of taking turns is fairer than majority rule. The unfairness of majority rule is compounded in a segmented society where the majority wins and the minority loses on all the issues of major importance to the two groups. In addition, the question of whether there is a substantive common good or fair bargain in any given situation will always be contested. In practice, some citizens will often vote for a substantive common good, some for a fair bargain, and some for their self-interest, producing a problem in aggregation. (See Barry, 1965 for the first statement of this problem.) To the degree to which a vote aggregates such qualitatively different "apples and oranges," the legitimacy of the resulting law is lowered, as it is for deficits in equality and liberty. The fairness of the boundaries of the polity is an important, but separate, issue.

33. They note that this year may have provided a "best case," as it included a close, hotly contested Presidential election and considerable agitation over the war in Iraq.

34. See Drysek, 2001 on the competition of discourses. Fraser's "subaltern counterpublics" are narrower than the bounds of everyday talk, as these arenas function as "bases and training grounds of agitational activities directed toward wider publics" (Fraser, 1990: 124). They are not themselves the wider public.

35. See Chambers, 1995: 322 for "a definite expansion of the sorts of things that could be considered arguments and reasons," Bohman, 1998: 400, Guttman and Thompson,1996, Drysek, 2001, esp. 661 and Warren, this volume.

13
Institutionalizing Deliberative Democracy

Mark E. Warren

Research into the deliberative dimensions of democracy has been remarkably productive over the last decade or so, spawning new insights into how deliberation functions within the many political venues that constitute contemporary democracies. Normative theories of deliberative democracy have justified and sometimes inspired a wide range of new institutional developments, from citizen juries, stakeholder meetings, deliberative polling, and deliberative forums to the Freedom of Information legislation that enhances public deliberation (Chambers, 2003; Gastil and Levine, 2005; Parkinson, 2006). The key claim of deliberative theories of democracy is simple and compelling: deliberative approaches to collective decisions under conditions of conflict produce better decisions than those resulting from alternative means of conducting politics: coercion, traditional deference, or markets. The decisions resulting from deliberation are likely to be more legitimate, more reasonable, more informed, more effective, and more politically viable (Cohen, 1996; Habermas, 1996; Gutmann and Thompson, 1996; Bohman, 1998).

The strengths that come with shifting the analytic center of democratic theory away from institutions and toward the medium of decision-making, however, has come with costs to understanding the institutional architecture that supports deliberation. Much of the intellectual energy that has gone into developing the theories of deliberative democracy has focused on the relationship between democratic norms and the general sociological insight that deliberation is, in principle, a viable approach to conflict. It is true that the institutional dimension of deliberative democratic theory – the dimension that would transform it from a theory of *deliberation* into a *democratic* theory – has gained much more attention over the last decade or so, most notably with the publication of Habermas's *Between Facts and Norms* (1996), and especially with respect to constitutionalism (see also Gutmann and Thompson, 1996; Bohman, 1998; Elster, 1998; Sunstein, 2001; and James, 2004). But deliberative approaches remain underdeveloped in at least two other areas that affect the relationship between deliberation and institutional design: (a) the social psychology of deliberation under conditions of conflict, and (b) institutional structuring of incentives to deliberate. These two problem areas focus my comments on the chapters in this volume. In Section 13.1, I suggest why centering democratic theory on deliberation as a medium of decision-making and organization produces a distinctive and normatively powerful approach. I note in Section 13.2 that there is nothing necessary about attractive normative outcomes: they depend upon careful institutional design. In Section 13.3, I make a methodological claim: Whereas deliberative democratic theorists often focus on the motivations of participants – in particular, to enter into reasonable deliberations with the intention of developing a consensus – I suggest that from an institutional perspective, we should remain agnostic about intentions, and instead focus on the question of whether deliberative interactions sway participants through the forces of persuasion. The importance of the distinction, I shall argue, is that it refocuses attention toward institutional structuring of talk, and allows us to think about the transformations of whatever strategic or manipulative intent participants may bring to an interaction into persuasive force. It follows that deliberative democratic theory focuses on the question of how institutions structure incentives for participants to win through the forces of persuasion rather than other kinds of force. Section 13.4 follows up this point by focusing on the social psychology of deliberation under conditions of conflict. In Section 13.5, I detail several key considerations for the design of deliberative institutions. I conclude in Section 13.6 by noting the importance of thinking about deliberative *systems* consisting of complementary institutions that specialize in the multiple kinds of deliberation necessary for a democratic politics and society.

13.1 Why deliberative theories of democracy are different

Most of our received democratic theories are centered on the institutions which enable the rule of the people: voting and elections, separation of power, distribution of rights, and representation. Democratic theories constructed in this way include direct democracy, participatory democracy, representative democracy, or pluralist democracy. A few democratic theories – particularly those inspired by classical republicanism – are explicitly ethical in structure: they posit the goods of civic virtues or communal solidarity and then view specific institutions as means to these ethical goals (Held, 1996). In contrast, deliberative theories of democracy are defined neither by commitments to any particular institutional device nor by ethical commitments to civic virtues or community. Rather, they seek to advance a particular medium of political conflict resolution and organization – that is, communicative influence. Because they are not comparable in the same plane of analysis, then, we should not think of theories of deliberative democracy as alternatives to other democratic theories, particularly those focused on institutions. Within theories of deliberative democracy, institutional analysis, critique, and recommendation follow from the view that deliberation, broadly conceived and all other things being equal, is a better way of making collective decisions under conditions of conflict within post-traditional societies than other possible ways and means, including power, money, and tradition-based authority. Institutions should be judged, therefore, not just by many of the standard mechanisms of democracy (such as majority rule, checks and balances, and rights), but also (and more fundamentally) by whether they serve to enable the medium of deliberation, which is in turn valued because of its intrinsically desirable normative properties relative to other possible means of doing politics.

Two inherent strengths of this medium-based approach account for the broad attractiveness and rapid development of deliberative democratic theory. The first involves its normative immanence to liberal-democratic political cultures. Critics notwithstanding, as an ideal within today's societies, it is virtually impossible to be "against deliberation," not only because to take this position is to be *for* some other way of conducting politics – and, when something is at stake, the alternatives violate the norms of liberal-democracy. Indeed, most critics are not, literally, "against deliberation" (Sanders, 1997), but rather against narrowly cognitivist or rationalist understandings of communicative influence (Dryzek, 2000; Young, 2000). Stated positively, the notion that deliberation is a good way to conduct politics has wide-spread legitimacy based on democratic as well as liberal norms. With respect to *egalitarian* norms, most forms of democratic egalitarianism are entailed in relations of mutual communicative influence. Speaking and listening assumes equality, while inequalities of status, power, and condition undermine mutual influence through speech. Likewise, the notion that those who are affected by collective decisions ought to be involved in making collective decisions through deliberation is inherently *inclusive*. When individuals are excluded from deliberations about matters that affect them, by default they are subject to other kinds of force – an inherent violation of the norm that conflicts ought to be settled through talk. With respect to liberal ideals of *freedom*, collective decisions that are deliberated and accepted are more likely to reflect individual choices, and less likely to be experienced as limitations on freedom. With respect to liberal ideals of *autonomy*, decisions that are collectively reasoned are likely to enhance individual reason and judgment than decisions made in other ways. Collective self-government through speech is closely linked with individual self-government through considered judgments. With respect to liberal ideals of *respect for individuals*, resolving political conflict through speech requires mutual recognition of participants as speakers – that is, as individuals who can be subject to communicative influence, and who are agents of communicative influence.

The second strength of the deliberative medium is that it is increasingly immanent to the social organization. Contemporary societies are becoming more resistant to bureaucratic administration, in part owing to their political complexity: hierarchical, rule-based governance works poorly in multi-stakeholder environments, or for collective projects that require extensive information and cooperation. Likewise, the cultures of contemporary societies are increasingly postmodern: individuals place an increasing value on self-governance and self-realization (Inglehart, 1997) as well as to their post-traditional cultures. For at least these reasons, today's societies favor *marketization*, owing to the ability of markets to handle complexity – a problem that goes beyond the topic here (Lindblom, 2002). But they also favor *communication*, not only as information becomes more central to production and social organization, but also because complexity in itself favors structures that transmit information. *Deliberation* builds on these postmodern social developments, as the "natural" medium through which these social transformations might link with the formation of public wills (Beck, 1997; see also Mansbridge, 1999).

Two chapters in this volume provide evidence for these broad theoretical expectations. Cook, Delli Carpini, and Jacobs (Chapter 2) suggest that when political participation is defined to include "discursive participation," citizens turn out to be more engaged and active than previous research suggests. Importantly, discursive participation is more broadly and equitably "distributed" than other resources: the strongest predictor of discursive participation is neither income nor education but rather social capital: being connected within society predicts discursive participation. Although this study does not tell us what is happening over time, it is consistent with the "critical citizen" hypothesis development by Norris and Dalton: political culture is changing in directions that are consistent with deliberative expectations (Dalton, 1999, 2000, 2007; Norris, 1999).

In Chapter 8, Fung notes that these cultural changes are matched by the emergence of multiple institutional experiments in deliberative democracy – what he calls "minipublics." While the chapter does not provide quantitative evidence about changes in the reach and effectiveness of bureaucratic/administrative sources of governance, Fung's case studies suggest a widespread experimentalism, driven by attempts to increase the legitimacy and effectiveness of governance. Other studies support Fung's suggestion that the increasing experimentalism with deliberative institutions is not a passing fad. Rather, it is deeply rooted in a growing gap between the governance demands of complex, pluralistic, postmaterial societies, and what the standard institutions of electoral democracy are able to deliver (Cain, Dalton, and Scarrow, 2003; Warren and Pearse, forthcoming).

13.2 Where deliberative democratic theories are lacking

While the culture and practices of deliberative democracy have been evolving rapidly, deliberative democratic theory is not as well positioned to provide guidance and analysis as it should be, in part owing to an abstractness of expectations. Critics of deliberative democracy commonly note, for example, that citizens are rarely as reasonable, self-aware, respectful, and enthusiastic about politics as deliberative ideals might suggest. Rosenberg's study (Chapter 7) of a deliberative setting that should bring out the best in citizens – deliberations about schools by a homogeneous group of educated, high-income parents in Laguna Beach, California – finds that "rational discourse" was rare, and the "transformative discourse" necessary to bridge what differences in cultural assumptions, styles, and capacities existed was non-existent.

Should deliberative democrats view such findings as a fundamental challenge to deliberative ideals? Yes – but not in the way critics might suggest. It is not that the ideals are "unrealistic." Rather, it may be, as Mansbridge argues (Chapter 12), that much deliberative work is being done through nonverbal and emotive forms of communication, for which deliberative theory does not yet have codeable concepts. But it is also likely that deliberative democrats have not paid enough attention to the exceptional, demanding, and fragile qualities of deliberation – which in turn would require a close focus on the institutional requirements for enabling and protecting deliberation. Many chapters in this volume begin to focus on these requirements, particularly those by Walsh (Chapter 3), List (Chapter 4), Bächtiger et al. (Chapter 5), and Mendelberg and Karpowitz (Chapter 6).

This particular weakness of deliberative theories of democracy reflects the inertia of its origins in the theory of communicative action. In developing the theory, Habermas (1984) argued persuasively that communication is an autonomous force in social organization that can (and often does) provide the social infrastructure for deliberative responses to politics. But at the same time, these origins left the mistaken impression that it is possible to generalize from the capacities of *everyday* communication to communication under conditions of *political* conflict – producing a misplaced set of expectations for political deliberation. Habermas does not himself misplace expectations: politics represents, in some sense, failures of everyday forms of communication – owing to power differentials, cultural divisions, or other incapacities (Warren, 2002). Deliberation is, therefore, already *exceptional* as a form of communication: it is a response to failed or missing social relations, failed institutions and systems, shifting injustices, and other circumstances that are not, as it were, ideal for deliberation. For these same reasons, deliberation is *demanding* of participants: they must elevate other participants to the status of speakers whose arguments will be given responses; it requires that participants seek to influence others through arguments; it supposes that participants are able to focus their speaking and listening upon validity claims, so that conversation can be about claims rather than about the participants. Deliberation, in other words, requires maturity from participants. Finally, deliberation is *fragile*: deliberation is vulnerable to unequal power, cultural and linguistic differences and inequalities, market forces, threats, and time constraints

(Warren, 2006a). Add to these features the fact that deliberation is embedded within complex incentive structures, normative frameworks, subtle systems of social signaling, any of which may indicate to participants that the costs of deliberation to social solidarity are higher than any conceivable benefits. Last but not least, politics tends to select for contexts and psychological affects that are not conducive to deliberation, including misunderstandings, differences, and ill-will. Thus, despite the many features of deliberation that make it an attractive alternative to other ways of doing politics – its capacities to align public and individual will-formation, its consistency with freedom and pluralism, its creativity – the exceptional, demanding, and fragile features of deliberation also make it a difficult medium to institutionalize.

While the challenges are considerable, they are not insurmountable. From the theory side, a number of thinkers have made considerable advances, especially in relating constitutional design to deliberative processes (Habermas, 1996; Nino, 1996; Elster, 1998; Sunstein, 2001; James, 2004; Urbinati, 2006). The general structural strategy is clear: political institutions should establish spaces and incentives for deliberation precisely where it is difficult or unlikely. From the empirical side, deliberative democracy benefits from the fact that it is not purely stipulative. Even though most communication in politics is not deliberation, actual instances of deliberation are common enough so that we have a wealth of cases from which to learn. In addition, the payoffs of successful deliberations are so high that many institutions have evolved ways of encouraging and protecting deliberation.

13.3 A definitional consideration: deliberation v. deliberative institutions

Connecting normative expectations to empirical studies of institutions will be easier if we distinguish "deliberation" from the institutions that enable deliberation. Simone Chambers provides a broadly agreed conception of deliberation when she writes that

> Generally speaking, we can say that deliberation is debate and discussion aimed at producing reasonable, well-informed opinions in which participants are willing to revise preferences in light of discussion, new information, and claims made by fellow participants. Although consensus need not be the ultimate aim of deliberation, and participants are expected to pursue their interests [and] an overarching interest in the legitimacy of outcomes (understood as justification to all affected) ideally characterizes deliberation. (2003: 309)

This concept of deliberation is, in part, based on intentions: participants deliberate when they seek to influence one another through argument, and to do so in ways that respond to the arguments of others. This approach is important for distinguishing deliberation from other kinds of communication, in particular, the strategic use of talk to manipulate others. However, we should not use this kind of distinction to identify the institutions of deliberative democracy for two reasons. First, it is true that institutions depend upon rules supported by norms, and norms depend upon intent. But in the case of democratic institutions the normative bar should be lower than deliberative intent. It is sufficient that participants agree to make decisions through talking and voting. A higher bar would define away the functions of deliberative institutions serve in transforming the strategic features of politics into communicative interaction. Thus, although we should not refer to manipulative speech as "deliberation," neither should we define the institutions of deliberative democracy in ways that would proscribe manipulative speech. Indeed, as a theoretical matter, we should expect participants to enter into communication with strategic intent: it is part of what defines an issue as "political" that participants disagree, and yet have stakes that motivate them to win. Institutions should be designed to channel strategic intent into talk, with the hope that when participants can *only* get their way through talk, they will seek to persuade.

Thus, from the point of view of democratic institutions and systems, we should be more interested in the outcomes of communication than communicative intent. If angry demonstration is necessary to persuade others that they should notice unpleasant facts, that is a contribution to deliberation – although the initial intentions may not be "deliberative." Likewise, strategic and hypocritical communications may induce a dynamic of communicative influence that produces deliberative outcomes (Elster, 1998). Institutionalizing deliberative democracy turns, in part, on structuring incentives in such a way that communicative utterances that are not necessarily deliberative *in intention* are captured to produce dynamics that are deliberative *in function*. This is way deliberative institutions should not depend upon, or be defined by, the deliberative intentions of participants. Rather, we should be interested in deliberative functions of institutional norms, rules, and constraints.

Getting the normative judgements in the right place will help to connect a variety of empirical observations and experiments to the broader generalizations that are already well developed. While there are a variety of approaches that lend themselves to developing this "middle-level" theory (Fung, Chapter 8), it is likely that the most successful will involve a combination of attributes. They will be problem-driven rather than theory-driven – seeking to generalize from real-world issues and experiments. They will involve analysis of incentive structures following from the problems as well as the institutional forms within which they are addressed. They will not use "high level" theory "descriptively," but rather to define the normative significance of the empirical work and to guide normative judgments of outcomes. At the same time, "middle level" theory development will avoid generalizing from single cases or examples, but rather seek to identify the attributes of the cases that produce the outcomes of significance. Fung's chapter is exemplary of the kind of systematic middle level theory development that will enable more sophisticated democratic practices as well as refine high-level theories (see also Warren, 2001; Warren and Pearse, forthcoming; Parkinson, 2006).

13.4 The social psychology of deliberation

The cases, problems, and theoretical insights gathered in this volume are especially valuable for those areas of middle-level theorizing having to do with the interrelationships between social psychology and institutional contexts. I was struck by three problem areas.

Difference and homogeneity

Deliberative democratic theory has long been troubled by questions of difference: What do participants need to share to engage in deliberation? Rosenberg's typology of discursive interactions – *egocentric, conventional, rational,* and *transformative* – provides a valuable tool for beginning to answer this question (Chapter 7). The first two kinds are limiting cases of deliberation. In the case of egocentric "proto-discourse," too little commonality exists. Participants are not really addressing one another but rather expressing positions that are, perhaps, evoked by conflict, but fail to connect. There would seem to be two possible reasons for this kind of failure. The first might be psychological: participants may have personalities overburdened, as it were, with everyday insecurities and common narcissistic desires, leading them to enter into conversation seeking psychological securities rather than discursive interactions. Because the psychological purpose of talk is about self-confirmation, conversation is not attuned to the autonomous existence of others. Deliberation is, as it were, derailed by verbal acting-out – ego-centric proto-discourse.

A second possible reason for proto-discourse is cultural rather than psychological: participants may lack common speaking styles, languages, or cultural norms, so that expressions, although evoked by conflict, fail to result in the mutual recognition and comprehensibility necessary for deliberation. In contrast, "conventional" discourse fails to count as deliberation because it functions simply to affirm what is already shared – experiences, conventions, normative expectations, and cultural styles.

Failures of deliberation, then, may be the result of (a) psychological disconnection; (b) too much cultural difference; or (c) too much social homogeneity. The first two kinds of failure are familiar. The third kind, however, is a bit more surprising. We often assume that social homogeneity provides the background of commonalities that makes deliberation easier. Rosenberg followed this assumption in selecting a "best case" situation to study: discussions among parents involved in schools who share culture, ethnicity, and language, and who have high levels of education. But he found very little rational deliberation (meaning "reasonable" in this context rather than "instrumental" as in rational choice usage) and no transformative deliberation. Why? Perhaps rather than favoring deliberation, homogeneity produced a high degree of initial agreement on basic values and goals. Lacking fundamental disagreements and feeling comfortable with convention, participants may not have experienced the need for deliberation. Or, alternatively, it may be that the scale of the context – local schools – favored the pressure of convention over conflict. As Mansbridge (1980) noted in her study of New England town meetings, participants were keenly aware of the high stakes of conflict, since conflict trades off against local solidarities. So, it may be that more difference is more conducive to deliberation. Given that too much difference also makes deliberation unlikely, the question for middle level theory may be one of understanding (a) what the optimal kinds and degrees of difference are, and (b) how institutions can compensate for less than optimal circumstances.

Mendelberg and Karpowitz (Chapter 6) add an intriguing refinement to these possibilities, finding that group norms can either encourage or suppress deliberation, depending upon the mix of men and women, and the kind of decision rule. Decision rules requiring unanimity tend to increase the pressure of group norms on dissenters. Interestingly, whereas dissenting men are alienated by group norms, women tend to increase their levels of deliberation, presumably seeking consensus. Thus, as Mendelberg and Karpowitz argue, not only do group norms need to be taken into account, but also their interactions with decision rules and gender mixes.

Recognition and reason

Rosenberg's fourth type, *transformative* discourse, is necessary when differences of culture or discursive style make reasonable discourse impossible. Transformative discourse occurs when participants seek to establish the understandings necessary for rational discourse. While Rosenberg found that no transformative discourse occurred within the group he studied, the "civic dialogues" studied by Walsh (Chapter 3) consist almost entirely of transformative discourse. Walsh does not use this term: she distinguishes between *deliberation* (Rosenberg's rational discourse) and *dialogue* (transformative discourse). Once we translate the terminology, however, one of the important impressions left by Walsh's chapter is that practitioners already know a lot about transformative discourse (see e.g., Saunders, 1999). Interestingly, Walsh's examples challenge the sequence suggested by Rosenberg: even though transformative discourse may be the highest developmental stage, from the perspective of temporal and developmental sequencing, it is a condition of rational discourse, which depends upon a prior recognition of speakers *qua* speakers (Warren, 2006a). Dialogue establishes this kind of equality by enabling each to establish themselves before others. Individuals do so in part by revealing their perceptions, interests, prejudices, fears, and hopes, and asking others to recognize each one in their full particularity. "Rationality" in the sense of reasonableness requires participants to have secured their identities in such a way that validity claims can become the objects of discourse. That is, deliberations are about the "what" of statements rather than about the "who" of participants. But the "who" can be bracketed, psychologically speaking, only on the basis of prior and on-going mutual recognition. These considerations suggest that, among other matters, middle-level theory will need to focus on: (a) the co-dependence of complementary forms of discourse, and (b) the temporal sequencing of forms of discourse (Fung, this volume; see also Saunders, 1999; Parkinson, 2006: chap. 7).

The bracketing of the "who" should not be understood, of course, as a bracketing of the person in favor of a stylized reason-giving – a criticism often leveled at theories of deliberative democracy. Rather, "bracketing" is an attitude of mutual recognition achieved in ways that enable discussions to proceed on the basis of mutual psychological security. Bessette (1994: 147–149) studied some of these effects in Congress, finding that deliberation works better when informal rules and norms are strong, including those that support mutual recognition and prohibit political embarrassment. More generally in small group contexts, mutual recognition should enable non-cognitive elements – situation, appearance, empathetic intuitions, experiences – to be expressed (thus becoming cognitive) in such a way that they can become a topic of conversation without evoking the kinds of identity-threatening discomforts and threats that can make deliberation impossible. Mendelberg and Karpowitz's (Chapter 6) study of the interaction between gendered norms and decision rules shows, however, that successful deliberation does not depend upon norms alone: discussions of distributive justice were more likely to occur in predominantly female groups working under unanimous (as opposed to majority) decision-rules. At the very least, these findings underscore the importance of research into the relationship between institutional design and the psychology of deliberators.

Publicity

We typically think of deliberation as a *public* process. Publicity is justified by the notion that speakers should be held accountable for their claims and representations, before the audiences potentially affected by them (Bohman, 1996: ch. 1; Gutmann and Thompson; 1996: ch. 3; Habermas, 1996). Within deliberative democratic theory, non-public deliberations have little place or justification beyond, say, necessary exceptions for matters of security (cf. Chambers, 2004; Bohman, 1998: 420–422).

Yet there may be important roles for non-public deliberation beyond the typical exceptions. Walsh makes the interesting observation that civic dialogue processes are typically non-public for the reason that building mutual recognition and trust among those who do not share backgrounds could not survive the glare of publicity. Likewise, many kinds of professional, scientific, and policy-related deliberations have non-public phases, without which it is difficult to imagine participants engaging in frank discussions motivated by validity claims (see also Bessette, 1994: 144–147).

Whether or not these observations are troubling for theories of deliberative democracy depends upon how we construe the democratic functions of publicity. It is clear that publicity is especially important when participants in deliberation are serving as representatives of one sort or another (Parkinson, 2006: ch. 4). Citizens need to be able to judge their representatives' speech and actions, and publicity is a condition for their judgments. Publicity is also important when there are reasons to believe that publicity is required for inclusion – that is, that secrecy would result in the exclusion of those with legitimate claims (Warren, 2004). Finally, publicity seems especially important when deliberation is fused with power, since the legitimacy of binding decisions should meet a higher threshold.

But these roles of public deliberation are not exhaustive of the democratic functions of deliberation, and under some circumstances may conflict with these functions. By its very nature, publicity introduces strategic elements into language use which will tend to trump (a) the self-revealing aspects of language use typical of transformative discourse, and (b) the frank discussion of validity claims. The social-psychology of (a) is straightforward: people do not reveal much of themselves under conditions of conflict. Under these conditions, participants will be unsure of the good-will of one another. This is why dialogue (transformative discourse), typically operates under strict rules of engagement and revelation, often enforced by facilitators. In this respect, dialogue is more akin to therapy than to political discourse. With respect to (b) scientific and related kinds of rational discourse usually operate under closed circumstances: discussion and testing of claims requires not only a shared sense of the particular rational enterprise, but also strong assurances that, for example, thinking out loud for the sake of deliberation will not be used by other participants for strategic purposes. A challenge for the design of democratic institutions is to balance the necessary non-public conditions of transformative and other creative discourses with the accountability and inclusion that are necessary for deliberation to function democratically, particularly within representative democracies (Chambers, 2004). In many cases, such a balance can be struck by holding participants in a non-public dialog about matters of public concern accountable for the results of their deliberative processes, while sheltering the process itself.

13.5   Institutional design

Insofar as deliberative theories of democracy have focused on institutions, they have focused mostly on constitutional distributions of rights and powers rather than these "middle level" questions about the interactions between norms, incentives, and social psychology (Preuss, 1995; Habermas,

1996; cf. Sunstein, 2001; Elster, 1998; Parkinson, 2006.). This volume develops a number of important middle-level insights. Fung's chapter is the most systematic and ambitious in this respect, focused on basic design choices about who participates, about what, when, how, and for what reasons, all of which affect the goals of democratic processes. And, indeed, the possible goals of deliberative approaches to politics are many, including increasing the legitimacy of decisions, increasing citizen participation, increasing the quality of decision-making, informing officials, informing citizens, developing democratic skills of citizens, holding government officials accountable, increasing justice, and creating more effective policies. But these goals include many trade-offs – for example, between the extent of participation and the quality of deliberation. One key task for middle level theory, nicely exemplified by Fung's chapter, is to combine hypothetically theorized connections between design choices and outcomes with analyses of cases that lend evidence to the generalizations.

While Fung focuses on institutional experiments that are mostly small-scale and policy-specific, two chapters are especially illuminating at the macro-institutional level. List (Chapter 4) borrows deliberative insights to address Condorcet's and Arrow's impossibility theorems. It has long been argued by deliberative democrats that deliberation clarifies preferences, but the focus has usually been on either the consequences of preference clarification for the autonomy of the individual or the consequences for stabilizing public opinion. By relating deliberation to the impossibility theorems, however, List shows that it may have an important function in enabling voting to consistently return majority preferences. The reason, List argues, is that impossibility theorems apply only when voters have incommensurable scales in terms of which they understand their preferences. By clarifying issues, deliberation may enable voters to place their differing preferences on the same scale – what List calls "meta-agreement" – a condition necessary for voting to reflect majority preferences (see also Riker, 1982; Knight and Johnson, 1994). Although List does not frame his contribution in this way, we could say that the inclusiveness of voting depends upon the inclusiveness of agendas, which is in turn dependent upon options that are sufficiently deliberated for citizens to recognize an option they favor.

Bächtiger et al.'s nicely-designed study of legislatures (Chapter 5) develops a robust set of middle-level theoretical expectations which they test with a comparative case study. Relative to presidential systems, deliberation in parliamentary systems is likely to be dampened by strong party discipline (see also Uhr, 1998: ch. 4). Because second chambers are less constrained by electoral pressures, they are also more deliberative. The more legislative business is conducted in public as opposed to closed-door committees, the less likely decision-making will be deliberative (see also Bessette, 1994: 144–147). And highly polarized issues are likely to be less conducive to deliberation than less polarized issues. Testing these factors by looking at legislatures in the United States, Britain, Switzerland, and Germany, Bächtiger and his colleagues find that differing institutional designs directly affect the quality of deliberation – respect, justification of arguments, openness, and reasoning – in the predicted ways, while more deliberation tended to produce consensus-based outcomes. On issues where there are clear majorities, however, deliberation had less impact on substantive outcomes: "power trumps process." Deliberation had more impact in cases where it was unclear where the majorities were. The broad lesson here, of course, is that legislative design choices make a difference for the constitution of deliberative processes, as indicated by comparative institutional research (Lijphart, 1999; Powell, 2000). But because legislative deliberations are not independent of the political contexts they are supposed to represent, deliberation is not the only force that affects decisions, and we should not expect deliberation to approximate the high quality that can be achieved in the sheltered venues designed for deliberative purposes.

Another lesson has to do with incentives: like many authors in this collection, Bächtiger and his colleagues are closely attentive to the ways in which institutional structures provide incentives for participants to deliberate. Owing to the inertia of its origins, however, theories of deliberative democracy have been handicapped in analyzing institutional incentives. Consistent with liberal views of deliberation, theories have focused mostly on how to protect talk from other kinds of power. When combined with democratic concerns, the theory has focused primarily upon *empowered inclusion*, conceived primarily as institutional protections and supports against coercive powers and economic vulnerabilities. Finally, many theories have followed Habermas by dichotomizing actions with strategic and communicative intent, with the former boxed off, as it were, from the transformative elements of deliberation.

Of course none of these theoretical emphases is "mistaken": communicative influence requires protection from other powers; participants require empowerment; and communicative intent is still preferable to strategic intent. Nonetheless, without further development, these same points can stunt institutional analysis in two ways. First, deliberative democratic theories have made the implicit assumption that if other powers are kept at bay, then deliberative influence would flow into the space leftover. Second, because the theory dichotomized strategic and communicative intent, it has been slow to grasp the obvious: because politics is about conflict, it selects for strategic interactions. A large part of the point of the theory of communicative action was to show that reason is not simply instrumental in nature, and, in particular, that normative reasoning has its own forms of validity, not reducible to the maximized preferences of individuals (Habermas, 1987). It seemed to follow that *if* we think of individuals as strategic actors, *then* we are also buying into the truncated views of human reasoning and motivation typical of rational choice theory. But the conclusion doesn't necessarily follow: it is possible to hold to the basic premises of the theory of communicative action and nonetheless hold that certain contexts tend to evoke strategic actions from individuals. Such an approach would be truer to political contexts, which, in contrast to everyday social interactions, tend to be characterized by low trust, high threat, and, hence, a bias toward the strategic uses of communication. Once these points are granted, the door is open to thinking about how institutions structure strategic incentives for actors to gain the upper hand through the "force of the better reasons."

Some incentives follow from factors that are relatively well analyzed, such as questions of the scale, the duration of processes, and the complexity of the issue. The contributions to this volume underscore a host of other key institutional effects on deliberative incentives, including the following:

Deliberation within elected institutions: As Bächtiger and his colleagues show, the structure of electoral systems of representation systems introduces differing incentives to deliberate. In addition to the factors analyzed by Bächtiger et al. (level of party discipline, levels of electoral pressure, levels of publicity, and issue polarization), it is worth noting the constraints on deliberation imposed by the electoral form itself. As Carl Schmidt (1988) first pointed out, simply the fact of electoral accountability, whatever its other democratic virtues, constrains deliberation within elected bodies. Thus, even under the incentive structures most inclined toward deliberation, we are likely to find that deliberation is constrained by electoral positioning, power brokering, and bargaining – as Bächtiger et al. observe (see also Mansbridge, 2004, Warren and Pearse, forthcoming). At the same time, our judgments of the deliberative virtues of electoral bodies might be quite different were we to ask about its role in focusing deliberation within the broader polity. So, while disciplined parties may limit deliberation within parliaments, discipline enables parties to communicate clearer messages to the broader public they represent, which may make it easier for citizens to participate in public deliberations, and then to use the vote to hold their representatives accountable. This point is, however, theoretical speculation: as far as I know, the research remains to be done.

Decision rules alter the incentives to deliberate. Following the lead of Mendelberg and Karpowitz, we might guess that unanimous decision rules increase the incentives for deliberation, since under these circumstances dissent can only be registered through voice or exit. In contrast, majoritarian rules allow dissenters to express their positions through the vote, without deliberating. In light of these expectations, however, Mendelberg and Karpowitz's findings about the impact of gender are particularly interesting: men are alienated rather than engaged by strong group norms, an effect that is strengthened by unanimous rules, while the same group pressures and rules encourage women to deliberate. These interactions between rules, gender, and group norms suggest there may be optimal mixes of men and women in deliberative bodies, justified not just by representative considerations, but also as a design element intended to increase the amount and quality of deliberation.

Publicity alters deliberative incentives. As Walsh suggests, when people know their words are public, they weigh them for their strategic as well as their communicative impact. This point suggests that the question as to how public any particular deliberative process should be is best determined by its goal. If the goal is one of establishing common ground, for example, closed deliberations may enable the kinds of sincerity and truth-speaking necessary for a transformative process. If, however, words are representative of positions for which the speaker should be held to account, publicity is important – but, as suggested above, accountability may come at a cost to deliberation.

Empowerment alters deliberative incentives, as observed by both Fung and Weatherford (see also Mansbridge, Chapter 12). Most citizen deliberative bodies are not empowered. A common assumption is that participants in empowered bodies are more likely to take their responsibilities seriously, and to see their investment as worthwhile. Likewise, it is often assumed that, for the same reasons, deliberation that is consequential will be more responsive and responsible to conflicting positions and opinions. Both assumptions are probably well founded, but they are for the most part based on impressions rather than comparative case studies (but see Warren and Pearse, forthcoming). In addition, empowered deliberation may very well be less imaginative (because it is defined by specific tasks), less principled (empowered decisions require brokering), and less clear (brokered compromises are often less clear than principled positions) than deliberation aimed at influence through the public sphere. So even if the assumptions about the effects of empowerment are well founded, it does not follow that empowered deliberations are "better" – but simply that they are different, and will have differing functions within a democracy.

Do high *stakes* alter the nature of deliberation? Theoretically, the differences between "hot" (high stakes) and "cold" (low stakes) deliberation should be important (Fung, this volume). At least since Madison, an argument for representative rather than directly democratic decision-making has been that personal interests tend to bias judgments. Institutions should therefore separate judge and cause. The same principle has been applied to legislative bodies: If legislators have personal stakes in decisions, their judgments will be corrupted, a principle that is at the root of conflict of interest and other kinds of anti-corruption legislation (Warren, 2004). On this principle, legislatures should be designed to remove personal stakes, except those that tie the chances of re-election to public justification. But, as Fung argues, the investments necessary for deliberation outside of legislatures may be quite different: because citizens are not professionals (it is not their job to deliberate, though it may be their duty) it seems unlikely that deliberations could occur without high stakes to underwrite the attention and psychic investments, as well as to underwrite interests in consensus or compromise. And yet citizens who self-select into political venues often have such intensely held preferences that they have difficulty with deliberation. While the relationship between interests and representative roles are relatively well understood in electoral institutions, we lack a corresponding body of theory and evidence relating the stakes of citizens to their deliberative capacities.

13.6 Deliberative systems

Despite these many gaps, our current theories are refined enough to suggest the broad outlines of the next generation of deliberation democratic theories. First, we should be conceiving of deliberation as one medium of decision-making and organization within broader democratic systems. Following Habermas (1996), we should continue to think about the ways in which deliberative media complement and guide other media of decision-making – administrative rules and markets. Each medium has its strengths and weaknesses: markets handle high levels of complexity and react rapidly to changing conditions, but have no "agency" and so cannot react directly to normative visions, problems, and social planning. Rule-based administrative power can benefit from authority, universality, and decisive timeliness, but tends to have limited capacities to handle complexity, produce innovations, and generate legitimacy. Deliberation can bestow normative direction and legitimacy, generate social capital, stabilize conflicts, and produce plus-sum resolutions. But deliberation is also costly of time and attentiveness, and has built-in limitations of scale. Successful deliberative institutions will be embedded within these other systems, responding to their weaknesses and benefiting from their strengths. For example, without the security provided by strong sovereign states through regimes of rights, the relatively fragile powers of deliberation are unlikely to grow and to be effective (Warren, 2006b). And without elected representatives, public deliberation would be isolated from state power. Thus, deliberative theories of democracy need to trace these interdependencies, with the aim of maximizing decision-making virtues of each.

The contributions in this volume, however, go to another, somewhat less appreciated point: no single design can suit all deliberative purposes and potentials, and, indeed, it is clear that "deliberative democracy" will really mean a *deliberative system* within which multiple kinds, modes, and levels of deliberation are distributed throughout other institutions and systems (Mansbridge, 1999; Walsh, this volume). Ideally, each kind, mode, and level of deliberation would be matched to justified purposes or goals (see e.g., Fung, 2006). Because trade-offs exist among goals, deliberative institutions should be complementary: those that generate consensus should be balanced by those that harbor and refine dissent. Those that are closed in order to generate trust and respect among participants should be balanced by those that are open, within which the same participants might approach the rough and tumble of public dialog with new skills, confidence, knowledge, and understandings. But to understand how to get such a system "right," in the sense that it maximizes a range of broadly agreed process goods – will require a good deal more theory building and empirical investigation of the kind represented in this volume.

Bibliography

Abers, Rebecca. 2003. "Reflections on What Makes Empowered Participatory Governance Happen," in Fung and Wright, *Deepening Democracy: Institutional Innovations in Empowered Participatory Governance.* London: Verso.

Abramson, Paul. 1983. *Political Attitudes in America.* San Francisco: Freeman.

Ackerman, Bruce. 1989. "Why Dialogue?" *The Journal of Philosophy* 86: 5–22.

Ackerman, Bruce and James Fishkin. 2004. *Deliberation Day.* New Haven, CT: Yale University Press.

Allport, Gordon W. 1954. *The Nature of Prejudice.* Reading, MA: Addison-Wesley.

Altshuler, Alan. 1970. *Community Control: The Black Demand for Participation in Large American Cities.* New York: Pegasus.

Andersen, Kristi. 1996. *After Suffrage: Women in Partisan and Electoral Politics before the New Deal.* Chicago, IL: University of Chicago Press.

Anderson, Rob, Leslie A. Baxter, and Kenneth N. Cissna. 2004. "Texts and Contexts of Dialogue." In Anderson, Baxter, and Cissna (eds.), *Dialogue: Theorizing Difference in Communication Studies,* Thousand Oaks, CA: Sage.

Arendt, Hannah. [1958] 1998. *The Human Condition,* 2nd edition. Chicago, IL: University of Chicago Press.

——. [1963] 1965. *On Revolution.* New York: Viking.

Aries, Elizabeth. 1976. "Interaction patterns and themes of male, female, and mixed groups." *Small Group Behavior* 7: 7–18.

——. 1996. *Men and Women in Interaction: Reconsidering the Differences.* New York: Oxford University Press.

——. 1998. "Gender Differences in Interaction: A Reexamination." In Daniel J. Canary and Kathryn Dindia (eds.), *Sex Differences and Similarities in Communication: Critical Essays and Empirical Investigations of Sex and Gender in Interaction.* Mahwah, NJ: Lawrence Erlbaum.

Arrow, Kenneth. 1951/1963. *Social Choice and Individual Values.* New York: Wiley.

Asch, Solomon E. 1952. *Social Psychology.* Englewood Cliffs, NJ: Prentice Hall.

Austen-Smith, David. 1990. "Information Transmission in Debate." *American Journal of Political Science* 34: 124–152.

——. 1992. "Strategic Models of Talk in Political Decision-Making." *International Political Science Review* 13: 124–152.

Babcock, Linda and Sara Laschever. 2003. *Women Don't Ask: Negotiation and the Gender Divide.* Princeton, NJ: Princeton University Press.

Babcock, Linda, Sara Laschever, Michele Gelfand, and Deborah Small. 2003. "Nice Girls Don't Ask." *Harvard Business Review* 81(10): 14–16.

Bächtiger, André. 2005. *The Real World of Deliberation. A Comparative Study of its Favorable Conditions in Legislatures,* Bern: Haupt Verlag.

Bächtiger, André and Steenbergen, Marco. 2004. "The Real World of Deliberation. A Comparative Study of Its Favorable Conditions in Legislatures." IUE Working Paper SPS No. 2004/17.

Baier, Annette C. 1987. "Hume, the Woman's Moral Theorist?" In Eva Feder Kittay and Diana T. Meyers (eds.), *Women and Moral Theory.* Totowa, NJ: Rowman & Littlefield.

Baiocchi, Gianpaolo. 2001. "Participation, Activism, and Politics: The Porto Alegre Experiment and Deliberative Democratic Theory." *Politics and Society* 29: 43–72.

Baiocchi, Gianpaolo. 2005. *Militants and Citizens: The Politics of Participatory Democracy in Porto Alegre*. Stanford, CA: Stanford University Press.

Barabas, Jason. 2004. "How Deliberation Affects Policy Opinions." *American Political Science Review* 98: 687–701.

Barber, Benjamin R. 1984. *Strong Democracy*. Berkeley: University of California Press.

——. 1998. *A Place for Us: How to Make Society Civil and Democracy Strong*. New York: Hill and Wang.

Barry, Brian, 1965, *Political Argument*, London: Routledge & Kegan Paul.

——. [1979] 1989. "Is Democracy Special?" In *Democracy, Power and Justice: Essays in Political Theory*. Oxford: Oxford University Press.

Beck, Ulrich. 1997. *The Reinvention of Politics: Rethinking Modernity in the Global Social Order*. Cambridge: Polity Press.

Benhabib, Seyla. 1992. *Situating the Self: Gender, Community and Postmodernism in Contemporary Ethics*. New York: Routledge.

——. 1996. "Toward a Deliberative Model of Democratic Legitimacy." In Benhabib (ed.), *Democracy and Difference: Contesting the Boundaries of the Political*. Princeton, NJ: Princeton University Press, pp. 67–94.

——. 2002. *The Claims of Culture: Equality and Diversity in the Global Era*. Princeton, NJ: Princeton University Press.

Bennett, Stephen. 1995. "Comparing Americans' Political Information in 1988 and 1992." *Journal of Politics* 57 (May): 521–532.

Berry, Jeffrey M., Kent E. Portney, and Ken Thomson. 1993. *The Rebirth of Urban Democracy* Washington, D.C.: Brookings.

Bessette, Joseph M. 1982. "Is Congress a Deliberative Body?" In Dennis Hale (ed.), *The United States Congress: Proceedings of the Thomas P. O'Neill Symposium*. Chestnut Hill, MA: Boston College.

——. 1994. *The Mild Voice of Reason: Deliberative Democracy and American National Government*. Chicago, IL: University of Chicago Press.

Black, Duncan. 1948. "On the Rationale of Group Decision-Making." *Journal of Political Economy* 56: 23–34.

Black, Jay (ed.). 1997. *Mixed News: The Public/Civic/Communitarian Journalism Debate* NJ: Lawrence Erlbaum.

Blum, Laurence A. 1982. "Kant and Hegel's Moral Rationalism: A Feminist Perspective." *Canadian Journal of Philosophy* 12 (1982): 287–302.

——. 1988. "Gilligan and Kohlberg: Implications for Moral Theory." *Ethics* 98 (1988): 472–491.

Boder, David P. 1940. "A New Apparatus for Voice Control of Electric Timers." *Journal of Experimental Psychology* 26: 241–247.

Bohman, James. 1996. *Public Deliberation: Pluralism, Complexity, and Democracy*. Cambridge, MA: MIT Press.

——. 1997. "Deliberative Democracy and Effective Social Freedom: Capabilities, Resources and Opportunities." In James Bohman and William Rehg (eds.), *Deliberative Democracy: Essays on Reason and Politics*. Cambridge, MA: MIT Press, pp. 321–348.

——. 1998. "The Coming of Age of Deliberative Democracy." *The Journal of Political Philosophy* 6: 400–425.

——. 2003. "Deliberative Toleration." *Political Theory* 31(6): 757–779.

Bolce, Louis, Gerald De Maio, and Douglas Mazzio. 1996. "Dial-In Democracy: Talk Radio and the 1994 Election." *Political Science Quarterly* 111 (3): 457–481.

Bond, R. and P. B. Smith. 1996. "Culture and Conformity: A Meta-Analysis of Studies Using Asch's Line Judgment Task." *Psychological Bulletin* 119: 111–137.

Boyte, Harry C. 2002. "A Different Kind of Politics: John Dewey and the Meaning of Citizenship in the 21st Century." www.cpn.org/crm/contemporary/different.html.

——. 2003. "Civic Populism." *Perspectives on Politics* 1: 737–742.

Boyte, Harry C. and Nancy N. Kari. 1996. *Building America: The Democratic Promise of Public Work*. Philadelphia, PA: Temple University Press.

Brady, Henry. 1999. "Political Participation." In J. P. Robinson, P. R. Shaver, and L. S. Wrightsman (eds.), *Measures of Political Attitudes*. San Diego, CA: Academic Press.

Brennan, Geoffrey. 2001. "Collective Coherence?" *International Review of Law and Economics* 21: 197–211.

Brewer, Marilynn B. and Norman Miller. 1984. "Beyond the Contact Hypothesis: Theoretical Perspectives on Desegregation." In Miller and Brewer (eds.), *Groups in Contact: The Psychology of Desegregation*. Orlando: Academic Press.

Brown, Rupert. 2000. *Group Processes: Dynamics within and between Groups*. Oxford: Blackwell.

Buchanan, James and Gordon Tullock. 1965. *The Calculus of Consent: Logical Foundations of Constitutional Democracy*. Ann Arbor: University of Michigan Press.

Burke, Edmund. 1987. *Reflections on the Revolution in France*. New York: Macmillan.

Burkhalter, Stephanie, John Gastil, and Todd Kelshaw. 2002. "A Conceptual Definition and Theoretical Model of Public Deliberation in Small Face-to-Face Groups." *Communication Theory* 12 (4): 398–422.

Burnstein, E. and A. Vinokur. 1973. "Testing Two Classes of Theories about Group Induced Shifts in Individual Choice." *Journal of Experimental Social Psychology* 9 (2): 123–137.

——. 1975. "What a Person Thinks Upon Learning He Has Chosen Differently from Others: Nice Evidence for the Persuasive-arguments Explanation of Choice Shifts." *Journal of Experimental Social Psychology* 11(5): 412–426.

——. 1977. "Persuasive Argumentation and Social Comparison as Determinants of Attitude Polarization." *Journal of Experimental and Social Psychology* 13 (4): 315–332.

Button, Mark and Kevin Mattson. 1999. "Deliberative Democracy in Practice: Challenges and Prospects for Civic Deliberation." *Polity* 31(4): 610–637.

Cain, Bruce, Russell Dalton, and Susan Scarrow. 2003. "Democratic Publics and Democratic Institutions." In *Democracy Transformed? Expanding Political Opportunities in Advanced Industrial Democracies*. Oxford: Oxford University Press, pp. 251–75.

Campbell, Andrea L. 2003. *How Policies Make Citizens: Senior Political Activism and the American Welfare State*. Princeton, NJ: Princeton University Press.

Carlie, L. L. 1990. "Gender, Language, and Influence." *Journal Personality and Social Psychology* 59: 941–951.

Chambers, Simone. 1995. "Discourse and Democratic Practices." In Stephen K. White (ed.), *The Cambridge Companion to Habermas*. Cambridge: Cambridge University Press.

——. 1996. *Reasonable Democracy: Jürgen Habermas and the Politics of Discourse*. Ithaca, NY: Cornell University Press.

——. 1999. *Talking versus Voting: Legitimacy, Efficiency, and Deliberative Democracy*. Unpublished manuscript. University of Colorado.

——. 2003. "Deliberative Democratic Theory." *Annual Review of Political Science* 6: 307–326.

Chan, Sewell. 2001. "D.C. Residents Dish Out Ideas; 3,500 Citizens Provide Criticism, Suggestions for City Leaders at Summit." *Washington Post*, October 7: C1.

Chapman, Bruce. 1998. "More Easily Done than Said: Rules, Reason and Rational Social Choice." *Oxford Journal of Legal Studies* 18: 293–303.

——. 2002. "Rational Aggregation." *Politics, Philosophy, and Economics* 1: 337–354.

Chickering, Arthur W. and Linda Reisser. 1993. *Education and Identity*. San Francisco: Jossey-Bass.

Cialdini, Robert B. and Melanie R. Trost. 1998. "Social Influence: Social Norms, Conformity, and Compliance." In D. T. Gilbert, S. T. Fiske, and G. Lindzey (eds.), *The Handbook of Social Psychology*. New York: Oxford University Press.

Cissna, Kenneth N. and Rob Anderson. 2002. *Moments of Meeting: Buber, Rogers, and the Potential for Public Dialogue*. Albany, NY: SUNY Press.

Cohen, Joshua. 1989. "Deliberation and Democratic Legitimacy." In Alan Hamlin and Philip Pettit (eds.), *The Good Polity: Normative Analysis of the State*. Oxford: Basil Blackwell.

——. 1996. "Procedure and Substance in Deliberative Democracy." In S. Benhabib (ed.), *Democracy and Difference: Contesting the Boundaries of the Political*. Princeton, NJ: Princeton University Press.

——. 1997. "Deliberation and Democratic Legitimacy." In J. Bohman and W. Rehg (eds.), *Deliberative Democracy: Essays on Reason and Politics*. Cambridge, MA: MIT Press.

Cohen, Joshua and Rogers, Joel. 1983. *On Democracy*. New York: Penguin Books, 1983.

——. 1992. "Secondary Associations and Democratic Governance." *Politics and Society* 20 (4): 393–472.

——. 2003. "Power and Reason." In Archon Furg and Eric Olin Wright, eds., *Deepening Democracy*. London: Verso.

Cohen, Joshua and Sabel, Charles. 1997. *European Law Journal* 3 (4): 313–342.

Connolly, William. 1983. *The Terms of Political Discourse*. Princeton, NJ: Princeton University Press.

Cook, F. L. and Jacobs, L. R. (1998). *Evaluation of Americans Discuss Social Security: Deliberative Democracy in Action*. Report to the Pew Charitable Trusts. Evanston, IL: Institute for Policy Research, Northwestern University.

——. 1998. *Evaluation of Americans Discuss Social Security: Deliberative Democracy in Action*. Evanston, IL: Institute for Policy Research.

Cooper, H. M. 1979. "Statistically Combining Independent Studies: A Meta-Analysis of Sex Differences in Conformity Research." *Journal of Personality and Social Psychology* 37: 131–146.

Corcoran, Robert L. and Karen Elliott Greisdorf. 2001. *Connecting Communities*. Washington, DC: Initiatives for Change.

Cottman, Michael H. 1999. "A View From the Summit: D.C. Residents Turn Out to Hash out Their City's Future." *Washington Post* (November 21): C1.

Courtright, J. A. 1978. "A Laboratory Investigation of Groupthink." *Communication Monographs* 45: 229–246.

Crosby, Ned. 1995. "Citizens Juries: One Solution for Difficult Environmental Questions." In Ortwin Renn, T. Webler and P. Wiedemann (eds.), *Fairness and Competence in Citizen Participation: Evaluating Models for Environmental Discourse*. Dordrecht, Netherlands: Kluwer Academic Publishers.

Cross, S. E. and L. Madson. 1997. "Models of the Self: Self-construals and Gender." *Psychological Bulletin* 122: 5–37.

Dahl, Robert A. 1967. "The City in the Future of Democracy." *American Political Science Review* 61: 953–970.

——. 1970. *After the Revolution? Authority in a Good Society*. New Haven, CT: Yale University Press.

——. 1989. *Democracy and Its Critics* (New Haven, CT: Yale University Press).

Dahl, Robert A. and Edward R. Tufte, 1973. *Size and Democracy*. Stanford, CA: Stanford University Press.

Dalton, Russell. 1999. "Political Support in Advanced Industrial Democracies." In P. Norris (ed.), *Critical Citizens: Global Support for Democratic Governance.* Edited Oxford: Oxford University Press.

Dalton, Russell. 2000. "Value Change and Democracy." In S.J. Pharr and R. Putnam (eds.), *Disaffected Democracies: What's Troubling the Trilateral Countries?* Princeton, NJ: Princeton University Press, pp. 252–269.

———. 2007. *Citizenship in America.* Washington, DC: Congressional Quarterly Press.

Davis, J. H., R. M. Bray, and R. W. Holt. 1977. "The Empirical Study of Decision Processes in Juries: A Critical Review." In J. L. Tapp, and F. J. Levine (eds.), *Law, Justice, and the Individual in Society.* New York: Holt, Rinehart, and Winston.

Davis, J. H., M. Stasson, K. Ono, and S. Zimmerman. 1988. "Effects of Straw Polls on Group Decision-Making: Sequential Voting Pattern, Timing, and Local Majorities." *Journal of Personality and Social Psychology* 55: 918–926.

Davis, J. H, T. Kameda, C. Parks, M. Stasson, and S. Zimmerman. 1989. "Some Social Mechanics of Group Decision Making: The Distribution of Opinion, Polling Sequence, and Implications for Consensus." *Journal of Personality and Social Psychology* 57: 1000–1012.

Davis, Richard and Diana Owen. 1998. *New Media and American Politics.* New York: Oxford University Press.

Delli Carpini, Michael X., and Scott Keeter. 1996. *What Americans Know about Politics and Why It Matters.* New Haven, CT: Yale University Press.

Delli Carpini, Michael X., Fax Lomax Cook, and Lawrence R. Jacobs. 2004. "Public Deliberation, Discursive Participation, and Citizen Engagement: A Review of the Empirical Literature." *Annual Review of Political Science* 7: 315–344.

Deutsch, Morton. 1973. *The Resolution of Conflict: Constructive and Destructive Processes.* New Haven, CT: Yale University Press.

———. 1975. "Equity, Equality, and Need. What Determines Which Value Will Be Used as the Basis of Distributive Justice?" *Journal of Social Issues* 31: 137–149.

Deveaux, Monique. 2003, "A Deliberative Approach to Conflicts of Culture." *Political Theory* 31(6): 780–807.

Dewey, John. [1927] 1954. *The Public and Its Problems.* Athens, Ohio: Swallow Press.

Dietrich, Franz. forthcoming. "Judgment Aggregation: (Im)Possibility Theorems." *Journal of Economic Theory* (forthcoming).

Dindia, Kathryn and M. Allen. 1992. "Sex Differences in Self-Disclosure: A Meta-Analysis." *Psychological Bulletin* 112: 106–124.

Döring, Herbert (ed.). 1995. *Parliaments and Majority Rule in Western Europe.* Frankfurt: Campus Verlag.

Druckman, James N. and Kjersten R. Nelson. 2003. "Framing and Deliberation: How Citizens' Conversations Limit Elite Influence." *American Journal of Political Science* 47: 729–745.

Dryzek, John S. 1990. *Discursive Democracy: Politics, Policy, and Political Science.* Cambridge: Cambridge University Press.

———. 2000. *Deliberative Democracy and Beyond: Liberals, Critics, Contestations.* New York: Oxford University Press.

———. 2001. "Legitimacy and Economy in Deliberative Democracy." *Political Theory* 29 (5): 651–669.

———. 2005a. "Handle with Care: The Deadly Hermeneutics of Deliberative Instrumentation." *Acta Politica* 40: 197–211.

Dryzek, John S. 2005b. "Deliberative Democracy in Divided Societies: Alternatives to Agonism and Analgesia." *Political Theory* 33: 218–242.

Dryzek, John, and C. List. 2003. "Social Choice Theory and Deliberative Democracy: A Reconciliation." *British Journal of Political Science* 33: 1–28.

Dryzek, John S. and Simon Niemeyer. 2003. "Pluralism and Consensus in Political Deliberation." Paper presented at the annual meeting of the American Political Science Association, Philadelphia.

Dryzek, John, and C. List. 2004. "Social Choice Theory and Deliberative Democracy: A Response to Aldred." *British Journal of Political Science* 34: 752–758.

Du Bois, Paul Martin, and Jonathan J. Hutson. 1997. *Bridging the Racial Divide: A Report on Interracial Dialogue in America*. Brattleboro, VT: Center for Living Democracy.

Eagly, Alice H. 1987. *Sex Differences in Social Behavior: A Social-Role Interpretation*. Hillsdale, New Jersey: L. Erlbaum.

Eagly, Alice H. and L. L. Carli. 1981. "Sex of Researchers and Sex-Typed Communications As Determinants of Sex Differences in Influenceability: A Meta-Analysis of Social Influence Studies." *Psychological Bulletin* 90: 1–20.

Eagly, Alice H. and B. T. Johnson. 1990. "Gender and Leadership Style: A Meta-analysis." *Psychological Bulletin* 108: 233–256.

Easton, David. 1953. *The Political System*. New York: Knopf.

Eavey, Cheryl and Gary J. Miller. 1984. "Fairness in Majority Rule Games with a Core." *American Journal of Political Science* 28: 570–586.

Edelman, Murray J. 1964. *The Symbolic Uses of Politics*. Urbana, IL: University of Illinois Press.

Ellis, D. G. 1982. "Relational Stability and Change in Women's Consciousness-Raising Groups." *Women's Studies in Communication* 5: 77–87.

Elster, John. 1986. "The Market and the Forum." In J. Elster and A. Hylland (eds.), *Foundations of Social Choice Theory*. Cambridge: Cambridge University Press.

———. 1997. "The Market and the Forum: Three Varieties of Political Theory." In J. Bohman and W. Rehg (eds.), *Deliberative Democracy: Essays on Reason and Politics*. Cambridge, MA: MIT Press.

———. 1998. *Deliberative Democracy*. Cambridge: Cambridge University Press.

Erikson, Robert S. and Kent L. Tedin. 2001. *American Public Opinion*. New York: Macmillan.

Esther Duflo and Raghabendra Chattopadhyay. 2004. "Women as Policy Makers: Evidence from a Randomized Policy Experiment in India," *Econometrica* 72 (5) (September 2004): pp. 1409–1443.

Estlund, David. 1997. "Beyond Fairness of Deliberation: The Epistemic Dimension of Democratic Authority." In James Bohman and William Rehg (eds.), *Deliberative Democracy: Essays on Reason and Politics*. Cambridge, MA: MIT Press.

———. 2006. "Depoliticizing Democracy," in Samantha Besson and José Luis Marti, *Deliberative Democracy and its Discontents*. London: Ashgate.

Etzioni, Amitai. 1996. *The New Golden Rule: Community and Morality in a Democratic Society*. New York: Basic Books.

Fearon, James D. 1998. "Deliberation as Discussion." In J. Elster (ed.), *Deliberative Democracy*. Cambridge: Cambridge University Press.

Fischer, Frank. 1993. "Citizen Participation and the Democratization of Policy Expertise: From Theoretical Inquiry to Practical Cases." *Policy Sciences* 26: 165–187.

Fisher, F. and Forester, J. (eds.) 1987. *The Argumentative turn in Policy Analysis and Planning*. Durham, NC: Duke University Press.

Fisher, Roger and William Ury. 1981. *Getting to Yes*. New York: Penguin, 1983.

Fishkin, James. 1991. *Democracy and Deliberation: New Directions for Democratic Reform*. New Haven, CT: Yale University Press.

——. 1992. *The Dialogue of Justice*. New Haven, CT: Yale University Press.

——. 1995. *The Voice of the People*. New Haven, CT: Yale University Press.

——. 1997. *The Voice of the People: Public Opinion and Democracy*. New Haven, CT: Yale University Press.

FOCUS St. Louis. 2002. *Bridges across Racial Polarization: A Handbook to Get You Started*. St. Louis, Missouri.

Follett, Mary Parker. [1925] 1942. "Constructive Conflict." In H. Metcalf and L. Urwick (eds.), *Dynamic Administration: The Collected Papers of Mary Parker Follett*. New York: Harper.

Forester, John. 1999. *The Deliberative Practitioner: Encouraging Participatory Planning Processes*. Cambridge, MA: MIT Press.

Forsyth, Don R. 1999. *Group Dynamics*. Belmont, CA: Wadsworth.

Fraser, Nancy. 1990. "Rethinking the Public Sphere: A Contribution to the Critique of Actually Existing Democracy." *Social Text* 25/26: 56–80.

——. 1992. "Rethinking the Public Sphere: A Contribution to the Critique of Actually Existing Democracy." In C. Calhoun (ed.), *Habermas and the Public Sphere*. Cambridge, MA: MIT Press.

Frohlich, Norman and Joe Oppenheimer. 1990. "Choosing Justice in Experimental Democracies with Production." *American Political Science Review* 84: 461–477.

——. 1992. *Choosing Justice*. Berkeley, CA: University of California Press.

Frohlich, Norman, Joe Oppenheimer and Cheryl Eavey. 1987. "Choices of Principles of Distributive Justice in Experimental Groups." *American Journal of Political Science* 31: 606–636.

Fung, Archon. 2001. "Accountable Autonomy: Toward Empowered Deliberation in Chicago Schools and Policing." *Politics and Society* 29: 73–104.

——. 2004. *Empowered Participation: Reinventing Urban Democracy*, Princeton, NJ: Princeton University Press.

——. 2006. "Varieties of Participation in Complex Governance." *Public Administration Review* 36: 65–74.

Fung, Archon and Erik Olin Wright. 2001. "Deepening Democracy: Innovations in Empowered Participatory Governance." *Politics and Society* 29(1): 5–41.

——. 2003. *Deepening Democracy: Institutional Innovations in Empowered Participatory Governance*. London: Verso.

Gaertner, Samuel L., John F. Dovidio, Jason A. Nier, Christine M. Ward, and Brenda S. Banker. 1999. "Across Cultural Divides: The Value of A Superordinate Identity." In D. Prentice and D. T. Miller (eds.), *Cultural Divides: Understanding and Overcoming Group Conflict*. New York: Russell Sage.

Gambetta, Diego. 1998. "Claro!" In J. Elster (ed.), *Deliberative Democracy*. Cambridge: Cambridge University Press, pp. 19–43.

Gamson, William. 1992. *Talking Politics*. New York: Cambridge University Press.

Gargarella, Roberto. 1998. "Full Representation, Deliberation, and Impartiality." In J. Elster (ed.), *Deliberative Democracy*. New York: Cambridge University Press.

Gastil, John. 1988. "Gender and Support for Reagan: A Comprehensive Model of Presidential Approval." *American Journal of Political Science* 32: 19–49.

——. 1993. *Democracy in Small Groups: Participation, Decision Making, and Communication*. Philadelphia, PA: New Society.

——. 2000. *By Popular Demand*. Berkeley, CA: University of Berkeley Press.

Gastil, John and Dillard, James. 1999. Increasing Political Sophistication through Public Deliberation." *Political Communication* 16: 3–23.

Gastil, John and Peter Levine (eds.). 2005. *The Deliberative Democracy Handbook: Strategies for Effective Civic Engagement in the Twenty-first Century* (San Francisco, CA: Jossey-Bass).

Gehrlein, William. 2000. "Social Homogeneity and Condorcet Winners: A Weak Connection." Paper presented at the annual meeting of the Public Choice Society, Charleston, South Carolina, March 2000.

Gehrlein, William. 2004. "Probabilities of Election Outcomes with Two Parameters: The Relative Impact of Unifying and Polarizing Candidates." Working paper, University of Delaware.

Giles, Howard, Anthony Mulac, James J. Bradac, and Patricia Johnson. 1987. "Speech Accommodation Theory: The First Decade and Beyond." *Communication Yearbook* 10: 13–48.

Gilens, Martin. 1998. "Gender and Support for Reagan: A Comprehensive Model of Presidential Approval." *American Journal of Political Science* 32: 19–49.

Goering, John. 2001. "An Assessment of President Clinton's Initiative on Race." *Ethnic and Racial Studies* 24 (3): 472–484.

Goethals, George R. and Mark P. Zanna. 1979. "The Role of Social Comparison in Choice Shifts." *Journal of Personality and Social Psychology* 37: 1469–1476.

Goodin, Robert E. 2000. "Democratic Deliberation Within," *Philosophy and Public Affairs* 29 (1): 81–109.

——. 2002. *Reflective Democracy*. Oxford: Oxford University Press.

——. 2005. "Sequencing Deliberative Moments." *Acta Politica* 40: 182–196.

Gould, Carol C. 1976. "Philosophy of Liberation and Liberation of Philosophy." In Carol C. Gould and Marx W. Wartofsky (eds.), *Women and Philosophy*. New York: Capricorn/G.P. Putnam.

——. 1996. "Diversity and Democracy: Representing Differences." In Seyla Benhabib (ed.), *Democracy and Difference: Contesting the Boundaries of the Political*. Princeton, NJ: Princeton University Press, pp. 171–186.

Graham, Keith. 2002. *Practical Reasoning in a Social World: How We Act Together* Cambridge: Cambridge University Press.

Greenstone, J. David, and Paul Peterson. 1981. *Race and Authority in Urban Politics*. Chicago, IL: University of Chicago Press.

Grimshaw, Jean. 1986. *Philosophy and Feminist Thinking*. Minneapolis: University of Minnesota Press.

Guinier, Lani. 1994. *The Tyranny of the Majority: Fundamental Fairness in Representative Democracy*. New York: Free Press.

Gunderson, Adolph G. 1995. *The Environmental Promise of Democratic Deliberation*. Madison: University of Wisconsin Press.

Gutmann, Amy. 2000. "Why Should Schools Care about Civic Education?" In L. M. McDonnell, P. M. Timpane, and R. Benjamin (eds.), *Rediscovering the Democratic Purposes of Education*. Lawrence: University Press of Kansas, pp. 73–90.

Gutmann, Amy and Dennis Thompson. 1996. *Democracy and Disagreement*. Cambridge, MA: Belknap Press.

——. 2004. *Why Deliberative Democracy?* Princeton, NJ: Princeton University Press.

Guzzetti, Barbara J. and Wayne O. Williams. 1996. "Changing the Pattern of Gendered Discussion: Lessons from Science Classrooms." *Journal of Adolescent and Adult Literacy* 40: 38–47.

Habermas, Jürgen. 1962 [1989]. *The Structural Transformation of the Public Sphere: An Inquiry into a Category of Bourgeois Society*. Cambridge, MA: MIT Press.

——. 1962 [1989]. *The Structural Transformation of the Public Sphere*. Trans, Thomas Burger with Frederick Lawrence. Cambridge, Mass: MIT Press.

——. 1973. *Legitimation Crisis*. Boston, MA: Beacon Press.

——. 1979. *Communication and the Evolution of Society*. Baston: Beacon Press.

——. 1982. "A Reply to My Critics." In John B. Thompson and David Held (eds.), *Habermas: Critical Debates*. Cambridge, MA.: MIT Press.

——. 1983. *Moralbewusstsein und kommunikatives Handeln*. Frankfurt a. M.: Suhrkamp.

——. [1976] 1985. "Hannah Arendt: On the Concept of Power." In *Philosophical-Political Profiles*. Trans. Frederick G. Lawrence. Cambridge, MA: MIT Press.

——. 1984/1987. *The Theory of Communicative Action: Volumes 1 & 2*. Boston, MA: Beacon.

Habermas, Jürgen. 1991. *Erläuterungen zur Diskursethik*. Frankfurt a. M.: Suhrkamp.

——. 1992. *Faktizität und Geltung: Beiträge zur Diskurstheorie des Rechts und des demokratischen Rechtsstaats*. Frankfurt a. M.: Suhrkamp.

——. 1992. "Further Reflections on the Public Sphere." In Craig Calhoun (ed.), *Habermas and the Public Sphere*. Cambridge, MA: MIT Press, pp. 422–461.

——. 1996. *Between Facts and Norms: Contributions to a Discourse Theory of Law and Democracy*. Cambridge, MA: MIT Press.

Hajer, Maarten A. and Hendrik Wagenaar. 2003. *Deliberative Policy Analysis: Understanding Governance in the Network Society*. Cambridge, Cambridge University Press.

Hamilton, Alexander, James Madison, and John Jay. [1788] 1961. *The Federalist Papers*. Clinton Rossiter (ed.) New York: New American Library.

Hansen, Susan B. 1997. "Talking about Politics: Gender and Contextual Effects on Political Proselytizing." *Journal of Politics* 59: 73–103.

Hanushek, Eric A. and John E. Jackson. 1977. *Statistical Methods for Social Scientists*. New York: Academic Press.

Harris-Lacewell, Melissa. 2004. *Barbershops, Bibles, and BET: Everyday Talk and Black Political Thought*. Princeton: Princeton University Press.

Hart, Roderick P. 2000a. *Campaign Talk*. Princeton, NJ: Princeton University Press.

——. 2000b. *DICTION 5.0: The Text-Analysis Program*. Thousand Oaks, CA: Scolari / Sage Publications.

Hasnain, Romana and Michael Garland. 1990. *Health Care in Common: Report of the Oregon Health Decisions Community Meetings Process*. Portland: Oregon Health Decisions.

Hastie, R., S. D. Penrod, and N. Pennington. 1983. *Inside the Jury*. Cambridge, MA: Harvard University Press.

Hegel, G. W. F. [1820] 1952. *The Philosophy of Right*. Oxford: Oxford University Press.

Held, David. 1996. *Models of Democracy*. Stanford, CT: Stanford University Press.

Held, Virginia. 1970. *The Public Interest and Individual Interests*. New York: Basic Books.

Herzog, Don. 1998. *Poisoning the Minds of the Lower Orders*. Princeton, NJ: Princeton University Press.

Hibbing, John R. and Elizabeth Theiss-Morse. 2002a. *Stealth Democracy: Americans' Beliefs about How Government Should Work*. Cambridge: Cambridge University Press.

——. 2002b. "The Perils of Voice: Political Involvement's Potential to De-Legitimate." Paper presented at the annual meeting of the American Political Science Association, Boston.

Hirst, Paul. 1994. *Associative Democracy: New Forms of Economic and Social Governance*. Amherst: University of Massachusetts Press.

Holmes, Janet. 1995. *Women, Men, and Politeness*. London: Longman.

Holzinger. Katharina. 2001. "Verhandeln statt Argumentieren oder Verhandeln durch Argumentieren? Eine empirische Analyse auf der Basis der Sprechakttheorie." *Politische Vierteljahresschrift* 42: 414–446.

Houlé, Kristin and Rona Roberts. 2000. *Toward Competent Communities: Best Practices for Producing Community-Wide Study Circles*. Lexington, KY: Roberts & Kay, Inc.

Huckfeldt, Robert and John Sprague. 1995. *Citizens, Politics, and Social Communication: Information and Influence in an Election Campaign*. Cambridge: Cambridge University Press, ch. 9.

Huckfeldt, Robert, Jeffrey Levine, William Morgan, and John Sprague. 1998. "Election Campaigns, Social Communication, and the Accessibility of Discussant Preference." *Political Behavior* 20: 263–294.

Huff, Archie V., Jr. 1995. *Greenville: The History of the CityaAnd County in the South Carolina Piedmont.* Columbia: University of South Carolina Press.

Inglehart, Ronald. 1997. *Modernization and Postmodernization: Cultural Economic, and Political Change in 43 Countries.* Princeton: Princeton University Press.

Immerwahr, John. 1997. *What Our Children Need: South Carolinians Look at Public Education.* New York: Public Agenda.

Jacobs, Lawrence, Theodor Marmor, and Jonathan Oberlander. 1998. "The Political Paradox of Rationing: The Case of the Oregon Health Plan." John F. Kennedy School of Government, Harvard University.

Jacobs, Lawrence R., Fay Lomax Cook, and Michael Delli Carpini. 2000. *Talking Together: Public Deliberation and Discursive Capital. A Report to the Pew Charitable Trusts* (report on file with author).

Jacobs, R. C. and D. T. Campbell. 1961. "The Perpetuation of an Arbitrary Tradition through Several Generations of a Laboratory Microculture." *Journal of Abnormal and Social Psychology* 62: 649–658.

James, Michael Rabinder. 2004. *Deliberative Democracy and the Plural Polity.* Lawrence: University of Kansas Press.

James, Rita. 1959. "Status and Competence of Jurors." *The American Journal of Sociology* 64: 563–570.

Janis, Irving L. 1982. *Groupthink: Psychological Studies of Policy Decisions and Fiascos.* Boston, MA: Houghton Mifflin.

Jones-Correa, Michael. 2000. "Immigrants, Blacks, and Cities." In Yvette M. Alex-Assensoh and Lawrence J. Hanks (eds.), *Black and Multiracial Politics in America.* New York: New York University Press.

Josephs, R., II. Markus, and R. Tafarodi. 1992. "Gender and self-esteem." *Journal of Personality and Social Psychology* 63: 391–402.

Kanra, Bora. 2005. Deliberation across Difference: Bringing Social Learning into the Theory and Practice of Deliberative Democracy in the Case of Turkey." Unpublished PhD thesis, Research School of Social Sciences, Australian National University.

Kant, Immanuel. [1785] 1949. *Fundamental Principles of the Metaphysic of Morals.* Trans. Thomas K. Abbott. Indianapolis: Bobbs-Merrill.

———. [1763] 1960. *Observations on the Feeling of the Beautiful and the Sublime.* Trans. John Goldthwait. Berkeley: University of California Press.

Kaplan, M. F. and C. E. Miller. 1987. "Group Decision-Making and Normative Versus Informational Influence: Effects of Type of Issue and Assigned Decision Rule." *Journal of Personality and Social Psychology* 53: 306–313.

Kapuscinski, Anne, Robert Goodman, Stuart Hahn, Lawrence R. Jacobs, Emily Pullins, Charles Johnson, Jean Kinsey, Ronald Krall, Antonio La Viña, Margarent Mellon, and Vernon Ruttan. 2003. "Making 'Safety First' a Reality for Biotechnology Products." *Nature Biotechnology.* 21 (June): 599–601.

Karpowitz, Christopher and Jane Mansbridge. 2005. "Deliberation, Disagreement, and Consensus: The Importance of Dynamic Updating in Public Deliberation." In John Gastil and Peter Levine (eds.), *The Deliberative Democracy Handbook*, San Francisco, CA: Jossey-Bass.

Kathlene, Lyn. 1994. "Power and Influence in State Legislative Policymaking: The Interaction of Gender and Position in Committee Hearing Debates." *American Political Science Review* 88(3): 560–576.

Keenan, Alan. 2003. *Democracy in Question: Democratic Openness in a Time of Political Closure*. Stanford, CT: Stanford University Press.

Keeter, Scott, Cliff Zukin, Molly Andolina, and Krista Jenkins. 2002. *The Civic and Political Health of the Nation: A Generational Portrait*. Washington DC: Center for Information and Research on Civic Learning and Engagement.

Kennedy, Ellen. 1988. "Introduction: Carl Schmitt's *Parlamentarism* in Its Historical Context." In Carl Schmitt, *The Crisis of Parliamentary Democracy*. Cambridge, MA: MIT Press.

Keohane, Robert O. 2001. "Governance in a Partially Globalized World." Presidential Address, American Political Science Association. *American Political Science Review* 95: 1–13.

Kim, Claire Jean. 2000. "Clinton's Race Initiative: Recasting the American Dilemma." *Polity* 33 (2): 175–197.

Knight, G. P. and A. F. Dubro. 1984. "Cooperative, Competitive, and Individualistic Social Values: An Individualized Regression and Clustering Approach." *Journal of Personality and Social Psychology* 46: 98–105.

Knight, Jack. 1999. "Constitutionalism and deliberative democracy." In S. Macedo (ed.), *Deliberative Politics: Essays on Democracy and Disagreement*. New York: Oxford University Press, pp 159–169.

Knight, Jack and James Johnson. 1994. "Aggregation and Deliberation: On the Possibility of Democratic Legitimacy." *Political Theory* 22: 277–296.

———. 1997. "What Sort of Political Equality Does Deliberative Democracy Require?" In James Bohman and William Rehg (eds.), *Deliberative Democracy: Essays on Reason and Politics*. Cambridge, MA: MIT Press.

Kramer, Ralph M. 1969. *Participation of the Poor: Comparative Community Case Studies in the War on Poverty*. Englewood Cliffs: Prentice-Hall.

Kriesi, Hanspeter. 2001. "Die Rolle der Öffentlichkeit im politischen Entscheidungsprozess. Ein konzeptueller Rahmen für ein international vergleichendes Forschungsprojekt." Veröffentlichungsreihe der Arbeitsgruppe Politische Öffentlichkeit und Mobilisierung. Wissenschaftszentrums Berlin für Sozialforschung.

Ladd, Carll Everett. 2000. *The Ladd Report: Startling New Research Shows How an Explosion of Voluntary Groups, Activities, and Charitable Donations is Transforming Our Towns and Cities*. New York: Free Press.

Lamm, H. and D. G. Myers. 1978. "Group-Induced Polarization Of Attitudes And Behavior." *Advances in Experimental Social Psychology* 11: 145–195.

Lascher, Edward L. 1996. "Assessing Legislative Deliberation: A Preface to Empirical Analysis." *Legislative Studies Quarterly* 21: 501–519.

Latour, Bruno. 1996. "On interobjectivity." *Mind, Culture and Activity* 3(4): 228–245.

Lehr, R. L., Guild, W., Thomas, D. L., and Swezey, B. G. 2003. *Listening to Consumers: How Deliberative Polling Helped Build 1,000 MW of New Renewable Energy Projects in Texas*. Golden, CO: National Renewable Energy Laboratory.

Leighninger, Matt and Martha McCoy. 1998. "Mobilizing Citizens: Study Circles Offer a New Approach to Citizenship." *National Civic Review* 87(2): 187.

Lemann, Nicholas. 1989. "The Unfinished War, Part II." *Atlantic Monthly* (January): 58.

Leventhal, G. S. and D. W. Lane. 1970. "Sex, Age, and Equity Behavior." *Journal of Personality and Social Psychology* 15: 312–316.

Lewin, Kurt. 1951. *Field Theory in Social Science; Selected Theoretical Papers*. D. Cartwright (ed.). New York: Harper & Row.

Lewis, Catherine H. 1998. *Horry County, South Carolina, 1730–1993*. Columbia: University of South Carolina Press.

Lewis-Beck, Michael. 1988. *Economics and Elections: The Major Western Democracies,* Ann Arbor: University of Michigan Press.

Lhotta, Roland. 2000. "Konsens und Konkurrenz in der konstitutionellen Oekonomie bikameraler Verhandlungsdemokratie: Der Vermittlungsausschuss als effiziente Institution politischer Deliberation." In Holtmann, Everhard und Voelzkow, Helmut (Hg.), *Zwischen Wettbewerbs- und Verhandlungsdemokratie.* Opladen/Wiesbaden: Westdeutscher Verlag.

Lindblom, Charles. 2002. *The Market System: What It Is, How It Works, and What to Make of It.* New Haven, CT: Yale University Press.

Lijphart, Arend 1999. *Patterns of Democracy. Government Forms and Performance in Thirty-Six Countries.* New Haven, CT: Yale University Press.

———. 2002. "The Wave of Power-Sharing Democracy." In Reynold, A. (ed.), *The Architecture of Democracy. Constitutional Design, Conflict Management, and Democracy.* Oxford: Oxford University Press, pp. 37–54.

Lindeman, Mark. 2002. "Opinion Quality and Policy Preferences in Deliberative Research." In M. Delli Carpini, L. Huddy, and R. Shapiro (eds.), *Research in Micropolitics: Political Decisionmaking, Deliberation and Participation.* Greenwich, CT: JAI Press.

Lippmann, Walter. 1927. *Public Opinion.* New York: Free Press.

List, Christian. 2002. "Two Concepts of Agreement." *The Good Society* 11: 72–79, reprinted in an extended form as "Substantive and Meta-Agreement." In A. van Aaken, C. List and C. Luetge (eds.) (2003) *Deliberation and Decision.* Aldershot: Ashgate.

———. forthcoming. "A Possibility Theorem on Aggregation over Multiple Interconnected Propositions." *Mathematical Social Sciences* 45: 1–13.

———. 2004a. "A Model of Path-Dependence in Decisions over Multiple Propositions." *American Political Science Review* 98: 495–513.

———. 2004b. "The Discursive Dilemma and Public Reason." Working paper, London School of Economics.

———. forthcoming. "The Probability of Inconsistencies in Complex Collective Decisions." *Social Choice and Welfare* (forthcoming).

List, Christian and R. E. Goodin. 2001. "Epistemic Democracy: Generalizing the Condorcet Jury Theorem." *Journal of Political Philosophy* 9: 277–306.

List, Christian, R. C. Luskin, J. S. Fishkin, and I. McLean. 2000/2005. "Can Deliberation Induce Single-Peakedness: Evidence from Deliberative Polls." Paper presented at the 2000 conference of the American Political Science Association.

List, Christian and P. Pettit. 2002. "Aggregating Sets of Judgments: An Impossibility Result." *Economics and Philosophy* 18: 89–110.

———. 2004. "Aggregating Sets of Judgments: Two Impossibility Results Compared." *Synthese* 140: 207–235.

Lloyd, Genevieve. 1983. "Reason, Gender and Morality in the History of Philosophy." *Social Research* 50: 491–513.

Lodge, Milton and Patrick Stroh. 1993. "Inside the Mental Voting Booth: An Impression-Driven Process Model of Candidate Evaluation." In S. Iyengar and W. McGuire (eds.), *Explorations in Political Psychology.* Durham: Duke University Press.

Lodge, Milton and Kathleen McGraw (eds.). 1995. *Political Judgment: Structure and Process.* Ann Arbor: University of Michigan Press.

Loewenberg, Gerhard and Thomas C. Mans. 1988. "Individual and Structural Influences on the Perception of Legislative Norms in Three European Parliaments." *American Journal of Political Science* 32: 155–177.

Loomis, Burdett A. 1990. *Dear Colleagues, Civility and Deliberation in the U.S. Senate.* Washington, DC: Brookings Institution.

Los Angeles Region NCCJ. 1995. "Neighbor to Neighbor Dialogue Series and Skills Training for Facilitating Interracial Dialogue." Los Angeles, California.

Lukes, Steven. 1974. *Power: A Radical View*. New York: Macmillan.

Luskin, Robert C. and James Fishkin. 1998. "Deliberative Polling, Public Opinion, and Democracy: The Case of the National Issues Convention." Paper presented at the annual meeting of the American Association of Public Opinion Researchers. St. Louis.

Luskin, Robert C. and James Fishkin (eds). 1999. "Symposium on Deliberative Democracy." *The Good Society* 9: 1–85.

——. 2002. "Deliberation and 'Better Citizens'". Paper Presented at the ECPR Joint Sessions, Turin, March 23–27.

Luskin, Robert C., James S. Fishkin, and Dennis L. Plane. 1999. "Deliberative Polling and Policy Outcomes: Electric Utility Issues in Texas." Paper delivered at the 1999 meetings of the Association for Policy Analysis and Management, Washington, DC.

Luskin, Robert C., James S. Fishkin, and Roger Jowell. 2002. "Considered Opinions: Deliberative Polling in Britain." *British Journal of Political Science* 32: 445–487.

Maccoby, E. E. 1998. *The Two Sexes. Growing Up Apart, Coming Together*. Cambridge, MA: Harvard University Press.

Macedo, Stephen. 1999. "Introduction." In Stephen Macedo (ed.), *Deliberative Politics. Essays on "Democracy and Disagreement."* New York: Oxford University Press, pp. 3–14.

Mackie, Gerry. 2002. "Does Democratic Deliberation Change Minds?" Paper presented at the annual meeting of the American Political Science Association, Boston.

MacNeil, M. K. and M. Sherif. 1976. "Norm Change over Subject Generations As a Function of Arbitrariness of Prescribed Norms." *Journal of Personality and Social Psychology* 34: 762–773.

Macpherson, C.B. 1977. *The Life and Times of Liberal Democracy*. New York: Oxford University Press.

Manin, Bernard. 1987. "On Legitimacy and Political Deliberation." *Political Theory* 15: 338–368.

Mansbridge, Jane. 1980. *Beyond Adversary Democracy*. Chicago, IL: University of Chicago Press.

——. 1988. "Motivating Deliberation in Congress." In Sarah Baumgartner Thurow (ed.), *Constitutionalism in America*, vol. 2. New York: University Press of America.

——. 1991. "Democracy, Deliberation, and the Experience of Women." In Bernard Murchland (ed.), *Higher Education and the Practice of Democratic Politics*. Dayton, OH: Kettering Foundation.

——. 1993. "Feminism and Democratic Community." In John W. Chapman and Ian Shapiro (eds.), *Democratic Community: NOMOS XXXV*. New York: New York University Press.

——. 1995. "Does Participation Make Better Citizens?" *The Good Society* 5 (2): 1–7.

——. 1998. "On the Contested Nature of the Public Good." In Walter W. Powell and Elisabeth S. Clemens (eds.), *Private Action and the Public Good*. New Haven, CT: Yale University Press.

Mansbridge, Jane. 1999a. "Everyday Talk in the Deliberative System." In Stephen Macedo (ed.), *Deliberative Politics: Essays on Democracy and Disagreement*. Oxford: Oxford University Press, pp. 211–239.

——. 1999b. "On the Idea that Participation Makes Good Citizens." In Stephen L. Elkin and Karol E. Soltan (eds.), *Citizen Competence and Democratic Institutions*. University Park: Pennsylvania State University Press.

——. 2004. "Representation Revisited: An Introduction to the Case against Electoral Accountability." *Democracy and Society* 2(1): 1, 12–13.

Mansbridge, Jane. 2006. "Deliberation and Self-Interest." In Samantha Besson and José Luis Marti, eds. *Deliberative Democracy and its Discontents*. London: Ashgate.

Mansbridge, Jane, Matthew Amengual, Janette Hartz-Karp, and John Gastil. 2006. "Norms of Deliberation: An Inductive Study," *Journal of Public Deliberation* 2(1): 1–47.

Marcus, George E. 2002. *The Sentimental Citizen: Emotion in Democratic Politics*. University Park: Pennsylvania State University Press.

Marcus, George E., W. Russell Neuman, and Michael MacKuen. 2000. *Affective Intelligence and Political Judgment*. Chicago, IL: University of Chicago Press.

Marder, Nancy S. 1987. "Gender Dynamics and Jury Deliberations." *Yale Law Journal* 96 (3): 593–612.

Markell, Patchen. 2000. "Making Affect Safe for Democracy: On Constitutional Patriotism." *Political Theory* 28: 38–63.

Marris, Peter and Martin Rein. 1973. *Dilemmas of Social Reform: Poverty and Community Action in the United States*. Chicago, IL: Aldine.

Mathews, David. 1999. *Politics for People: Finding a Responsible Public Voice*. Urbana: University of Illinois Press.

McCarrick, A. K., R. W. Manderscheid, and S. Silbergeld. 1981. "Gender Differences in Competition and Dominance during Married-Couples Group Therapy." *Social Psychology Quarterly* 44: 164–177.

McClintock, C. G. and L. J. Keil. 1983. "Social Values: Their Definition, Their Development, And Their Impact upon Human Decision Making in Settings of Outcome Interdependence." In H. Blumberg, A. Hare, V. Kent, and M. Davies (eds.), *Small Groups and Social Interaction*. New York: John Wiley and Sons.

McClosky, Herbert and Jon Zaller. 1984. *The American Ethos: Public Attitudes toward Capitalism and Democracy*. Cambridge, MA: Harvard University Press.

McClurg, Scott. 2003. "Social Networks and Political Participation: The Role of Social Interaction in Explaining Political Participation." *Political Research Quarterly* 56: 448–464.

McCoy, Martha and Patrick L. Scully. 2002. "Deliberative Dialogue to Expand Civic Engagement: What Kind of Talk Does Democracy Need?" *National Civic Review* 91: 117–135.

McDonald, Michael P. and Samuel Popkin. 2001. "The Myth of the Vanishing Voter." *American Political Science Review* 95: 963–974.

McDonnell, Lorraine M. and M. Stephen Weatherford. 1999. "State Standards-Setting and Public Deliberation: The Case of California". National Center for Research on Evaluation, Standards, and Student Testing (CRESST); Center for the Study of Evaluation (CSE); Graduate School of Education & Information Studies, University of California, Los Angeles.

——. 2000. "Varieties of Practical Deliberation: Purposes, Organization, Context." Paper prepared for presentation at the 2000 Annual Meeting of the Western Political Science Association, San Jose, California, March 24–26, 2000.

McPhail, Mark Lawrence. 2004. "Race and the (Im)Possibility of Dialogue." In Rob Anderson, Leslie A. Baxter, and Kenneth N. Cissna (eds.), *Dialogue: Theorizing Difference in Communication Studies*. Thousand Oaks, CA: Sage, pp. 209–224.

Mendelberg, Tali and John Oleske. 2000. "Race and Public Deliberation." *Political Communication* 17: 169–191.

——. 2002. "The Deliberative Citizen: Theory and Evidence." In M. delli Carpini, L. Huddy, and R. Shapiro (eds.), *Research in Micropolitics: Political Decisionmaking, Deliberation and Participation*. Greenwich, CT: JAI Press.

Merelman, Richard M., Greg Streich, and Paul Martin. 1998. "Unity and Diversity in American Political Culture: An Exploratory Study of the National Conversation on American Pluralism and Identity." *Political Psychology* 19: 781–807.

Merkle, Daniel M. 1996. "The National Issues Convention Deliberative Poll." *Public Opinion Quarterly* 60: 588–619.

Merritt, Davis. 1998. *Public Journalism and Public Life: Why Telling the News Is Not Enough*. Mahwah, NJ: Lawrence Erlbaum.

Mettler, Suzanne. 2002. "Bringing the State Back in to Civic Engagement: Policy Feedback Effects of the G.I. Bill for World War II Veterans." *American Political Science Review* 96 (June): 351–365.

Michelman, Frank. 1988. "Law's Republic." *Yale Law Journal* 97: 1493–1537.

Milbrath, Lester W. and M.L. Goel. 1977. *Political Participation*. Chicago, IL: Rand McNally.

Mill, John Stuart. [1859] 1956. *On Liberty*. Currin V. Shields (ed.) New York: Liberal Arts Press.

——. 1861/1991. *Considerations on Representative Government*. Buffalo, NY: Prometheus Books.

——. 1998. *Utilitarianism*. Oxford: Oxford University Press.

Miller, David. 1992. "Deliberative Democracy and Social Choice." *Political Studies* 40: 54–67.

Miller, J. B. 1985. "Patterns of Control In Same-Sex Conversations: Differences between Women and Men." *Women's Studies in Communication* 8: 62–69.

Miller, Patrice M., Dorothy L. Danaher and David Forbes. 1986. "Sex-Related Strategies for Coping with Interpersonal Conflict in Children Aged five and seven." *Developmental Psychology* 22(4): 543–548.

Morone, James A. 1990. *The Democratic Wish: Popular Participation and the Limits of American Government*. New York: Basic Books.

Moscovici, Serge. 1985. "Innovation and Minority Influence." In G. Lindsey and E. Aronson (eds.), *The Handbook of Social Psychology*, NewYork: Random House.

Mouffe, Chantal. 2000. *The Democratic Paradox*. London: Verso.

Moynihan, Daniel P. 1969. *Maximum Feasible Misunderstanding: Community Action in the War on Poverty*. New York: Free Press.

Mueller, Dennis C. 1989. *Public Choice II*, Cambridge: Cambridge University Press.

Mutz, Diana C. 2002. "Cross-cutting Social Networks: Testing Democratic Theory in Practice." *American Political Science Review* 96(1): 111–126.

Myers, D. G. 1978. "Polarizing Effects of Social Comparison." *Journal of Experimental Social Psychology* 14: 554–563.

——. 1982. "Polarizing Effects of Social Interaction." In H. Brandstatter, J. Davis, and G. Stocker-Kreichbauer (eds.), *Group Decision Making*. New York: Academic Press.

Myers, D.G. and H. Lamm. 1975. "The Polarizing Effects of Group Discussion." *American Scientist* 63: 297–303.

——. 1976. "The Group Polarization Phenomenon." *Psychological Bulletin* 83: 602–662.

Nagel, Jack H. 1987. *Participation*. New York: Prentice Hall.

——. 1992. "Political Accountability: Combining Deliberation and Fair Representation in Community Health Decisions." *University of Pennsylvania Law Review* (May): 1965–1985.

National Conference for Community and Justice (NCCJ). 2002. "Risks, Rights, and Responsibilities of Dialogue."

Neck, C. P. and G. Moorhead. 1995. Groupthink Remodeled: The Importance of Leadership, Time Pressure, and Methodical Decision-Making Procedures. *Human Relations* 48: 537–557.

Nelson, Barbara J., Linda Kaboolian and Kathryn A. Carver. 2004. "Bridging Social Capital and an Investment Theory of Collective Action: Evidence from the Concord Project." Paper presented at the annual meeting of the American Political Science Association, Chicago, Illinois.

Nemeth, C., J. Endicott, and J. Wachtler. 1976. "From the '50s to the '70s: Women in Jury Deliberations." *Sociometry* 38: 193–204.

Niemeyer, Simon. 2004. "Deliberation in the Wilderness: Displacing Symbolic Politics." *Environmental Politics* 13: 347–372.

Niemi, Richard G. 1969. "Majority Decision-Making with Partial Unidimensionality." *American Political Science Review* 63: 488–497.

Niño, Carlos Santiago. 1996. *The Constitution of Deliberative Democracy.* New Haven, CT: Yale University Press.

Norris, Pippa. 1999. "Introduction: The Growth of Critical Citizens?" In *Critical Citizens: Global Support for Democratic Governance.* Edited by Pippa Norris. Oxford: Oxford University Press.

Nussbaum, Martha. 1995. "Emotions and Women's Capabilities." In Martha Nussbaum and Johnathan Glover (eds.), *Women, Culture, and Development.* Oxford: Oxford University Press.

——. 1996. "Aristotle on Emotions and Rational Persuasion." In Amelie Rorty (ed.), *Essays on Aristotle's Rhetoric.* Berkeley: University of California Press.

Oliver, Leonard P. 1990. "Study Circles: New Life for an Old Idea." *Adult Learning* 2 (3): 20–22.

Olson, Mancur. 1971. *The Logic of Collective Action: Public Goods and the Theory of Groups.* Cambridge, MA: Harvard University Press.

One America. 1998. One America in the Twenty-First Century: The President's Initiative on Race – One America Dialogue Guide. Washington, DC: The White House.

Oskamp, Stuart and James M. Jones. 2000. "Promising Practices in Reducing Prejudice: A Report from the President's Initiative on Race." In Stuart Oskamp (ed.), *Reducing Prejudice and Discrimination.* Mahwah, NJ: Lawrence Erlbaum.

Ostrom, Elinor. 1998. "A Behavioral Approach to the Rational Choice Theory of Collective Action." *American Political Science Review* 92: 1–22.

Page, Benjamin. 1996. *Who Deliberates?* Chicago, IL: University of Chicago Press.

Pangle, Lorraine S. and Pangle, T. L. 2000. "What the American Founders Have to Teach Us about Schooling for Democratic Citizenship." In L. M. McDonnell, P. M. Timpane, and R. Benjamin (eds.), *Rediscovering the Democratic Purposes of Education.* Lawrence: University Press of Kansas.

Parkinson, John. 2005a. "Legitimacy Problems in Deliberative Democracy." *Political Studies,* 51: 180–196.

——. 2003b. "The Legitimation of Deliberative Democracy." Unpublished PhD thesis, Research School of Social Sciences, Australian National University.

——. 2006. *Deliberating in the Real World: Problems of Legitimacy in Democracy.* Oxford: Oxford University Press.

Pateman, Carole. 1970. *Participation and Democratic Theory.* Cambridge: Cambridge University Press.

Patterson, Thomas E. 2002. *The Vanishing Voter: Public Involvement in an Age of Uncertainty.* New York: Alfred A. Knopf.

Pauly, Marc, and M. van Hees. 2005. "Logical Constraints on Judgment Aggregation." *Journal of Philosophical Logic.* 35 (6): 560–585.

Pearce, W. Barnett and Stephen W. Littlejohn. 1997. *Moral Conflict: When Social Worlds Collide.* Thousand Oaks, CA: Sage.

Penrod, S., and Hastie, R. 1980. "A Computer Simulation of Jury Decision-Making." *Psychological Review* 87: 133–159.

Peterson, Paul E. 1981. *City Limits.* Chicago, IL: University of Chicago Press.

Pettigrew, Thomas F. and Linda R. Tropp. 2000. "Does Intergroup Contact Reduce Prejudice? Recent Meta-Analytic Findings." In Stuart Oskamp (ed.), *Reducing Prejudice and Discrimination.* Mahwah, NJ: Lawrence Erlbaum.

Pettit, Philip. 2001. "Deliberative Democracy and the Discursive Dilemma." *Philosophical Issues* 11: 268–299.

Pharr, Susan J. and Robert D. Putnam (eds.). 2000. *Disaffected Democracies: What's Troubling the Trilateral Countries.* Princeton, NJ: Princeton University Press.

Pharr, Susan J., Robert D. Putnam, and Russell J. Dalton. 2000. "Trouble in the Advanced Democracies? A Quarter Century of Declining Confidence." *Journal of Democracy* 11: 5–25.

Pilisuk, M., B. Brands, and D. van den Hove. 1976. "Deceptive Sounds: Illicit Communication in Laboratory." *Behavioral Science* 21: 515–523.

Polletta, Francesca. 2002. *Freedom is an Endless Meeting: Democracy in American Social Movements.* Chicago, IL: University of Chicago Press.

Powell, Bingham G., Jr. and Whitten, Guy D. 1993. "A Cross-National Analysis of Economic Voting: Taking Account of the Political Context." *American Journal of Political Science* 37: 391–411.

——. 2000. *Elections as Instruments of Democracy: Majoritarian and Proportional Visions.* New Haven and London: Yale University Press.

Pollins, N. P., R. L. Montgomery, and T. G. Smith. 1975. "Autokinetic Paradigms: Reply." *Sociometry* 38: 358–373.

Preuss, Ulrich. 1995. *Constitutional Revolution: The Link between Constitutionalism and Progress.* Atlantic Highlands: Humanities Press.

Price, Vincent and P. Neijens. 1998. "Deliberative Polls: Toward Improved Measures of 'Informed' Public Opinion?" *International Journal of Public Opinion Research* 10: 145–176.

Price, Vincent and Joseph N. Cappella. 2001. "Online Deliberation and its Influence: The Electronic Dialogue Project in Campaign 2000." Paper presented at the annual meeting of the American Association for Public Opinion Research, Montreal, Canada.

——. 2002. "Online Deliberation and Its Influence: The Electronic Dialogue Project in Campaign 2000." *IT Soc.* I: 303–328.

Price, Vincent, D. Goldthwaite, J. Cappella, and A. Romantan. 2003. "Online Discussion, Civic Engagement, and Social Trust." Working Paper, University of Pennsylvania, Philadelphia.

Prothro, James W. and Charles W. Grigg. 1960. "Fundamental Principles of Democracy: Bases of Agreement and Disagreement." *Journal of Politics* 22: 276–294.

Pruitt, D. G. 1971. "Choice Shifts in Group Discussion: An Introductory Review." *Journal of Personality and Social Psychology* 20: 339–360.

Przeworski, Adam. 1998. "Deliberation and Ideological Domination." In Jon Elster (ed.), *Deliberative Democracy.* New York: Cambridge University Press, pp. 140–160.

Putnam, Robert D. 1993. *Making Democracy Work: Civic Traditions in Modern Italy.* Princeton, NJ: Princeton University Press.

Putnam, Robert. 2000. *Bowling Alone: The Collapse and Revival of American Community.* New York: Simon and Shuster.

Rahn, Wendy and John Transue, 1998. "Social Trust and Value Change: The Decline of Social Capital in American Youth." *Political Psychology*: 545–565.

Rawls, John. 1971. *A Theory of Justice*. Cambridge, MA: Belknap Press of Harvard University Press.

Rawls, John. 1985. "Justice as Fairness: Political not Metaphysical." *Philosophy and Public Affairs* 14: 223–251.

——. 1993. *Political Liberalism*. New York: Columbia University Press.

——. 1996. *Political Liberalism*. New York: Columbia University Press.

——. 1997. "The Idea of Public Reason"; "Postscript." In James Bohman and William Rehg (eds.), *Deliberative Democracy: Essays on Reason and Politics*. Cambridge, MA: MIT Press, pp. 93–143.

——. 1999. *The Law of Peoples*. Cambridge, MA: Harvard University Press.

Reich, Robert. 1988. "Policy Making in a Democracy." In Robert Reich (ed.), *The Power of Public Ideas*. Cambridge: Ballinger.

Reichler, Patricia and Polly B. Dredge. 1997. *Governing Diverse Communities: A Focus on Race and Ethnic Relations*. Washington DC: National League of Cities.

Riker, William H. 1982. *Liberalism against Populism: A Confrontation between the Theory of Democracy and the Theory of Social Choice*. San Francisco: Freeman.

Risse, Thomas. 2000. "Let's argue! Communicative Action in World Politics." *International Organization* 54: 1–39.

Rorty, Amélie Oksenberg. 1985. "Varieties of rationality, varieties of emotion." *Social Science Information* 24: 343–353.

Rosenbaum, Walter A. 1978. "Public Involvement as Reform and Ritual." In Stuart Langton (ed.), *Citizen Participation in America*. Lexington, MA: Lexington Books.

Rosenberg, Shawn W. 2002. *The Not So Common Sense: How People Judge Social and Political Life*. New Haven, CT: Yale University Press.

——. 2004. "Reconstructing the Concept of Deliberation." Paper prepared for the annual meeting of the Midwest Political Science Association, Chicago, April 15–18.

——. (forthcoming). "Rethinking Democratic Deliberation: The Limits and Potential of Citizen Participation." *Polity*.

——. 2005. "The Empirical Study of Deliberative Democracy: Setting a Research Agenda." *Acta Politica* 40: 212–224.

Rosen, Michael. 1999. "Utopia in Frankfurt: Realism and Optimism in the Life's Work of Jürgen Habermas." *Times Literary Supplement*, Oct. 8: 3–4.

Rosenstone, Steven J. and John Mark Hansen. 1993. *Mobilization, Participation, and Democracy in America*. New York: Macmillan.

Rothstein, Bo. 2005. "Is Political Science Producing Technically Competent Barbarians?" *European Political Science* 4 (1): 3–13.

Ryan, Susan, Anthony S. Bryk, Gudelia Lopez, Kimberly Williams, Kathleen Hall, and Stuart Luppescu. 1997. "Charting Reform: LSCs Local Leadership at Work." (Report sponsored by the Consortium on Chicago School Research, December.)

Ryfe, David. 1998. "What is Good Public Discourse? A Review of the Literature." A Report submitted to the Penn National Commission on Society, Culture, and Community. October 15, 1998.

——. 2002. "The Practice of Deliberative Democracy: A Study of 16 Deliberative Organizations." *Political Communication* 19: 359–377.

Safier, Paul. 2006. "Rationing the Public: The Oregon Health Plan." In Amy Gutmann and Dennis Thompson (eds.), *Ethics and Politics: Cases and Comments*. Belmont, CA: Thomson-Wadsworth.

Sanders, G. S. and R. S. Baron. 1977. "Is Social Comparison Irrelevant for Producing Choice Shifts?" *Journal of Experimental Social Psychology* 13: 303–314.

Sanders, Lynn M. 1997. "Against Deliberation." *Political Theory* 25: 347–376.

Santos, Boaventura de Sousa. "Participatory Budgeting in Porto Alegre: Toward a Redistributive Democracy." *Politics and Society* 26 (4, Dec. 1998): 461–510.

Sapiro, Virginia. 1999. "Considering Political Civility Historically: A Case Study of the United States." Paper presented at the annual meeting of the International Society of Political Psychology, Amsterdam, The Netherlands.

———. 2002. "Seeking Knowledge and Information as Political Action: A U.S. Historical Case Study." Paper prepared for presentation at the meeting of the European Consortium for Political Research, Turin, March.

———. 2003. "Theorizing Gender in Political Psychology Research." In David O. Sears, Leonie Huddy, and Robert Jervis (eds.), *Oxford Handbook of Political Psychology*. New York: Oxford University Press.

Saunders, Harold H. 1999. *A Public Peace Process: Sustained Dialogue to Transform Ethnic and Racial Conflicts*. New York: St. Martin's Press.

Scharpf, Fritz W. 1997. *Games Real Actors Play. Actor-Centered Institutionalism in Policy Research*. Boulder, CO: Westview Press.

Schattschneider, E. E. 1960. *The Semi-Sovereign People*. New York: Holt, Rinehart, and Winston.

Schkade, David, Cass Sunstein, and Daniel Kahneman. 2000. "Deliberation about Dollars: The Severity Shift." *Columbia Law Review* 100: 1139–1175.

Schmitt, Carl. [1923] 1985. *The Crisis of Parliamentary Democracy*. Trans. Ellen Kennedy. Cambridge, MA: MIT Press.

Schoem, David and Sylvia Hurtado (eds). 2001. *Intergroup Dialogue: Deliberative Democracy in School, College, Community and Workplace*. Ann Arbor: University of Michigan Press.

Schudson, Michael. 1997. "Why Conversation is Not the Soul of Democracy." *Critical Studies in Mass Communication* 14: 297–309.

———. 1998. *The Good Citizen: A History of American Civic Life* (Cambridge, MA: Harvard University Press).

———. 2003. "How people Learn to be Civic." In E. J. Dionne, Kayla Meltzer Drogosz, and Robert E. Litan (eds.), *United We Serve: National Service and the Future of Citizenship*.Washington, DC: Brookings, pp. 263–277.

Scott, John T., Richard E. Matland, Philip A. Michelbach, and Brian H. Bornstein. 2001. "Just Deserts: An Experimental Study of Distributive Justice Norms." *American Journal of Political Science* 45 (4): 749–767.

Sears, David O. and Leonie Huddy. 1990. "On the Origins of Political Disunity among Women." In Louise A. Tilly and Patricia Gurin (eds.), *Women, Politics, and Change*. New York: Russell Sage Foundation.

Shapiro, Ian. 1999. "Enough of Deliberation. Politics is about Interests and Power." In Stephen Macedo (ed.), *Deliberative Politics. Essays on "Democracy and Disagreement."* Oxford University Press, pp. 28–38.

Shapiro, Robert Y. and Harpreet Mahajan. 1986. "Gender Differences in Policy Preferences: A Summary of Trends From the 1960s to the 1980s." *Public Opinion Quarterly* 50: 42–61.

Sherif, Muzafer. 1966. *In Common Predicament: Social Psychology of Intergroup Conflict and Cooperation*. Boston, MA: Houghton Mifflin.

Sidanius, Jim and Felicia Pratto. 1999. *Social Dominance: An Intergroup Theory of Social Hierarchy and Oppression*. New York: Cambridge University Press.

Silverberg, Helene. 1990. "What Happened to the Feminist Revolution in Political Science? A Review Essay." *The Western Political Quarterly* 43: 887.

Sirianni, Carmen and Lewis Friedland. 2001. *Civic Innovation in America: Community Empowerment, Public Policy, and the Movement for Civic Renewal.* Berkeley: University of California Press.

Skocpol, Theda. 1999. "How American Became Civic." In *Civic Engagement in American Democracy.* Washington, DC: Brookings Institution Press, pp. 27–80.

———. 2003. *Diminished Democracy: From Membership to Management in American Civic Life.* Norman: Oklahoma University Press.

Skocpol, Theda and Morris Fiorina (eds.). 2000. *Civic Engagement in American Democracy.* Washington: Brookings Institution Press.

Skogan, Wesley G. and Hartnett, Susan M. 1997. *Community Policing: Chicago Style.* New York: Oxford University Press.

Smith, Eric R. A. N. 1989. *The Unchanging American Voter.* Berkeley: University of California Press.

Sniderman, Paul M., Richard A. Brody, and Philip E. Tetlock. 1991. *Reasoning and Choice: Explorations in Political Psychology.* New York: Cambridge University Press.

Soss, Joe, 1999. "Lessons of Welfare: Policy Design, Political Learning, and Political Action." *American Political Science Review* 93: 363–380.

Spörndli, Markus. 2003. "Discourse Quality and Political Decisions: An Empirical Analysis of Debates in the German Conference Committee." WZB Discussion Paper FS IV 03–101. Berlin: Wissenschaftszentrum Berlin für Sozialforschung.

———. 2004. *Diskurs und Entscheidung. Eine empirische Analyse kommunikativen Handelns im deutschen Vermittlungsausschuss,* PhD dissertation, Institute of Political Science, University of Bern.

Stech, F. and C. G. McClintock. 1981. "Effects of Communication Timing on Duopoly Bargaining Outcomes." *Journal of Personality and Social Psychology* 40: 664–674.

Steenbergen, Marco R., André Bächtiger, Markus Spörndli, and Jürg Steiner. 2003. "Measuring Political Deliberation." *Comparative European Politics* 1: 21–48.

Steiner, Jürg, André Bächtiger, Markus Spörndli, and Marco R.Steenbergen. (forthcoming, 2004). *Deliberative Politics in Action. Analysing Parliamentary Discourse.* Cambridge: Cambridge University Press.

Street, M. D. 1997. "Groupthink: An Examination of Theoretical Issues, Implications, and Future Research Suggestions." *Small Group Research* 28: 72–93.

Strodtbeck, F. L. and R. D. Mann. 1956. "Sex Role Differentiation in Jury Deliberations." *Sociometry* 19: 3–11.

Strodtbeck, F. L., R. James, and C. Hawkins. 1957. "Social Status In Jury Deliberations." *American Sociological Review* 22: 713–719.

Strom, Kaare. 2000. "Delegation and Accountability in Parliamentary Democracies." *European Journal of Political Research* 37: 261–289.

Study Circles Resource Center (SCRC). 1997. *Facing the Challenge of Racism and Race Relations: Democratic Dialogue and Action for Stronger Communities,* 3rd ed. Pomfret, Connecticut.

Sullivan, John L., James Pierson, and George E. Marcus. 1979. "An Alternative Conceptualization of Political Tolerance: Illusory Increases 1950s–1970s." *American Political Science Review* 73: 781–794.

Sunstein, Cass R. 1994. *Political Conflict and Legal Agreement,* Tanner Lectures on Human Values, Harvard University.

———. 1996. *Legal Reasoning and Political Conflict.* New York: Oxford University Press.

———. 2000. "Deliberative Trouble: Why Groups Go to Extremes." *Yale Law Journal* 110: 71–119.

———. 2001. *Designing Democracy: What Constitutions Do.* Oxford: Oxford University Press.

——. 2002. "The Law of Group Polarization." *Journal of Political Philosophy* 10: 175–195.

Susskind, Lawrence. 1983. "Mediated Negotiation in the Public Sector: Mediator Accountability and the Public Interest Problem." *American Behavioral Scientist* 27: 255–279.

Susskind, Lawrence (ed.) 1999. *The Consensus Building Handbook.* Thousand Oaks, CA: Sage.

Susskind, Lawrence and Connie Ozawa. 1984. "Mediated Negotiation in the Public Sector: The Planner as Mediator." *Journal of Planning Education and Research* 4: 5–15.

Taylor, Charles. 1994. "The Politics of Recognition." In Amy Gutmann (ed.), *Multiculturalism: Examining the Politics of Recognition.* Princeton, NJ: Princeton University Press, pp. 25–74.

Teixeira, Ruy. 1992. *The Disappearing American Voter.* Washington, DC: Brookings Institution Press.

Theiss-Morse, Elizabeth, George Marcus, and John Sullivan. 1993. "Passion and Reason in Political Life: The Organization of Affect and Cognition and Political Tolerance." In George Marcus and Russell Hanson (eds.), *Reconsidering the Democratic Public.* University Park: The Pennsylvania State University Press, pp. 249–272.

Tocqueville, Alexis de. 1969. *Democracy in America,* trans. George Lawrence, ed. J. P. Mayer. New York: Harper and Row.

Tomz, Michael, Jason Wittenberh, and Gary King. 2003. *Clarify: Software for Interpreting and Presenting Statistical Results.* Available at http://gking.harvard. edu/stats.shtml.

Tullock, Gordon and Colin D. Campbell. 1970. "Computer Simulation of a Small Voting System." *Economics Journal* 80: 97–104.

Uhr, John. 1998. *Deliberative Democracy in Australia.* Melbourne: Cambridge University Press.

Unger, Roberto. 1987. *False Necessity: Anti-Necessitarian Social Theory in the Service of Radical Democracy.* Cambridge: Cambridge University Press.

U. S. Bureau of Census. 1995. *Statistical Abstract of the United States.* Washington, DC: Government Printing Office.

Urbinati, Nadia. 2006. *Representative Democracy: Principles and Genealogy.* Chicago: University of Chicago Press.

Vanberg, Viktor and James M. Buchanan. (1989). "Interests and Theories in Constitutional Choice." *Journal of Theoretical Politics* 1: 49–62.

Van Mill, David. 1996. "The Possibility of Rational Outcomes from Democratic Discourse and Procedures." *Journal of Politics,* 58: 734–752.

Varshney, Ashutosh. 2002. *Ethnic Conflict and Civic Life: Hindus and Muslims in India.* New Haven, CT: Yale University Press.

Verba, Sidney and Norman Nie. 1972. *Participation in America,* New York: Harper and Row.

Verba, Sidney, Kay Lehman Schlozman, and Henry E. Brady. 1995. *Voice and Equality: Civic Voluntarism in American Politics.* Cambridge, MA: Harvard University Press.

Vinokur, Amiram and Eugene Burnstein. 1974. "Effects of Partially Shared Persuasive Arguments on Group Induced Shifts: A Group Problem-Solving Approach." *Journal of Personality and Social Psychology* 29: 305–315.

——. 1978. "Depolarization of Attitudes in Groups." *Journal of Personality and Social Psychology* 36: 872–885.

Walsh, Katherine Cramer. 2003. "The Democratic Potential of Civic Dialogue on Race." Paper presented at the annual meeting of the Midwest Political Science Association, Chicago, Illinois, April 3–6.

Walsh, Katherine Cramer. 2004. *Talking about Politics: Informal Groups and Social Identity in American Life.* Chicago, IL: University of Chicago Press.

Walsh, Katherine Cramer. 2005. "Communities, Race, and Talk: The Correlates of Civic Intergroup Dialogue." Paper prepared for presentation at the Midwest Political Science Association annual meeting, Chicago, Illinois, April 7–10.

——. 2007. *Talking about Race: Community Dialogues and the Politics of Difference.* Chicago: University of Chicago Press.

Walzer, Michael. 1997. *On Toleration.* New Haven, CT: Yale University Press.

——. 1999. "Deliberation, and What Else?" In Stephen Macedo (ed.), *Deliberative Politics.* New York: Oxford University Press.

Warren, Mark E. 1992. "Democratic Theory and Self-Transformation." *American Political Science Review* 86(1): 8–23.

——. 2002. "Deliberative Democracy." In Geoffrey Stokes and April Carter (eds.), *Democratic Theory Today.* Cambridge: Polity Press.

——. 2004. "What Does Corruption Mean in a Democracy?" *American Journal of Political Science* 48: 327–342.

——. 2006a. "What Should and Should Not Be Said: Deliberating Sensitive Issues." *Journal of Social Philosophy* 37: 165-183.

——. (2006b). "Democracy and the State." In John Dryzek, Bonnie Honig, and Anne Phillip (eds.), *The Oxford Handbook of Political Theory.* Oxford: Oxford University Press.

Warren, Mark Russell. 2001. *Dry Bones Rattling: Community-Building to Revitalize American Democracy,* Princeton, NJ: Princeton University Press.

Weber, Edward. 2003. *Bringing Society Back In: Grossroots Ecosystem Management, Accountability, and Sustainable Communities.* Cambridge: MIT Press.

Weigold, Michael F. and Barry R. Schlenker. 1991. "Accountability and Risk-Taking." *Personality and Social Psychology Bulletin* 17: 25–29.

Weatherford, M. Stephen and McDonnell, L.M. (forthcoming). "Deliberation with a Purpose: Reconnecting Communities and Schools." In S.W. Rosenberg (ed.), *Can the People Deliberate? An Encounter between Theory and Research on Democratic Deliberation.* London: Palgraves McMillan.

West, C. and D. Zimmerman. 1987. "Doing Gender." *Gender and Society* 1: 125–151.

Williams, Melissa. 2000. "The Uneasy Alliance of Group Representation in Deliberative Democracy." In Will Kymlicka and Wayne Norman (eds.), *Citizenship in Diverse Societies.* Oxford: Oxford University Press, pp. 124–154.

Yankelovich, D. 1991. *Coming to Public Judgment: Making Democracy Work in a Complex World.* Syracuse, NY: Syracuse University Press.

Yin, Robert and Douglas Yates. 1975. *Street Level Governments: Assessing Decentralization and Urban Services.* Lexington, MA: Lexington Books.

Young, Iris Marion. 1996. "Communication and the Other: Beyond Deliberative Democracy." In Seyla Benhabib (ed.), *Democracy and Difference: Contesting the Boundaries of the Political.* Princeton, NJ: Princeton University Press, pp. 120–136.

——. 1997. "Difference as a Resource for Democratic Communication." In James Bohman and William Rehg (eds.), *Deliberative Democracy: Essays on Reason and Politics.* Cambridge, MA: MIT Press, pp. 383–406.

——. 2000. *Inclusion and Democracy.* Oxford: Oxford University Press.

——. 2001. "Activist Challenges to Deliberative Democracy." *Political Theory* 29(5): 670–690.

Index